Linguistische
Arbeiten

Herausgegeben von Klaus von Heusinge
Ingo Plag, Beatrice Primus, Elisabeth Sta

Bert Botma, Roland Noske (Eds.)

Phonological Explorations

Empirical, Theoretical and Diachronic Issues

De Gruyter

ISBN   978-3-11-029516-0
e-ISBN 978-3-11-029517-7
ISSN   0344-6727

Library of Congress Cataloging-in-Publication Data
A CIP catalog record for this book has been applied for at the Library of Congress.

Bibliographic information published by the Deutsche Nationalbibliothek
The Deutsche Nationalbibliothek lists this publication in the Deutsche Nationalbibliografie;
detailed bibliographic data are available in the Internet at http://dnb.d-nb.de.

© 2012 Walter de Gruyter GmbH & Co. KG, Berlin/Boston

Gesamtherstellung: Hubert & Co. GmbH & Co. KG, Göttingen
∞ Gedruckt auf säurefreiem Papier

Printed in Germany

www.degruyter.com

Contents

VI

Notes on contributors

Diana Apoussidou
Diana Apoussidou works as a 'Referent' at the *Stiftung für Hochschulzulassung* in Dortmund, Germany. She completed her PhD at the University of Amsterdam in 2006 and held postdocs at the University of Amsterdam, the University of Massachusetts Amherst, and the University of Utrecht. Her research focuses on computational approaches to phonology and issues of learnability.

Diana Archangeli
Diana Archangeli is a professor of Linguistics at the University of Arizona. She completed her PhD at Massachusetts Institute of Technology in 1984. Her main research interests include understanding language sound systems from the abstract phonological level to the concrete details of articulation, with special emphasis on vowel harmony.

Paul Boersma
Paul Boersma is professor of Phonetic Sciences at the University of Amsterdam. He received a PhD from the University of Amsterdam in 1998. His research focuses on modelling and simulating the acquisition, evolution and typology of the production and comprehension of phonology and phonetics. He is also the designer and main author of Praat, the world's most used computer program for the analysis and manipulation of speech.

Geert Booij
Geert Booij is a professor of Linguistics at the University of Leiden. He took his PhD at the University of Amsterdam in 1977. He was previously professor of General Linguistics and dean of the Faculty of Arts at the Free University of Amsterdam. His research interests include phonology, morphology, and the architecture of grammar.

Bert Botma
Bert Botma is a lecturer of English Language and Linguistics at the University of Leiden and holds a postdoc at the same university. He completed his PhD at the University of Amsterdam in 2004. His main research interest is in segmental phonology.

Janet Grijzenhout
Janet Grijzenhout is professor of English Linguistics and director of the Baby Speech Laboratory (BSL) at the University of Konstanz. She obtained her

PhD from Utrecht University in 1995 and her habilitation from the Heinrich-Heine-Universität, Düsseldorf in 2001. Her main research interests include all areas of phonology, morphology, English linguistics, comparative linguistics, historical linguistics, first and second language acquisition, and infant speech perception and production.

Carlos Gussenhoven

Carlos Gussenhoven was professor of General and Experimental Phonology at the Radboud University Nijmegen and professor of Linguistics at Queen Mary, University of London until his retirement in 2011. He took his PhD at the University of Nijmegen in 1984. His research has been on the intonation and tone structure of languages, including British English, Standard Nigerian English, and standard and non-standard varieties of Dutch.

Camiel Hamans

Camiel Hamans studied Dutch Language and Literature at the University of Amsterdam. After teaching at the Universities of Leiden and Poznań he left academic life to pursue a career in journalism and politics, which led to his appointment as Secretary General of the Dutch Social Democrats in the European Parliament. He has continued to publish on topics relating to the phonology-morphology interface.

Ben Hermans

Ben Hermans is a Senior Researcher at the Meertens Instituut of the Royal Netherlands Academy of Arts and Sciences. He obtained his PhD from the Free University of Amsterdam in 1994. He is interested in the synchronic and diachronic phonology of Limburgian dialects.

Frans Hinskens

Frans Hinskens is a Senior Researcher at the Meertens Instituut of the Royal Netherlands Academy of Arts and Sciences and professor of Language Variation and Language Change at VU University Amsterdam. He completed his PhD at the University of Nijmegen in 1993. Between 1998 and 2002 he was chair of the Department of Dutch at the University of Leipzig.

Harry van der Hulst

Harry van der Hulst is a professor of Linguistics at the University of Connecticut. He obtained his PhD from the University of Leiden in 1984. His main research interests are feature systems and segmental structure, syllable structure, word accent systems, vowel harmony and sign language phonology.

John J. McCarthy
John J. McCarthy is Distinguished University Professor, Vice-Provost for Graduate Education, and Dean of the Graduate School at the University of Massachusetts Amherst. He completed his PhD at Massachusetts Institute of Technology in 1979. His research interests lie in the areas of phonology, morphology, and their interface.

Jeff Mielke
Jeff Mielke is an associate professor of Linguistics at the University of Ottawa. He completed his PhD in 2004 at the Ohio State University and held a postdoc at the University of Arizona. He uses laboratory and computational techniques to study language sound patterns at the typological level and at the level of the individual.

Kevin Mullin
Kevin Mullin is a doctoral student in the Department of Linguistics at the University of Massachusetts Amherst. He does experimental research on speech perception and formal theoretical phonology in Serial Harmonic Grammar and Harmonic Serialism.

Roland Noske
Roland Noske is an associate professor at the Department of Foreign Languages and Cultures (Dutch section) at the University of Lille and a member of the Joint Research Group (CNRS) STL. He completed his PhD at the University of Tilburg in 1992 and his habilitation at Denis Diderot University (Paris 7) in 2001. His research interests include Dutch linguistics, French linguistics, syllable structure, typology, and historical linguistics.

Marc van Oostendorp
Marc van Oostendorp is a Senior Researcher at the Meertens Instituut of the Royal Netherlands Academy of Arts and Sciences and professor of Phonological Microvariation at the University of Leiden. He obtained his PhD from the University of Tilburg in 1995. His research interests include the phonology of varieties of Dutch, language policies, and the interface between phonology and morphosyntax.

Krisztina Polgárdi
Krisztina Polgárdi is a Senior Research Fellow at the Research Institute for Linguistics at the Hungarian Academy of Sciences. She took her PhD at the University of Leiden in 1998. Her research focuses on syllable structure issues in Hungarian, Turkish, Dutch and English.

Douglas Pulleyblank
Douglas Pulleyblank is Head of the Department of Linguistics at the University of British Columbia. He completed a PhD in Linguistics at the Massachusetts Institute of Technology in 1983. His main research interests are phonology and the interface between phonology and phonetics. He has a long-standing interest in Nigerian languages, particularly Yoruba, as well as African languages in general.

Brian W. Smith
Brian W. Smith is a doctoral student in the Department of Linguistics at the University of Massachusetts Amherst. His research deals with theoretical approaches to phonological variation and the phonology-morphology interface, especially in the framework of Harmonic Grammar.

Irene Vogel
Irene Vogel is Full Professor at the University of Delaware. She received her PhD from Stanford University. Her research focuses on the various interfaces of phonology with other components of grammar.

Jeroen van de Weijer
Jeroen van de Weijer is Full Professor of English Linguistics at Shanghai International Studies University. He took his PhD at the University of Leiden in 1994. His research focuses on combining models of theoretical phonology with psycholinguistics.

Bert Botma & Roland Noske

Introduction

This collection of phonological papers grew out of the editors' realization, back in 2010, that Norval Smith would soon reach the age of 65, when he would be due to retire from his post at the University of Amsterdam. Our intention was to present him with this book on the day of his retirement (September 30, 2011). As it turns out, the project took almost exactly a year longer than we had anticipated.

The contributors to this volume include former colleagues, collaborators and students of Norval's. Their contributions explore a broad range of topics. We believe that this reflects not only Norval's own research interests (for which 'broad' is perhaps an understatement), but that it also offers a good representation of current phonological thinking, from different empirical, theoretical and diachronic angles.

In "Allomorphy and the architecture of grammar", Geert Booij considers a number of patterns of Dutch allomorphy. He observes that only a small part of these can be accounted for in terms of a common underlying form, with the surface forms being derived by phonological rules. For example, while it has been claimed that the relation between words like *rode* [roːdə] and *rooie* [roːjə] 'red (inflected)' is the result of a process of $d > j$ weakening (see e.g. Smith 1973), such a view is in fact problematic. Not only is $d > j$ weakening lexically restricted, but words with *j* may also have idiosyncratic meanings. For instance, *rooie* has the additional, unpredictable meaning of 'communist', suggesting that the word is stored. On the basis of such observations, Booij concludes that most allomorphs have to be listed in the lexicon, as words or as constituents of words. Booij goes on to show that this view of allomorphy has important consequences for the architecture of grammar.

In "From *prof* to *provo*", Camiel Hamans explores the interaction between phonology and morphology from the perspective of Dutch clippings. Hamans observes two distinct patterns: monosyllabic clippings (e.g. *prof* < *professor*) and a more recent pattern of disyllabic clippings ending in *-o* (e.g. *provo* < *provocateur*). A further development is that this *-o* is now also added to full forms, as in *suffo* 'silly person' (compare English *sicko*). Hamans examines two previous analyses of Dutch clipping, Van de Vijver (1997) and Hinskens (2001), and a more recent proposal for English in Lappe (2007). He observes that the analyses of Van de Vijver and Hinskens can be applied to the change from a monosyllabic to a disyllabic clipping template (with the change itself involving constraint reranking), while Lappe's approach can be applied to the extension of *-o* to full forms.

Is recursion restricted to the syntactic component of the grammar, or is it also a property of the phonological component? This question has recently met with renewed interest (see esp. Van der Hulst 2010). In "Recursion in phonology?", Irene Vogel focuses on an area where recursion has often been claimed to be relevant, viz. in structures involving Phonological Words. Vogel evaluates these claims and shows that the recursive structures that have been proposed introduce problems with regard to both phonological structure (e.g., they violate the Strict Layer Hypothesis) and linguistic structure in general (recursion in Phonological Words exhibits different properties than recursion in syntax). Vogel goes on to consider two alternative recursion-free proposals: a string-based analysis, and an analysis which retains the prosodic hierarchy. The latter account assumes an additional 'Composite Group', a constituent between the Phonological Word and the Phonological Phrase. The Composite Group permits skipping of prosodic levels (subject to several restrictions), and therefore avoids the problems with the Strict Layer Hypothesis. Vogel evaluates this analysis against a range of crosslinguistic data and psycholinguistic experiments.

The next two contributions are concerned with chain shifts in the history of Germanic. In "The Grimm-Verner push chain and Contrast Preservation Theory", Roland Noske shows that the adoption of the Glottalic Theory of the Proto-Indo-European obstruent inventory makes it possible to analyze Grimm's Law and Verner's Law as a single, bifurcating chain shift. This analysis resolves a number of problems associated with the traditional Neogrammarian view, in which Verner's Law applied at a later time than Grimm's Law. The assumption of a bifurcating chain shift explains why the undergoers of Verner's Law are properly included in those of Grimm's Law. It also replaces the peculiar chronological development that is traditionally assumed for Germanic (voiceless plosive > *voiceless fricative > *voiced fricative > voiced plosive) by a scenario in which voiced plosives derive directly from voiceless ones, without unattested intermediate forms. In the second part of his paper, Noske shows that the proposed scenario receives a natural account in Contrast Preservation Theory (Łubowicz 2003, 2012; see also Montrueil 2006).

In "Segmental structure and vowel shifts", Janet Grijzenhout accounts for a number of historical developments in Germanic vowel systems, including vocalic chain shifts. In Grijzenhout's model, vowels are specified in terms of the elements |I|, |U|, |A|, |@|, and combinations of these. Such combinations involve head/dependency relations between elements, such that one element is the head (and so phonetically more prominent) and the other the dependent (and so phonetically less prominent). Grijzenhout's approach offers a straightforward interpretation of a number of diachronic changes. Most importantly, since elements are privative, they offer an inherent evaluation metric to measure the complexity of segments. This allows a natural account of such processes as unrounding of front vowels. For example, the change /yː/ > /iː/, as has occurred in e.g. Old Icelandic, involves the loss of the |U| element, viz. |I,U| > |I|, yielding a less marked structure. Grijzenhout provides a dependency-based analysis of this change and a host of other vowel changes from Proto-Indo-European to Proto-Germanic, and from English and Icelandic.

Turning to synchronic issues, in "The distribution of vowels in English and trochaic proper government", Krisztina Polgárdi presents an account of the distribution of RP English vowels (short tense, long tense, short lax, and long lax) in terms of a loose CV framework, a representational approach that builds on earlier work in Government Phonology, in particular Lowenstamm (1996). An important ingredient of Polgárdi's analysis is that stressed rhymes must properly govern an empty nucleus to their right. Polgárdi shows that this assumption helps to explain the complementary distribution of short and long vowels: the former do not occur in open syllables (e.g. *[bræ], where the short lax vowel cannot properly govern) while the latter cannot occur in closed syllables (e.g. *[viːktə], where the second part of the long vowel cannot properly govern the following empty nucleus). Polgárdi assumes that apparently open syllables with short lax vowels (e.g. the first syllable in *city*) are closed by the first part of a 'virtual geminate'. This allows the generalization that short lax vowels must be followed by a consonant cluster. Support for this comes from Welsh English, where virtual geminates are realized as long phonetically, e.g. *city* ['sɪtːɪ] and *hook* [hʊkː].

In "A propos of the Dutch vowel system 21 years on, 22 years on", Bert Botma and Marc van Oostendorp take a fresh look at the phonological specification of the two sets of Dutch monophthongs (viz. /aː, eː, øː, oː, i, y, u/ vs. /ɑ, ɛ, ɪ, ɔ, ʏ/). In doing so, they build on insights from Smith et al. (1989), who were themselves inspired by the work of Rudolf de Rijk (cf. De Rijk 1967). Botma and Van Oostendorp identify three approaches to the Dutch vowel system: one in which the contrast is in terms of length, one in which the contrast is in terms of quality (between 'tense' and 'lax' vowels), and one in which the contrast is between 'strongly cut' and 'weakly cut' syllables. After reviewing the evidence, Botma and Van Oostendorp argue in favour of the last option, a view which originated in the work of Sievers and Trubetzkoy. Botma and Van Oostendorp point out that an advantage of a syllabic approach is that the contrast between the two sets of vowels need no longer be made in terms of a feature [tense] or [lax], for which phonetic support has not been forthcoming.

Harry van der Hulst's "A minimal framework for vowel harmony" is couched in the framework of Radical cv Phonology, a minimalist offshoot of the dependency-based approach to segmental structure. After outlining the general background of the framework, Van der Hulst applies RcvP to a number of processes of vowel harmony. His main proposal is that vowels in a harmonic domain contain the harmonic element as a variable element. Variable elements surface only when they are 'licensed', either positionally (e.g. because they are in word-initial position) or laterally (i.e. because of a preceding or following instance of the same element). This approach has a number of interesting consequences. One concerns the status of 'transparent' vowels. Consider Finnish, a language with progressive palatal harmony. Van der Hulst formalizes the Finnish harmony pattern in terms of variable |I|, which, when present, is positionally licensed in the first vowel of a word and laterally in every following vowel (e.g. *tyhmæ-stæ* 'stupid-ILL'). Finnish /i e/ have traditionally been described as 'transparent' (e.g. Van der Hulst & Smith 1986), since they occur in both front and back words, and do not impose their frontness on a following back vowel (e.g. *tuoli-lla* 'chair-ADESS', where /i/ is followed by a back vowel in the suffix). In Van der Hulst's analysis, back words do not contain any instance of variable |I| (the [i] in *tuolilla* is argued to derive from underlying /ɨ/), so that here no harmony takes place. In front words, /i e/ simply participate in the harmony, as their specification for variable |I| is licensed either positionally or laterally (e.g. *velje-llæ* 'brother-ADESS'). Hence, in Van der Hulst's account 'transparent' vowels do not in fact exist.

A quite different perspective on vowel harmony is presented in Diana Archangeli, Jeff Mielke and Douglas Pulleyblank's "Greater than noise: frequency effects in Bantu height harmony". The authors contrast two fundamentally different theories of phonological competence, viz. Universal Grammar (UG) and Emergent Grammar (EG). These two theories make different predictions about how phonological patterns are reflected in a language's frequency data. Under UG, phonological patterns are expected to be (close to) categorical, predicting a tight statistical adherence to postulated patterns. Under EG, phonological patterns are expected to have more exceptions, predicting a looser statistical adherence. In addition, unlike UG, EG predicts that phonological patterns may be gradually extended to broader classes, with the relevant generalizations acting as 'data attractors'. Archangeli et al. test these predictions by comparing the frequencies of vowel co-occurrence patterns in 6 Bantu languages with a five-vowel system (/i, e, a, o, u/) and height harmony, against 6 control languages with a five-vowel system and no harmony. The canonical height harmony pattern is displayed by Ciyao. In this language, harmony is primarily a property of verbal stems (in root-suffix combinations). The pattern is asymmetric, in that high front vowels surface as high after high and low root vowels and as mid after mid vowels, while high back vowels surface as high after high and low root vowels and after front mid /e/, but lower to mid back after /o/. Thus, the sequences *e...i*, *o...i* and *o...u* (but not *e...u*) are expected to be virtually absent under a UG account, but merely under-represented under an EG account. The results of Archangeli et al.'s study are consistent with EG. The data indicate that height harmony in verbs is not categorical. It appears to extend morphologically to the class of nouns, and phonologically to any sequence of a mid plus high vowel sequence. Phonological extension is observed in nouns, which contain fewer *e...u* sequences than would be expected. This suggests that the harmony pattern is gradually extended in such a way that any high vowel lowers before a mid vowel.

The next two papers in the volume deal with Limburgian. While normally classified as a tone-accent language, both show that the phonological status of tone in Limburgian is in fact a matter of contention. In "The phonological representation of Limburgian tone accents", Ben Hermans argues that the two tonal word patterns in Limburgian, Accent 1 and Accent 2, are predictable from prosodic structure. Based on fieldwork data from the dialect of Maasbracht, Hermans observes a number of important regularities in the distribution of Accents 1 and 2. One is that a non-high vowel requires Accent 1 in a preceding syllable, while a high vowel requires Accent 2 in a preceding syllable. To account for this difference, Hermans adopts a model similar to that of Halle & Vergnaud (1987), but in which syllables are located in the same dimension as feet. In Hermans' model, trochees can be bisyllabic or monosyllabic; the former have Accent 2, the latter have Accent 1. In this way, Hermans accounts for the distribution of the two accents. For example, a non-high vowel in the second syllable of a word is sufficiently sonorous to project its own foot. The initial syllable will therefore form a foot on its own (a monosyllabic trochee), which receives Accent 1. In contrast, a high vowel in the second syllable of a word is not sufficiently sonorous to project its own foot. Therefore, it forms a foot together with the initial syllable (a bisyllabic trochee), which receives Accent 2. In this analysis, there is thus no need to posit tones underlyingly, as in previous accounts of Limburgian tone.

In "Quantity or durational enhancement of tone: the case of Maastricht Limburgian high vowels", Carlos Gussenhoven offers further support for the claim that the high vowels of Maastricht Limburgian contrast in terms of length rather than tone (see Gussenhoven & Aarts 1999). Gussenhoven reports on a production experiment in which the length difference between tonal minimal pairs and minimal pairs with high vowels is compared. The results show that the length difference in high vowels, i.e. between /i, u/ and /iː, uː/, is treated differently from the length difference that is due to tone, in non-high vowels. The results of this experiment raise the question of how Maastricht Limburgian can maintain its tone contrasts along with the other vocalic contrasts that it employs. Gussenhoven suggests that the language is in the process of losing lexical tone. In the past, the situation in Maastricht

Limburgian was similar to that in the dialect of Cologne, where both high and non-high vowels can bear contrastive tone. The Maastricht dialect is probably developing towards the situation found in the dialect of nearby Weert, which has lost all lexical tone contrasts.

In "Using constraint conjunction to discover constraints: the case of Mandarin Chinese", Jeroen van de Weijer discusses a hitherto unnoticed restriction in Mandarin Chinese. Barring very few exceptions, this language lacks syllables with a voiced stop followed by a vowel with (a rising) tone 2 and a nasal (e.g. *dán, *bíŋ). As Van de Weijer points out, at least part of this restriction is phonetically natural, since the low tone that is associated with the voiced onset stop is antagonistic to the high tone of the following vowel. (It is less clear whether a similar antagonistic relation obtains between the high toned vowel and the nasal.) Van de Weijer analyzes the restriction in terms of two conjoined OT constraints, one banning sequences of a voiced onset and a high toned vowel, and one banning sequences of a high toned vowel and a nasal. By themselves these constraints are relatively low-ranked, but the conjunction of the two constraints is ranked high in the grammar of Mandarin Chinese.

In "Implications of harmonic serialism for lexical tone association", John McCarthy, Kevin Mullin and Brian Smith compare tone association in two versions of OT, parallel OT (Prince & Smolensky 1993[2004]) and Harmonic Serialism (e.g. McCarthy 2010). In parallel OT, output candidates may show the effect of several phonological changes simultaneously. Harmonic Serialism, on the other hand, is derivational: here output candidates show the effect of one change at a time, with the winning candidate being run through the grammar once again so that it can accumulate additional changes. McCarthy et al. observe that although there is growing support for Harmonic Serialism, the model is unable to account for the tonal pattern of languages like Kikuyu, if these tones are construed of as being lexically linked. This leads the authors to return to an assumption of early work in autosegmental phonology, viz. that tones are never associated in underlying representations — a position that is in accordance with the OT principle of Richness of the Base.

In "A constraint-based explanation of the McGurk effect", Paul Boersma provides an OT account of the McGurk effect, a phenomenon that illustrates the low-level interaction of visual and auditory cues in speech perception. Boersma formalizes the interaction between cue constraints (which evaluate the relation between sensory and phonological representations) and structural constraints (which evaluate phonological representations) using perception tableaux. The procedure of lexicon-driven perceptual learning then explains how the constraints come to be ranked as they are. Boersma goes on to show that the same cue constraints and structural constraints are used in production by speakers.

Frans Hinskens' "Liquids in a case of unfolding early L1 Dutch" describes the development of /l/ and /r/ in a Dutch acquiring girl between the ages of 1;5 and 3;3. Hinskens shows that that the liquid system develops from one in which neither /l/ nor /r/ is realized, via free variation and a phase in which the realizations are probabilistically conditioned by internal constraints, into the prevalent adult system, where /l/ and /r/ are fully contrastive. Hinskens relates his case study to what is known about the unfolding of consonant inventories in the early L1 acquisition of Dutch, as well as to more general aspects of the phonology of liquids.

In "The Tibetan numerals segmentation problem and how virtual learners solve it", Diana Apoussidou compares the performance of two models in the acquisition of the morphological segmentation of Tibetan numerals. One model combines OT with the Gradual Learning Algorithm (GLA, Boersma 2008); the other model combines Harmonic Grammar (HG, Boersma & Pater 2008) with GLA. HG differs from OT in that it uses positive weights as well constraint violations represented by negative integers. Candidate forms are evaluated by multiplying the violations of a constraint with its corresponding weight. Apoussidou shows that her two groups of virtual learners (one using using OT/GLA, the other HG/GLA) acquire the Tibetan system, but do so in different ways. The OT/GLA learners use a restrictive lexicon, and so assign a greater role to the grammar. The HG/GLA learners, on the other hand, fall into two groups: one group uses a restrictive lexicon (like the OT/GLA learners) while the other makes extensive use of allomorphy. The difference between the latter group and the group of OT/GLA learners results from an important difference between OT and HG: in HG, the cumulative effect of lighter-weighted constraints can outweigh a heavier-weighted constraint. Apoussidou suggests that in the Tibetan numerals case, faithfulness and the respective lexical constraints together outweigh a heavier-weighted lexical constraint. This results in the production of more errors, which leads the latter group of HG/GLA learners to resort more to allomorphy.

It remains for us to thank the contributors to this volume for meeting our rather stringent deadlines. We are also grateful to 35 anonymous reviewers for constructive comments and for their willingness to review papers at such short notice. Some of the papers in this volume were presented at a workshop at the University of Amsterdam, on the day of Norval's retirement. We would like to thank the speakers, and Enoch Aboh and Kees Hengeveld for helping to organize the workshop research.

References

Boersma, Paul (2008): "A programme for bidirectional phonology and phonetics and their acquisition and evolution." ROA-868.

Boersma, Paul & Joe Pater (2008): "Convergence properties of a gradual learning algorithm for Harmonic Grammar." ROA-970.

De Rijk, Rudolf (1967): "A propos of the Dutch vowel system." Ms., MIT (electronic edition at http://dbnl.nl/tekst/rijk004apro01_01/).

Gussenhoven, Carlos & Flor Aarts (1999): "The dialect of Maastricht." – In: *Journal of the International Phonetic Association* 29, 55–66.

Halle, Morris & Jean Roger Vergnaud (1987): *An Essay on Stress.* – Cambridge, Mass.: MIT Press.

Hinskens, Frans (2001): "Hypocoristische vormen en reductievormen in het hedendaagse Nederlands." – In: *Neerlandica Extra Muros* 39: 37–49.

Lappe, Sabine (2007): *English Prosodic Morphology.* – Dordrecht: Springer.

Lowenstamm, Jean (1996): "CV as the only syllable type." – In: Durand, Jacques & Bernard Laks (eds.), *Current Trends in Phonology: Models and Methods*, 419–441. CNRS/ESRI, Paris X.

Łubowicz, Anna (2003): *Contrast Preservation in Phonological Mappings.* PhD dissertation, University of Massachusetts Amherst – Amherst, Mass.:GSLA. ROA-554.

– (2012): *The Phonology of Contrast.* – London: Equinox.

McCarthy, John J. (2010): "An introduction to Harmonic Serialism." – In: *Language and Linguistics Compass* 4, 1001–1018.

Montrueil, Jean-Pierre (2006): "Contrast Preservation Theory and historical change." – In: Gess, Randall S. & Deborah Arteaga (eds.), *Historical Romance Linguistics. Retrospective and Perspectives*, 111–129. Amsterdam/Philadelphia: John Benjamins.

Prince, Alan & Paul Smolensky (1993[2004]): *Optimality Theory: Constraint Interaction in Generative Grammar* – Malden, Mass./Oxford, UK: Blackwell.

Smith, Norval S. H. (1973): "The phenomenon of D-deletion in Dutch." – In: *Spektator* 2, 421–437.

Smith, Norval S. H., Roberto Bolognesi, Frank van der Leeuw, Jean Rutten & Heleen de Wit (1989): "A propos of the Dutch vowel system 21 years on." – In: Bennis, Hans & Ans van Kemenade (eds.), *Linguistics in the Netherlands 1989*, 219–230. Dordrecht: Foris.

Van der Hulst, Harry (ed.) (2010): *Recursion and Human Language.* Berlin: Mouton de Gruyter.

Van der Hulst, Harry & Norval S.H. Smith (1986): "On neutral vowels." – In: Bogers, Koen, Harry van der Hulst & Maarten Mous (eds.), *The Phonological Representation of Suprasegmentals*, 233–279. Dordrecht: Foris.

Vijver, Ruben van de (1997): "The duress of stress: On Dutch clippings." – In: Coerts, Jane & Helen de Hoop (eds.): *Linguistics in the Netherlands*, 219–230. Amsterdam: John Benjamins.

Geert Booij

Allomorphy and the architecture of grammar*

1 Introduction

One of the tasks of phonology is to provide an adequate theory of how allomorphy, the variation in the phonological shape of morphemes and words, should be accounted for in the grammar of natural languages. In this article, I will argue that lexically governed allomorphy, and even allomorphy in general, should be accounted for primarily in the lexicon. This view has various implications for the nature of the lexicon and the architecture of grammar, as we will see below.

One of the reasons for choosing this topic is that my esteemed colleague Norval Smith wrote some articles on this issue at the start of his linguistic career at the University of Amsterdam, in the 1970s. In those days, the phonological analysis of allomorphy received a new impetus through the rise of generative phonology, and in particular through the publication of Chomsky & Halle (1968). This also applies to the study of Dutch allomorphy, the topic of the present chapter and also of some of Norval Smith's early publications. The classical generative approach to allomorphy is that all allomorphs of a morpheme are derived from a common underlying form by means of a set of (possibly ordered) phonological rules.

A nice example of applying this idea of a common underlying form and a set of ordered rules to Dutch allomorphy phenomena can be found in Smith (1973). In this article (probably the first English contribution to *Spektator*, the journal for Dutch language and literature), Smith dealt with two types of allomorphy: the alternation between /d/ and the glides /j, w/, and the alternation between /də/ and ∅. The two types of alternation are illustrated in (1):

---

* The research for this article was supported by a fellowship from the Alexander von Humboldt-Stiftung, which is gratefully acknowledged here. I thank Matthias Hüning (FU Berlin) and two anonymous reviewers for their comments on an earlier version of this article.

(1)   a.   /d/-*glide alternation*

kwade	[kʋaːdə]	kwaaie	[kʋaːjə]	'angry(inflected)'
rode	[roːdə]	rooie	[roːjə]	'red (inflected)'
houden	[hɑudən]	houwen	[hɑuwən]	'to keep'
gouden	[ɣɑudən]	gouwen	[ɣɑuwən]	'golden'

        b.   /də/-∅ *alternation*

slede	[sleːdə]	slee	[sleː]	'sledge'
lade	[laːdə]	la	[laː]	'drawer'
broeder	[brudər]	broer	[bruːr]	'brother'
veder	[veːdər]	veer	[veːr]	'feather'

Smith proposed to account for these alternations by means of two rules: a rule that deletes /d/, followed by a rule that inserts a glide. In those cases where glide insertion does not apply, a rule of schwa deletion removes the unwanted post-vocalic schwa, as in *sled[ə] > sle[ə] > slee*.

This analysis was criticized in Zonneveld (1975), and Smith replied in Smith (1975). Zonneveld developed his analysis in more detail in his dissertation (Zonneveld 1978). Zonneveld's basic objection was that the two alternations cannot be subsumed under one rule of /d/-deletion. Instead, there is one rule turning /d/ into a glide, and another one that deletes /də/ inter-vocalically and at the end of a word. The details of this debate will not concern us here. Instead, I will comment on the underlying methodology of these analyses, and the problems that they evoke.

The major problem of these analyses lies in the leading idea of classical generative phonology that all alternation patterns have to be accounted for by rules. These rules apply to underlying forms, and derive the various surface alternants. As far as the alternations in (1) go, a problem for this approach is that the relevant rules are lexically governed. That is, they do not apply to all words that meet the structural description of the relevant phonological rules, but only to a subset of them. For instance, the word *slede* 'sledge' cannot be realized as *sleje* [sleje], nor the word *broeder* 'brother' as *broeier* [brujər]. Also, the word *woede* 'rage' cannot be realized as *woe* [wu]. Therefore, a rule-based analysis is forced to mark all relevant individual words with a rule feature [+R*n*], and to make that feature part of the structural description of Rule *n*. Alternatively, if the majority of words undergo the rule, the words that do not undergo it must be marked with a negative rule feature [–Rn], marking these words as negative exceptions to the rule. In this way, phonological rules can be blocked from applying to the wrong words.

A second example of the rule-based approach to allomorphy in Dutch is the classical analysis of the phonological variation displayed by the diminutive suffix, with its five allomorphs *-tje, -je, -kje, -pje, -etje*: *traan-tje* 'tear-DIM', *kat-je* 'cat-DIM', *konin-kje* 'king-DIM', *riem-pje* 'belt-DIM', *zonn-etje* 'sun-DIM'. The choice of a specific allomorph is governed by the phonological shape of the stem. Hence, it was argued that these five allomorphs could be derived from one underlying form /tjə/, by means of a set of ordered phonological rules (Haverkamp-Lubbers & Kooij 1971). This topic has been extensively discussed by Dutch linguists; see the references in Booij (1995) and Van der Hulst (2008). The problem in this case is that certain diminutives have exceptional forms. For instance, the diminutive of *brug* 'bridge' is either the regular *brug-je*, or the unexpected *brugg-etje*. Similarly, for *bloem* 'flower' we find not only the regular diminutive noun *bloem-pje* but also the irregular form *bloem-etje*, with both the regular meaning 'small flower' and the idiosyncratic meaning 'bunch of flowers'.

In the case of diminutive allomorphy there is another problem: the rules that we need cannot be considered general phonological rules of Dutch, since they apply to diminutive words only. For instance, the allomorph *-pje* shows up after stems ending in /m/ preceded by a long vowel (*riem – riem-pje*). This looks like a rule of nasal place assimilation. However, whereas it is normally the case in Dutch (and universally) that the nasal consonant adapts its place of articulation to the following obstruent, in this case the order of assimilation is the reverse: the underlying /t/ assimilates to the preceding /m/. Therefore, the rules for the alternations in the diminutive suffix must be qualified as morpholexical rules (Booij 1995). A morpholexical rule is a rule whose application is governed by the presence of a specific lexical or morphological feature, in this case the feature [+diminutive]. Hence, two types of phonological rules have to be distinguished: automatic phonological rules, which apply whenever the phonological structural description of the rule is met, and morpholexical rules, which have a more restricted application. The distinction between these two types of rules, and its relevance for the organization of phonology, was argued for in detail by Anderson (1974). Anderson's claim is that normally morpholexical rules precede automatic phonological rules.

The non-automatic nature of the allomorphy of the diminutive suffix has prompted some Dutch linguists to come up with alternative analyses. For instance, Van der Hulst has recently proposed an analysis in which the five allomorphs are listed, but summarized in a schema with variables and a fixed common part *je* (/jə/) (Van der Hulst 2008). A similar solution is offered in Van Zonneveld (1978):

(2)   -(ə) ({[–son], ([+cor])}) je

The selection of the variable material in this schema is then determined by the phonological properties of the stem: the variable material of the suffix can be omitted if this is necessary for the well-formedness of the output form. The basic idea is therefore that the allomorphs of this suffix are listed, but that the choice of a particular allomorph is still governed phonologically. A similar approach to allomorphy in Polish, in the framework of Optimality Theory, has been proposed in Rubach & Booij (2001). This approach also reflects the idea that if there is a clash between the phonological properties of a stem and those of a suffix, those of the stem prevail (Borowsky 2000).

So far, it seems that the problem of restricted application of rules can be solved by means of the devices mentioned above: rules can be governed by lexical and/or morphological features. Alternatively, allomorphs may be listed, but selected by phonological constraints, in which case stem properties may be given precedence to suffix properties.

However, there is another type of analytical problem in dealing with allomorphy phenomena, which we have already seen for the diminutive pair *bloempje - bloemetje*: the two allomorphs of a lexical morpheme may differ in meaning, or in stylistic value. For instance, the Dutch words *broeder* and *broer* 'brother' do not have the same range of meanings. The word *broeder* does not only mean 'brother' in the literal sense, but also 'male nurse', 'male member of a religious order', and 'male member of a protestant church community'. These additional meanings are not available for the short form *broer*. In the case of the alternation *rode – rooie* mentioned in (1a), the second form is more informal. Moreover, it has a lexicalized meaning, i.e. 'socialist', that *rode* does not have. In such cases, the two forms must therefore be stored in the lexicon for non-phonological reasons, along with their specific meaning or stylistic value. The process of *de*-deletion is no longer productive, and the allomorphy is a relic of the past. This means that the *de*/∅ alternation can at best be expressed in terms of a redundancy rule which states that some words have a corresponding *de*-less form with the same or a similar meaning. The same holds for the *d*/glide alternation, which cannot be extended to new words. However, while these alternations can be expressed in terms of redundancy rules, it is not obvious that speakers of Dutch do so. In fact, they do not need to do this, if we allow for the possibility that allomorphy can be lexically stored.

As mentioned above, in diminutive allomorphy there are some words with two diminutive forms, e.g. *kip-je – kipp-etje* 'chicken-DIM' and *brug-je – brugg-etje* 'bridge-DIM'. Moreover, there may be semantic differences between the two forms, as in *bloem-pje* 'small flower' vs. *bloem-etje* 'bunch of flowers, bouquet'. This implies lexical listing of the diminutive nouns with the various suffix allomorphs. There are also diminutive nouns without corresponding base words, such as *meis-je* 'girl', for which the base word *meis* is not available (except for some speakers as the result of back formation). These words must be listed, despite the fact that the diminutive suffix has the regular shape *-je* that is required after an obstruent.

How can we do justice to regularities in alternation patterns, and at the same time to the non-automatic and lexicalized nature of this allomorphy? This seems impossible in the classical approach sketched above. The problem is caused by the rule–list fallacy (Langacker 1987), viz. the idea that information that is stored cannot at the same time be specified as instantiating a regularity, and vice versa. Current views of the lexicon avoid this fallacy, by specifying both the various lexical forms and the abstract alternation patterns that they instantiate in the lexicon (see e.g. Booij (2010); Jackendoff (2002), and the references mentioned there). This means in effect that rules may function as redundancy rules that specify to what extent the information on lexical entries is predictable, redundant information (Jackendoff 1975). In the case of *broeder – broer*, for instance, both words are stored in the lexicon. They can be related by means of a phonological schema that specifies in which contexts this *də*/∅ alternation can occur. Each word is a combination of three types of information, phonological (PHON), morpho-syntactic (SYN), and semantic (SEM). The lexical information about the words *broeder* and *broer* will therefore have the following structure (with arbitrary lexical indices 9 and 10):

(3) /brudər/$_9$ ↔ SYN$_9$ ↔ SEM$_{9a}$, SEM$_{9b}$, SEM$_{9c}$
    /brudər/$_9$ ↔ SYN$_9$ ↔ SEM$_{9a}$

These two lexical entries share one meaning, i.e. the literal meaning of 'brother'(SEM$_{9a}$), whereas the other meanings are unique for the long word form *broeder*. The syntactic properties are identical. The phonological redundancy schema that expresses the relevant pattern may then be formulated as follows:

(4) Redundancy schema

</X V:də(r)/ ↔ SYN$_i$ ↔ SEM$_i$ > ≈ </X V:(r)/ ↔ SYN$_i$ ↔ SEM$_i$>

The parts between angle brackets are schemas (i.e. correlations of phonological form, morphosyntactic form, and meaning), and '≈' stands for 'is paradigmatically related to'. Hence, (4) expresses a generalization about all pairs of lexical entries of the sort exemplified in (3): for words with a long vowel followed by /dər/ or /də/ there may be a corresponding word without /də/. This rule has to be labeled explicitly as being a redundancy rule, since it cannot be applied productively to new cases.

A precursor of this conception of the lexicon in relation to phonological alternations can be found in Leben & Robinson's (1977) theory of 'upside-down phonology'. Phonological rules may work upside-down, to undo the effect of rules. The idea is that, given the strong lexical governedness of many phonological rules, it is preferable to store complex words in the lexicon in their surface forms. Phonological rules then have a redundancy rule function, and can be used to determine the relatedness of various lexical items by undoing the effect of phonological rules. For instance, in their approach the English rule of Trisyllabic Laxing would serve to relate *sanity* [sænɪti] to *sane* [seɪn], despite the fact that these words have different initial vowels. In the case of the deadjectival noun *obesity*, an exception to Trisyllabic Laxing, this rule is not necessary to relate the word to the adjective *obese*. Robinson also applied this idea to the allomorphs of Dutch diminutives (Robinson 1980). For instance, Dutch *riem-pje* 'belt-DIM' is computed back to *riem-tje*, and consequently recognizable as the diminutive form of *riem* 'belt'. In the case of *broeder – broer*, undoing the rule of *de*-deletion would mean that *broeder* is reconstructed by inserting *de*, which can then be related to the word *broeder* with the same meaning. However, notice that this incorrectly predicts that *broer* has the same range of meanings as *broeder*. Therefore, the upside-down phonology approach cannot be the whole solution, as it cannot deal with semantic differences between allomorphs.

After this short introductory sketch of the issues that allomorphy raises with respect to the architecture of grammar, the next sections will discuss in more detail how allomorphy should be accounted for. The leading idea is that allomorphy is to a remarkably large extent a matter of the lexicon and of morphology, and not of phonology. Section 2 shows how the selection of an allomorph may be governed by morphological rather than phonological considerations. Section 3 argues that in a model which assumes paradigmatic word formation, selection of the appropriate allomorph is a straightforward affair. Section 4 discusses the role of phonological output conditions in the choice between allomorphs. Section 5 considers briefly the implications of allomorphy for the issue of storage vs. computation. Finally, section 6 summarizes my conclusions as to what allomorphy implies for the architecture of grammar.

2 Morphological implications of allomorphy

Morphemes may vary in their phonetic shape due to the effect of automatic phonological rules. An example is the rule of syllable-final devoicing in Dutch; this explains why the lexical morpheme *hoed* 'hat' has the shape [hut] when used as a singular form, and [hud] in the plural form *hoed-en* /hudən/. The standard analysis is that the morpheme *hoed* has the underlying form /hud/. However, in many cases allomorphy has lost its synchronic motivation. This is the case for the words in (1b): these words were subject to a historical phonological process of *de*-deletion that affected words one by one. Synchronically, we end up with two different words that may still be synonymous. However, in most cases there is independent evidence (semantic, pragmatic, stylistic, or other) for their status as separate lexical items. In some cases, language users may feel that the two words are no longer related, as is the case for a word pair like *ijdel* 'vain' – *ijl* 'thin'. The same applies to Dutch words that differ in the presence vs. the absence of a final schwa, such as those in (5):

(5) aard[ə]   aard   'earth'
     eind[ə]   eind   'end'
     er[ə]   eer   'honour'
     keuz[ə]   keus   'choice'
     leuz[ə]   leus   'slogan'
     wijz[ə]   wijs   'manner'

There is no automatic rule of word-final schwa-deletion in present-day Dutch, and speakers of Dutch have to learn in which case this alternation applies. The process of word-final schwa-deletion is no longer productive. Therefore, we have to assume that both words are stored in the lexicon, and that they may be related by a phonological redundancy schema which states that nouns that end in a schwa may have a correspondent without schwa, with the same meaning. This schema, which expresses a paradigmatic relationship between two sets of words, will have the format shown in (4). Since this schema is not productive, language users can do without it, as they will have stored all relevant cases.

When words of the kind in (5) function as constituents of compounds, it may be that one of the allomorphs has to be chosen obligatorily. For instance, the word *eind* 'end' can function as first part of a compound, as in the forms in (6):

(6) eind-bedrag   'final amount of money'
     eind-gesprek   'final discussion'
     eind-oordeel   'final judgment'
     eind-verslag   'final report'

In these compounds, the allomorph *eind* cannot be replaced with the long allomorph *einde*: a word like **einde-bedrag* is ill-formed. On the other hand, the long form does occur as the rightmost constituent (i.e. as the head) of compounds, in forms as in (7):

(7) gespreks-eind(e)   'discussion end, end of discussion'
     levens-eind(e)   'life end, end of life'

In these words, the long form may be replaced with the short form; for instance, we also find *levens-eind*, as shown in (7).

The data in (6) imply that compounds with initial *eind-* have to be stored in the lexicon. This is an interesting conclusion in relation to the debate on the balance between storage and computation. These compounds are quite regular as to form and meaning. However, even though their meaning is fully transparent, they must be stored in order to specify the correct choice of allomorph. The regularity that it is the short form *eind* that has to be used in compounds can be expressed by a subschema for NN compounds of the following type (Booij 2005, 2009a, 2010):

(8) $<[\text{eind}_i \ N_j]_{Nk} \leftrightarrow [\text{final}_i \ N_j]_k>$

In this schema, the double-arrowed symbol denotes the correlation between form and meaning. The meaning 'final' correlates with this use of the short form *eind*.

The preceding discussion shows that the choice of a particular allomorph may be morphologized, i.e. depend on its position in a complex word. This form of lexicalization may go hand in hand with the development of allo-morphs into affixoids. For instance, the word *eind-* in the compounds in (3) has acquired the specific meaning 'final', and we might therefore claim that Dutch has acquired a prefix *eind-* with this meaning (Booij 2005). The term 'affixoid' is used here to denote words with a 'bound' meaning, i.e. a meaning linked to a word that is part of a complex word. This affixoid behaviour can also be observed in the distribution of the words *ere* [e:rǝ] and *eer* [e:r], both meaning 'honour'. In isolation, the short form *eer* is preferred to the long form *ere* (which has an archaic flavour). However, when used with the meaning 'honorary', it is always the long form that is used, while the short form is used when other meanings are involved:

(9)   a.   ere-lid   'honorary member' (litt. 'honour member')
            ere-voorzitter   'honorary chairman' (litt. 'honour chairman')

      b.   eer-betoon   'mark of honour' (litt. 'honour show')
            eer-bied   'respect' (litt. 'honour offering')

This regularity concerning *ere-* can be expressed by a morphological subschema for NN compounds with *ere* as their first constituent.

(10) $[\text{ere}_i \ N_j]N_k \leftrightarrow [\text{honorary}_i \ N_j]_k$

This kind of variation is reminiscent of the morphomic phenomena discussed in Aronoff (1994). In many languages, a lexical item may have various stems that are used in inflection and word formation. In Latin, for instance, verbs have three different stem allomorphs, and the choice of a particular stem variant is determined by purely morphological considerations. In the case of

Dutch, the choice of allomorph may also be conditioned semantically, as shown in (9): one allomorph, used in a particular morphological structure, carries one meaning from the set of meanings of a lexical item.

We have seen, therefore, that an allomorph which results from a historical phonological process of schwa-deletion may receive a new interpretation as an affixoid, that is, as a word with a specific meaning in a specific morphological structure.

3 Morphological selection of allomorphs

The data discussed in section 2 show that the selection of allomorphs may shift from phonology to morphology (cf. also Booij 2002, Chapter 5.3). The morphological selection of allomorphs can also be observed in the systematic difference between native and non-native allomorphs of Dutch words. Consider the following sets of related words:

(11) *Base word*   *Native suffix*   *Non-native suffix*

   a. filter /fɪltər/ 'filter'   filter-en 'to filter'   filtr-eer   'to filter'
   b. regel /reːɣəl/ 'rule'   regel-en 'to arrange' regul-eer 'to regulate'
   c. orkest /ɔrkɛst/ 'orchestra' orkest-en 'orchestras' orkestr-eer 'to orchestrate'

In (11a), the word *filter* has the allomorph *filtr-* in words coined with a non-native suffix; in (11b), the word *regel* has *regul-* as its allomorph before the non-native suffix *-eer*; in (11c), the word *orkest* has the allomorph *orkestr-* before the non-native suffix *-eer*. This may seem to imply that for each of these three words we have to list two stem allomorphs, a native stem that is the form when used as a word by itself (or in combination with a prefix, as in *ge-regel* '(the act of) arranging things'), and a non-native stem allomorph that is used before non-native suffixes. In some cases, it may look as though the relation between the two allomorphs can be captured by the phonology. Suppose we assume the underlying form /fɪltr/ for the word *filter*. From this underlying form we may derive the word *filter* by means of schwa insertion, a phonological rule that rescues the unsyllabifiable coda cluster /tr/. In *filtreer*, schwa insertion does not apply since the syllabification is *fil.treer* (the dot indicates a syllable boundary), with /tr/ forming an onset. However, this does not explain why a schwa is inserted in the (infinitive form of the) verb *filteren*, as *fil.tren* would also be well formed prosodically. That is, the presence of schwa within the stem is not due to phonological requirements. In the case of *orkest*, we might assume an underlying form with final /r/, i.e. *orkestr*. However, here the /r/ cannot be rescued by schwa-insertion (as is the case for German: *Orchester*) since the word in isolation is not *orkester*, but *orkest*. In the case of *regel*, with its non-native stem allomorph *regul-* , the situation is even more complex.

What can be achieved as a descriptive generalization is that we assign the allomorphy to the stem, and not to the suffix. Consider the following Dutch complex adjectives and their base words:

(12)	moment	'moment'	moment-eel	'at this moment'
	tekst	'text'	tekstu-eel	'textual'
	ratio	'ratio'	ration-eel	'rational'
	positie	'position'	position-eel	'positional'
(13)	muziek	'music'	muzik-aal	'musical'
	rabbi	'rabbi'	rabbin-aal	'rabbinal'
	ras	'race'	raci-aal	'racial'
	dictator	'dictator'	dictatori-aal	'dictatorial'

These facts are described in De Haas & Trommelen (1993) as cases of suffix allomorphy. The suffix *-eel* is said to have the allomorphs *-ueel* and *-oneel*, and the suffix *-aal* is described as having the allomorphs *-naal* and *-iaal*. Such a description misses the generalization that the extra elements *i, u, n* and *on* recur in the different types of non-native complex words. For instance, *on* also shows up in *position-eer*, and the *n* also appears in *rabbin-aat* 'position of a rabbi' and in *rabbin-isme* 'teachings of the rabbis'. Hence, these extra 'bits of sound' are stem extensions rather than initial parts of suffixes.

It will now be clear that these alternations do not belong to the domain of phonology proper. Does this mean that the stem allomorphs of the relevant words have to be listed as such? This would mean that speakers of Dutch memorize allomorphs such as *regul-* and *position-*. The question is: how do speakers acquire these allomorphs? The obvious answer is: as part of the complex words that they come across and memorize. In other words, a stem allomorph like *rabbin-* is not stored in isolation, but as part of complex words such as *rabbinaal* and *rabbinaat*.

The only reason why one might think that such stem allomorphs are stored as such is that they can be used for coining new words. For example, if we want to derive a word in *-ist* from the word *positie* 'position', the word will be *positionist*, not *positist*. However, we do not need to list a stem allomorph in isolation, because new words can be coined on the basis of paradigmatic relations between existing words (Booij 2002, 2010). That is, we can derive *positionist* from *positioneel* by replacing the suffix *-eel* with the suffix *-ist*.

The necessity of assuming paradigmatic relationships is clear for independent reasons, from cases where there is no base word that is shared by the word pairs (Booij 2010). Consider the following English word pairs in *-ism* and *-ist*:

(14) altru-ism   altru-ist
      aut-ism   aut-ist
      bapt-ism   baptist
      commun-ism   communist
      pacific-ism   pacif-ist

Even though they have no corresponding base word, the meaning of one member of a pair can be defined in terms of that of the other member. In particular, the meaning of the word with *-ist* can often be paraphrased as 'person with the ability, disposition, or ideology denoted by the word in *-ism*'. Hence, the following paradigmatic relationship can be defined for these two schemas:

(15) <[x-ism]Ni↔SEMi>≈<[x-ist]N$_j$↔[person with property Y related to SEM$_i$]$_j$>

where SEM$_i$ represents the meaning of the word in *-ism*, and the angle brackets mark the edges of a constructional schema. Thus, an altruist has a disposition for altruism, and a pacifist adheres to the ideology of pacifism. The paradigmatic relationship between these two schemas may lead to the coining of new words. For instance, if we know what *determinism* is, we can easily coin the word *determinist*, which predictably denotes a person adhering to determinism.

In sum, stem allomorphy can easily be recognized and recovered on the basis of existing and hence listed complex words, from which other complex words can be derived by means of affix substitution.

What remains to be accounted for is when and how language users recognize various allomorphs as being formal variants of the same word. I will not discuss this issue in this chapter; see Booij (2010: Chapter 10) for a brief discussion. Our focus here is on the implications of allomorphy for the architecture of grammar, and the facts discussed above lead to the conclusion that allomorphy is massively stored in the lexicon and encoded in the lexical representation of existing, listed complex words.

4 Phonological selection of allomorphs

If the various allomorphs of a morpheme cannot be derived from one underlying form, this does not mean that their distribution cannot be governed by phonological conditions, as pointed out by Carstairs (1988): the two competing forms may be phonologically completely unrelated, yet their selection may be determined phonologically. A good example of this situation is the competition between the Dutch suffixes *-er* and *-aar*, discussed in another article by Norval Smith (Smith 1976). These two suffixes have a common historical origin; according to the *Woordenboek der Nederlandsche Taal*, the suffix *-aar* is a later, strengthened form of *-er*. Synchronically, it does not make sense to assume a rule that can derive *-er* from *-aar* or vice versa, as there is no independent evidence for such rules apart from the *-er/-aar* alternation. If we tried to capture such alternations in phonological terms, we would end up with a very complicated, and very probably unlearnable phonological system. Therefore, it is a better idea to come up with an analysis in which the phonological complementary distribution of allomorphs is captured in a more insightful way. For instance, the selection of allomorphs can be modeled as the result of a set of ranked phonological output conditions. This is proposed for *-er* and *-aar* in Booij (1998), and for certain types of allomorphy in Polish by Rubach & Booij (2001). The basic generalization for the Dutch cases is that *-aar* occurs after a stem ending in an unstressed syllable with a final coronal sonorant, and *-er* elsewhere (with the variant *-der* after /r/) (Booij 2002: 183):

(16) a. eet   'to eat'   et-er   'eater'
      judo   'to do judo'   judo-er   'judoist'
      Amsterdam   'id.'   Amsterdamm-er 'inhabitant of Amsterdam'
      wetenschap   'science'   wetenschapp-er 'scientist'

    b. vereer   'to worship' vereer-der   'worshipper'
      vier   'to celebrate' vier-der   'celebrator'
      Bijlmermeer   'id.'   Bijlmermeer-der 'inhabitant of Bijlmermeer'

    c. looch[ə]n   'to deny'   loochen-aar   'denier'
      luist[ə]r   'to listen'   luister-aar   'listener'
      knuts[ə]l   'to tinker'   knutsel-aar   'tinkerer'
      Diem[ə]n   'id.'   Diemen-aar   'inhabitant of Diemen'
      Udd[ə]l   'id.'   Uddel-aar   'inhabitant of Uddel'

The use of *-aar* instead of *-er* after an unstressed syllable avoids the creation of a sequence of two unstressed syllables; the use of *-der* avoids the ill-formed phonological sequence /rər/. Hence, the selection of the various allomorphs can be stated in terms of phonological output conditions (Booij 1998). As in other cases of allomorphy, one finds irregular forms such as *ler-aar* 'teacher', derived from *leer* 'to teach, to learn' (we would expect *leer-der*, which is the correct form for the meaning 'learner'), and *dien-aar* 'servant' instead of the expected *dien-er* (there is also the irregular word *dien-der* 'police officer', with the allomorph *-der*). Again, this shows that the allomorphs have to be considered as different, competing suffixes, with a certain degree of phonological similarity, and that lexical listing of complex words with the correct allomorph is necessary.

This type of interaction between morphology and phonology receives a natural interpretation in a tripartite parallel architecture of grammar, as proposed in Jackendoff (2002), with three levels of representation: phonology, morpho-syntax, and semantics (as was illustrated in section 1), and interface components specifying the systematic relations between these levels. In the case of the competition between *-er*, *-aar* and *-der* discussed here, this means that at the level of morphology, morphological schemas will create words of the types X-*er*, X-*aar* (the restriction that *-aar* is allowed only after stems ending in a coronal sonorant reflects another type of interface between morphology and phonology, viz. phonological subcategorization) and X-*der*. The relevant interface principle is defined as follows: 'from the set of competing complex words, choose the word with the optimal corresponding phonological form'. This explains why we have *et-er* 'eater' instead of *et-aar or *eet-der, as *eter* has the optimal prosodic form of a trochee and the simplest syllable contact possible; and it explains why we have *loochen-aar* 'denier' instead of *loochen-er: the latter word has a final unstressed syllable that cannot be parsed as the right constituent of a trochaic foot, given that *loochen* /loxən/ already forms a trochee on its own. Existing exceptional words such as *ler-aar*, *dien-der* and *opener* 'opener' (instead of the expected *openaar*) are listed, and thus override this general selection principle.

5 Storage versus computation

Allomorphy phenomena have interesting consequences for the issue of what kind of information is stored, and which information is computed by the grammar. As was shown above, complex words must be listed in the lexicon if they behave irregularly with respect to allomorphy, a conclusion also reached by Zuraw (2010) on the basis of an analysis of lexical variation in allomorphy in Tagalog. Therefore, some complex words must be listed, despite the fact that they are morphologically regular.

From a psycholinguistic point of view, it is obvious that storage of regular forms is quite normal: if regular word forms exhibit frequency effects, they must be lexically stored (Baayen et al. 2003). This conclusion is supported by the facts mentioned in (1): the morphologically fully regular inflected adjectives *kwaaie*, *rooie* and the infinitive *houwen* must be listed in the lexicon because they allow for $d > j$ weakening. This weakening does not apply to all inflected adjectives with a stem ending in /d/, as shown in (17a);

similarly, (17b) shows that not all relevant infinitives in *-en* allow for *d-*weakening.

(17) a. rode   'red'   > ro[j]e *but* wred-e 'cruel' > *wreje
       b. lijden 'suffer'> lij[j]en *but* mijden 'avoid' > *mij[j]en

In classical generative phonology, one would have to assign negative rule features to all words whose inflected forms do not undergo the weakening rule. A more adequate conception of the mental lexicon is one in which language users can store inflected forms. Storage makes it possible for such form to acquire idiosyncratic properties, e.g. that they belong to an informal stylistic register or that they have a special meaning (for example, *rooie* has the additional meaning of 'socialist', which *rod-e* does not have).

The claim that the outputs of phonological rules can be stored in lexical representations is supported by the observation that allomorphy is preserved even after the relevant phonological process has disappeared. This is for example the case for the early Germanic rule of vowel lengthening in open syllables (Prokosch' Law). Relics of this alternation are found in some nouns, and also in some diminutives:

(18) sch[ɪ]p 'ship'   sch[eː]p-en 'ships'   sch[eː]p-je 'ship-DIM'
     p[ɑ]d   'path'   p[aː]d-en   'paths'   p[aː]d-je   'path-DIM'

These facts, and their implication for what is stored in the lexicon, are discussed in more detail in Booij (2009b).

6 Conclusion

Allomorphy is a pervasive phenomenon in the grammar of Dutch. Only a small part of it can be accounted for in terms of a common underlying form for the allomorphs, with phonological rules deriving the surface forms (but even there one might assume storage of surface forms, cf. Booij (2009b)). Most allomorphs have to be listed in the lexicon, as words or as word constituents. The choice of allomorph may depend on morphological structure (section 2), on paradigmatic relations (section 3), or on prosodic output conditions (section 4). There is positive evidence that regular complex words, even inflected ones, are stored in the lexicon. This allows us to specify allomorphs in the lexicon without the formal machinery of exception features. In our approach, stylistic and semantic differentiation between allomorphs finds a natural interpretation, reflecting the old idea ('Humboldt's universal') that if there is difference in form, there may also be difference in meaning. The preservation of the effect of phonological rules after their disappearance also implies the lexical storage of allomorphy (section 5).

In sum, our conclusion is that a proper architecture of the grammar of natural languages has four basic ingredients: a tripartite parallel architecture with interface conditions, storage of complex words (whether regular or irregular), morphological schemas that specify allomorphs, and paradigmatic relations between complex words that can be actuated by coining new complex words.

References

Anderson, Stephen R. (1974): *The Organization of Phonology.* – New York: Academic Press.

Aronoff, Mark (1994): *Morphology by Itself: Stems and Inflectional Classes.* – Cambridge, MA: MIT Press.

Baayen, R. Harald, James M. McQueen, Ton Dijkstra & Rob Schreuder (2003): "Frequency effects in regular inflectional morphology: revisiting Dutch plurals." – In: Baayen, R. Harald & Rob Schreuder (eds.): *Morphological Structure in Language Processing*, 355–90. Berlin: Mouton de Gruyter.

Booij, Geert (1995): *The Phonology of Dutch.* – Oxford: Clarendon Press.

– (1998): "Prosodic output constraints in morphology." – In: Kehrein, Wolfgang & Richard Wiese (eds.): *Phonology and Morphology of the Germanic Languages*, 143–163. Tübingen: Niemeyer.

– (2002): *The Morphology of Dutch.* – Oxford: Oxford University Press.

– (2005): "Compounding and derivation: evidence for Construction Morphology." – In: Dressler, Wolfgang, Dieter Kastovsky, Oskar Pfeiffer & Franz Rainer (eds.): *Morphology and its Demarcations*, 109–132. Amsterdam/Philadelphia: John Benjamins.

– (2009a): "Construction morphology and compounding." – In: Rochelle Lieber & Pavol Stekauer (eds.): *The Handbook of Compounding*, 201–216. Oxford: Oxford University Press.

– (2009b): "Lexical storage and phonological change." In: Hanson, Kristin & Sharon Inkelas (eds.): *The Nature of the Word. Essays in Honor of Paul Kiparsky*, 497–505. Cambridge MA: MIT Press.

– (2010): *Construction Morphology.* – Oxford: Oxford University Press.

Borowsky, Toni (2000): "Word-faithfulness and the direction of assimilation." – In: *The Linguistic Review* 17, 1–28.

Carstairs, Andrew (1988): "Some implications of phonologically conditioned suppletion." – In: Booij, Geert & Jaap van Marle (eds.): *Yearbook of Morphology 1988*, 67–94. Dordrecht: Foris.

Chomsky, Noam & Morris Halle (1968): *The Sound Pattern of English.* – New York: Harper and Row.

De Haas, Wim & Mieke Trommelen (1993): *Morfologisch Handboek van het Nederlands. Een Overzicht van de Woordvorming.* Den Haag: SDU.

Haverkamp-Lubbers, Roos & Jan Kooij (1971): *Het Verkleinwoord in het Nederlands.* – Amsterdam: Instituut voor Algemene Taalwetenschap, Universiteit van Amsterdam.

Jackendoff, Ray (1975): "Semantic and morphological regularities in the lexicon." – In: *Language* 51, 639–671.

– (2002): *Foundations of Language.* – Oxford: Oxford University Press.

Langacker, Ronald (1987): *Foundations of Cognitive Grammar.* Vol. 1: Theoretical prerequisites. – Stanford, CA: Stanford University Press.

Leben, William R. & Orrin W. Robinson (1977): "'Upside-down' phonology." – In: *Language* 53, 1–20.

Robinson, Orrin W. (1980): "Dutch diminutives over easy." – In: Zonneveld, Wim, Frans van Coetsem & Orrin W. Robinson (eds.): *Studies in Dutch Phonology,* 139–57. The Hague: Martinus Nijhoff.

Rubach, Jerzy & Geert Booij (2001): "Allomorphy in Optimality Theory: Polish iotation." – In: *Language* 77, 26–60.

Smith, Norval S. H. (1973): "The phenomenon of D-deletion in Dutch." – In: *Spektator* 2, 421–437.

– (1975): "In suppport of D-deletion." – In: *Spektator* 5, 17–22.

– (1976): "-Aar." – In: *Leuvense Bijdragen* 65, 485–96.

Van der Hulst, Harry (2008): "The Dutch diminutive." – In: *Lingua* 118, 1288–1306.

Van Zonneveld, Ron (1978): "Verkleinwoordvorming." – In: Van Berkel, A., W. Blok, G. Brummel & Th.A.J.M. Janssen (eds.): *Proeven van Neerlandistiek, Aangeboden aan Prof. Dr. Albert Sassen,* 279–302. Groningen: Nederlands Instituut Groningen.

Zonneveld, Wim (1975): "A reanalysis of D-deletion in Dutch." – In: *Spektator* 4, 231–239.

– (1978): *A Formal Theory of Exceptions in Generative Phonology.* – Lisse: Peter de Ridder Press.

Zuraw, Kie (2010): "A model of lexical variation and the grammar with application to Tagalog nasal substitution." – In: *Natural Language and Linguistic Theory* 28, 417–472.

Camiel Hamans

From *prof* to *provo*: some observations on Dutch clippings*

1 Introduction

Traditionally, clipping (also called shortening, abbreviation or truncation) of lexical material has been viewed as an irregular and rather eccentric process of word formation. For example, Stockwell & Minkova (2001: 10) observe that

> shortening may take any part of a word, usually a single syllable, and throw away the rest, like quiz from inquisitive, phone from telephone, plane from airplane, flu from influenza ...The process often applies not just to an existing word, but to a whole phrase. Thus mob is shortened from mobile vulgus "fickle rabble". Zoo is from zoological gardens. Ad and British advert are transparently based on advertisement ... Many shortenings have entered the language and speakers have lost track of where they came from. How many people would recognize gin and tonic as coming from Genève?

According to Marchand (1969: 441), clipping is not a regular grammatical process but a stylistic and sociolinguistic phenomenon belonging to informal registers and special jargons. This leads him to claim that clipping forms part of the *parole* (speech) instead of the *langue* (system). The same claim, in a different theoretical framework, is made by Aronoff (1976: 20–21). However, the examples provided by Marchand (e.g. *fridge* for *refrigerator*, *plane* for *airplane*, *maths* for *mathematics*) show how common clipped forms are in Standard English.

Marchand distinguishes between four types of clipping:

(i) *Back clipping*	temp	<	temperature
	ad		advertisement
(ii) *Fore clipping*	van		caravan
	plane		airplane
(iii) *Fore and back clipping*	fridge		refrigerator
	flu		influenza

---

* Frans Hinskens, Richard Wiese and the editors of this volume were kind enough to comment on an earlier draft of this article, which has resulted in quite a few additions and improvements. I want to thank them for their suggestions.

(iv) *Compound clipping*   Amerind   American Indian
                                 modem   modulator-demodulator

Given this scheme, it will be clear that there is no immediately clear rule or
set of rules which governs the process of clipping. The overall picture seems
to be irregular: sometimes the right part of a word is truncated, as in (i),
sometimes the left part, as in (ii), and sometimes truncation applies at both
sides, as in (iii). For this reason, clipping has long been neglected in the
theoretical literature, in spite of its suprisingly high productivity, in English
as well as in a host of other languages (see e.g. Augst 2000; Bauer 1994,
2001; Hamans 1997, 2004a, 2008; Kuitenbrouwer 1987; Rey-Debove & Rey
1993).

2 Productivity

Clipping has recently begun to attract more attention, in particular because of
the recent emergence of a new form of clipping which consists of a trochaic
foot with a final full vowel. Some English examples are given in (1).

(1) *English*   psycho   <   psychopath
                 homo   homosexual
                 nympho   nymphomaniac

Jespersen (1942: 223) was one of the first to provide examples of this type of
clipping, which is characterized by an added *-o* in the second syllable, as in
(2):

(2)   journo   <   journalist
                 commo   commissary
                 afto   afternoon

Another quite frequent pattern involves truncated forms with final *-y, -ie* or *-i*
(examples from Lappe 2007).

(3)   assy   <   asphalt
                 skelly   skeleton
                 veggies   vegetables

The question of whether the forms in (2) and (3) involve the same type of
clipping as those in (1), or whether they present a special case of truncation
followed by derivation, is discussed below.

As Moore (2010: 144) notes, the patterns illustrated in (2) and (3) are
especially frequent in Australian English:

This use of the *-ie* or (*-y*) and *-o* suffix with abbreviated forms of words is not exclusive to Australia, although it is more common in Australia than elsewhere, and it is used in distinctive ways in Australia.

The same point is made by Gunn (1972: 60):

> Aren't we reaching the inane, when we Australians start accepting *beddie, cardie,* (cardigan), *Chrissie, pressie, ciggie, habbie* (haberdashery), *leckie* (lecture), *prossie* (prostitute), *sandie* (sandwich), *tabbie* (tablet), *weepie,* and *yewie* (U-turn)? Of course, these and other habits are not restricted to Australia, but the increase in their popularity here is phenomenal.

A similar development has been observed for Dutch (e.g. Kuitenbrouwer 1987; Fisiak & Hamans 1997; Hamans 2004b). First, Dutch, like English, has an older class of monosyllabic clippings. As in English, this class consists mainly of back clippings, as in (4).

(4)	Jap	<	Japanner	'Japanese person'
	prof		professor	'professor'
	mees		meester	'teacher'

In addition, Dutch, again like English, has a more recent, productive class of disyllabic clippings ending in *-o*, as in (5).

(5)	alto	<	alternatief	'alternative'
	lesbo		lesbisch	'lesbian'
	provo		provocateur	'member of the anarchistic Provo movement of the 1960s in Amsterdam'

Dutch also has a small number of clippings ending in *-i*, as in (6) (examples from Hinskens 2001).

(6)	obi	<	ober	'waiter'
	studi		student	'student'
	omi		oma	'grandmother'

Unlike in German, where clippings regularly end in *-i* (Féry 1997; Wiese 2001), the Dutch *-i* class is small and only marginally productive. As Van de Vijver (1997: 229) has argued, in Dutch *-o* can be seen as the default vowel in this context. In the remainder of this paper, I will ignore clipped forms ending in *-i*.

Clipping is not restricted to the Germanic languages. Hamans (2004b) and Fisiak & Hamans (1997) cite a number of examples from French, noting that the French truncation patterns are in fact much richer than those of English, Dutch and German. Some examples are given in (7).

(7)   bac(calaureat)   appart(ement)   ado(lescent)
       fac(ulté)   manif(estation)   promo(tion)
       pub(licité)   coop(érative)   diapo(sitive)

       mégalo(mane)   sympa(thique)   ciné(rama)
       écolo(giste)   fana(tique)   télé(vision)
       biblio(thèque)   giga(ntesque)   pédé(raste)

The description of Spanish clipping in Rainer (1997: 679–701) shows that it is similar to French clipping. In both French and Spanish, clipped forms are not restricted to a final *-o* but may end in a range of vowels. In addition, clippings may consist of either one or two syllables, and the final syllables may be closed or open.

(8)   dex(erina)   fac(ultad)   ape(tito)
       box(eo)   diver(tido)   bibe(rón)
       fut(bol)   sacris(tán)   dire(ctor)

       bici(cleta)   coca(ína)   choco(late)
       combi(nacion)   compa(ñero)   crono(metro)
       pisci(na)   contra(revolucion)   saxo(fono)

3 Clipping or derivation?

Let us now address the question posed earlier, viz. whether the data in (2), (3), (5) and (6) should be considered as instances of clipping similar to those in (1), or whether they present a special case of truncation followed by derivation. Of course, it is immediately clear that the processes operating in (2), (3), (5) and (6) cannot be described in terms of truncation alone. Clipping of e.g. *commissary* would lead to a form like **com* or **commis*, and cannot produce the correct form ending in *-o*. In cases such as this one, clipping is only the first step in the process; the truncation 'rule' must be followed by suffixation of *-o*.

On the other hand, there are good arguments for why the 'suffix' *-o* (cf. Lappe 2007) should not be distinguished from the ending *-o* in the examples in (1). The first, and most important, argument for this is that forms like *psycho*, *homo* and *nympho* share certain semantic and stylistic features (see Hamans 2004b for extensive discussion of the semantic, stylistic and sociolinguistic aspects of clippings):

- they belong to an informal register
- they have a certain negative connotation

The second, semantic aspect may be due to "the not always and everywhere appreciated denotation" of these clippings (Hamans 2004b: 162), which has become an integral part of the connotative meaning of the *-o* ending. In (2) and (5), the 'suffix' *-o* has an explicitly informal and negative meaning, even in those cases where the base form has no negative associations itself. Jespersen (1942: 223) notes the "slangy, often also hypocoristic, character of the suffix *-o*, which does not really change the sense of the root-word itself." It is doubtful whether this is correct, however; a form like *journo* conveys far less respect and appreciation than its non-truncated counterpart *journalist*.

In French, where the same process operates, the situation appears to be quite similar:

(9)   catho   <   catholique   'Roman Catholic'
           clepto   cleptomane   'kleptomaniac'
           neuro   neurologue   'neurologist'

(10)   stalo   <   stalinien   'Stalinist'
           prolo   prolétaire   'prole/proletarian'
           intello   intellectuel   'intellectual'

According to Antoine (2000a: xliv), the *-o* ending strengthens the negative association, not just in words from the 'political domain' but also in e.g. *intello*. While *intellectual* has a positive meaning, *intello* is not only clearly informal but also has an (exclusively) pejorative meaning. The same holds for the Dutch example *alto*, in (5) above. Whereas non-truncated *alternatief* has a neutral association, *alto* has a pejorative meaning only.

This brings us to the preliminary conclusion that distinguishing between the ending *-o* and the 'suffix' *-o* leads to a methodological problem: if we make this distinction, we miss the generalisation that the two forms share certain stylistic and semantic aspects. Below, we will also see that the two forms display the same phonological behaviour: combining them with the truncated base almost always results in a trochee. This, too, is a strong argument for not distinguishing between the two *-o* endings. With Ockham's razor in mind, forms like (English) *journo* and (Dutch) *alto* are therefore best analyzed on a par with 'real' clippings like *dipso* (< *dipsomaniac*) and *psycho* (< *psychopath*).

In section 6, I will discuss a number of examples with *-o* which do not involve any truncation, e.g. *sicko* (< *sick*) in (17) and Dutch *suffo* 'fathead' (< *suf* 'silly') in (19). (Another example is Swedish *fyllo* 'drunkard' (< *full* 'full').) In these forms, the 'suffix' *-o* plays exactly the same role as in (1) and (2). This provides us with a third argument against a distinction between the ending *-o* and the suffix *-o*, and suggests instead that the three instances of *-o* should receive a unified treatment. However, it will be clear that for the derivation of the second and third 'type' of *-o*, an extra suffixation rule is required, whereas the first type of -*o* is a direct result of the clipping process itself.

One question that remains is whether a form like *veggies* (see (3)) should be analyzed along the same lines. Antoine (2000b: xxxi–xxxii) discusses final -*ie*/-*y* at length:

> '-ie/y' is a true suffix, with a hypocoristic meaning, which was first used in Scots; … it was used very early in combination with clipping (*hussy, chappy*). This suffix is commonly used with clippings of Christian names (*Andy, Cathy, Eddie, Ronnie* etc.) or of family names (*Fergie, Gorby, Schwarzy*, etc.). It is also used in the coining of nicknames (*Fatty, Froggie*, etc.) or of endearing terms (*dearie*, sweetie, etc.) … It can serve, as in the case of proper nouns to obtain a hypocoristic diminutive (e.g.: *pressie, shortie, woodie, biccy, chewie, hottie, preemie*) though such words can also be used humorously, or ironically, or even pejoratively. It is to be noted further that the suffix '-ie/-y' is added to clippings of words that already have negative overtones – the change of ending often results in an even more pejorative word; -ie/-y thus serves to enhance the negative trait in words that designate individuals whose social or political behaviour is frowned upon by the speaker, character traits or behaviours that are deemed to be and presented as pathological ones. The political lexicon offers instances of this, with words like *commie, lefty, rightie*, but other fields also do.

Although there is a clear difference between -*ie*/-*y* and -*o* (-*ie*/-*y* does not result from clipping[1] and functions as a diminutive/affective suffix with a hypocoristic meaning), the two forms have something in common: both can be combined with a truncated form, and both may have a pejorative meaning.

I will not discuss clipping followed by -*ie*/-*y* suffixation any further here. I will therefore not attempt to answer the question to what extent forms like *veggies* must be treated on a par with forms like *psycho* and *journo*. For discussion of this, see Lappe (2007). For a unified approach to German *i*-formation (which includes clipping, as in *Sani* (< *Sanitäter* 'medical assistant') and hypocoristic formation, as in *Rudi* (< *Rudolf*) and *Ossi* (< *Ostdeutscher* 'person from East Germany'), see Féry (1997).

4 Prosodic Morphology

The advent of Prosodic Morphology (McCarthy & Prince 1986, 1994) provided an impetus to the analysis of clipping, since this framework makes

---

[1] *Callie* (from *California*) and *combie* (from *combination*), taken from Lappe (2007), may be counterexamples to this.

it possible to account for phenomena which cannot be straightforwardly handled in 'regular morphology'. As Wiese (2001: 131–132) notes, traditional concatenative morphology cannot account for clipping because the phenomenon "does not rely on the chaining of morphemes". A further problem for traditional approaches is that it is often unclear how truncation operates. The cut-off point in clipping may be a morphological boundary (e.g. *tram* < *tramway*), a syllable boundary (e.g. Dutch *auto* < *automobiel* 'car'), or it may not coincide with any boundary, as in *info* (< *information*) and *temp* (< *temporary*). This problem is obviated in Prosodic Morphology, where the focus is shifted to the output of the truncation process, which is assumed to be prosodically conditioned.

Approaches to clipping in Prosodic Morphology include Weeda (1992) for English, Piñeros (1998) for Spanish, Féry (1997) and Wiese (2001) for German, Simpson (2001, 2010) for Australian English, and Van de Vijver (1997) and Hinskens (2001) for Dutch. This paper is not the place for an extensive discussion of these works; below, I restrict my attention to the analyses of Van de Vijver and Hinskens, and I consider briefly a recent approach to English clippings by Lappe (2007).

Van de Vijver considers a number of different types of Dutch clippings and hypocoristics. These include monosyllabic forms, which invariably end in a consonant (see (4) above), and disyllabic forms. The latter include clippings that consist of two open syllables, as in (11), and clippings that consist of a closed syllable followed by an open syllable, as in (12). (Van de Vijver also discusses disyllabic clippings consisting of a closed syllable preceded by either an open or a closed syllable; since these occur with names only, they will not be discussed here.)

(11)	aso	<	asociaal	'antisocial'
	brabo		Brabant	'person from Brabant'
	depro		depressief	'depressed person'

(12)	alto	<	alternatief	'alternative'
	lesbo		lesbisch	'lesbian'
	limbo		Limburg	'person from Limburg'

Van de Vijver develops an Optimality-theoretic analysis in which two constraints are undominated. The first of these is ANCHOR-LEFT, which requires the left edge of the clipping to match the left edge of the base, i.e. "the first segment of the base is also the first segment of the clipping" (Van de Vijver 1997: 223). In earlier work (cf. Hamans 1996: 72) I have shown that there are very few counterexamples to this left-anchoring, one being *bus* 'bus' (< *autobus*). However, such cases of 'non-back clipping' are clearly exceptional.

The second undominated constraint is CONTIGUITY, which requires the relative order of segments in the clipped form to be identical to that in the base. Van de Vijver (1997: 223) further assumes a constraint ALIGN (σ, PrWd) ("Some edge of every syllable must be aligned to some edge of the prosodic word"). This constraint bans clippings that are larger than two syllables, since such forms will necessarily have at least one syllable that is not aligned with the edge of a prosodic word. ALIGN (σ, PrWd) outranks MAX-IO, the correspondence constraint which requires input segments to be retained in the output.

Van de Vijver's analysis is based on names only, and so we may wonder whether it can be straightforwardly extended to the kinds of clippings under discussion here. It would seem that this is not the case. One general problem is Van de Vijver's (1997: 221) assertion that "all monosyllabic clippings have disyllabic bases". This claim is incorrect, as is shown by the existence of forms like *provo* (< *provocateur*), *prof* (< *professor*), and many more. Van de Vijver (1997: 228) himself notes the counterexample *bieb* (< *bibliotheek* 'library'). He suggests that clipping here involves an intermediate form *biblio* (*-theek* is treated as a bound morpheme) in which the final syllable falls outside the disyllabic template (i.e. *bibliotheek* > *bibli(o)* > *bieb*). Aside from the fact that this seems an ad hoc solution, it is unclear what the intermediate forms of *provo* and *prof* would be, and why. The problem with Van de Vijver's account, it seems, is simply that clipping from longer bases is much more frequent than he claims.[2]

Another problem with Van de Vijver's account is that it incorrectly predicts **provoc* (['provɔk]) as the optimal clipping of *provocateur*, rather than *provo* ['provo]. The constraints introduced so far predict two pairs of possible clippings for *provocateur* and *professor*: *provo* and *provoc*, and *profes* [pro'fɛs] and *profe* ([pro'fɛ]). Of these, *provoc*, *profes* and *profe* are unattested. One way to rule out *provoc* and *profes* would be to invoke the well-known markedness constraint NOCODA and rank it above MAX-IO. However, Van de Vijver (1997: 224) instead prefers a constraint which compares the syllabic role of a segment in the base with that in the clipping, viz. STROLE ("Segments in the clipping and their correspondents in the base should have identical syllabic roles"), originally proposed in McCarthy & Prince (1994). *Provok* and *profes* violate this constraint, since the final consonants in these forms occupy the coda position of the second syllable, while in the base they occupy the onset position of the third syllable.

This leaves the non-optimal candidate *profe*, with a final [ɛ]. Observing

---

[2] The same holds for English, where we find even larger inputs with monosyllabic clippings, e.g. *vet* (< *veterinarian*, *veteran*), *lab* (< *laboratory*) and *ad* (< *advertisement*).

that Dutch word-final syllables are not usually stressed, Van de Vijver proposes the dominant constraint FINALSTRESSCLOSED (FSC), which requires the final stressed syllable of a clipping (which corresponds to a stressed syllable in the base) to be closed. FSC rules out *profe*, but sanctions outputs like *profes* and *prof*.[3] However, the problem is that FSC predicts the wrong outcome for *provocateur*, since it prefers **'provoc* to *'provo*. This is illustrated in the tableau in (13).

(13) Incorrect selection of *provoc* (instead of *provo*) due to high-ranking FSC

provocateur	FSC	ALIGN (σ, PrWd)	STROLE	MAX-IO
a. *provoca*		*!		*teur*
b. *provoc*			*	*ateur*
c. *provo*	*!			*cateur*

Thus, while the ranking in (13) accounts for the presence of final consonants in hypocoristics like *A'leid* (< *A'leida*) and *Pa'tries* (< *Pa'tricia*), it makes an incorrect prediction for clippings. We may conclude, therefore, that Van de Vijver's analysis cannot be easily extended to this type of truncation.

Like Van de Vijver, Hinskens (2001) takes disyllabic clippings as his starting-point. Rather than present a theoretical analysis, his concern is to provide an inventory of possible Dutch clippings, along with their sociolinguistic and stylistic properties. His corpus consists of a collection of Dutch neologisms from Kuitenbrouwer (1987). Hinskens observes that most of the clipped forms in the corpus are trochaic. This supports Kooij & Van Oostendorp's (2003) observation that the 'ideal' Dutch word consists of exactly one trochaic foot (a preference that can be seen even more clearly in abbreviated forms; cf. Kooij & Van Oostendorp 2003: 80). In Optimality Theory, trochaic feet can be derived by the constraints FOOT-BINARITY ("Feet are binary") and FOOT-FORM (trochee) ("Align the left edge of a foot with the left edge of its head"), TROCHEE in short. See Piñero (1998) for an application of these constraints to clipping in Spanish.[4]

Hinskens is not explicit about the constraints that are necessary to derive the appropriate clipped outputs, except to note that ANCHOR-LEFT must outrank TROCHEE. The output **profes* violates TROCHEE, while **fessor* violates ANCHOR-LEFT; the fact that the correct form is monosyllabic *prof*

---

[3] Note that **[pro'fɛ] is ruled out in any case because it ends in a lax vowel, which is impossible in Dutch; all of Van de Vijver's examples contain final tense vowels and diphthongs.

[4] Van de Vijver achieves the same result with ALIGN (σ, PrWd) and WSP ('Weight-to-Stress', i.e. 'stressed syllables are heavy').

suggests that the ranking is ANCHOR-LEFT >> TROCHEE (cf. Hinskens 2001: 46). To ensure that e.g. *provo* is favoured over **provoc*, Hinskens assumes NOCODA (rather than Van de Vijver's constraint STROLE).

While Hinskens' analysis accounts for a range of data, his constraint ranking incorrectly derives **prof* ([prɔf], with final devoicing) from *provocateur*. We have seen that this problem cannot be circumvented by reversing the ranking of TROCHEE and ANCHOR-LEFT, since this would incorrectly derive **fessor* from *professor*. The only way to avoid this, it seems, is to relinquish Van de Vijver's claim that ANCHOR-LEFT is inviolable in clipped forms. Hinskens' use of NOCODA is also in need of refinement, since it favours the clipped form **pro* ([pro], a possible but not preferred Dutch word form; cf. Kooij & Van Oostendorp 2003: 92) over *prof*.[5] To ensure that the optimal clipping is disyllabic, one possibility is to assume that NOCODA operates on polysyllabic words only (which would be a very unattractive stipulation), or to assume Van de Vijver's FSC constraint.

5 Lappe's alternative

Lappe (2007) does not consider Dutch clippings; her focus is on English clippings, name truncation (e.g. *Rube* < *Ruben*, *Di* < *Diana*), and what she terms 'suffixed' hypocoristics and clippings. Examples of suffixed hypocoristics include *Izzy* (< *Isidore*), *Callie* (< *California*) and *Mandy* (< *Amanda*). Suffixed clippings include such forms as *hammy* (< *hamster*), *limo* (< *limousine*), and also *avo* (< *avocado*) and *condo* (< *condominium*).[6] Lappe's examples of clippings include *mes* (< *mescaline*) and *pro* (< *professional*), in addition to unsuffixed disyllabic clippings such as *detox* (< *detoxification*) and *accad* (< *academy*).

Given that English truncation is similar to Dutch truncation, it may be useful to consider some aspects of Lappe's account here. Lappe's starting-point is quite different from what we have seen so far. She argues that since clippings usually consist of a single heavy syllable, and since truncation does not display 'emergence-of-the-unmarked' effects (for this notion, see

---

[5] The form **pro* would end in a tense vowel, since Dutch bans final lax vowels (i.e. **[prɔ]). If a lax vowel in a base ends up in word-final position due to clipping, it is realized as tense, e.g. *info* (< *informatie* 'information'), *demo* (< *demonstratie* 'demonstration') and *afko* (< *afkorting* 'abbreviation'). Here the full forms have lax [ɔ] and the clippings tense [o].

[6] *Avo* and *condo* could also be treated as simple disyllabic clippings.

McCarthy & Prince 1994), the basic structure of clippings is monosyllabic (see Lappe 2007: 7–13).[7] In Lappe's (2007: 163) view, "monosyllabic clipping, *y*-suffixed clipping and *o*-suffixed clipping, and unsuffixed clipping are truncatory processes in their own right". Disyllabic clipped forms like *barbie* (< *barbecue*) and *alkie* (< *alcohol*) are viewed as consisting of a monosyllabic root plus an affix (-*y* or -*o*). The same holds for forms like *combie* (< *combination*) and for the forms *avo* and *condo* mentioned above.

Lappe's (2007: 46; see also 2003) main argument for this view comes from a consideration of the constraint MAX:

> The main problem for a MinWd approach to English truncation … comes from the fact that the proposed ranking of the prosodic markedness constraints with respect to MAX predicts that only one of the two possible minimal word structures will surface in truncation: the disyllabic minimal word. Monosyllabic minimal words, by contrast, can never be optimal. The reason is that MAX, even though lowly ranked, will always prefer a disyllabic candidate over a monosyllabic candidate. The basic prediction of this ranking is that the amount of segmental material preserved from the base will be maximal; disyllables will always preserve more material from their bases than monosyllables.

This is also the reason why Van de Vijver (1997: 225) claims that "clipped forms do not have an underlying form of their own", and that faithfulness constraints therefore do not play a role. The same view is implicit in Hinskens (2001), where monosyllabic outputs are favoured by ANCHOR-LEFT, with MAX playing no role in this aspect of the analysis.

This paper is not the place to review Lappe's analysis in any detail. In what follows, my focus will be on the diachrony of clipping phenomena (see section 6), and not so much on the synchronic grammatical system that produces them. Here I will note only that Lappe proposes an important markedness constraint that restricts the size of outputs, viz. COINCIDE-σ (stress), which requires "every element of the output [to be] in the main stressed syllable" (Lappe 2007: 179). This constraint favours the creation of monosyllabic outputs, and at the same time penalizes each segment which is not part of the output of the clipping. COINCIDE-σ (stress) is dominated by the constraint MAX (affix), which requires every affix in the input to have a correspondent in the truncated form" (Lappe 2007: 187). One effect of MAX (affix) is therefore that it forces the presence of -*o* and -*y* in the output, if these vowels are also part of the input.

---

[7] One of Lappe's arguments for this is that in unsuffixed disyllabic clippings like *celeb*, *exec* and *ident* (with final stress), the "word structure cannot be explained in terms of unmarked prosodic word structure" (Lappe 2007:13). An unmarked prosodic word structure would have resulted in a trochaic pattern instead. In Dutch, this kind of clipping is restricted to names, and is not considered here.

6 Diachronic aspects

Lappe is certainly correct when she notes that the majority of clippings
consists of a single heavy syllable. However, the preponderance of
monosyllabic clippings in Lappe's corpus obscures the observation that
truncation to a disyllabic template is a recent phenomenon in (American)
English. In earlier work, I have also observed that older clippings tend to be
monosyllabic (see Hamans 1996, 2004a, 2004b). However, both English and
Dutch also display a more recent pattern of disyllabic clipping, which is
likely due to the fact that the two languages are predominantly trochaic.

The emergence of disyllabic clippings is one argument for taking the
trochee to be the unmarked metrical pattern in modern Dutch (see Kooij &
Van Oostendorp 2003 for other arguments). However, the preferred Dutch
minimal word has not always been trochaic, as is evidenced for instance by
the historical apocope process illustrated in (14).

(14)	stemme	>	stem	'voice'
	vrouwe	>	vrouw	'woman'
	kribbe	>	krib	'crib'

Stress used to fall on the first syllable of the older variants in (14), which
contain a schwa in the second syllable. At some point in the history of Dutch,
apocope no longer applied; from this point onwards, trochaic forms remained
unaffected (cf. Kooij & Van Oostendorp 2003: 80). The forms in (15), for
example, did not undergo apocope.

(15)	boete	>	*boet	'fine'
	vrede	>	*vreed	'peace'
	rede	>	*reed	'speech'

These data could suggest a change from a non-trochaic to a trochaic metrical
pattern. Further support for this comes from the accommodation of loans, e.g.
pijler 'pillar' from Latin *pila*, with stress shift and subsequent
diphthongization.

Not all the evidence points in the same direction, however. Another
loanword from the same base, *pilaar*, retained stress on the final syllable. In
addition, the preference for a trochaic pattern is not manifested in allegro
speech, where instead of an expected stress shift we find complete vowel
reduction and concomitant monosyllabification (Awedyk & Hamans 1998),
as in (16).

(16)	ba.'naan	>	bnaan	'banana'
	par.'tij	>	p(r)tij	'party'
	ka.'non	>	knon	'cannon'

These data suggest that there is more variability in preferred minimal word structure than is sometimes assumed (though whether it is justified to compare the effects of fast speech with 'normal' grammatical patterns is an open question).

These considerations aside, we can observe two competing clipping patterns in modern Dutch: an older pattern, illustrated in (4), of mainly monosyllabic forms, and a relatively recent pattern, illustrated in (5), (11) and (12), of mainly disyllabic trochees with a final, possibly suffixed, -*o*. The recent pattern emerged in the mid 1980s, due to influence of American English (Kuitenbrouwer 1987; Hamans 1996, 2004a, 2004b). Dutch has only two disyllabic clipped nouns with final -*o* that are older, viz. *indo* 'Indonesian-Dutch half-breed' (first attested in 1898) and *provo* (introduced by the criminologist Wouter Buikhuisen in 1965). (The clipped form *prof*, from *professor*, was first attested in 1875.)

As noted, the preponderance of monosyllabic clippings in Lappe's corpus masks the recent emergence of disyllabic truncation in (American) English. Lappe's corpus consists of three dictionaries (one of standard English and two slang dictionaries) from the early 1980s, a few years before -*o* clipping became fashionable. The pattern was already productive in Australian English earlier, but the influence of Australian English on American and British English is small, and its influence on Dutch negligible.

To date, no satisfactory explanation has been advanced for the emergence of -*o* clippings in American English, owing to the lack of reliable data. Since clipped forms, and in particular -*o* clippings, belong to informal registers, a reasonable scenario is that this pattern originated in the street jargons of youngsters in the big American cities, with a possible influence from Hispanic and perhaps Italian (see Hamans 2004b). It is interesting to observe in this respect that the -*o* ending has subsequently spread to full words which form part of and originated in youngsters' slang:

(17)	sicko	<	sick
	weirdo	<	weird
	creepo	<	creep

Hamans (1996, 2004a, 2004b) proposes an American English influence for languages such as Dutch, Swedish and Polish, which have all acquired -*o* clippings fairly recently and, for Dutch and Swedish at least, on a massive scale.

7 Conclusion

If the diachronic and contact-based scenario sketched in section 6 is correct, then the approach of Van de Vijver (1997) or Hinskens (2001) would offer a reasonable explanation for the change from a mono- to a disyllabic clipping template. The development from an initial stage with a preference for monosyllabic clippings to a later stage with an influx of *-o* clippings, and a subsequent extension of *-o* suffixation to 'full words' (as in *sicko*), can be expressed in terms of a re-ranking of constraints, as in (18).

(18)   Old system: ANCHOR-LEFT >> TROCHEE
        New system: TROCHEE >> ANCHOR-LEFT

However, the Dutch preference for disyllabic trochaic minimal words, which predates the change from mono- to disyllabic clippings, has not yet become absolute, and most likely never will. This means that the language system displays some variability (which is not problematic in Prosodic Morphology). Unfortunately, we do not yet have sufficient diachronic data to refine this very sketchy picture.

The account offered by Lappe also contributes to our understanding of the change, in particular because the change did not just involve truncation, but was also extended to full forms, with suffixation of *-o*. English examples of this were given in (17). Some Dutch examples are provided in (19) and (20):

(19)   lullo   <   lul   'penis'
        duffo   duf   'dull'
        suffo   suf   'silly'

(20)   lokalo   <   lokaal   'local'
        gewono   gewoon   'normal'
        positivo   positief   'positive'

A detailed description of this process is beyond the scope of this paper. However, it will be clear that in Lappe's approach, these data can conceivably be treated by extending the constraints COINCIDE-σ (stress) and MAX (affix).

In sum, the three theoretical approaches considered in this paper take different perspectives on clipping. Lappe's point of departure is the older pattern of monosyllabic clipping, while Van de Vijver and Hinskens focus primarily on the more recent, disyllabic pattern. More diachronic data are required to evaluate which of these perspectives is ultimately the more appropriate. This is an issue for further research.

References

Augst, Gerhard (2000): "Gefahr durch lange und kurze Wörter." – In: Stickel, Gerhard (ed.): *Neues und Fremdes im deutschen Wortschatz. Aktueller Lexikalischer Wandel*, 210–238. Berlin: De Gruyter.

Antoine, Fabrice (2000a): *Dictionnaire français-anglais des mots tronqués*. – Louvain-La-Neuve: Peeters.

– (2000b): *An English-French Dictionary of Clipped Words*. – Louvain-La-Neuve: Peeters.

Aronoff, Mark (1976): *Word Formation in Generative Grammar*. – Cambridge, Mass: MIT Press.

Awedyk, Wiesław & Camiel Hamans (1998): "How allegro speech ruins the principles of universal grammar or are universal constraints universal?" – In: Caron, Bernard (ed.): *Proceedings of the 16th International Congress of Linguists*. Oxford: Pergamon (CD-ROM Paper No. 0155).

Bauer, Laurie (1994): *Watching English Change. An Introduction to the Study of Linguistic Change in Standard Englishes in the Twentieth Century*. – London & New York: Longman.

– (2001): *Morphological Productivity*. – Cambridge: Cambridge University Press.

Gunn, Jeannie (1972): "Change in Australian idiom." – In: Turner, George (ed.): *Good Australian English and Good New Zealand English*, 47–63. Sydney: Reed Education.

Féry, Caroline (1997): "*Uni* und *Studis*: Die besten Wörter des Deutschen." – In: *Linguistische Berichte* 172, 461–489.

Fisiak, Jacek & Camiel Hamans (1997): "Memento for a Lefto." – In: Ahlqvist, Anders & Věra Čapková (eds.): *Dán do oide. Essays in Memory of Conn R. Ó Cléirigh*, 157–163. Dublin: Institiúid Teangeolaíochta Éireann.

Hamans, Camiel (1996): "A Lingo of Abbrevs." – In: *Lingua Posnaniensis* 38, 69–78.

– (1997): "Clippings in modern French, English, German and Dutch." – In: Hickey, Raymond & Stanisław Puppel (eds.): *Language History and Linguistic Modelling. A Festschrift for Jacek Fisiak on his 60th Birthday*, 1732–1741. Berlin & New York: Mouton de Gruyter.

– (2004a): "From *rapo* to *lullo*." – In: Duszak, Anna & Urszula Okulska (eds.): *Speaking from the Margin. Global English from a European Perspective*, 69–75. Frankfurt am Main: Peter Lang.

– (2004b): "The relation between formal and informal style with respect to language change." – In: Dabelsteen, Christine & J. Normann Jørgensen (eds.): *Languaging and Language Practices*, 162–187. Copenhagen: University of Copenhagen.

– (2008). "Why clipped forms should be accepted as nouns." – In: *Lingua Posnaniensis* 50, 95–109.

Hinskens, Frans (2001): "Hypocoristische vormen en reductievormen in het hedendaagse Nederlands." – In: *Neerlandica Extra Muros* 39, 37–49.

Jespersen, Otto (1942): *A Modern English Grammar. Part 4: Morphology*. – Copenhagen: Ejnar Munksgaard.

Kooij, Jan & Marc van Oostendorp (2003): *Fonologie. Uitnodiging tot de Klankleer van het Nederlands.* – Amsterdam: Amsterdam University Press.

Kuitenbrouwer, Jan (1987): *Turbotaal. Van Socio-babbel tot Yuppiespeak.* – Amsterdam: Aramith.

Lappe, Sabine (2003): "Monosyllabicity in Prosodic Morphology: the case of truncated personal names in English." – In: Booij, Geert & Jaap van Marle (eds.): *Yearbook of Morphology* 2002, 135–186. Dordrecht: Kluwer.

– (2007): *English Prosodic Morphology.* – Dordrecht: Springer.

McCarthy, John J. & Alan Prince (1986): *Prosodic Morphology.* – Technical Report #32, New Brunswick: Rutgers University Center for Cognitive Science.

– (1994): "The emergence of the unmarked: Optimality in prosodic morphology." – In: Gonzalez, Mercé (ed.): *Proceedings of NELS* 24, 333–379. Amherst: MA: GLSA Publications.

Marchand, Hans (1969): *The Categories and Types of Present-Day English Word-Formation.* – München: C.H. Beck.

Moore, Bruce (2010): *What's their story? A History of Australian Words.* – Melbourne: Oxford University Press Australia & New Zealand.

Piñeros, Carlos (1998): *Prosodic Morphology in Spanish: Constraint Interaction in Word Formation.* – Ph.D. dissertation, Ohio State University.

Rainer, Franz (1993): *Spanische Wortbildungslehre.* – Tübingen: Niemeyer.

Rey-Debove, Josette & Alain Rey (1993). *Nouveau Petit Robert. Préface.* – Paris: Dictionnaires Le Robert.

Simpson, Jane (2001): "Hypocoristics of place-names in Australian English." – In: Blair, David & Peter Collins (eds.): *English in Australia*, 89–112. Amsterdam: John Benjamins.

– (2010): "Hypocoristics in Australian English." – In: Burridge, Kate & Bernd Kortmann (eds.): *Varieties of English 3. The Pacific and Australasia*, 398–414. Berlin/New York: De Gruyter.

Stockwell, Robert & Donka Minkova (2001): *English Words. History and Structure.* – Cambridge: Cambridge University Press.

Vijver, Ruben van de (1997): "The duress of stress: On Dutch clippings." – In: Coerts, Jane & Helen de Hoop (eds.): *Linguistics in the Netherlands*, 219–230. Amsterdam: John Benjamins.

Weeda, Donald (1992). *Word Truncation in Prosodic Morphology.* – PhD dissertation, University of Texas.

Wiese, Richard (2001): "Regular morphology vs. prosodic morphology? The case of truncation in German." – In: *Journal of Germanic Linguistics* 13, 131–177.

Irene Vogel

Recursion in phonology?

1 Introduction

Recursion has been from the outset of generative theory the basis of a crucial distinction between the syntactic and phonological components of grammar: the former characterized by recursion and the latter not. The issue of recursion has recently become a topic of discussion again (cf. among others Hauser, Chomsky and Fitch (2002), Pinker and Jackendoff (2005), Jackendoff & Pinker (2005), Neeleman & Van de Koot (2006), Van der Hulst (2010b); see also Lobina (2011) for a review of the issues). Alongside, and largely independently of, the general discussions about the overall structure of human language, a number of phonological analyses have been proposed that involve recursive structures, perhaps facilitated by apparent similarities between (prosodic) phonological and syntactic trees.[1]

This paper focuses on an area in which recursion has often been introduced into phonology: structures involving Phonological Words. Both the motivation for this recursion and the resultant structures are evaluated. It is shown that the proposed recursive structures introduce problems with regard to both phonological structure and linguistic structure more generally. For example, the proposed structures fail to exhibit the properties of recursion as generally defined in linguistic theory. This in turn leads to a conflict with the widely accepted concept of linguistic constituent as a string with a particular set of properties independent of its internal structure.

Two alternative proposals that avoid recursion are considered: Neeleman & Van de Koot's (2006) string-based analysis and an alternative that retains the model of prosodic phonology but with a constituent that replaces the Clitic Group between the Phonological Word and the Phonological Phrase, the Composite Group (cf. Vogel 2009, 2010). Aspects of the geometry of the prosodic hierarchy are reconsidered, and then general conclusions are drawn regarding the nature of both phonology and grammar in general.

---

[1] Despite the various ways in which recursive structures have appeared in phonology, the broader implications of such a move are typically not addressed, though notable exceptions include Neeleman & Van de Koot (2006) and Van der Hulst (2010a), discussed below.

2 Prosodic phonology and the introduction of recursive structures

The prosodic hierarchy was developed to provide phonological constituents that could serve as the domains for phonological phenomena since the constituents of the other components of grammar were often found to be inadequate as phonological domains (among others Selkirk 1972, 1980; Nespor & Vogel 1986). The 'interface' constituents, representing a mapping from morpho-syntactic to phonological structure, generally include varieties of the following: Phonological Word < Clitic Group < Phonological Phrase < Intonational Phrase < Phonological Utterance (Nespor & Vogel 1986). While some form of most of these constituents is widely accepted, the Clitic Group has often been the object of controversy and excluded from the hierarchy. Interestingly, this exclusion tends to be coupled with the introduction of a recursive Phonological Word structure, although these options are in fact independent of each other.

2.1 The Clitic Group and the Strict Layer Hypothesis

The Clitic Group (CG), originally proposed in Hayes (1989 [1984]), essentially consisted of a Phonological Word (PW) plus elements such as "#" or 'level 2' affixes which combined as sisters of the PW (Nespor & Vogel 1986: 154). As a result of the highly constrained geometry of the prosodic hierarchy, these elements were attributed PW status. Specifically, an aspect of the Strict Layer Hypothesis (SLH), the principle of 'Strict Dominance' (or 'Strict Succession'), only permitted (non-terminal) constituents to dominate constituents of the immediately lower prosodic level, so that every element the CG dominated had to be a PW. Structures in which a constituent dominates constituents more than one level lower were excluded, as were recursive structures in which a constituent dominated constituents of the same or higher levels.

2.2 Problems with the Clitic Group and Strict Layer Hypothesis

Objections to the CG were raised with regard to a) its overlap with the PW, and b) the assignment of PW status to affixes and clitics. The first situation arises sporadically in many languages (e.g. $[[giant]_{PW}]_{CG}$ $[[pandas]_{PW}]_{CG}$ $[[love]_{PW}]_{CG}$ $[[bamboo]_{PW}]_{CG}$, and commonly in so-called isolating languages (e.g. Vietnamese: $[[tôi]_{PW}]_{CG}$ $[[thich]_{PW}]_{CG}$ $[[con]_{PW}]_{CG}$ $[[ngựa]_{PW}]_{CG}$ $[[đen]_{PW}]_{CG}$ 'I like CLASSIFIER horse black' = 'I like the black horse'). Even complete overlap is not a crucial argument against the CG, however, on the assumption that the prosodic hierarchy is part of Universal Grammar and elements may be present in a language without overt manifestation (cf. Hayes 1995; Itô & Mester 2008).

The second situation is quite common, and more problematic (e.g. ... $[[of]_{PW}$ $[the]_{PW}$ $[pre]_{PW}$ $[season]_{PW}]_{CG}$; Italian: $[[lo]_{PW}$ $[si]_{PW}$ $[ri]_{PW}$ $[sostituisce]_{PW}]_{CG}$ '(he) re-substitutes it for himself'). In these structures, the clitics and affixes are labeled as PWs to satisfy the requirements of the Strict Layer Hypothesis, not due to properties of the items themselves, which do not, in fact, exhibit the typical properties of PWs (e.g. stress, minimality).

2.3 The introduction of the Recursive Phonological Word

A number of researchers have proposed to resolve the problems with the SLH by modifying Strict Dominance, rather than rejecting the SLH altogether. One widely proposed modification involves the introduction of structures in which a constituent may dominate constituents more than one level lower in the prosodic hierarchy (e.g. Itô & Mester 2003; Selkirk 1996; Anderson 2005; Vogel 2008, 2009). An additional, independent, modification is the introduction of 'recursive' structures (cf. among others Selkirk 1996; Peperkamp 1997; Booij 1996; Hall 1999; Anderson 2005), illustrated with the Italian example in (1).

1. a. *[lo si ri [sostituisce]$_{PW}$]$_{PW}$*   or   b. *[lo [si [ri [sostituisce]$_{PW}$]$_{PW}$]$_{PW}$]$_{PW}$*
    '(he) re-substitutes it for himself'

Both the 'core' and outer constituent(s) are labeled PW here, although in some analyses a diacritic is used to label the outer constituent: PW' or PW^{max}. The first structure, with only two levels of PW, is more commonly adopted than the latter, which introduces a potentially infinite number of constituents and depth into phonological trees (e.g. Bickel & Hildebrandt 2007; Schiering et al. 2007; Bickel et al. 2009; Schiering et al. 2010).

The most common Recursive Phonological Words (RPWs) involve affixes and clitics. In some cases, however, it is also proposed that compounds constitute recursive PWs as in *[[water]$_{PW}$ [tower]$_{PW}$]$_{PW}$* (see also Wheeldon & Lahiri 2002 for Dutch, Peperkamp 1997 for Italian, Vigário 2003 for Portuguese). The motivation for treating compounds as RPWs is the necessity of grouping the constituents in a way that is distinct from simply joining them into a Phonological Phrase (PPh). For example, in English, it is well known that compounds typically stress the first element of a string while phrases stress the last element (e.g. **green** *house* and *green* **house**).[2]

3 Problems with the Recursive Phonological Word

3.1 Recursion in the phonological component

As mentioned, since recursion has typically been the basis of a crucial distinction between phonology and syntax, its elimination would require us to revise our view of the components of grammar and their interactions. Moreover, examination of the proposed recursive phonological structures reveals that they do not observe the usual definitions of *recursion* and *linguistic constituent*, so it would be necessary to either abandon these concepts or recognize distinct definitions in the phonology and syntax.[3]

3.2 The Recursive Phonological Word is not recursive

A general definition of recursion is given in (2) (Pinker & Jackendoff 2005: 211). (See the papers in Van der Hulst (2010b) for other views of recursion.)

(2) Recursion consists of *embedding a constituent in a constituent of the same type*,[4] for example a relative clause inside a relative clause [...], which automatically confers the ability to do so *ad libitum*.

They go on to mention that "[t]his does not exist in phonological structure: a syllable [...] cannot be embedded in another syllable."[5]

Despite this proposed difference between syntax and phonology, recursive structures have been proposed in phonological analyses. As indicated above,

---

[2] See Plag et al. (2008) for a detailed discussion of the position of stress in compounds.

[3] Phonological phenomena are presented here in derivational rule format, however, many of the points are also relevant for a constraint-based approach. In fact, in some OT analyses there is indirect recognition of the problem of introducing recursive structures and it is proposed that they are a marked option, surfacing only when a constraint such as *NonRecursive(C_i)* is ranked lower than certain other constraints (cf. Anderson 2005; Itô & Mester 2009, among others).

[4] The italics have been added here.

[5] Van der Hulst (2010a) argues that syllables might in fact be recursive, however, this is not a widely held view.

Recursive Phonological Words have often been proposed to account for con-
structions involving clitics and affixes, and compounds.[6] As can be seen with
the Italian examples below (i.e. (3a) repeated from (1) and the compound in
(3b)), however, these structures differ in fundamental ways from this
standard view of recursion.

(3) a. [lo si ri [sostituisce]$_{PW}$]$_{PW}$ '(one) re-substitutes it'
     b. [[gira]$_{PW}$ [sole]$_{PW}$]$_{PW}$ 'sunflower'

The structures in (3) contain several strings labeled "PW". According to the
definition of recursion, the embedded PWs should be the same type of
constituent as the ones in which they are embedded, and thus exhibit the
same properties. The rule of Intervocalic s-Voicing (ISV) in northern
varieties of Italian shows that this view is problematic. ISV results in the
pronunciation of intervocalic 's' as [z] between vowels within a PW, so if all
PWs are the same type of constituent, we would expect ISV to apply to the
various instances of 's' in (3). This prediction is incorrect, however (i.e. *[lo
[z]i ri [[z]ostituisce]$_{PW}$]$_{PW}$, [[gira]$_{PW}$ [*[z]ole]$_{PW}$]$_{PW}$*). Thus, despite the
claim that such structures are recursive, the fact that the properties of the
inner and outer PWs are different conflicts with the usual definitions of
recursion and constituent. That is, we do not observe the *"embedding [of] a
constituent in a constituent of the same type."*

Indeed, with regard to compounds it is not only observed that the components do not combine like sequences of words to form Phonological Phrases,
but also that the properties of the individual members of a compound differ
from those of the entire compound. Assigning the same PW label to both
obscures this difference. For example, Vowel Harmony (VH), as well as
other types of phonological phenomena commonly apply within a PW, but
not across the PWs of a compound (cf. among others Nespor & Vogel 1986;
Booij 2007). Hungarian offers a well-known case, *Budapest*, where the first
element (*Buda*) is a back vowel word, while the second (*Pest*) is a front
vowel word. A similar situation arises in many other languages. For example,
in the Gur language Dagbani, ATR harmony applies within a PW but not
across the members of a compound, as in [no sɔ-ɣʊ] 'hen coop' ('fowl' +
'stall-sg'), where the first element is [+ATR] and the second (followed by a
suffix) is [−ATR] (Olawsky 2002: 210).

Admittedly, the nature of, and relationship between, phonological and
grammatical words is complex, as amply demonstrated in Dixon & Aikhen-

---

[6] It has also been proposed that higher level structures such as Intonational Phrases
may be recursive (e.g. Ladd 1996), however, since they may more directly refer to
syntactic structures they appear to be a reflection of the recursive property of syntax
rather than phonology (cf. Van der Hulst 2010a).

vald (2002a), however, on the assumption that prosodic constituents are part of Universal Grammar, it is crucial to establish common mapping principles applicable across languages. Dixon & Aikhenvald's (2002b) analysis of Fijian raises challenges to this view, not only in their adoption of the Recursive Phonological Word, but in the nature of the strings they permit to form PWs. The Fijian PW is defined on the basis of phonological rules such as Diphthongization: sequences of *ai, ei, oi, au, eu* and *ou* are realized as diphthongs within a single PW, but as V-V otherwise (pp. 36-37). Thus, certain affixes, function words, and their combinations may constitute PWs, as in (4), where the bracketings below each example show the grammatical categories in the PWs .

(4) a. $[[a - ona]_{PW} [i - talanoa]_{PW}]_{PW}$ 'his story'
       (i.e. $[[art - poss]_{PW} ...]$)
     b. $[[i - na]_{PW} [ona]_{PW} [i - talanoa]_{PW}]_{PW}$ 'in his story'
       (i.e. $[[prep - article]_{PW} [poss]_{PW} ...]$)
     c. $[[i - na - j]_{PW} [talanoa]_{PW}]_{PW}$ 'in the story'
       (i.e. $[[prep - article - nom pref]_{PW} ...]$)[7]

These structures correctly predict Diphthongization in (4c) where the sequence a+i is in a single PW, and its absence in the other items. They also, however, introduce several problems. First, it is not accurate to claim that the PW is the domain for Diphthongization since it only applies to the inner PWs, not throughout the outer PW. In addition, if such varied types of strings constitute PWs, it is not clear what type of mapping principles would account for PW construction cross-linguistically (cf. Vogel 2009).[8]

3.3 How many PWs are there?

The structure in (1a) above tends to be more widely used than that in (1b), however, the latter is adopted in certain typological analyses. The potentially unlimited number of PW levels of (1b) is exploited by Bickel & Hildebrandt (2007) and Schiering et al. (2007), for example in Lhasa, Burmese and Kham, claimed to have eleven or more PW levels. (See also Bickel et al. 2009; Schiering et al. 2010.)

---

[7] The boundaries used by Dixon & Aikhenvald are replaced here by '-'.

[8] Dixon & Aikhenvald (2002b) suggest that there might not be general principles that relate morpho-syntactic (grammatical) and phonological words across languages. Given the view taken here, however, that prosodic constituents are part of UG, it is crucial that there be at least some core principles for mapping morpho-syntactic structure onto phonological (here PW) structure.

Analyses with large numbers of PW levels exhibit the same problems as those with two levels with regard to recursion in the phonological component and the violation of the usual linguistic definitions of recursion and constituent. Moreover, if each language defines PWs on the basis of its own idiosyncratic properties, we are again unable to establish a consistent, cross-linguistically valid, set of mapping principles responsible for the interfaces between phonology and the other components of grammar.

This being said, the appearance in some languages of a large number of phonological phenomena, each seeming to apply in a different context, nevertheless raises an interesting challenge. In fact, it is essentially this issue that led to the proliferation of boundary types in earlier generative analyses, and levels in lexical phonology (cf. Vogel 2009). Any proposal that considers prosodic constituents universal must account for such cases, as discussed below.

4 Recursion-free phonology: string-based alternative

As mentioned, the RPW was introduced to resolve problems in the geometry of the prosodic hierarchy. However, this solution comes at a 'cost' to linguistic theory. We must thus ask whether the only possible solutions require the introduction of 'recursive' structures. An alternative that avoids recursion is proposed by Neeleman & Van de Koot (2006) who argue that recursion, as well as certain other properties, crucially distinguish syntax from phonology. Their view of phonology, moreover, differs from the widely assumed hierarchical constituent structure making use, instead, of sequences of strings, enriched and structured by an ordered set of boundary symbols.

One main concern with the prosodic hierarchy expressed by Neeleman & Van de Koot is the diacritic nature and potential proliferation of constituent types, however, it should be noted that the use of boundaries in their model appears to be subject to an analogous concern. In fact, many models of prosodic phonology offer specific definitions of the constituents, so there is in reality little room for their proliferation. The choice of a label in phonology, as in syntax, is arbitrary, serving as a means of referring to a specific type of string. Thus, phonological node labels in any framework are no more 'diacritic' than node labels in syntactic structures. What is crucial in both phonology and syntax is that strings delimited by the labels define a set of constituent types with identifiable properties that are part of Universal Grammar.

It is noteworthy, moreover, that the boundary symbols in Neeleman & Van de Koot's proposal essentially correspond to the constituent labels of the prosodic hierarchy. Closer examination, in fact, shows that the resulting structures encode a hierarchical organization that bears a striking resemblance to the hierarchical structure of prosodic phonology. For example, an item might be structured in the string-based approach as in (5), where '111, 222, etc.' indicate unanalyzed strings (cf. Neeleman & Van de Koot 2006: 1533). The symbols 'ω', 'F' and 'σ' stand for Phonological Word, Foot and Syllable, and represent the nature of the boundaries in given positions (i.e. before, between and after portions of a string). Brackets are not used, since Neeleman & Van de Koot argue that there is no need for prosodic constituents.

$$(5) \quad \omega \ 111 \ \sigma \ 222 \qquad \left\{ \begin{matrix} F \\ \sigma \ 333 \ \sigma \end{matrix} \right\} \omega$$

Here, the portion of the string '111 σ 222' is a Foot when F follows, while the last syllable, if present, is directly included in the Phonological Word without Foot structure. Thus, this representation permits the skipping of levels, a possibility that was discussed above in relation to the weakening of the Strict Layer Hypothesis. Indeed, (5) is easily represented in a prosodic framework that permits the skipping of levels: $[\ [\sigma \ \sigma]_F \ \sigma \ ]_{PW}$.

Again addressing the difference between syntax and phonology, Neeleman & Van de Koot argue that the string-based approach offers an additional advantage over a prosodic phonology approach, claiming that the former automatically excludes several properties of syntax from the phonological component. For example, they argue that their system excludes from phonology c-command relations as well as operations involving non-adjacent items. While the proposed strings do, in fact, exclude these properties, it is not clear that such distinctions between syntax and phonology are necessarily a result of the string structures. In addition to recursion, it has generally been accepted that phonology and syntax are governed by different principles. In fact, what seems more interesting than the absence of c-command in phonology is its presence in syntax. By the same token, adjacency would appear to be the default for interactions; so again, what is of interest is the specific property of syntax that permits operations involving relationships between non-adjacent items.

Whether or not we accept a string-based analysis of phonology, Neeleman & Van de Koot's analysis presents arguments for maintaining a distinction between the syntax and phonology, including limiting recursion to syntax. Moreover, if skipping of levels is permitted in prosodic phonology the differences between the string-based and prosodic hierarchy approaches are not as great as they at first appear.

5 Recursion-free phonology: Composite Group alternative

Another type of analysis that excludes recursion retains the prosodic hierarchy, but replaces the original Clitic Group with the Composite Group (CompG) (cf. Vogel 2009, 2010). The CompG includes ('level 2') affixes that are excluded from the PW, clitics, and the members of compounds. While at first glance it may appear surprising that a single constituent comprises both compounds and affixes and clitics, it should be noted that precisely the same set of items is grouped together by the Recursive Phonological Word approach.

5.1 The Composite Group Geometry

The RPW, the string-based, and the CompG approaches all share the possibility of skipping levels, however, the first two also involve additional changes that are avoided with the CompG. The need for skipping levels is well motivated in phonology, for example, in accounting for extrasyllabic consonants (e.g. *stream*: $[s[trim]_{\sigma/F}]_{PW}$), and extrametrical syllables (e.g. *lavender*: $[[laven]_F \ der]_{PW}$). In some analyses a 'superfoot' has been proposed for the latter (i.e. $[[laven]_F \ der]_{F'}$). Interestingly, the superfoot is similar to the RPW, involving the embedding of a phonological constituent (C) in an enhanced constituent claimed to be of the same type (C'). In this case, too, several drawbacks are observed. As Itô & Mester (2003: 31) point out, the superfoot appears to maintain the original SLH by "incorporating the categorical non-uniformity of the string 'Fσ' in its very definition." In reality, the result is an enrichment of the prosodic hierarchy with a distinct constituent between the Foot and the PW, although as with the RPW this is obscured by the use of the same term at two levels (i.e. F and F'; PW and PW').

The CompG analysis captures the skipping of levels with structures such as those in (6).

(6) a. $[\ [\ ]_{PW} \ \sigma]_{CompG}$ b. $[\sigma [\ ]_{PW}]_{CompG}$

    c. $[\ [\ ]_{PW} \ F]_{CompG}$ d. $[F [\ ]_{PW} \ ]_{CompG}$

The Italian examples in (7a, b) illustrate (6a, b), and show that more than one syllable may join with the PW in a CompG, as in (7c).

(7) a. [[lava]$_{PW}$ li]$_{CompG}$ 'wash them'
    b. [li [lava]$_{PW}$]$_{CompG}$ '(he) washes them'
    c. [lo si ri [sostituisce]$_{PW}$]$_{CompG}$ '(he) re-substitutes it for himself'

The structures in (6c, d) involving feet may include larger function words, where the head of the foot exhibits some prominence (e.g. *[[delle]$_F$ [stampe]$_{PW}$]$_{CompG}$* 'of the/some prints'). Similar prominence is not exhibited with multiple (unfooted) syllables (e.g. *[te li [stampa]$_{PW}$]$_{CompG}$* '(he) prints them for you', *[ti ri [stampa]$_{PW}$]$_{CompG}$* '(he) reprints for you').[9]

While structures involving the PW' and F' have a number of similarities, a different outcome seems to be required with respect to the outer constituent in the two cases. In the case of the Foot, Itô & Mester (2008) argue that no additional constituent is motivated, but in the case of the PW, as has been seen, an additional constituent seems to be required. For example, it was seen that in Italian Intervocalic *s*-Voicing applies within a PW, but not in strings with a prefix or clitics, or in compounds. By recognizing the distinctness of the larger (outer) CompG constituent, we automatically account for the observed phonological pattern: ISV applies within the PW, and nothing further needs to be stated. With the RPW analysis, by contrast, it is necessary to stipulate that ISV applies within the inner PWs but not the outer one.

5.2 Restrictions on Composite Group geometry

In the CompG approach, the Strict Layer Hypothesis continues to substantially restrict prosodic structures, with a single crucial modification – the possibility of skipping levels. All that is required is that a constituent C contain at least one constituent of the next lower level, as expressed by the principle of Proper Headedness in (8). Unless demonstrated to be otherwise, this should considered to be an unviolable property of prosodic structure.

(8) *Proper Headedness*: Every (nonterminal) prosodic category of level i must have a head, that is, it must immediately dominate a category of level C_{i-1} (cf. Itô & Mester 2003: 37).

One possible complication with this principle is that it potentially allows any number of levels to be skipped, as long as a constituent has a head. It is proposed that the possibilities are nevertheless limited, for example by Itô & Mester's (2003: 38) Maximal Parsing constraint.

---

[9] General principles of Eurhythmy may introduce additional prominences in strings of unstressed syllables (cf. Nespor & Vogel 1989), however this phenomenon would be distinct from the stress associated with the head of a Foot.

(9) *Maximal Parsing*: Prosodic structure is maximally parsed, within the limits imposed by other (universal and language-particular) constraints on prosodic form.

Thus, two syllables originally excluded from a constituent of the next higher level may be restructured to form such a constituent (foot), yielding a more thoroughly parsed structure (i.e. *Fσσ* would be reanalyzed as *FF*).

While this accounts for the Japanese cases discussed by Itô & Mester, it does not yield the correct structure for Italian cases such as *lo si ri sostituisce* '(he) re-substitutes it for himself'. Grouping the first and second clitics, or the second clitic and the prefix, into a Foot would incorrectly predict stress on the Foot head, shown in bold in (10).

(10) a. [[**lo** si]$_{Ft}$ ri [sostituisce]$_{PW}$]   b. [lo [**si** ri]$_{Ft}$ [sostituisce]$_{PW}$]

Moreover, any grouping of *lo* and *si* into a PW (as a Foot or not), or of *ri-* and the stem, would predict the application of the PW level Intervocalic s-Voicing rule, yielding an ungrammatical result:
*[lo [z]i ri [[z]ostituisce]$_{PW}$]$_{PW}$.

Alternatively, we may formulate the principle of Minimal Distance in (11) which requires any element excluded from a prosodic constituent to be parsed at the first available level *after* that one.

(11) *Minimal Distance*: An unparsed phonological element is parsed at the next (higher) available constituent level.

Thus, an element (e.g. clitic, 'level 2' affix, extrametrical syllable, extra-syllabic segment) that has been excluded from some constituent will not subsequently form such a constituent; it will be adjoined as a sister of that constituent at the next higher level. For example, in *[lo si ri [sostituisce]$_{PW}$]$_{CompG}$*, the clitics and 'level 2' affix become sisters of the PW within the CompG.

In some analyses clitics are prosodically attached to larger constituents such as the Phonological Phrase (e.g. Anderson 2005). It seems, however, that only the placement of the clitics is sensitive to the larger constituents. That is, once a clitic is in place, its phonological behavior is the same as if it were attached to a smaller (e.g. PW) host. This can be seen in (12), where the distribution of [s, z, əz] is the same whether it represents a plural or posses-sive form, or the reduced (clitic) form of the auxiliaries *is* and *has*.

(12) a. *Plural*   the moon[z] appeared
     b. *Possessive*   the moon[z] appearance
     d. *Aux 'is'*   the moon[z] appearing as we talk
     d. *Aux 'has'*   the moon[z] appeared already
     e. *Aux 'has'*   the Earth's one and only moon[z] appeared brighter lately

The first two elements are placed after a PW and join with it in the next higher constituent, the CompG. The placement of the auxiliaries, by contrast, refers to a larger structure that includes the entire subject of a sentence. If we attribute different prosodic structures to the 's' of the auxiliaries and the 's' of the plural and possessive, however, we would (incorrectly) expect this difference in structures to manifest itself with different phonological behaviors. Instead, these various forms of 's' are similar, and distinct from an 's' which is part of a PW. The latter does not exhibit the same distributional requirements since both [s] and [z] appear after voiced segments (e.g. *lance*, *lens*). Following the principle of Minimal Distance, the different types of 's' in (12) may be grouped into a CompG with their host, once their placement is determined, as illustrated in (13).

(13)   a. *Plural*   [the [moon]$_{PW}$ s]$_{CompG}$ appeared
       b. *Aux 'has'*   [the [moon]$_{PW}$ s]$_{CompG}$ appeared already

Since the prosodic hierarchy involves an interface with other components of grammar, a further restriction may be formulated to ensure the possibility of cross-linguistic generalization, and to avoid the construction of idiosyncratic PWs as seen above in Fijian. Thus, in addition to a phonological head, a PW must have a "morphological core", as stated in (15).

(14)   *Morphological Core*: A PW must contain a morphological core.

It should be noted that the core is not necessarily the morphological head, which may be an affix in certain frameworks, but corresponds to what is commonly referred to as a 'root'. This makes it possible to prevent affixes, clitics, or other bits of words from becoming PWs, even if they exhibit Foot structure.[10]

5.3 The CompG is not isomorphic to morphological structure

Prosodic phonology crucially admits constituents that are distinct from those of the other components of grammar, and the CompG is no exception. In this way, it provides the necessary phonological grouping for so-called 'ordering paradoxes', as illustrated with the following well-known examples.

(15)   a. ungrammaticality   b. transformational grammarian

In (15a), the problem is the ordering of affixation of 'level 2' *un-* before 'level 1'-*ity*, and in (15b), it is the morphological attachment of the 'level 1'

---

[10] It should be noted that 'meaningless' roots may constitute a core, such as the first element of *huckleberry*, or the components of many Chinese compounds.

-ian to the entire compound. Since the CompG includes phonological material that may not coincide with the related morpho-syntactic structure, *-ity* and *-ian* join into the PWs to their left, regardless of the organization of the other elements, as in (16).

(16) a. [un [grammatical ity]$_{PW}$]$_{CompG}$
      b. [[transformational]$_{PW}$ [grammar ian]$_{PW}$]$_{CompG}$

Finally, it should be noted that the CompG is the prosodic constituent associated with idiosyncrasy, most likely due to the CompG's interface with morphology, the component of grammar typically associated with exceptionality (cf. Vogel 2008, 2009). With the formulation of appropriately restricted contexts, rules that apply under specific, limited conditions may apply within the CompG domain, even if they do not apply consistently throughout the constituent. Thus, it is possible to avoid the proliferation of PW types or levels of embedded PWs such as those posited in Bickel & Hildebrandt (2007); Bickel et al. (2009); Schiering et al. (2007, 2010), or lexical levels and boundaries in earlier models of phonology.

6 Test Cases

6.1 Other Languages

The test of any proposal is its applicability to phenomena of other languages. First, let us consider European Portuguese (e.g. Vigário 2003) and Dutch (e.g. Booij 1999, 2007, 2010 among others), for which it has been proposed that certain affixes may constitute PWs on their own, illustrated in (17) and (18), where the affixes are bolded.

(17) *Portuguese* a. [[**pos**]$_{PW}$ [sintactico]$_{PW}$]$_{CompG}$ 'post-syntactic'
                   b. [alegre]$_{PW}$ [**mente**]$_{PW}$]$_{CompG}$ 'happily'

(18) *Dutch*   [[rood]$_{PW}$ [**achtig**]$_{PW}$]$_{CompG}$ 'reddish'

While such affixes may be excluded from the PW containing the word's root, and even meet phonological minimality requirements, since they are not roots themselves, they would not fulfill the Morphological Core requirement in (14) above. The CompG avoids this problem by simply labeling the affixes as Feet and parsing them as sisters of the associated PW, as in (19) and (20).

(19) *Portuguese*   a. [[**pos**]$_{Ft}$ [sintactico]$_{PW}$]$_{CompG}$
                      b. [alegre]$_{PW}$ [**mente**]$_{Ft}$]$_{CompG}$

(20) *Dutch*   [[rood]$_{PW}$ [**achtig**]$_{Ft}$]$_{CompG}$

These structures have the advantage of allowing the affixes to exhibit prominence on the Foot head, without considering them PWs. Moreover, by taking the CompG, as opposed to the RPW, as the domain for combining the affixes and their morphological bases, we avoid the problems of recursion and definition of linguistic constituent described earlier.

The failure of PW rules to apply throughout a compound is also handled straightforwardly with the CompG. For example, in the Hungarian and Dagbani compounds mentioned above, the first two elements constitute the base compound, but they do not exhibit Vowel Harmony. The suffixes harmonize with the linearly adjacent roots, showing that they are part of the PW while being morpho-syntactically associated with the entire compound.

The failure of PW rules to apply throughout a compound is also handled straightforwardly with the CompG. For example, in the Hungarian and Dagbani compounds mentioned above, the first two elements constitute the base compound, but they do not exhibit Vowel Harmony. The suffixes harmonize with the linearly adjacent roots, showing that they are part of the PW while being morpho-syntactically associated with the entire compound.

(21) a. [[Buda]$_{PW}$ [pest-nek]$_{PW}$]$_{CompG}$ 'Budapest-dat'
      b. [[no]$_{PW}$ [sɔ-ɣʊ]]$_{PW}$]$_{CompG}$ 'hen coop' (= 'fowl' + 'stall-sg')

Given that Vowel Harmony is a PW domain, if the entire structure is a (recursive) PW, we would incorrectly expect to find harmony throughout the compound, not just between the root and adjacent suffix.

Another type of situation is seen in Dutch, where it has been proposed that parts of words that do not correspond to morphemes may constitute PWs, and then form RPWs (e.g. Booij 2010), as in (22).

(22) a. [[ant]$_{PW}$ [woord]$_{PW}$]$_{PW}$ 'answer'   b. [[aal]$_{PW}$ [moes]$_{PW}$]$_{PW}$ 'alms'

Due to space limitations, it is not possible to do justice to Booij's motivation for his proposed analysis, however, one arguent for these structures is that the words exhibit the stress pattern of compounds, so if compounds are RPWs, then these words should also be RPWs. While the second elements happens to correspond to roots (*woord* 'word', *moes* 'pulp'), they are not roots in the items in question; moreover, the first elements are neither affixes nor other roots. Consequently, the full structures are neither derived nor compound forms based on the "roots", but rather lexical items of their own. As with the affixes seen in (17) and (18), labeling the portions of words here as PWs leads to a violation of the principle of the Morphological Core.

Since such items are distinctly atypical forms for Dutch, making them look like another type of structure can be misleading. Alternatively, their exceptionality may be represented directly, for example with pre-specified Foot prominence relations in a PW, as in (23).[11]

(23)   a. [[ant]$_{Ft(s)}$ [woord]$_{Ft(w)}$]$_{PW}$ b. [[aal]$_{Ft(s)}$ [moes]$_{Ft(w)}$]$_{PW}$

Finally, let us return briefly to the atypical PW structures of Fijian. A drawback of these structures is that their idiosyncrasy does not allow us to formulate cross-linguistic generalizations for the mapping between morpho-syntactic and phonological structure. By contrast, the CompG can account for the same data, and also retain more consistent definitions of the prosodic con-stituents in question. While the possessor *ona* may constitute a PW since it is bisyllabic and meets the minimality requirement of two moras (cf. Dixon & Aikhenvald 2002a), this is not the case for the other function words. The lat-ter, as well as the prefix *i-*, are individual syllables, and as such join with an available PW in a CompG, as in (24).

(24)   a.   [a [ona]$_{PW}$]$_{GC}$ [i [talanoa]$_{PW}$]$_{GC}$ 'his story'
       b.   [i na [ona]$_{PW}$]$_{GC}$ [i [talanoa]$_{PW}$]$_{GC}$ 'in his story'
       c.   [i na j [talanoa]$_{PW}$]$_{GC}$ 'in the story'

Diphthongization can now be assigned to the CompG instead of the PW domain. It applies in (24c) where the *ai* sequence is in a single CompG, but not in (24a, b) where it is split into different CompGs.

---

[11] Accounting for exceptions is a complex subject. Booij's stipulating that the parts of words in such cases are PWs is one way of addressing their exceptionality. The proposal advanced here, however, offers the advantages of a) using the mechanism of pre-specification, a widely used means for representing exceptionality, and b) allowing us to maintain stringent restrictions on PW structure, something that is necessary if we are to have mapping principles that apply across languages. This approach would, however, require subsequent adjustments when certain affixes are added, as pointed out by a reviewer. It is then suggested that there is yet another alternative, a series of statements for stress within different constituents, for example: a) within the PW, the rightmost foot is strong [(Àla)$_{Ft}$ (*báma*)$_{Ft}$] $_{PW}$; b) within the CompG, the leftmost PW is strong {[gréén]$_{PW}$ [house]$_{PW}$}$_{CompG}$; {[óóg]$_{PW}$ [lid]$_{PW}$}$_{CompG}$ or{[ánt]$_{PW}$ [woord]$_{PW}$}$_{CompG}$; c) unless the rightmost PW branches {(ver) [ant]$_{PW}$ (wóór).(de.lijk)]$_{PW}$} $_{CompG}$, and so forth. While capturing some of the observed patterns, such an analysis still falls short since there are exceptions to these generalizations as well such as stress on the first foot in words such as *cátamaran* and right stress in compounds such as *Fifth Ávenue* (cf. Plag et al. 2008). Clearly, the means of treating stress (and other) exceptions requires continued investigation. (See Simon & Wiese (2011) for detailed discussion of exceptions.)

6.2 Psycholinguistic data: response latencies

A different type of evidence also supports the CompG over Recursive PW
structures. Based on a series of experiments with Dutch speakers, Wheeldon
& Lahiri (1997, 2002) argue that the unit of phonological encoding for
speech production is the Phonological Word (cf. Levelt 1989). The underlying assumption is that as one prepares to speak, an utterance consisting of
more PWs will cause a longer delay than one with fewer PWs. A problem
arises, however, leading Wheeldon & Lahiri to resort to the RPW to account
for their findings, while the CompG offers a simple interpretation of the data.
As shown below, data from a subsequent study with Italian also support the
latter analysis.

In a prepared speech paradigm, Wheeldon & Lahiri presented a series of
words and phrases with different structures, shown in (25) and (26)[12], on a
computer screen. A beep followed each item, signaling to the subjects to
begin their response using the item just seen. The response latency, or time to
onset of speech, was measured.

(25) *Study 1 (Wheeldon & Lahiri 1997)*

     a. *Clitic Sentence*   [Ik zoek het] [water]   'I seek the water.'
     b. *(Stressed) Pronoun Sentence* [Ik zoek] [het] [13]   'I seek it.'
     c. *Adjective-Noun Sentence*   [Ik zoek] [vers] [water] 'I seek fresh water.'
     d. *Control Sentence*   [Ik zoek] -----   'I seek'

(26) *Study 2 (Wheeldon & Lahiri 2002)*

     a. *Compound Sentence*   [Het was] [oog] [lid]   'It was eyelid.'
     b. *Matched Phrase*   [Het was] [oud] [lid]   'It was old member.'
     c. *Simple Word (sw / ws)* [Het was] ['orgel] / [or'kaan] 'It was organ /
                                                        hurricane.'

It was predicted that the fastest responses would occur with the control, a
single PW. The slowest responses were expected with (24c) and (25a, b),
with three PWs. The remaining structures were predicted to have intermediate response latencies.

The fastest responses were, indeed, observed with (24d), and intermediate
latencies were observed for Clitic and Pronoun Sentences in Study 1, and for
Simple Word Sentences in Study 2. It was also correctly predicted that the
Adjective-Noun Sentences in both studies would exhibit significantly longer
response latencies. A problem arose, however, with the Compound Sentences
and their Matched Phrases in the second study. While both structures were

---

[12] The brackets are the PWs posited by Wheeldon & Lahiri.
[13] The pronoun *het* 'it' was stressed, so it was assigned PW status.

analyzed as having three PWs, leading to the prediction that they would require the same preparation time, the Compound Sentences showed significantly faster responses, patterning with the Simple Words, rather than with the phrasal targets. The account offered by Wheeldon & Lahiri (2002) was that compounds must be construed as recursive PWs, and a stipulation was then required to ensure that only the outer PWs are counted in determining the response latencies; the inner PWs are used for other phonological phenomena.

A similar experiment with Italian further examined this issue (Vogel & Wheeldon 2010). The stimuli consisted of 12 of each of the following structures, all with four syllables and penultimate stress.

(27) a. *V-N compound*   guastafeste   'killjoy'
      b. *V-N phrase*   guida treni   '(he) drives trains'
      c. *non-derived wd.* Guatemala   'Guatemala'
      d. *derived wd.*   guarnizione   'trimming'

The crucial comparison is between the compounds and matching phrases since these structures yielded the originally unexpected results in Dutch. The single PW lexical items served as a basis for comparison. Both derived and non-derived words were included, to verify that morphological complexity itself is not what determines the response behaviors.

The Italian findings were essentially the same as the Dutch findings. Overall, the compounds patterned with single words rather than phrases, and when the matched pairs of compound and phrase were examined within subjects, the effect was even stronger. The onset latencies for the compounds, non-derived and derived words did not differ significantly (cf. Vogel & Wheeldon 2010).

It is noteworthy that languages with substantially different prosodic patterns behave similarly with respect to the prosodic units relevant for speech encoding, combining a set of structures not originally expected to pattern together. While Wheeldon & Lahiri proposed that the relevant prosodic constituent is the PW, the items that show similar response latencies involve one PW in some cases (i.e. single words, stressed pronouns), but two in other cases (i.e. compounds). The number of Composite Groups, however, correctly predicts the response patterns: all the structures that show the same, intermediate, response latencies consist of a single CompG, regardless of their internal structure, including number of PWs, as shown in (28).

(28) *CompG Structures – intermediate response latency*
     Dutch
     a. [[water]]$_{CompG}$ 'water'   b. [[het]]$_{CompG}$ 'it'
     c. [[oog] [lid]]$_{CompG}$ 'eyelid'   d. [['orgel]/[or'kaan]]$_{CompG}$
                                                    'organ / hurricane'

Italian
a. [[Guatemala]]$_{CompG}$ 'Guatemala'   b. [[guarnizione]]$_{CompG}$ 'trimming'
c. [[guastafeste]]$_{CompG}$ 'killjoy'

Significantly longer latencies are observed only with phrases which were matched with the compounds for PWs, but also contained two CompGs (i.e. [[oud]]$_{CompG}$ [[lid]]$_{CompG}$ 'old member'; [[guida]]$_{CompG}$ [[treni]]$_{CompG}$ '(he) drives trains').

Thus, if we consider the CompG, and not the PW, to be the prosodic constituent that is relevant for planning in speech production, the results follow automatically. No additional stipulation is required for certain types of structure.

7. Conclusions

The introduction of recursion into the phonological component, despite the fact that it was traditionally considered a crucial distinction between syntax and phonology, was examined from several perspectives. It was shown, however, that the 'recursion' in the Recursive Phonological Word does not exhibit the properties associated with recursion in syntax - the embedding of a constituent of a particular type (i.e. characterized by specific properties) within another constituent of the same type. Thus if the RPW is taken as evidence of recursion in phonology, we can no longer maintain the definitions of two core aspects of linguistics, linguistic constituent and recursion, itself. e same type. The alternative advanced here rests on the presence of a prosodic constituent between the Phonological Word and the Phonological Phrase, the Composite Group. Since the problems that led to the introduction of the RPW were caused by a component of the Strict Layer Hypothesis, the prohibition against the skipping of levels in the prosodic hierarchy (i.e. Strict Dominance or Succession), the CompG permits levels to be skipped, subject to several restrictions. This proposal was tested with a variety of languages and psycholinguistic data from Dutch and Italian.

References

Anderson, Stephen (2005): *Aspects of the Theory of Clitics.* – Oxford: Oxford University Press.

Bickel, Balthasar & Kristine Hildebrandt (2007): Word domains. Ms. University of Leipzig.

Bickel, Bakthasar, Kristine Hildebrandt & René Schiering (2009): "The distribution of phonological word domains." – In: Janet Grijzenhout & Barış Kabak (eds.): *Phonological Domains: Universals and Deviations*, 47–75. Berlin: Mouton de Gruyter.

Booij, Geert (1996): "Cliticization as prosodic integration: the case of Dutch." – In: *The Linguistic Review.* 13, 219–242.

– (1999): "The role of the prosodic word in phonotactic generalizations." – In: Hall, Tracy A. & Ursula Kleinhenz (eds.): *Studies on the Phonological Word.* Philadelphia: John Benjamins. pp. 47–72.

– (2007): *The Grammar of Words.* Second edition. – Oxford: Oxford University Press.

– (2010): "Compound construction: rules or analogy? A construction morphology perspective." – In: Scalise, Sergio & Irene Vogel (eds.): *Cross-disciplinary Issues in Compounding*, 93–107. Amsterdam/Philadelphia: John Benjamins.

Dixon, Robert M.W. & Alexandra Y. Aikhenvald (eds.) (2002a): *Word.* – Cambridge: University Press.

– (2002b): "Word: a typological framework. – In: Dixon & Aikenvald (2002a), 1-41.

Hall, Tracy A. (1999): "The phonological word: a review." – In: Hall, Tracy A. & Ursula Kleinhenz (eds.): *Studies on the Phonological Word*, 1–22. Philadelphia: John Benjamins.

Hauser, Marc D., Noam Chomsky & W. Tecumseh Fitch (2002): "The faculty of language: what is it, who has it, and how did it evolve?" – In: *Science.* 298: 1569–1579.

Hayes, Bruce (1989 [1984]): The Prosodic Hierarchy in Meter. – In: Kiparsky, Paul & Gilbert Youmans (eds.): *Rhythm and Meter.* 201–260. Orlando, Florida: Academic Press.

– (1995): *Metrical stress theory: Principles and case studies.* – Chicago: The University of Chicago Press.

Itô, Junko & Armin Mester (2003): "Weak layering and word binarity" – In: Takeru Honma, Masao Okazaki, Toshiyuki Tabata & Shin-ichi Tanaka (eds.): *A New Century of Phonology and Phonological Theory. A Festschrift for Professor Shosuke Haraguchi on the Occasion of His Sixtieth Birthday,* 26–65. Tokyo: Kaitakusha.

– (2008): Prosodic adjunction in Japanese compounds. – In: *Proceedings of Formal Approaches to Japanese Linguistics.* MIT Working Papers in Linguistics, 97–112.

– (2009): The extended prosodic word. In Grijzenhout, Janet & Bariş Kabak (eds.): *Phonological Domains: Universals and Deviations*, 135–194. Berlin: Mouton de Gruyter.

Jackendoff, Ray & Steven Pinker (2005): "The faculty of language: what's special about it?" – In: *Cognition*. 95: 201–236.

Ladd, D. Robert (1996): *Intonational Phonology*. – Cambridge: Cambridge University Press.

Levelt, Willem (1989). *Speaking: From Intention to Articulation*. – Cambridge, Mass.: MIT Press.

Lobina, David J. (2011): "'A running back' and forth: a review of *Recursion and Human Language*." – In: *Biolinguistics* 5.1–2, 151–169.

Neeleman, Ad & Johannes van de Koot (2006): "On syntactic and phonological representations." – In: *Lingua*. 116, 1524–1552.

Nespor, Marina & Irene Vogel (1986; 2nd edition 2007): *Prosodic Phonology*. – Dordrecht: Foris.

– (1989): "On clashes and lapses." – In: *Phonology* 6, 69–116.

Olawsky, Knut (2002): "What is a word in Dagbani?" – In: Dixon & Aikenvald (eds.): (2002a), 205-226. Cambridge: University Press.

Peperkamp, Sharon (1997): *Prosodic Words*. – The Hague: Holland Academic Graphics.

Pinker, Steven & Ray Jackendoff (2005): "The nature of the language faculty and its implications for the evolution of language. (Reply to Fitch, Hauser, and Chomsky)." – In: *Cognition*. 97: 211–225.

Plag, Ingo, Gero Kunter, Sabine Lappe & Maria Braun (2008): "The role of semantics, argument structure, and lexicalization in compound stress assignment in English" – In: *Language* 84, 760–794.

Schiering, René, Baltahsar Bickel & Kristin Hildebrandt (2010): "The prosodic word is not universal, but emergent." – In: *Journal of Linguistics* 46, 657–710.

Schiering, René, Kristin Hildebrandt & Balthasar Bickel (2007): Cross-linguistic challenges for the prosodic hierarchy: evidence from word domains. Ms. University of Leipzig.

Selkirk, Elisabeth (1972): *The Phrase Phonology of English and French*. – Ph.D. Dissertation, Massachusetts Institute of Technology. (Published 1980 by Garland Press, New York)

– (1980): "Prosodic domains in phonology: Sanskrit revisited." – In: Aronoff, Mark & Marie L. Kean (eds.): *Juncture*, 107-129. Saratoga: Anma Libri.

– (1996): "The prosodic structure of function words." – In: Morgan, James L. & Katherine Demuth (eds.): *Signal to Syntax: Bootstrapping from Syntax to Grammar in Early Acquisition*, 187-213. Mahwah, NJ: Erlbaum

Simon, Horst J. & Heike Wiese (eds.) (2011): *Expecting the Unexpected: Exceptions in Grammar*. – Berlin: Mouton de Gruyter.

Van der Hulst, Harry (2010a): "A note on recursion in phonology. – In: Van der Hulst (ed.) (2010b), 301–341.

Van der Hulst, Harry (ed.) (2010b): *Recursion and Human Language*. Berlin: Mouton de Gruyter.

Van Oostendorp, Marc (2010): "Sigma strikes back." Abstract for Old World Conference in Phonology 7. Nice, France.

Vigário, Marina (2003): *The Prosodic Word in European Portuguese*. – Berlin: Mouton de Gruyter.

Vogel, Irene (2008): "Universals of prosodic structure." – In: Scalise, Sergio, Elisabetta Magni & Antonietta Bisetto (eds.): *Universals of Language Today*, 59-82. Berlin: Springer.

– (2009): "The status of the Clitic Group." – In: Grijzenhout, Janet & Barış Kabak (eds.): *Phonological Domains: Universals and Deviations,* 15–46. Berlin: Mouton de Gruyter.

– (2010): "The phonology of compounding." – In: Scalise, Sergio & Irene Vogel (eds.): *Compounding: Theory and Analysis*, 145-163. Amsterdam: John Benjamins.

Vogel, Irene & Linda Wheeldon (2010): "Units of speech production in Italian." – In: Colina, Sonia, Antxon Olarrea & Ana M. Carvalho (eds.): *Romance Linguistics 2009*, 95–110. Philadelphia: John Benjamins.

Wheeldon, Linda & Aditi Lahiri (1997): "Prosodic Units in Speech Production." – In: *Journal of Memory and Language* 37, 356–381.

– (2002). "The minimal unit of phonological encoding: prosodic or lexical word." In: *Cognition* 85: B31–B41.

Roland Noske

The Grimm-Verner push chain and Contrast Preservation Theory*

1 Introduction

Traditional textbooks from before the 1980s treat Grimm's Law and Verner's Law as essentially four different historical changes (i.e. three separate changes known as the three 'acts' of Grimm's Law, and Verner's Law). In these descriptions not much attention, if any, is given to the idea that the changes are systematically linked. Nevertheless, the idea of a systematic link, at least for the three parts of Grimm's Law, was advanced by Grimm himself in his *Geschichte der deutschen Sprache*, where he writes (1848: 393):

> One can appropriately compare the Sound Shift with vehicles that move in a circle: as soon as a wheel arrives at the place of the preceding one, then its own place has already been taken by a following wheel, but no wheel will overtake another one. In their movement there cannot remain space anywhere that is not immediately filled. [My translation, R.N.][1]

Grimm describes here something what we would now call a chain shift. From the above cited passage, it cannot be concluded whether Grimm saw the three changes as a push or a pull chain.

In the period after the publication of these words, the Neogrammarian doctrine became prevalent. This doctrine states that every sound change should be phonetically motivated, or be caused by analogy. Such a stance is incompatible with the idea of a chain shift, where a part of the shift is due to systemic pressure, caused by the need to maintain contrast. The Neogram-

---

* I would like to thank Joaquim Brandão de Carvalho, Olga Fischer, Piotr Gąsiorowski, Janet Grijzenhout, Martin-Joachim Kümmel, Jean-Pierre Montreuil, Cédric Patin, Christopher Piñón, Norval Smith and Janet Watson for valuable discussions and suggestions. I also wish to thank two anonymous reviewers for their useful comments. Remaining errors are mine. The analysis presented in this paper was presented in various stages of development to audiences in Amsterdam, Lille, Nantes, Orléans, Gniezno and Manchester.

[1] "Man mag die lautverschiebung passend wagen vergleichen, die in einem kreise umlaufen: sobald ein rad die stelle des vorangehenden erreicht ist seine eigne bereits von einem folgenden eingenommen, aber keins ereilt das andere, bei ihrer bewegung kann nirgend raum bleiben, der nicht alsbald ausgefüllt würde."

marian stance must be the explanation why this passage in Grimm (1848) did not receive any attention in the late 19th century.

It took a long time for the idea of Grimm's Law as a chain shift to re-emerge. Eighty-four years later, Kretschmer (1932: 274) describes Grimm's Law clearly as a push chain:

> Hence, the process was the following: when the aspirated voiced stop approached the plain voiced stop and threatened to coincide with it, speakers made an effort to differentiate the plain voiced stop from it: the realization of this phoneme then led to a fortis articulation. But as soon as the plain voiced stop came close to the former voiceless stop, the latter also changed in order to avoid a merger, such that it was aspirated and finally became spirantized. [My translation, R.N.][2]

Kretschmer's insight is repeated by Luick (1940: 802–803). Later, Kiparsky (1971) analyzes Grimm's Law as a pull chain using the SPE (Chomsky & Halle 1968) framework. Also Fox (1976), Bynon (1977) and Campbell (1994, [2]2004) see Grimm's Law as a chain shift.

In this article, I will show that Verner's Law must have been part and parcel of the same chain shift. For this I will make use of an independently needed modification of the traditionally assumed Proto-Indo-European (PIE) obstruent inventory. I will then show how the Grimm-Verner push chain can be expressed formally in modern phonological theory. But first, I will give an overview of the traditional view.

2 An outline of the traditional view

2.1 The Proto-Indo-European obstruent system

The Neogrammarian view on the PIE obstruent inventory as put forth by Brugmann (1897) and modified in later research involves a series of 12 stops and a single fricative, cf. the overview in (1) (*tenues*, *mediae* and *mediae aspiratae* are the traditional Neogrammarian terms for voiceless, voiced and breathy voiced stops respectively):

---

[2] "Der Vorgang war also folgender: als die Media aspirata sich der Media annäherte und mit ihr zusammenfallen drohte, bemühten sich die Sprechenden die Media von ihr zu differenzieren; die Realisation dieses Phonems führte dabei zur fortis-Artikulation. Sobald aber die Media dadurch der alten Tenuis nahkam, wurde diese auch differenziert, um den Zusammenfall zu vermeiden und zwar aspiriert und schließlich spirantisiert."

(1) *PIE obstruent inventory, traditional view*[3]

	voiceless stops (*tenues*)	voiced stops (*mediae*)	breathy voiced ('voiced aspirated') stops (*mediae aspiratae*)	fricative
labial	p	b	b^h	
dental	t	d	d^h	s
velar	k	g	g^h	
labiovelar	k^w	g^w	g^{wh}	

We can thus represent the PIE obstruent system in the following simplified diagram (where the uppercase characters generalize over the places of articulation):

(2) PIE obstruent system: T D D^h (in four places of articulation), *s*

2.2 The Proto-Germanic accent shift

In Proto-Germanic, there was an accent shift from the free, lexically determined stress system (as still found in, e.g., Russian) to a word or root initial stress. According to several authors adhering to the traditional view (e.g., Lehmann 1961: 69) this would have conditioned the Germanic sound shift (Grimm's Law, see section 2.3, below). An example of correspondences with other IE languages is given in (3), where Gothic and Old English (OE) represent PG in the relevant aspects:

(3) | *Sanskrit* | *Ancient Greek* | *Latin* | *Gothic, OE* |
| | pitár- | πατήρ [pa'te:r] | pater | fádar (*Gothic*) fǽder (*OE*) |

2.3 Grimm's Law

Grimm's Law consists of three 'acts': voiceless stops spirantize (act 1); breathy voiced stops become fricatives (act 2) and voiced stops become voiceless (act 3):

---

[3] I give here the traditional view as given by Lehmann (1952). Brugmann originally also posited a series of palatal stops. These were later shown to be allophones of the velars (although this remains a matter of debate). Brugmann further assumed that the PIE inventory also contained a series of voiceless aspirates in addition to the voiced aspirates. This idea was abandoned in subsequent research.

(4) *Grimm's Law (Rask 1818, Grimm 1822 and later amendments)*

    a. (act 1) $p > f$ $t > \theta$ $k > x \, (>h)$ $k^w > x^w \, (>h^w)$

    b. (act 2) $b^h > {*}\beta \, (> b)$ $d^h > {*}\eth \, (> d)$ $g^h > {*}\gamma \, (> g)$ $g^{hw} > {*}\gamma^w \, (> g^w)$

    c. (act 3) $b > p$ $d > t$ $g > k$ $g^w > k^w$

As one can see, act 2 leads to an unattested voiced fricative that is subsequently changed into a stop by a supposed occlusivization process. I will come back to this process below, in section 3.3. Grimm's Law can be represented schematically as in (5):

(5) *Diagram of Grimm's Law*

	Pre-PG		PG1		PG2
a. (act 1)	T	⟶	Þ	- - - ▸	Þ
b. (act 2)	Dʰ	⟶	*Đ	⟶	D
c. (act 3)	D	⟶	T	- - - ▸	T
		Grimm's Law		occlusivization	

Examples of the workings of the law can be shown by the correspondences between PIE and English (and Dutch for one example) in (6).[4]

(6) a. (act 1) *p̱ed > f̱oot   *trei̯ > ṯhree   *ḵāt- > ẖate
                  *ḵu̯od > w̱hat

     b. (act 2) *ḇʰrātēr > ḇrother *ḏʰugəter > ḏaughter *g̱ʰaidos > g̱oat
                  *g̱ʷʰermos > w̱arm

     c. (act 3) *ḇend- > p̱en   *ḏekm > ṯen   *gelə- > c̱old
                  *g̱ʷa- > c̱ome; > ḵwam (preterit, Dutch)

2.4 Verner's Law

Lottner (1862) lists a number of types of counter-examples to Grimm's Law. The most important class is that of voiced stop reflexes of voiceless stops, where one would expect voiceless fricatives. Examples are given in (7).[5]

---

[4] In these examples, we see some additional changes in the evolution from PG to English: *h* in *hate* is the result of change from the velar to the glottal fricative, which took place after spirantization (hence $k > x > h$). In act 2, in addition to the PIE>PG loss of aspiration, the PIE labiovelar aspirated stop lost its plosive character and became a glide, and in act 3, in addition to being devoiced, the labiovelar lost its labial character to become plainly velar. The labial character was maintained in the Dutch preterit form *kwam* 'came-SG'.

[5] In these examples, thorn (*þ*) represents [θ] (but intervocalically [ð], see note 7). The consonantal alternations in the verb paradigms in (7) are traditionally referred to as *grammatischer Wechsel* 'grammatical alternation'.

(7) a. *Original *p (no examples of the alternation in the modern languages)*
       OE hebban - hōf hōfon hafen ('lift' *cf.* heave)

   b. *Original *t (the alternation survives in modern German)*
      OE cweþan (cwiþþ) cwæþ - cwǣdon cweden ('say': *cf.* quoth)
      OE sēoþan (sīeþþ) sēaþ - sudon soden ('boil' *cf.* seethe)
      Modern German schneiden - schnitt geschnitten ('cut')

   c. *Original *k (survives in modern German and Dutch)*
      Modern German ziehen ziehe – zog gezogen ('pull')
      OE þēon (þīehþ) þēah - þigon þigen ('prosper' *cf. Modern Germ.* gedeihen)
      Modern Dutch zien zie gezien - zag zagen ('see', *Dutch lost intervocalic* **h**)
      Modern Dutch slaan sla - sloeg sloegen geslagen ('beat')

Verner (1876) analyzes these alternations as being related to alternations of
the position of the original PIE accent. His law states (1876: 114):

> IE *k, t, p* first shifted to *h, þ, f* in all environments; the voiceless fricatives thus
> originating, together with the voiceless fricative *s* inherited from Indo-European,
> then became voiced medially in voiced environments, but remained voiceless
> when they were the final sounds of accented syllables. [Translation by Lehmann
> 1967][6]

Verner uses here the expression 'final sounds of accented syllables' because
he believes that intervocalic consonants belong to the former syllable (Verner
1876: 117; I will briefly come back to this assumption below in footnote 23).
The effect of the law can be illustrated by the forms in (8):

(8)

Proto-Indo-European (reconstructed)	*Sanskrit*	*Ancient Greek*	*Gothic, Old English (OE)*	*Modern High German*
*bʰrátēr	bʰrátar-	φράτηρ (['pʰra:te:r])	brōþar (*Gothic*) brōþor (*OE*)	Bruder
*pətḗr	pitár-	πατήρ ([pa'te:r])	fadar (*Gothic*) fæder (*OE*)	Vater

In the word for 'brother', *t* in PIE, Sanskrit and Ancient Greek corresponds to
þ in Gothic (where it represents [θ]) and OE (where it represents [ð])[7]
according to act 1 (spirantization) of Grimm's Law. Verner's Law does not

---

[6] "Indogerm. *k, t, p* gingen erst überall in *h, þ, f* über; die so entstandenen tonlosen
fricativae nebst der vom indogermanischen ererbten tonlosen fricativa *s* wurden
weiter inlautend bei tönender nachbarschaft selbst tonend, erhielten sich aber als
tonlose im nachlaute betonter silben."

[7] In intervocalic position, *þ* in OE represents [ð]. The voiced character is the result of
a voicing process that took place only in the early stages of Old English, and that
was independent from Verner's Law (Campbell 1959: 179–180).

apply here, because the preceding vowel is stressed. By contrast, in the word for 'father', PIE, Sanskrit and Ancient Greek *t* corresponds not to *θ*, but to *d*. In most modern Germanic languages, like Dutch, English and Icelandic, this contrast has levelled out, but it remained in High German, despite additional shifts.

As Verner mentions in his own description of the law, cited above, the law applies only medially. However, many scholars, like Jespersen (1933: 230), assume that the law applies also word-finally. I will come back to this below, in section 7.4.2.

The functioning of Grimm's Law and Verner's Law combined is shown in the diagram in (9):

(9)   *Diagram of Grimm's Law and Verner's Law*

		PIE	Pre-PG	PG1	PG2
a.	(act 1)	T ⟶	Þ ⤎--→	Þ ----→	Þ
b.	(act 2)	Dʰ ⟶	*Ð ----⤏	*Ð ⟶	D
c.	(act 3)	D ⟶	T ----→	T ----→	T
		Grimm's Law	Verner's Law	occlusivization	

Verner mentions that he cannot derive *D* at PG2 directly from *T*, "for this would be a sound innovation *directly counter to the main direction of the sound shift* [i.e., act 3 of Grimm's Law, *D > T*, RN], which produced a voiceless stop from the Indo-European voiced stop" (1876: 101, translation by Lehmann 1967, italics mine).[8] It is for this reason that he has to assume that his law applies after that of Grimm, and that occlusivization applied across the board.

3 Problems related to the traditional view

The traditional view of the PIE obstruent system and the PG sound changes has given rise to a number of problems. They concern (i) the typology of the PIE obstruent system, (ii) the alleged occlusivization process, (iii) the fact that the changes are not monotonic, (iv) the fact that *s* does not undergo occlusivization and (v) the number of changes Germanic must have under-

---

[8] "Dagegen kann man die germanische tönende explosiva nicht auf directem wege durch mittönen der stimme aus der indogermanischen explosiva entstanden sein, denn dies würde ein lautübergang sein, der gerade gegen die hauptrichtung der lautverschiebung die aus der indogermanischen tönenden explosiva tonlose explosiva hervorbrachte, gehen würde."

gone vis-à-vis PIE, compared to the classical languages like Sanskrit and Greek. I will briefly treat each of these problems.

3.1 The typological improbability of the traditional obstruent inventory

The first problem concerns the typological improbability of the alleged PIE obstruent inventory. As mentioned by several authors (e.g., Pedersen 1951; Martinet 1955; Jakobson 1958), the occurrence of *mediae aspiratae*, i.e. voiced aspirates (in fact breathy voiced or "murmured" stops), without voiceless aspirated stops is typologically very strange.[9] To make matters worse, there are also problems regarding the fact that the occurrence of *b* is rare in PIE, and that there is an apparent constraint against the combination: voiced stop-vowel-voiced stop (the so-called **deg constraint*) in PIE. Under the traditional model these facts remain unexplained. For more details on these points, see Salmons (1993: 16–18).

3.2 The alleged occlusivization process

A second problem concerns Verner's Law and the invoked occlusivization process. Here one important problem is that the intermediate stage of voiced fricatives, which should have resulted after the application of Verner's Law and before occlusivization, has not been unambiguously attested. It is true that certain PIE voiceless stops occur as voiced fricatives in historical data. However, it is more straightforward to derive these from voiced stops than vice versa because occlusivization is much less common than spirantization. On top of that, there are several indications that the examples of the original *mediae aspiratae* (voiced aspirates) which indeed show up as voiced fricatives in historical records, probably have gone through a stage where they were voiced stops (Luick 1940: 800–801).

3.3 The absence of monotonicity

As mentioned above, Verner cannot derive D directly from T as this would go against the 'main direction' D > T (Grimm's Law, act 3). Therefore, he has to assume the complicated derivation T > Þ > Ð > D (Grimm's Law, act 1, followed by Verner's Law and occlusivization). However, on closer

---

[9] Kelabit, a language of Northern Borneo, is reported as an exception by Blust (1974, 2006).

inspection we see that this also goes against a main direction: first there is a spirantization T > Þ, and then, after application of Verner's Law, exactly the opposite development, i.e. a despirantization (or: occlusivization) in the change Ð > D. Hence, we have a change [– cont] > [+ cont] > [– cont]. This is likewise true for act 2 of Grimm's Law, which is followed by occlusiviza-tion (Dʰ > Ð > D). In both cases, the change is not monotonic because there is a reversal of an earlier change. So, under this scenario too, there are developments against a 'main direction'. In generative terms, because these changes are not monotonic, they are of the so-called Duke of York Gambit[10] type, which suggests the possibility of a faulty analysis (see Pullum 1976).[11]

3.4 The absence of occlusivization concerning *s*

There is yet another problem connected to occlusivization: precisely the only certain fricative in PIE, *s*, which changed to *z* in PG after a non-stressed vowel by Verner's Law, did not undergo the alleged occlusivization. This casts further doubt on the assumption that occlusivization took place at all. To my knowledge, this problem regarding the traditional view has hitherto gone unnoticed.

3.5 The position of Proto-Germanic and Sanskrit compared to Proto-Indo-European

Under the traditional view, the 'classical languages' (especially Sanskrit) seem close to PIE but Germanic seems to have undergone substantial sound changes in the transition from PIE. In their focus on and admiration of Sanskrit and other classical languages, the Neogrammarians gave no attention to the logical possibility that it is Sanskrit that has undergone substantial changes compared to PIE.

---

[10] "The Grand Old Duke of York / He had ten thousand men / He marched them up a great high hill / And he marched them down again."

[11] The lack of monotonicity in Verner's scenario was first noticed by F.L. Wells (1903–1905: 523) who stated: "[t]he chronological relation of Verner's law to Grimm's law is not to be dismissed so lightly as Verner himself dismissed it. It will not suffice to accept unquestioningly Verner's dictum that voicing must have occurred after spirantization, since *f-v* [specified as bilabial in a footnote, R.N.] is quite as much against the Hauptrichtung [main direction, R.N.] – if it has any – as *p-b* or *ph-bh*."

4 Glottalic Theory and its consequences for Verner's Law

Due to the typological improbability of the classic view on the PIE obstruent inventory (as mentioned in the previous section), this view has come increasingly under attack. Emonds (1972), Hopper (1973, 1997a, b, 1982), Gamkredlidze & Ivanov (1973, 1995), Haudricourt (1975), Vennemann (1984), Kortlandt (1985, 1988) and Haider (1985) have all produced alternatives to the classic inventory, whereby, with the exceptions of Emonds and Haider, the voiced stops were replaced by voiceless glottalized stops (ejectives).[12] These models are subsumed under the name of 'Glottalic Theory'. For ease of exposition I give here Hopper's (1973, 1997a, 1997b, 1982) model, but the point made here also holds for the other models of the Glottalic Theory, and *mutatis mutandis,* for Emonds' and Haider's models.[13]

(10) Hopper's (1973, 1997a, b, 1982) glottalic model compared to the traditional model (Lehmann 1952)

	Series I	Series II	Series III
Traditional model (Lehmann 1952)	b, d, g	bʰ, dʰ, gʰ	p, t, k
Glottalic model (Hopper 1973, 1997a, b, 1982)	p', t', k'	b, d, g	p, t, k

With this model, the typological problems concerning the obstruent inventory have been resolved: there are no longer voiced aspirates, the rarity of the occurrence of *b* (which is *p'* under the glottalic model) is in accordance with typological observations (labials are often absent in ejective series), and the glottalic equivalent to the **deg* constraint (now: *ejective-vowel-ejective) is typologically straightforward.[14]

---

[12] Emonds (1972) replaces the voiced stops of the traditional model by plain voiceless ones and the plain voiceless stops by aspirated voiceless ones. Haider (1985: 11ff) replaces the voiced stops by implosives (or, rather, "nonexplosives". The 'implosive' version of the theory copes with a number of objections that have been raised against Glottalic Theory. For further discussion, see Kümmel (2012).

[13] For an overview of the different models within the Glottalic Theory see Salmons (1993: 31) and Vennemann (2006: 130).

[14] A general criticism of the Glottalic Theory is is that it makes the analysis of Germanic and some other branches of IE simpler, but that of other branches more complicated. In this paper I cannot go into the complexities of this discussion, but I refer the reader to Salmons (1993) for arguments in favour of the Glottalic Theory and to Job (1995) for arguments against it. A broad spectrum of discussions of the Glottalic Theory by various researchers can be found in Vennemann (ed., 1989).

This model has important consequences for Verner's Law. As noted by Vennemann (1984: 20–22, 1985: 533–535), Verner's Law can now be assumed to have taken place before the spirantization part of Grimm's Law, and so it simply changes voiceless plain obstruents into voiced ones, i.e. mostly voiceless plain stops into voiced plain stops, but also *s* to *z*. This is so because the change T > D does not go anymore against the 'main direction' (see section 2.4), i.e. act 3 of Grimm's Law, which has now become *T'* > *T*. This assumption, which has been endorsed by Kortlandt (1985), solves three major problems mentioned in section 3: that of the relative chronology of the laws of Grimm and Verner, that of the non-monotonicity of the shifts, as well as that of the non-application of occlusivization to *s*. Fourthly, it can now be assumed that a spirantization process has applied to certain voiced stops, rather than that a less likely occlusivation process applied to voiced fricatives. Thus, the diagram of the Germanic sound changes in (9) can now be modified and simplified:

(11) *Diagram of Grimm's Law and Verner's Law under the Glottalic Theory and the relative ordering proposed by Vennemann (1984)*

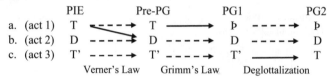

		PIE	Pre-PG	PG1	PG2
a.	(act 1)	T	T	þ	þ
b.	(act 2)	D	D	D	D
c.	(act 3)	T'	T'	T'	T
		Verner's Law	Grimm's Law	Deglottalization	

Concerning Grimm's Law, it can be concluded that act 2 (which was *Dʰ* > *Đ* > *D*) has disappeared, because PIE *Dʰ* has been replaced by *D*, so there is no change (*D* remains *D*). Concerning act 3, we see that PIE *D* has been replaced by a glottalized stop, *T'*, so act 3 now represents a deglottalization process instead of a devoicing process. From now on, we will refer to act 1 of the now less complex Grimm's Law as 'Germanic Spirantization, and to act 3 as '(Germanic) Deglottalization'.

5 The laws of Verner and Grimm from a synchronic perspective

As we have just seen, there are many advantages to the Glottalic Theory and the chronological ordering of Verner's Law before Grimm's Law. As we

---

Kümmel (2007: 47–54 & 189–192) shows that it is difficult to find typological parallels to a change from glottalized stops to plain stops, which the Glottalic Theory has to assume for nearly all branches.

have seen, the assumption of the new ordering is motivated by the problems that arise if one assumes the reverse ordering. There is no principled reason, however, not to assume that both processes applied at the same time. If we make this assumption, and if we formalize the two processes as synchronic phonological rules, then a very interesting picture emerges. (12) and (13) are rules in the model of Chomsky & Halle (1968) (SPE) representing Verner's Law and act 1 of Grimm's Law (Germanic Spirantization) respectively:[15]

(12) *Verner's Law*[16]

$$\begin{bmatrix} -\text{voice} \\ -\text{constr.gl.} \end{bmatrix} \rightarrow [+\text{voice}] \; / \; \begin{bmatrix} V \\ -\text{stress} \end{bmatrix} \; ([+\text{voice}]) \underline{\quad} V$$

(13) *Grimm's Law, act 1: Germanic Spirantization*

$$\begin{bmatrix} -\text{voice} \\ -\text{constr.gl.} \end{bmatrix} \rightarrow [+\text{cont}] \quad (\text{no context})^{17}$$

The feature [–constricted glottis] is used here to restrict the class of undergoers of the shifts to voiceless plain stops, thus excluding glottalized stops. This means, therefore, that Germanic Spirantization is in an *Elsewhere relationship* with Verner's Law; that is, the context of Verner's Law is *properly included* in that of Germanic Spirantization. Hence, the order of application (i) Verner's Law, (ii) Germanic Spirantization follows automatically from Kiparsky's (1973, 1982) Elsewhere Condition (or from the principle of Proper Inclusion Precedence proposed by Koutsoudas et al. (1974)). According to these principles, Verner's Law has precedence over Germanic Spirantization because its domain of application is more specific.

In this experiment of regarding Germanic Spirantization and Verner's Law as part of a synchronic phonological system, the Elsewhere relationship between the structural descriptions of the Germanic Spirantization and

---

[15] As noted by an anonymous reviewer, the features [voice] and [constricted glottis] are nowadays mostly considered to be monovalent. Hence, in modern frameworks, it is not possible to refer to negative specifications of these features like I do in the SPE-style rules in (12 and (13). This matter, however, is immaterial to the present demonstration of the elsewhere relationship between the rules.

[16] The specification ([+ voice]) must be part of the rule in (12) because Verner's Law also applied after a non-stressed vowel followed by a voiced consonant, cf. the PG past participle **wurd-* 'turned' (which is followed by a stressed ending), where *d* results from the application of Verner's law).

[17] I abstract away from the fact that spirantization does not apply to the stop in question if a stop is preceded by *s* or if it is the second member of a cluster of stops. This is of no consequence for the matter discussed here (but see section 7.4.4, below).

Verner's Law reveals that these laws must be somehow related: it is striking that these two most famous Germanic sound laws have exactly the same undergoer, i.e. a voiceless plain obstruent, and that their order of application can be determined by a general principle. It is therefore tempting to investigate the hypothesis that the Germanic Spirantization and Verner's Law were in fact part of a single process, or were triggered by the same phenomenon. I will do this in the next section.

6 Grimm's Law and Verner's Law as a single bifurcating push chain

I now come to the central hypothesis of this article. In section 4 it was shown that with the adoption of Glottalic Theory, act 2 of Grimm's Law is eliminated. Grimm's Law then consists of only two processes, i.e. (i) context-sensitive spirantization of voiceless stops and (ii) deglottalization of glottalized stops. Verner's Law now simply involves voicing of voiceless stops in contexts in which spirantization did not apply.

This scenario, together with the elsewhere relationship between Grimm's Law and Verner's Law that we established in the previous section, suggests that the laws were part of a single, bifurcating chain shift:

(14) *The Grimm-Verner chain shift*

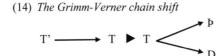

Ejectives deglottalized to voiceless full stops. Because of this, and in order to maintain contrast, original voiceless full stops were pushed to become either spirants or voiced stops, depending on their context.[18]

It can now be concluded that Vennemann's diagram in (11) can be greatly simplified:

---

[18] The idea of a single bifurcating push chain representing the laws of Grimm and Verner was first presented by me in Noske (2009). Bynon (1977: 83ff) also presents Grimm's and Verner's laws as a push chain, but because she uses the traditional obstruent system, she fails to solve the paradox noted by Verner himself, i.e. that a direct change from *T* to *D* would go against the main direction (as pointed out section 2.4).

(15) *The Germanic Sound Shift (my version)*[19]

	PIE		PG
a.	T	⟹	Þ
b.	D	----⇥	D
c.	T'	⟶	T

In the following section, I will show how this push chain can be formulated in a formal phonological framework.

7 The Grimm-Verner Chain Shift in Contrast Preservation Theory

7.1 Chain shifts and formal phonological theory

Chain shifts have traditionally been problematic for both input-driven models like SPE and output oriented models like Optimality Theory (OT). In the SPE framework, chain shifts cannot really be accounted for as a unitary phenomenon because they typically involve counter-feeding relationships. For a chain A > B, B > C, a rule changing B to C has to apply first, and hence there is no explanation for the shift.

In OT, the problem is the same, if not worse, since here chain shifts involve opaque and non-harmonic changes.[20] The opacity is incompatible with the idea of a single mapping which depends on a specific constraint ranking, since change tends to go into the direction of an optimum that is determined by that constraint ranking. I.e., it cannot be explained why in a chain A > B, B > C, there is no fusion between original A and original B, in other words, why B originating from original A does not end up as C, just original B has become C.

Opacity is a notorious problem for OT, and since the introduction of OT, many workarounds have been proposed, such as conjunction, sympathy, multiple strata, dispersion, etc., but none of them have dealt with systemic pressures, which typically result in chain shifts.[21] A proposal by Łubowicz

---

[19] This diagram is a simplified. As I mention in section 7.4.4 below, *T* before *s* did not spirantize and remained unchanged. A more precise rendering should therefore also contain an arrow between PIE *T* to PG *T*.

[20] An anonymous reviewer points out that classic OT cannot in fact model chain shifts, while SPE can model them but not explain them.

[21] Kirchner (1996) and Gnanadesikan (1997) have both proposed solutions for opaque chain shifts Kircher introduces a local constraint conjunction, while Gnanadesikan makes a distinction between classical IDENT-type constraints and novel IDENT-

(2003, 2012) does precisely this. She proposes a theory in which *scenarios* of changes are compared with one another. In addition, a new type of constraint is introduced, *constraints of contrast preservation (PC),* which exist alongside markedness constraints. The role of faithfulness constraints is reduced. This theory, termed Contrasts Preservation Theory (or PC Theory), is well-suited to account for chain shifts, as Łubowicz shows for synchronic processes in, among others, Finnish and Polish.

PC Theory differs from other theories on contrast like Dispersion Theory (Flemming 2002) in that it does not focus on (the maximization of) contrast itself, but on phenomena which involve neutralization of contrasts in some contexts and preservation of contrasts in others, as well as on the transparent vs. opaque nature of processes.

Montreuil (2006) has shown that PC Theory can be fruitfully used to provide formal accounts of historical chain shifts. He draws attention to the fact that contrast transformation, which is very frequent in the history of languages, is in fact a chain shift. A well-known example of such a contrast transformation is American English *writer* [ɹajɾəɹ] vs. *rider* [ɹaːjɾəɹ], where an original voicing contrast has been transformed into a length contrast.[22]

7.2 Some elements of Contrast Preservation Theory

Łubowicz proposes three types of PC constraints.[23] In the description of these types below, *P* represents a potentially contrastive phonological property, such as a distinctive feature, length, stress, presence vs. absence of a segment.

(16) $PC_{IN}(P)$
For each pair of inputs contrasting in P that map onto the same output in a scenario, assign a violation mark. (Łubowicz 2003: 18)
"If inputs are distinct in P, they need to remain distinct."

(17) $PC_{OUT}(P)$
For each output that corresponds to two or more inputs contrasting in P, assign a violation mark. (Łubowicz 2003: 20)
"Avoid outputs ambiguous in P property."

ADJACENT-type constraints on some scale of similarity. However, the notion of systemic pressure is not accounted for in either analysis.

[22] Using PC theory, Montreuil shows that in Gallo, an originally prosodic contrast was transformed into a segmental one.

[23] For reasons of space, my rendering of Łubowicz's fairly elaborate theory will have to be very limited.

(18) PC$_{REL}$(P)

For a pair of outputs minimally contrasting in P that does not correspond to a pair of inputs minimally contrasting in P, assign a violation mark. (Łubowicz 2003: 24)

"Avoid transformation of contrast."

The role of PC$_{REL}$(P) is to keep the segments in place and not to allow for random shifts.

7.3 A formal analysis of the Grimm-Verner push chain.

Let us now look how this type of constraints can be used to work out a formal scenario of the Grimm-Verner chain shift. To begin with, I propose three constraints, one PC$_{IN}$(P) and two PC$_{REL}$(P) constraints:

(19) PC$_{IN}$(CG)

(20) a. PC$_{REL}$(voice)   b. PC$_{REL}$(cont)

PC$_{IN}$(CG) states that a contrast in [constricted glottis] in an input pair (the feature which distinguishes ejective consonants from plain ones) should be present in the output (unless, of course, there are other contrasts between the members of that pair in the output). PC$_{REL}$(voice) says that for a pair of outputs, a minimal contrast in voicing in the output should also be present in the input, and PC$_{REL}$(cont) does the same for the feature [continuant].

I further assumed that PC$_{IN}$(CG) is ranked above PC$_{REL}$(voice) and PC$_{REL}$(cont), which are not ranked with respect to each other:

(21) PC$_{IN}$(CG) > {PC$_{REL}$(voice), PC$_{REL}$(cont)}

In Pre-Proto-Germanic, for a hypothetical input pair /at'a/, /ata/ the following evaluation will take place. I distinguish three stages: the *initial historical stage* (before the advent (or promotion to an undominated position) of a constraint against ejectives), the *intermediate historical stage*, with the advent of a constraint against ejectives), and a *final historical stage*. For each example of constraint evaluation that I give, the historical stage is indicated.

(22) . **Initial historical stage:** *Pre-Proto-Germanic*

(identity mapping) at'a, ata ⇒ at'a, ata

scenario	PC$_{IN}$(CG)	PC$_{REL}$(cont)	PC$_{REL}$(voice)
/at'a/ → at'a /ata/ → ata			

☞

(neutralization of the ejective/plain stop contrast:) at'a, ata ⇒ ata, ata

scenario	PC$_{IN}$(CG)	PC$_{REL}$(cont)	PC$_{REL}$(voice)
/at'a/ → ata /ata/ → ata	*! {/at'a/, /ata/}		

(contrast transformation) at'a, ata ⇒ ata, aθa

scenario	PC$_{IN}$(CG)	PC$_{REL}$(cont)	PC$_{REL}$(voice)
/at'a/ → ata /ata/ → ata			* {[ata], [ada]}

(contrast transformation) at'a, ata ⇒ ata, ada

scenario	PC$_{IN}$(CG)	PC$_{REL}$(cont)	PC$_{REL}$(voice)
/at'a/ → ata /ata/ → ata		* {[ata], [aθa]}	

What we see here is that identity mapping gives the right outcome, because
no constraint is violated. I now assume that in the transition from Pre-Proto-
Germanic to Proto-Germanic an undominated constraint against ejectives was
added (or that this constraint was promoted to an undominated position):
*CG (a constraint banning constricted glottis).

(23) . **Intermediate historical stage:** *Proto-Germanic, with introduction (or*
*promotion) of *CG*

(identity mapping) at'a, ata ⇒ at'a, ata

scenario	*CG	PC$_{IN}$(CG)	PC$_{REL}$(cont)	PC$_{REL}$(voice)
/at'a/ → at'a /ata/ → ata	*!			

(neutralization of the ejective/plain stop contrast:) at'a, ata ⇒ ata, ata

scenario	*CG	PC$_{IN}$(CG)	PC$_{REL}$(cont)	PC$_{REL}$(voice)
/at'a/ → ata /ata/ → ata		*! {/at'a/,/ata/}		

(contrast transformation) at'a, ata ⇒ ata, aθa

Scenario	*CG	PC$_{IN}$(CG)	PC$_{REL}$(cont)	PC$_{REL}$(voice)
/at'a/ → ata /ata/ → aθa				* {[ata], [ada]}

☞

(contrast transformation) at'a, ata ⇒ ata, ada

scenario	*CG	PC$_{IN}$(CG)	PC$_{REL}$(cont)	PC$_{REL}$(voice)
/at'a/ → ata /ata/ → ada			* {[ata], [aθa]}	

☞

We now see that the /at'a/, /ata/ pair can now show up either as {[ata], [aθa]} or as {[ata], [ada]}. That is, the *t* in /ata/ either undergoes spirantization (Grimm's Law, act 1 (Germanic Spirantization)) or undergoes voicing (Verner's Law). At this stage of the elaboration of the scenario, there is no way to choose between *aθa* and *ada* (both: < *ata*). As shown above in section 2.4, Verner's Law (voicing) applies only after unstressed vowels, while spirantization applies elsewhere. In order to account for the choice of the right process (voicing or spirantization), I introduce here two phonetically grounded constraints, a faithfulness constraint and a markedness constraint:

(24) IDENTPOSTSTRESS (Laryngeal) (IDENTPOSTSTRLAR).
    Consonants directly behind a stressed vowel should be faithful to the underlying laryngeal specification.

This faithfulness constraint is an expression of the view of De Jong et al. (1993) that coarticulation effects are reduced in stressed environments, thus impeding intervocalic voicing.[24] The markedness constraint concerns intervocalic voicing:

(25) INTERVOIVOI
    Consonants should be specified [voiced] if between other segments specified [voiced].

IntervoiVoi is an extended version of intervocalic voicing, because it also refers to voiced consonants.[25] The appropriate ranking of the constraints is IDENTPOSTSTRESSLAR > INTERVOIVOI, while both constraints are ranked below PC_{REL}(voice) and PC_{REL}(cont). This gives us the following constraint ranking at this point:

(26) *CG PC_{IN}(CG) > {PC_{REL}(voice), PC_{REL}(cont)} > IDENTPOSTSTRESSLAR > INTERVOIVOI

Let us now consider how the selection between spirantization and voicing given above in (22b) operates:

---

[24] An alternative to IDENTPOSTSTRESSLAR could be a constraint that states that a consonant following a vowel within the same syllable should be faithful to its laryngeal specification. This solution works if one adopts Hoard's (1971) view that a stressed vowel captures a following consonant into its syllable. This view is also adopted by Selkirk (1982) and J.C. Wells (1990). If it is correct, Verner's idea, mentioned in section 2.4, that intervocalic consonants belong to the former syllable is partially corroborated.

[25] This straightforward extension of Intervocalic voicing is needed because Verner's Law also applied after voiced consonants.

(27) **Intermediate historical stage:** *Selection of spirantization and voicing*

(contrast transformation) át'a, áta ⟹ áta, áθa

áta	*CG	PC$_{IN}$ (CG)	PC$_{REL}$(cont)	PC$_{REL}$(voice)	IDENTPOST- STRESSLAR	INTERVOI- VOI
☞ áθa			*{[áta], [áθa]}			*
áda				*{[áta], [áda]}	*!	

(contrast transformation) at'á, atá ⟹ atá, adá

atá	*CG	PC$_{IN}$ (CG)	PC$_{REL}$(cont)	PC$_{REL}$(voice)	IDENTPOST- STRESSLAR	INTERVOI- VOI
aθá			*{[áta], [áθa]}			*!
☞ adá				*{[áta], [áda]}		

We see that by ranking IDENTPOSTSTRESSLAR above INTERVOIVOI the bifurcation depicted in (14) can be accounted for in the framework of PC Theory.

This concludes my analysis of the Grimm-Verner push chain within PC Theory. However, it is necessary to defend it against potential counter-examples. This is the subject of the next section.

7.4 Residual issues

7.4.1 PIE initial voiceless stops

Initial and final T in Pre-Proto-Germanic always becomes Þ in Proto-Germanic (and not D). The above analysis does not account for this. Indeed, in the case of initial or final $T > Þ$ INTERVOIVOI is not violated; but if T had become D, IDENTPOSTSTRESSLAR would also not have been violated. My analysis would thus predict that Þ and D would both be possible outcomes. The solution to this problem is provided by the following a well-established correspondence constraint:

(28) **IDENTLAR:** Do not change the laryngeal specification of a segment

Now the following constraint ranking can be established:

(29) *CG PC$_{IN}$(CG) > {PC$_{REL}$(voice), PC$_{REL}$(cont)} > IDENTPOSTSTRESSLAR > INTERVOIVOI > IDENTLAR

The following evaluation can now be established for initial T:

(30) **Intermediate historical stage:** *initial PIE* T

/t'a/, /ta/	*CG	PC_IN (CG)	PC_REL (cont)	(voice)	IDENTPOST-STRESSLAR	INTER-VOIVOI	IDENT-LAR
t'a, ta	*!						
ta, ta		*!					*
ta, da				*			**!
☞ ta, θa			*				*

7.4.2 PIE final voiceless stops.

Another problem concerns the PIE final voiceless stops. According to the traditional version of Verner's Law, *T* turns into *D* when preceded by an unstressed vowel. However, the constraint IntervoiVoi (cf. (25)), combined with constraint ranking as given in (30), produces Þ whenever PIE *T* is in final position. This counterexample is not valid if one adopts Mańczak's (1990) stance that Verner's Law did not apply word-finally. Mańcak mentions no less than five arguments which show that the evidence for a word-final application of Verner's voicing is very scant or non-existent. This confirms a dictum by an early researcher on Verner's Law: "[a]nd if once the true nature of Verner's Law be sufficiently understood, it will be obvious that its conditions are exactly those most favorable to intervocalic voicing." (F.L. Wells 1903–1905: 526).

7.4.3 Possible fusion of *T* and *D*

Our third problem concerns the fact that in our model of the Grimm-Verner push chain, one does indeed find an instance of non-preservation of contrast. As one can see in the diagram in (15), *D* can have an ambiguous input: it is either *D* or *T*. It suffices to realize that here there is no highly ranked PC_IN constraint for the feature [voice] (or, rather, that the PC_IN(voice) constraint is low in the constraint hierarchy), and hence *T* can turn into *D* when IntervoiVoi blocks other outputs.

7.4.4 *T* does not spirantize before *s* or as second member of a stop cluster

A fourth apparent counter-example concerns the fact that, as is well known, PIE *T* did not spirantize in PG if it was preceded by *s,* or if it was the second member of a cluster of two plain voiceless stops (the first member of which did spirantize, like in Germ. *Haft* vs. Lat. *capt-*). A straightforward explanation for this is a tendency in the form of a non-dominated OCP constraint[26]

---

[26] The generally accepted Obligatory Contour Principle (OCP), proposed by McCarthy (1986, 1988), states that on the melodic level, identical elements are prohibited. Here, the OCP would apply to the melodic level where the feature [continuant] is located.

that excludes a sequence of two obstruents sharing the same feature specification for [continuant]. Such a constraint is needed for many languages as dissimulation processes regarding [continuant] abound across languages.[27]

7.5 The final historical stage

In the *final historical stage*, the processes were lost and the results were lexicalized. The underlying form containing T' in PIE contained T in this stage and those containing T in PIE now contained Þ or D (or still T for the cases mentioned in section 7.4.4). Hence there was now a new obstruent inventory:

> (31)   *The new PG obstruent inventory*
> T ($< T'$,T) , Þ ($< T$), D ($< T$,D), s

Later, there was additional intervocalic voicing. This has become possible because $PC_{REL}(cont)$ and $PR_{REL}(cont)$ did not play a role anymore: they refer to contrast transformation ($t'/t \rightarrow t/\theta$ and $t'/t \rightarrow t/d$), but the t' is no longer there. Therefore, we find z and $ð$ in later texts.

Finally, the conditioning factor of stress was destroyed, because of the stress shift to the initial position (see section 2.2).

8 Conclusions

In this paper, I have given a new interpretation of the history of the Proto-Germanic obstruent system. I have shown that Grimm's and Verner's laws can be analyzed as two subprocesses of a single system-driven process that was essentially a bifurcating sound shift under the influence of the pushing power of Deglottalization (which replaces act 3 of Grimm's Law). This pushing power resulted from the need to maintain contrastivity between original ejectives and original plain voiceless stops. In order to do this, the

---

[27] Examples of this type of dissimilation can be found in, e.g., Modern Greek, where this type of manner dissimilation is quite common, e.g. in φτηνός 'cheap', which is pronounced as [fθinos] in the learned (*Katherévousa*) variety of the language but as [ftinos] in the colloquial (*Demotikí*) variety, and in λεπτά 'minutes', which is pronounced as [lepta] in the learned variety but as [lefta] in the colloquial variety (Newton 1972: 88). Cf. also the English form *fifth* [fɪfθ], which is pronounced as [fɪft] in certain dialects, although θ shows up in other positions in these dialects.

Glottalic Theory was adopted, which enabled a change T > D without going 'against the main direction of the sound change'.

The major upshot of the above analysis is that Deglottalization, Germanic Spirantization (formerly act 1 of Grimm's Law) and Verner's Law are now related and therefore necessarily synchronous with each other. One does not, therefore, have to answer the question whether Grimm's Law preceded or followed Verner's Law. Neither does one have to wonder why in the transition from PIE to PG there were two processes that applied to the same original segments, i.e. the plain voiceless stops.

The second part of the paper presented a formal phonological analysis of this chain shift within Contrast Preservation Theory, building on work by Łubowicz (2003, 2012). Like the analysis presented in Montreuil (2006), this analysis shows that historical chain shifts can find their formal expression in modern phonological theory.

References

Baldi, Philip & Ronald N. Werth (eds.) (1970): *Readings in Historical Phonology: Chapters in the Theory of Sound Change.* – University Park, PA: Pennsylvania State University Press.

Blust, Robert (1974: 'A double counter-universal in Kelabit.' – In: *Papers in Linguistics* 7, 309–324.

– (2006): 'The origin of the Kelabit voiced aspirates: a historical hypothesis revisited.' – In: *Oceanic Linguistics* 45.2, 311–338.

Brugmann, Karl (1897): *Vergleichende Laut-, Stammbildungs- und Flexionslehre der indogermanischen Sprachen. Erster Band: Einleitung und Lautlehre.* 2nd ed. – Strassburg: Trübner.

Bynon, Theodora (1977): *Historical Linguistics.* – Cambridge: Cambridge University Press.

Campbell, Alistair (1959): *Old English Grammar.* – Oxford: Claredon Press.

Campbell, Lyle (2004): *Historical Linguistics: an Introduction* (2nd edition). – Edinburgh: Edinburgh University Press, and Cambridge, MA: MIT Press. [First edition published in 1994].

Chomsky, Noam & Morris Halle (1968): *The Sound Pattern of English.* – New York: Harper & Row.

De Jong, Kenneth, Mary E. Beckman & Jan Edwards (1993): "The interplay between prosodic structure and coarticulation". – In: *Language and Speech* 36, 197–212.

Emonds, Joseph (1972): "A reformulation of Grimm's Law". – In: Brame, Michael (ed.), *Contributions to Generative Phonology*, 108-122. Austin: University of Texas Press,

Flemming, Edward S. (2002): *Auditory Representations in Phonology.* – New York: Routledge.

Fox, Anthony (1976): "Problems with phonological chains." – In: *Journal of Linguistics* 12, 289–310.

Gamkrelidze, Thomas V. & Vjačeslav V. Ivanov (1973): "Sprachtypologie und die Rekonstruktion der gemeinindogermanischen Verschlüsse". – In: *Phonetica* 27, 150–156.

– (1995): *Indo-European and the Indo-Europeans.* – Berlin: Mouton de Gruyter.

Gnanadesikan, Amalia E. (1997). *Phonology with Ternary Scales.* – PhD dissertation, University of Massachusetts, Amherst.

Grimm, Jacob (1822): *Deutsche Grammatik.* vol. I. 2nd ed. – Göttingen: Dieterich.

– (1848): *Geschichte der deutschen Sprache.* – Leipzig: In der Weidmannschen Buchhandlung.

Haider, Hubert (1985): "The fallacy of typology. Remarks on the PIE stop-system." – In: *Lingua* 65, 1–27.

Haudricourt, André-Georges (1975): "Les mutations consonantiques (occlusives) en indo-européen". – In: Bader, Françoise et al. (eds.): *Mélanges offerts à Emile Benveniste*, 267–272. Paris: Société Linguistique de Paris.

Hoard, James. E. (1971): "Aspiration, tenseness and syllabification in English". – In : *Language* 47, 133–140.

Hogg, Richard M. (1992): *A Grammar of Old English. Vol. 1 Phonology.* – Oxford: Blackwell.

Hopper, Paul J. (1973): "Glottalized and murmured occlusives in Indo-European". – *Glossa* 7, 141-166.

– (1977a): "Indo-European consonantism and the 'new look'". – *Orbis* 26, 57–72.

– (1977b): "The typology of the Proto-Indo-European segmental inventory". – In: *Journal of Indo-European Studies* 5, 41–53.

– (1982): "Areal typology and the early Indo-European consonant system" – In: Edgar C. Polome´ (ed.): *The Indo-Europeans in the Fourth and Fifth Millennia*, 121–139. Ann Arbor: Karoma.

Jakobson, Roman. (1958): "Typological studies and their contribution to historical linguistics." – In: *Proceedings of the 8th International Congress of Linguists* (Oslo 1957), 17–35. Also published in: Jakobson, Roman (1971): *Selected Works, vol. I: Phonological Studies,* 523–532. – The Hague: Mouton.

Jespersen, Otto (1933): "Verners gesetz und das wesen des akzents". – In: *Linguistica: selected papers in English, French and German,* 228–248. København: Levin & Munksgaard,

Job, D. Michael (1995): "Did Proto-European have glottalized stops?" – In: *Diachronica* 12, 237–250.

Kiparsky, Paul (1971): *Phonological Change.* – Bloomington: Indiana University Linguistics Club [originally PhD dissertation, MIT, 1965].

(1973): "'Elsewhere' in phonology". – In: Anderson, Stephen & Paul Kiparsky (eds.): *A Festschrift for Morris Halle*, 93–106. New York, London [etc.]: Holt, Rinehart and Winston.

– (1982): "Lexical phonology and morphology". – In: *Linguistics in the Morning Calm*, 3–91. Edited by The Linguistics Society of Korea. Seoul: Hanshin Publishing Co.

Kortlandt, Frederik (1985): "Proto-Indo-European glottalic stops: the comparative evidence". – In: *Folia Linguistica Historica* 6, 183–201.

– (1988): "Proto-Germanic Obstruents". – In: *Amsterdamer Beiträge zur älteren Germanistik* 27, 3–10.

Koutsoudas, Andreas, Gerald Sanders & Graig Noll (1974): "The application of phonological rules". – In: *Language* 50, 1–28.

Kretschmer, Paul (1932): "Die Urgeschichte der Germanen und die germanische Lautverschiebung." – In: *Wiener prähistorische Zeitschrift* 19, 269–280.

Kümmel, Martin-Joachim. 2007. *Konsonantenwandel.* – Wiesbaden: Reichert Verlag.

– (2012): "Typology and reconstruction: the consonants and vowels of Proto-Indo-European." – In: Benedicte Nielsen Whitehead, Thomas Olander, Birgit Anette Olsen & Jens Elmegård (eds): *The Sound of Indo-European, Phonemics and Morphophonemics* (Copenhagen Studies in Indo-European 4), 291–312. Copenhagen: Museum Tusculanum.

Lehmann Winfred P. (1952): *Proto-Indo-European Phonology.* – Austin: University of Texas Press and Linguistic Society of America. Available online at: http://www.utexas.edu/cola/centers/lrc/books/piep00.html.

– (1961): "A definition of Proto-Germanic: a study in the chronological delimitation of languages." – In: *Language* 37, 67–74.

– (1967): *A Reader in Nineteenth-century Historical Indo-European Linguistics.* Ed. and transl. by Winfred P. Lehmann. – Bloomington, Indiana: Indiana University Press. Available online at: http://www.utexas.edu/cola/centers/lrc/books/readT.html.

Lottner, Carl (1862): "Ausnahmen der ersten Lautverschiebung." – In: *Zeitschrift für vergleichende Sprachforschung auf dem Gebiete des Deutschen, Griechischen und Lateinischen* 11.3, 161–205. English translation in Lehmann (1967).

Łubowicz, Anna. (2003): *Contrast Preservation in Phonological Mappings.* PhD dissertation, University of Massachusetts, Amherst. – Amherst, Mass.: GSLA. ROA-554.

– (2012): *The Phonology of Contrast.* – London: Equinox.

Luick, Karl (1940): *Historische Grammatik der englischen Sprache.* Bd. 1, Abt. 1–2. – Leipzig: Bernhard Tauchnitz.

McCarthy, John J. (1986): "OCP effects: gemination and antigemination". – In: *Linguistic Inquiry* 17, 207–263.

– (1988): "Feature geometry and dependency: a review." – In: *Phonetica* 45, 84–108.

Mańczak, Witold (1990): "La restriction de la règle de Verner à la position médiane et le sort du *s* final en germanique". – In: *Historische Sprachforschung* 103, 92–101.

Martinet, André (1955): *Economie des changements phonétiques. Traité de phonologie diachronique.* – Bern: Francke.

Montreuil, Jean-Pierre (2006): "Contrast preservation theory and historical change". – In: Gess, Randall S. & Deborah Arteaga (eds.), *Historical Romance Linguistics. Retrospective and Perspectives*, 111–129. Amsterdam/Philadelphia: Benjamins.

Newton, Brian (1972): *The Generative Interpretation of Dialect: a Study of Modern Greek Phonology*. – Cambridge: Cambridge University Press.

Noske, Roland (2009): "Verner's law, phonetic substance and form of historical phonological description". – In: *Proceedings JEL'2009 (dis)continu, 6th Nantes Linguistic Meeting*, 33–42.

Pedersen, Holger (1951): *Die gemeinindoeuropaischen und die vorindoeuropaischen Verschlußlaute*. – København: Munksgaard. Det kongelige Danske Videnskabernes Selskab 32(5).

Pullum, Geoffrey K. (1976): "The Duke of York gambit". – In: *Journal of Linguistics* 12, 83–102.

Rask, Rasmus (1818): *Undersögelse om det gamle Nordiske eller Islandske Sprogs Oprindelse: et af det Kongelike Danske Videnskabers Selskab kronet Prisskrift*. – Kjøbenhavn: Gyldendalske Boghandlings Forlag. Republished in 1999 by Routledge, London. English translation published in 1993 as: *Investigation of the Origin of the Old Norse or Icelandic language*. – Copenhagen: The Linguistic Circle of Copenhagen. German translation published in 1932, in: Rask, Rasmus, *Ausgewählte Abhandlungen*, vol. 1, ed. by Louis Hjelmslev. Kopenhagen: Levin & Munksgaard.

Salmons, Joseph C. (1993): *The Glottalic Theory. Survey and Synthesis*. – McLean, Virginia: Institute for the Study of Man.

Selkirk, Elisabeth O. (1982): "The syllable". – In: Van der Hulst, Harry & Norval Smith eds., *The Structure of Phonological Representations*, vol. II, 337–383. Dordrecht: Foris.

Vennemann, Theo (1984): "Hochgermanisch und Niedergermanisch". – In: *Beiträge zur Geschichte zur deutschen Sprache und Literatur* (Tübingen) 106, 1–45.

Vennemann, Theo (1985): "The bifurcation theory of the Germanic and German consonant shifts synopsis and some further thoughts". – In: Fisiak, Jacek (ed.): *Papers from the 6th International Conference on Historical Linguistics*, 527–547. Amsterdam: Benjamins,

– (2006): "Grimm's Law and loanwords". – In: *Transactions of the Philological Society* 104.2, 129–166.

– (ed.), (1989): *The New Sound of Indo-European: Essays in Phonological Reconstruction. Proceedings of a Workshop held during the Seventeenth International Conference on Historical Linguistics held on Sept 9–13 1985 at the University of Pavia*. – Berlin: Mouton de Gruyter.

Verner, Karl (1876): "Eine ausnahme der ersten lautverschiebung". – In: *Zeitschrift für vergleichende Sprachforschung auf dem Gebiete der indogermanischen Sprachen* 23, 97–130. English translations in Baldi & Werth (1978: 32–63) and Lehmann (1967).

Wells, Frederic L. (1903–1905): "Experimental phonetics and Verner's Law". – In: *Journal of English and Germanic Philology* 5, 522–527.

Wells, John C. (1990): "Syllabification and allophony." – In: Susan Ramsaran (ed.): *Studies in the Pronunciation of English, a Commemorative Volume in Honour of A.C. Gimson*. 76–86. London and New York: Routledge. Downloadable from: http://www.phon.ucl.ac.uk/home/wells.

Janet Grijzenhout

Segmental structure and vowel shifts*

1 Introduction

This paper explores the role of segmental representations in diachronic vowel change. It adopts a version of Dependency Phonology (e.g. Anderson & Ewen 1987, DP), which it applies to a number of unconditioned changes as have occurred in the history of Germanic. The interest in these changes is driven by a desire to understand why these vowels changed the way they did, and to explain why certain changes are more likely to occur than others. The focus of the paper is limited to internally motivated changes, i.e. changes within linguistic systems; we will not be concerned with external changes, i.e. those changes whose explanation involves reference to external factors, e.g. language contact.

In the languages of the world, consonant inventories seem to be more stable over time than vowel inventories. Diachronic changes affecting vowels include lengthening and shortening (i.e. changes in vowel quantity), and fronting, backing, rounding, unrounding, raising, lowering, tensing and laxing (i.e. changes in vowel quality). In addition, vowels that were realized as diphthongs at some point in time may at some later point come to be realized as monophthongs, or vice versa. Section 2 will present the view on the structural representation of vowel quantity and quality that will be assumed in this paper. Next, section 3 examines some of the changes that short vowels, long vowels, and diphthongs underwent in the transition from Proto-Indo-European to Proto-Germanic. Sections 4 and 5 concentrate on vowel shifts in Old Icelandic and Early Modern English, respectively. The final part of the paper offers a brief discussion of some other types of vowel shifts and attempts to account for these in terms of DP representations.

---

* This paper is inspired by Norval Smith, to whom I owe many thanks. He took a sincere interest in my work from the time I was a student onwards, and he always helped me with his patient guidance and advice. He was the first to ever refer to my work, and this demonstration of confidence was essential in my endeavour to follow in the phonological footsteps of my instructors in the 1980s: Colin Ewen, Harry van der Hulst, Jan Kooij, and Norval Smith. I am also grateful to the editors of this volume, and I thank Kristján Árnason and two anonymous reviewers for their helpful comments.

2 Theoretical preliminaries: vowel quantity and vowel quality

Before discussing specific cases of vowel changes, it is instructive to first consider what we mean by 'vowel quantity' and 'vowel quality'. With respect to quantity, I will follow Lass (1984) in distinguishing the 4 types of quantity systems given in (1).

(1) Types of vowel quantity systems (based on Lass 1984: 99)

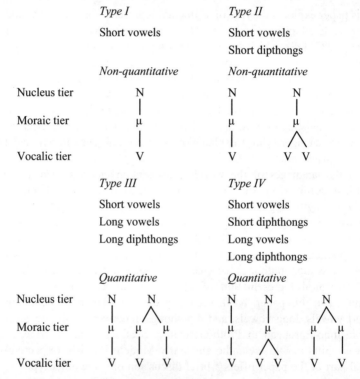

In non-quantitative systems, each syllabic peak (or nucleus, 'N') dominates one mora which in turn dominates one vocalic slot ('V') for a monophthong, and two V-slots for a diphthong. In quantitative systems, length is encoded by means of two moras. In Type III systems, short vowels are represented by one mora which is filled by one V-slot, whereas long vowels and diphthongs are represented by two moras (which dominate a sequence of two V-slots; these share their features/elements in long vowels, and differ in their featural/elemental content in diphthongs). In Type IV systems, short vowels and short diphthongs have the same representation as monophthongs and diphthongs in Type II systems, whereas long vowels and long diphthongs are represented by two moras in the nucleus.

I will make a further distinction between the representation of rising and falling diphthongs. The former involve diphthongs which start with a high vowel quality and end in a non-high vowel quality, so that the level of sonority rises within the segment, and diphthongs in which both parts are high but whose second element has greater intensity, as in English *few* [fjuː] and *new* [njuː]. The latter involve diphthongs which start with a mid or low vowel quality and end in a high vowel quality, so that the level of sonority drops within the segment, as well as diphthongs in which both parts have the same vowel height, but which are realized with more intensity on the first portion, as in Dutch *uw* [yw] 'your'). In type III and type IV systems, the final element is the head of the nucleus for rising diphthongs, whereas falling diphthongs are left-headed. This is shown in (2), where headedness is represented in terms of vertical dominance.

(2) The representation of quantity in rising and falling diphthongs

	Rising diphthong	Falling diphthong
Nucleus tier	N	N
Moraic tier	μ μ	μ μ
Vocalic tier	V V	V V

With respect to quality, we follow the main tenets of DP and assume that place properties are encoded by the components (or elements) |I|, |U| and |A| (see e.g. Anderson & Ewen 1987; Ewen 1995; Smith 2000). The presence of |I| in the representation of a vowel indicates the property 'front' or 'palatal'. The presence of |U| identifies a vowel as 'back' and/or 'round'. The presence of |A| reflects the fact that a vowel is 'low', and hence (relatively) 'sonorous'. We further assume that the component |@| represents 'centrality' or 'energy reduction' (e.g. Harris 1994). For vowel systems which display a broad range of quality distinctions, it is assumed that the representation of vowels involves head–dependency relations, symbolized here by '>' (where the element to the left of '>' dominates, or governs, the element on the right). This makes it possible to express vowel height as a scalar dependency relation in which |I| represents the highest front vowels, |I>A| vowels which are one degree less high, |I,A| vowels which occupy the 'mid' position in a system, |A>I| vowels that are lower, and |A| the lowest vowels in a system.[1]

---

[1] Using the components |U| and |@| instead of |I| in combination with the different dominance relations with |A| expresses the same height distinctions for back vowels

Consider (3), which illustrates the DP representation of a number of commonly attested vowels (and is roughly based on Durand's (2000) proposal for the vowel inventory of Danish).[2]

(3) A hypothetical vowel system and its representation in DP

/i/	|I|	/y/	|I>U|	/u/	|U|
/ɪ/	|I>@|	/ʏ/	|I>U,@|	/ʊ/	|U>@|
/e/	|I>A|	/ə/	|@>A|	/o/	|U>A|
/ø/	|I>A,U|			/ɤ/	|U>A,@|
/ɛ/	|I,A|	/ə/	|@,A|	/ɔ/	|U,A|
/œ/	|I,A>U|				
/æ/	|A>I|	/ɐ/	|A>@|	/ɒ/	|A>U|
/œ/	|A>I,U|	/ɑ/	|A|		

There is a long history of using the DP framework to represent historical vowel changes (e.g. Anderson 1980; Anderson & Jones 1977; Jones 1980). I will argue that the components |I, U, A, @| are also ideal for representing the historical data considered in this paper. In what follows, we will discuss examples of changes in vowel systems that were purely qualitative at first and in which the type of quantity changed at some later point; the changes under investigation are part of the development of the vowel system of late Proto-Indo-European (PIE) to that of early Proto-Germanic (PGmc), and the change from a North Germanic Type III quantity language (Old Icelandic) towards a Type II system.

3 The reconstructed vowel system of late PIE and early PGmc

Germanic languages are set apart from other Indo-European languages in that they underwent a series of consonant shifts, which allegedly started well

---

and central vowels, respectively. Where |I| and/or |@| dominate |U|, the front or central vowel is round. Where |I| does not dominate |U|, the front vowel is spread.

[2] Note that our interpretation of |@| differs slightly from that of Harris (1994). In the proposal put forward here, centrality can also be used with other components to indicate a scalar relationship in the front-central-back dimension: |I| without |@| represents the most front vowels, vowels specified as |I>@| are more front than central, vowels specified for |@| without |I| or |U| are central, |U>@| represents vowels that are more back than central, and |U| represents the most back vowels. As mentioned in footnote 1, all combinations of |I|, |@|, and/or |U| can be distinguished for height in terms of head–dependency relationships with the lowness component |A|.

before the 5th century BC and which were completed by the 2nd century BC. The consonantal changes in question are collectively referred to as the 'First Consonant Shift' or 'Grimm's Law'. The result of these changes is that Germanic languages have fricatives where Indo-European had aspirated plosives (cf. English *father*, Icelandic *faðir* vs. Latin *pater*), tense plosives where Indo-European had lax plosives (Dutch *tand* 'tooth' vs. Latin *dent-*), and voiced plosives where Indo-European had breathy voiced plosives (cf. English *brother*, Icelandic *bróðir* vs. Sanskrit *b^hratar*). In addition to these consonantal changes, Germanic languages also underwent a series of vocalic shifts. We discuss a number of these below.

A standard assumption about the late PIE vowel inventory is that it consisted of 4 short non-high vowels, 5 long monophthongs and possibly 8 short and 6 long falling diphthongs (e.g. Antonsen 1972; Lehmann 1993). With respect to quantity, PIE is considered a Type IV language. As we will see below, the most drastic changes in the transition from late PIE to early PGmc involved changes in vowel quality.

In PIE, the short high vowels [i] and [u] occurred as allophones of /y/ and /w/ only, and as the second element of diphthongs. The table in (4) presents the inventory of PIE monophthongs assumed by Antonsen (1972), Lehmann (1993), and many others:

(4)   Late PIE monophthongs (cf. Antonsen 1972: 136; Lehmann 1993: 95)

		Short			Long	
	Front	Central	Back	Front		Back
High				iː		uː
Mid	e	ə	o	eː		oː
Low			ɒ			ɒː

As can be seen in (4), the inventory of short and long vowels is asymmetric. The short vowels differ in the non-low vs. low dimension, and within the former there is a three-way contrast between front, central, and back. The long vowels display a three-way contrast in the high-mid-low dimension and a two-way place contrast between front spread vs. back round.

A question for which we will provide a speculative answer only is why this asymmetry in the height dimension should have existed. Typological work has established that the most common vowel in the languages of the world is the most sonorous one, i.e. a variant of the low vowel /a/. In the PIE vowel system, this vowel is indeed present, but the least sonorous vowels, viz. short high ones, are lacking. For a syllable to be well formed in the quantitative system of PIE, it either had to contain a short vowel with sufficient sonority (encoded in DP by the presence of |A|, as in (5)), a long vowel (which is intrinsically more sonorous than a short one), or a diphthong

whose first element was non-high. In other words, I speculate that the
asymmetry in the PIE inventory is due to minimal-sonority requirements of
syllable nuclei.

In establishing the phonological representation of vowels, we should first
consider which vowels are contrastive. I will tentatively assume that the
following vowel specifications express the contrasts between the vowels of
the late PIE system.[3] (As above, head–dependency relations are represented
in terms of vertical dominance; for example, in the representation of /e/, |I| is
the head, and thus dominates the dependent |A|.)

(5)   Late PIE vowels (e.g. Antonsen 1972: 136–140) and their DP representations

   a.   Short vowels

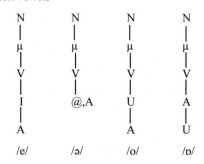

   b.   Long vowels

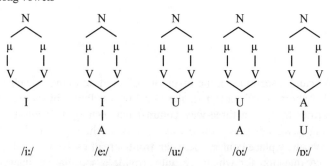

According to Antonsen, short high /i, u/ gradually developed from allophones
to phonemes in early PGmc while the distinction between PIE short /ə, o, ɒ/
was lost. These three vowels merged to a single central (or possibly back)

---

[3]   In (5), the four short vowels contain |A|, probably because short vowels require a
      sufficient degree of sonority to occupy the syllabic nucleus. This sonority
      requirement was possibly no longer active in early PGmc. The vowels of early
      PGmc are representationally less complex; see (7).

vowel, as is illustrated by the examples in (6a-c), where the relevant vowels are represented in boldface.

(6) Merger of non-front short vowels in PGmc (Antonsen 1972: 137)

	PIE		PGmc	
a.	pəteːr	>	fɑdæːr	'father'
b.	bʰondʰe	>	bɑnde	'he bound'
c.	pɒŋkonom	>	fɑnhɑnɑn	'to catch'

The following suggestion is tentative, but I will make it nonetheless, because the logic behind it might be insightful. Vowel shifts, which occur in typologically diverse languages, have mostly been analyzed as 'pull-chain' or 'push-chain' effects (Martinet 1952, 1955). I assume that the introduction of the short high vowels in PGmc 'pushed' the other short vowels to a lower position. This optimised the high vs. non-high contrast — in other words, it maximised the sonority distance between the high and non-high vowels). For the front vowel /e/, this might have involved just a single step down the height scale, to /ɛ/. For the central and back short vowels, the introduction of /ɪ/ and /ʊ/ resulted in lowering, which eventually led to a merger with the lowest vowel, i.e. /ɑ/.

In the DP model adopted here, lowering is formalised in terms of a greater prominence of the component |A|. That is, for the front vowel, the dominance relation |I>A| changes to |I,A|, while for the back vowel, the component |U| loses its prominence, so that |U>A| gradually changes to |U,A|, with |A| no longer in a governed position.[4] For schwa, the central element loses its prominence and becomes a dependent, i.e. |@,A| changes to |A>@|. The intermediate result of the gradual lowering of /o/ and /ə/ may have been segments like /ɔ/ and /ɐ/. Further lowering of short /ɔ/ would have resulted in short /ɒ/, which is perceptually similar to /ɐ/, while further lowering of /ɐ/ may have resulted in /ɑ/. The short low vowels /ɐ, ɑ, ɒ/ are perceptually similar and as far as I know, there are no languages which have a phonemic contrast between these vowels. In the absence of tangible evidence, we can only speculate about the precise nature of the vowel that resulted from the merger of PIE /ə, o, ɒ/, i.e. whether it was low central or back. For the purposes of this paper, nothing crucial hinges on this.[5]

---

[4] This analysis incorporates Stampe's (1972) observation that non-high vowels in particular tend to eliminate their palatal (or 'frontness') or labial (or 'round') constriction to increase their sonority. In the model adopted here, depalatalization involves a decrease in the prominence of |I|. Delabialization involves a decrease in the prominence of |U|.

[5] In PGmc, /i, u/ were lowered to [e, o] in the context of /ɑ/ or /ɔː/ in a following unstressed syllable. The assumption here is that this process can be accounted for in

(7) Early PGmc short vowels (Antonsen 1972: 136–140) and their representation
     in DP

high-front	/ɪ/	|I|
high-back	/ʊ/	|U|
mid-front	/ɛ/	|I,A|
low	/ɑ/	|U>A|

In the long vowel inventory, the high vowels remained stable (e.g. PIE
swiːnom > PGmc *swiːnan* 'swine'; PIE *muːs* > PGmc *muːs* 'mouse'), so that
these cannot be responsible for any 'pull chain' or 'push chain' effects. The
changes that took place in the non-high long vowels were as follows: long /eː,
oː/ lowered (perhaps in analogy with the lowering of short /e o/); /eː/ lowered
to /ɛː/ (e.g. Campbell 1983) or possibly to /æː/ (Antonsen 1972; see (8a)),
whereas /oː/ lowered to /ɔː/. At the same time, /ɒː/ was raised one degree in
height, to /ɔː/. Thus, lowering of /oː/ and raising of /ɒː/ led to a merger whose
result was a single vowel, viz. /ɔː/ (see (8b,c)).

(8) Lowering of /eː/ and merger of non-front non-high vowels in early PGmc
     (Antonsen 1972: 137)

	PIE		PGmc	
a.	bʰeːdʰmme	>	bæːdme	'we bade'
b.	ploːtus	>	floːduz	'flood'
c.	mɒːteːr	>	mɔːdæːr	'mother'

The changes that early PGmc had undergone in the long vowels (i.e. lowering
of /eː/ and merger of /oː/ and /ɒː/) resulted in a change from an original three-
way height distinction (i.e. high vs. mid vs. low; see (4)) to a two-way
distinction (high vs. non-high). The changes in the long vowels can be
represented as in (9):

(9) Transition from late PIE to early PGmc long monophthongs

/iː/	|I|	>	/iː/	|I|	(no change)
/uː/	|U|	>	/uː/	|U|	(no change)
/eː/	|I>A|	>	/ɛː/ (or /æː/)	|I,A|	(lowering)
/oː/	|U>A|	>	/ɔː/	|U,A|	(merger)
/ɒː/	|A>U|	>	/ɔː/	|U,A|	(merger)

Germanic languages have a tendency to simplify nuclei in unstressed
syllables. In this position, diphthongs are typically monophthongized, long
vowels shortened, and short vowels are lost. According to Antonsen (1972:

---

terms of spreading of |A| (which in the triggering vowels occupies the head
position), with spreaded |A| functioning as a dependent in the targeted vowels.

136–140), some PIE diphthongs were simplified in unstressed syllables first (e.g. /ai/ > /æː/, /au/ > /ɔː/).[6] Monophthongization is a change in which a diphthong (e.g. /au/, where |A| and |U| are dominated by separate V-slots) comes to be realized as a monophthong (e.g. as /ɔː/, where the two V-slots both dominate |A| and |U|).[7]

(10) PIE /au/ > PGmc /ɔː/ (in unstressed syllables)

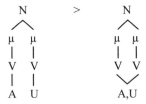

In stressed syllables, some diphthongs underwent merger. For example, the PIE falling diphthongs /ai/ and /oi/ survived as /ai/ in PGmc (PIE *gʰaids* > PGmc *gaitz* 'goat'; PIE *stoigʰa* > PGmc *staiga* 'I climbed'), and /au/ and /ou/ merged to /au/ (PIE *augonom* > PGmc *aukanan* 'to increase'; PIE *bʰougʰe* > PGmc *bauge* 'he bent'). The merger of falling diphthongs that start with a mid or low quality and end with a high offglide may be attributed to a general tendency to lower the first portion, so that e.g. /eɪ/ eventually becomes /aɪ/ while /oʊ/ develops into /aʊ/ (e.g. Labov 1994); the latter change is illustrated in (11).

---

[6] A similar monophthongization process took place in the history of Dutch (e.g. PGmc */au/ > /oː/ as in *oor* 'ear', *lopen* 'walk') and German (PGmc */au/ > German /oː/ as in *Ohr* 'ear', except before labials, hence *laufen* 'walk'). Anderson & Ewen (1987: 129) analyze the monophthongization of the Middle English falling diphthongs /aɪ, aʊ/ to late Middle English /ɛː ɔː/ as follows: the first part of the diphthong (containing the component |A|) is more prominent than the second part (containing |I| or |U|); the prominence relation is maintained after fusion, so that the resulting monophthongs are mid-low /ɛː, ɔː/, represented as |A>I| and |A>U|.

[7] The reverse process is also attested as a diachronic change. In diphthongization, two elements (or two features) which characterize a steady-state vowel (e.g. |I>U| for the monophthong /yː/) are 'broken up' in such a way that one element is associated with the first portion of the diphthong, and the other with the second portion (e.g. |I|, |U| for the diphthong [iu]). In section 6.2 we will see that such diphthongization always seems to produce diphthongs that have a single component (|I|, |U|, |A| or |@|) in either the first or the second portion (or in both).

(11) PIE /ou/ > PGmc /au/ (in stressed syllables)

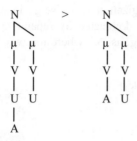

In this section, I have suggested that the change in the short vowel system of PGmc may have been triggered by the introduction of high short vowels. Once short /i/ and /u/ were established as full-fledged phonemes in the early PGmc vowel inventory, the front, central, and back mid short vowels lowered. This lowering is analyzed here as a change in the prominence of the |A| component. Lowering resulted in a system in which the short front high vowel /i/ contrasts in height with /ɛ/ and in which short back /u/ contrasts in height with /ɑ/.

The shift in the inventory of long vowels also involved lowering of mid vowels, resulting in a system in which the high vowels /iː/ and /uː/ contrast with the non-high vowels /ɛː/ (or /æː/) and /ɔː/. One change that affected diphthongs in unstressed syllables was monophthongization, while diphthongs in stressed syllables underwent mergers, with the resulting diphthongs having a greater height difference between the first and second element.

4 Vowel shifts in Old Icelandic

As there no oral records of the medieval period, we can only speculate about the precise quality and quantity of vowels in earlier stages of Icelandic. Fortunately, a manuscript survives in which an anonymous Icelandic author, who lived in the middle of the 12th century, provides important information about the consonantal and vocalic system of his language. The manuscript, called the *First Grammatical Treatise*, is available to us through a careful translation into modern English by Einar Haugen (Haugen 1950, 1972).[8] The anonymous author of the *First Grammatical Treatise* distinguishes 9 vowels.

---

[8] I am grateful to Allison Wetterlin for drawing my attention to this translation and presenting me with a copy.

Apart from the five vowel symbols <*a, e, i, o, u*> that are also used in Latin, he adds four more. The first additional vowel he mentions is *blandinn* ("mixed") between /a/ and /o/ "with the mouth less open than for *a*, but more than for *o*" (all quotations in this paragraph are from Haugen's (1972: 15) translation). This careful description allows us to identify the vowel in question as a low-mid back vowel which can be transcribed with the IPA symbol /ɔ/. The second vowel is a 'blending' as well, "spoken with the mouth less open than for *a*, but more than for *e*", i.e. /ɛ/.[9] The third sound "is made up from the sounds of *e* and *o*", i.e. /ø/, and the fourth sound "is a single sound made up from the sounds of *i* and *u*", i.e. /y/. The descriptions that the author provides reveal the intuition that some vowels are more 'basic', whereas others are 'blends' or 'combinations' of the properties of the basic vowels. It is striking that this intuition corresponds exactly to how these vowels are interpreted in DP.

Haugen (1972: 34–35) draws attention to the fact that the four additional vowels that the author of the 12th-century manuscript mentions had come into existence some 500 years earlier. /ɔ/ had been introduced into the phonemic system due to *u*-umlaut of /a/, while *i*-umlaut had caused fronting of /a, o, u/ to /ɛ/ (or possibly /æ/; cf. Antonsen 1972), /ø/ and /y/.

The author of the *First Grammatical Treatise* shows that each of these nine vowels "changes the meaning if they are precisely distinguished", e.g. when placed between the same two consonants. Each vowel may also induce a change in meaning "if it is spoken in the nose" (Haugen 1972: 16), i.e. if it is nasalized. A further aspect that induces a change in meaning is whether the vowel is long or short. We will see below that in contrast to Modern Icelandic, most Old Icelandic vowels were inherently short or long independent of syllable structure.

When combined with another vowel, the letters <i> and <e> may sometimes represent the consonant /j/ (as in *earn* 'iron') and <u> may represent /w/ in the same context (e.g. *uín* 'wine') in Old Icelandic. In the literature, it is suggested that other vowel combinations mentioned in the *First Grammatical Treatise* represent diphthongs: <au> in *austr* 'east' represents /au/, <ei> in *eir* 'copper' most probably represents /ei/, and <ey> in *eyrir* 'ounce' is the rounded diphthong /øy/ (e.g. Antonsen 1972: 119; Árnason 1980; Benediktsson 1959; Pétursson 2005). If we ignore nasality, the vocalic system of 12th-century Icelandic thus includes nine short vowels that each have a long counterpart, and three diphthongs; that is, it is a Type III language.

---

[9] Pétursson (2005: 1260) also assumes this vowel for Old Icelandic, whereas Antonsen (1972: 119) uses /æ/ instead.

(12)   Old Icelandic short and long vowels, and diphthongs

	Front		Back		Diphthongs	
	Spread	Round	Spread	Round	Spread	Round
High	i, iː	y, yː		u, uː		
High-mid	e, eː	ø, øː		o, oː	ei	øy
Low-mid	ɛ, ɛː			ɔ, ɔː		
Low			a, aː		au	

4.1 Shifts in Old Icelandic long vowels

Haugen (1972: 37) mentions that the first shift in the Old Icelandic vowel
system was that long /aː/ "was spontaneously rounded" and fell together with
/ɔː/; this occurred around the year 1200. We already encountered a similar
change in late PIE, with PIE /ɒː/ merging with /ɔː/ in early PGmc. I
tentatively assume that raising of /aː/ resulted in a back round rather than a
back spread vowel, given that rounding seems to be the unmarked state for
back vowels.[10] In Old Icelandic, the result of this early change was that a
four-way height distinction in the long vowels changed into a three-way
height distinction.

According to e.g. Pétursson (2005), long /yː/ was unrounded and merged
with /iː/, and long /øː/ merged with long /ɛː/.[11] A possible basis for this sound
change may be the fact that rounding contrasts in front vowels ([iː] vs. [yː],
[ɛː] vs. [øː]) are relatively difficult to perceive; such contrasts naturally
develop in the direction of a merger to the unmarked members of each pair,
i.e. /iː/ and /ɛː/.

Thus, the first major changes in the vowel system involved the dimension
of rounding: all contrasts in the long back vowels were resolved by having
rounded vowels only, while no rounding contrasts were maintained in the
front series.[12] In DP, the merger of front spread and round vowels implies

---

[10] An anonymous reviewer suggests that the low vowel may have been round already
(i.e. /ɒː/ rather than /aː/), in which case it already contained |U| as a dependent
component. Rounding can then be analyzed more straightforwardly as a promotion
of dependent |U| to head |U|.

[11] Long /eː/ (represented here as |I>A|) underwent diphthongization to /ie/ (represented
as a sequence of |I|, |I,A|). A subsequent shift in intensity resulted in the right-
headed diphthong /jɛ/.

[12] The changes in Norwegian, a language closely related to Icelandic, were slightly
different. After */aː/ > /ɔː/, the other back vowels underwent raising (e.g. PGmc
goːðr > Norwegian <god> /guː/ 'good'). As a result, the highest back vowel */uː/
was 'pushed up' as well, and since this vowel could not be raised any further, it

that |U| was removed from the representation of long front vowels. The relevant changes are given in (13). Note here that the mid vowel /øː/, represented as |I>A,U|, was unrounded and lowered to /ɛː/, suggesting that |A| no longer functioned as a dependent. As a result of the rounding of /aː/ to /ɔː/ and the loss of /yː/ and /øː/, rounding was eliminated as a distinctive property of long vowels.

(13)   Early changes in Old Icelandic long vowels

Front vowels

/iː/	|I|				
/yː/	|I>U|	>	/iː/	|I|	(unrounding)
/eː/	|I>A|				
/øː/	|I,A>U|	>	/ɛː/	|I,A|	(unrounding)
/ɛː/	|I,A|				

Back vowels

/uː/	|U|				
/oː/	|U>A|				
/ɔː/	|U,A|				
/aː/	|A|	>	/ɔː/	|U,A|	(rounding)

Next, the front vowel /ɛː/ was diphthongized to the fronting diphthong /ai/, the back vowel /ɔː/ developed into the backing diphthong /au/, while /oː/ was diphthongized to /ou/ (or /ɔu/). The question emerges why long non-high vowels diphthongized. In his article on the natural history of diphthongs, Stampe (1972) suggests that it is difficult to maintain steady air pressure for long vowels. If this is correct, it is not surprising that these vowels eventually came to be pronounced with an offglide. The Old Icelandic change from long non-high monophthongs to diphthongs is then the result of natural tendencies.[13] Diphthongization of non-high long vowels can be represented as follows:

---

fronted to /yː/ instead (e.g. PGmc *mus* > Norwegian <mus> /myːs/ 'mouse') (see e.g. Awedyk & Hamans 1989). In the DP model adopted here, raising is accounted for by gradually making |A| less prominent: */aː/ (|A|) > early Norwegian /ɔː/ (|A,U|); early /oː/ (|U>A|) > later /uː/ (|U|). Fronting involves the addition of |I|; thus, early /uː/ (|U|) > later /yː/ (|I>U|).

[13] An anonymous reviewer points out that hearers may also have difficulty distinguishing the high-mid [eː] vs. low-mid [ɛː] contrast; the contrast between [je] and [ai] is more salient perceptually.

(14)   Diphthongization of Old Icelandic non-high long vowels

Front vowels				Back vowels				
/iː/	|I|			/uː/	|U|			
/eː/	|I>A|	>	/je/	|I|, |I>A|	/oː/	|U>A|	>	/ou/ |U>A|, |U|
/ɛː/	|I,A|	>	/ai/	|A|, |I|	/ɔː/	|U,A|	>	/au/ |A|, |U|

Of the original Old Icelandic long vowels, only /iː, uː/ remained stable (cf. PGmc **huːs* > Icelandic *hús* [huːs] 'house'); all others had come to be realized as diphthongs by the 16th century.[14]

4.2 Shifts in Old Icelandic short vowels

According to Pétursson (2005: 1261), an early shift (which may have occurred in the 14th century) that took place in Icelandic short vowels was the lowering of short /i/ to /ɪ/. Thus, in contrast to the high long vowels, which remained stable over time, a change in the short high vowel occurred relatively early in the history of the vowel system. The short vowel system changes in accordance with Labov's 'principle 2', which states that short vowels "fall along a nonperipheral track" (cf. Labov 1994: 176). In a DP model, this change involves the centrality element @: the lowering of /i/ to /ɪ/ involves the emergence of \|@\| as a dependent (\|I>@\|). Subsequently (or possibly simultaneously), short /y/ unrounded and merged with the new /ɪ/. (Unrounding of front vowels was also observed for the long vowels; see section 4.1.) Next, short /e/ was lowered to lax /ɛ/, and short back /u/ was fronted and lowered to /ʏ/. Gradually, short /ø/ and /o/ were lowered to lax /œ/ and /ɔ/ (perhaps in that order), while short /a/ remained unchanged.

The high short vowels were lowered first, followed by the mid-high short vowels. The changes discussed thus far (lowering of short /i/, unrounding of front rounded vowels, fronting and lowering of short /u/ and lowering of mid short vowels) can be represented schematically as in (15):

---

[14] The vowels that were long in Old Icelandic had an accent in the spelling, which today indicates tenseness in high vowels, e.g. *tíma* [tʰiːma] 'time', *nýr* [niːr] 'new', *hús* [huːs] 'house'), and diphthongization otherwise (*ég* [jeːx] 'I', *blóð* [plouːð] 'blood', *ár* [auːr] 'year', *bátur* [pauːtʏr] 'boat'). Other diphthongs are spelled as <ei>/<ey> (*heita* [heiːta] 'to call', *hey* [heiː] 'hay'), <æ> (*ær* /aiːr/ 'ewe') and <au> (*auga* [œʏːɣa] 'eye'.

(15)   Changes in Icelandic short vowels (cf. Pétursson 2005: 1260–1261)

	Front		Lowered and centralized		Back
High	/i, y/	>	/ɪ, ʏ/	<	/u/
Mid	/e/	>	/ɛ/		
	/ø/	>	/œ, ɔ/	<	/o/

Summarizing, the account proposed for the respective changes involves the following changes in the representation f vowels:

(16)   Changes in Old Icelandic short vowels

Front vowels

/i/ |I|	>			>	/ɪ/ |I>@|	laxing
/y/ |I>U|	>	/i/ |I|	>	/ɪ/ |I>@|	unrounding, laxing
/e/ |I>A|			>		/ɛ/ |I,A>@|	lowering, laxing
/ø/ |I,A>U|			>		/œ/ |I,A>U,@|	laxing

Back vowels

/u/ |U|	>	y |I>U|	>	/ʏ/ |I>U,@|	fronting, laxing
/o/ |U>A|			>	/ɔ/ |U,A>@|	lowering, laxing

As a result of these changes, a system emerged with five diphthongs, two long vowels (/iː, uː/) and six short vowels (/ɪ, ʏ, ɛ, œ, ɔ, a/), given in (17).

(17) Modern Icelandic vowels (cf. Haugen 1958; Árnason 1980: 8; 2005: 30, 124)

	Front		Back		Falling diphthongs	
	Spread	Round	Spread	Round	Spread	Round
High	i			u		
High-mid	ɪ	ʏ				ou
Low-mid	ɛ	œ		ɔ	ɛi	œy
Low			a		ai, au	

Vowel length had lost its distinctive function by the 16th century. Hence, due to the changes in quality, the type of quantity system changed: Icelandic developed from a Type III system into a Type II system in which both monophthongs and diphthongs are short when followed by a long consonant or cluster, and long in stressed open syllables and in stressed syllables closed by a single consonant. Thus, vowel length in Modern Icelandic is determined by syllable structure and stress.

Of the original Old Icelandic long vowels, only /iː/ and /uː/ remained stable (cf. Old Icelandic *skína* [sciːna] 'to shine'; *hús* [huːs] 'house'). All other long vowels had become diphthongized by the 16th century. In section 5, the Icelandic changes will be compared with what is possibly the best-known change in a vowel system, viz. the English Great Vowel Shift.

5 The Great Vowel Shift

The Great Vowel Shift affected long vowels, and probably started with the diphthongization of high long vowels (e.g. PGmc *hu:s* > English *house*). It is not my intention to give an exhaustive overview of the history of English vowels; rather, I restrict my attention to a couple of changes which illustrate the role of segmental structure in inducing sound change.

According to e.g. Luick (1940: 549–591), the "primary impulse" for the Great Vowel Shift involved raising of mid /eː, oː/ to /iː, uː/. As a consequence, the original /iː, uː/ were 'pushed' from their position and were diphthongized to /aɪ, aʊ/. In reaction to Luick's thesis, Jespersen (1965) postulated instead that the primary change behind the Great Vowel Shift was the diphthongization of /iː/ and /uː/. Jespersen further assumed that after diphthongization of /iː, uː/, /eː, oː/ shifted to /iː, uː/, which in turn 'pulled' /ɛː, ɔː/ to the next higher position in the vowel system. A slightly different account is offered by Stampe (1972), to which we turn now.

Stampe (1972: 579) starts out by observing that in Middle English, the labiovelar glide /w/ (or /ʊ/) was inserted before the velar fricative /x/, as in *taght > taught* /taʊxt/. Gradually, this /x/ changed to /f/ or was lost. The glide was 'absorbed' by the homorganic /f/, but remained in those cases where /x/ was lost. Stampe suggests that the relevance of glide absorption in respect of the Great Vowel Shift has been underestimated, a point to which we return shortly. He further suggests that it is difficult to maintain steady air pressure for long vowels, so that these develop an offglide. Thus, apart from glide insertion before /x/, glides also emerge in the realization of /iː, uː/ as [iɪ, uʊ]. In our analysis, this change can be represented as a shift in intensity:

(18) Diphthongization of Middle English /iː/ to /iɪ/

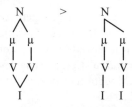

Next, /ɪ/ was absorbed by a following homorganic consonant (e.g. Old English /diːtʃ/ > Middle English /ditʃ/ 'ditch' vs. /diɪk/ > /diɪk/ 'dike'), while /ʊ/ was absorbed by labial and velar consonants (e.g. /pluʊme/ > /plum/

'plum', /duʊk/ > /duk/ 'duck' vs. /huʊs/ > /huʊs/ 'house').[15] In those cases where the glide was not absorbed, the diphthong remained in Middle English.

Stampe (1972: 580) suggests that after the high tense vowels had been diphthongized in this way, long front and back vowels were raised by one degree of height, i.e. /eː/ > /iː/ (e.g. /siː/ 'see'), /æː/ > /eː/ (e.g. /kleːn/ 'clean'), /oː/ > /uː/ (e.g. /duː/ 'do'), and /ɔː/ > /oː/ (e.g. /goːt/ 'goat'). In DP, these changes reflect a gradually less prominent role of |A|. This raising was probably completed by the 16th century. Next, low /aː/ was fronted to /æː/, and other long front vowels were subsequently raised by one degree (e.g. /sæːkə/ > /seːk/ 'sake', /kleːn/ > /kliːn/ 'clean'). This process applied to most words from the 17th century onwards, but left some high frequency words unaffected.

In the meantime, the homorganic diphthongs /iɪ/ and /uʊ/ changed as follows. The offglide retained its colour (i.e. its palatal and labial property, respectively), whereas the head (or 'syllabic element' in the terminology of Stampe 1972: 581), which carries the syllable pulse and its accentual features, increases its level of sonority by gradually lowering the vocalic element in question (i.e. |I| > |I>A| > |A|, |U| > |U>A| > |A|). In other words, Middle English /iɪ/ comes to be realized as /eɪ/ first and subsequently as /aɪ/, while /uʊ/ changes via /oʊ/ to present-day /aʊ/. According to Stampe (1972: 583), the resulting diphthongs are optimal cases of polarization of 'sonority' and 'colour'; Stampe notes that this is the reason why /aɪ, aʊ/ are the most commonly attested diphthongs in languages of the world.

Finally, Stampe (1972: 581) shows that long mid vowels have also been diphthongized to different degrees in different varieties of English since the 18th century (e.g. /seːk/ > /seɪk/ 'sake', /goːt/ > /goʊt/ 'goat') .

6 Vowel shifts

This section considers shifts and segmental representations of short vowels (section 6.1) and long vowels (section 6.2).

---

[15] The remaining short vowel was laxed and lowered in the development from Middle English to Early Modern English, e.g. /ditʃ/ > /dɪtʃ/, /plum/ > /plʌm/, /duk/ > /dʌk/.

6.1 Shifts in short vowels

The impulse for an unconditioned change in any system with short vowels may have different origins. I will discuss four possibilities here: (i) lowering of high-mid vowels after the introduction of high short vowels within a system, (ii) raising and rounding or fronting of the lowest back vowel in the system (which in turn may cause raising of mid back or front vowels), (iii) lowering and centralization of high short vowels (which in turn may cause lowering and centralization of other short vowels, so that the distinction between originally short and long vowels is turned into a lax/tense distinction), and (iv) loss of contrastive length; this may lead to a situation in which originally short vowels come to be realized with a homorganic offglide in stressed syllables, setting in motion a diphthongization process.

In section 3, I suggested that the gradual lowering of late PIE /e/ to early PGmc /ɛ/ may have been triggered by the introduction of short high vowels in the system. The introduction of high short vowels caused the lowering of the existing mid vowels, so as to optimize the height differences between the short vowels. For short non-front /ə, o, ɒ/, lowering resulted in the merger of these vowels to the lowest short vowel.

Antonsen (1972: 140) suggests that context-sensitive changes gave rise to the late PGmc system with short /i, e, ɑ, u/, long /iː, eː, æː, ɔː, uː/, and four falling diphthongs /iu, eu, ai, au/. In some Germanic systems, /ɑ/ undergoes a context-free change. In the ancestor of Frisian and English, for instance, /ɑ/ is fronted to /æ/ in all contexts, except before nasal consonants (by a process known as *Aufhellung*, 'brightening', 'fronting', or 'spontaneous palatalization').[16] In other systems, the lowest vowel changes in such a way that it acquires roundness (e.g. /ɑ/ > /ɔ/), as was the case when Old Icelandic /ɑː/ came to be realized as a round back vowel (see section 4.1).

In section 4, we saw that short non-low vowels lowered and centralized in Old Icelandic. We analyzed this development as involving the association of dependent |@| to the representation of the affected vowels. In this way, a system emerged in which originally long vowels were not specified by a centrality element, whereas originally short vowels were represented as lax ones. This change made the length contrast redundant, and eventually Icelandic lost contrastive length in its vowel system.

---

[16] In Old English, /ɑ/ is lengthened and merges with /ɔː/ before a nasal-fricative cluster, cf. early PGmc **/θɑnxtɔː/ > late PGmc **/θɑːnxtɔː/ > Old English /θɔːxtɑ/ 'thought'. In Old Frisian, short vowels were nasalized in this context. Afterwards, the nasal consonant disappeared with compensatory lengthening of the vowel, cf. PGmc **/unsɑ/ > Old Frisian /uːs/ 'our' (e.g. Bremmer 2009: 26).

Finally, another incentive for a change in short vowels may be the loss of a length contrast. Consider in this respect late Vulgar Latin, where vowel length was contrastive. When this contrast was subsequently lost, another system of oppositions emerged: the historically long vowels were raised slightly, while the historically short vowels were subject to other changes. For example, Penny (2002) suggests that short /ɛ, ɔ/ were lengthened in stressed syllables and developed into the semi-diphthongs /eɛ, oɔ/. Raising of the first part of these diphthongs (presumably to 'polarize' the two portions) led to the emergence of Romance /iɛ/ ([je]) and /uɔ/ ([wo]). In Italian, the diphthongization of short mid vowels seems to be restricted to stressed open syllables while in Spanish, it is less restricted. In Early Rumanian (e.g. Andersen (1972: 41) and references cited there), /ɛ, ɔ/ diphthongized to /ea, oa/. In DP, this can be analyzed as follows: in their underlying representations, the segments involve a combination of |A| and |I| (for /ɛ/) or |U| (for /ɔ/). Under stress, the vowel is lengthened and 'split' into a portion in which |I| or |U| becomes more prominent (by occupying the head position, with a dependent |A|) and a portion which contains |A| only; in other words, the initial portion of the diphthong is represented by |I>A| or |U>A|, and the final portion by |A| alone.

To conclude the discussion on shifts in short vowels, we have seen that one system-internal change involves lowering and/or centralization of non-low vowels. In the DP model adopted here, lowering involves a step-wise increase in the dominance of |A|, while centralization involves the association of a dependent |@|. The lowest vowel in a system may be raised, which involves the introduction of the back element |U| (/a/ > /ɔ/). Non-round low back vowels may also be fronted (i.e. they gain |I|), e.g. /a/ > /æ/.

In stressed syllables, historically short vowels may lengthen and eventually develop a homorganic offglide. This process is analyzed here as a shift in intensity, giving rise to a falling or rising diphthong; cf. (2) above. This may in turn set in motion a diphthongization process in which the head (or 'syllabic element') becomes more sonorous (i.e. it undergoes lowering) and/or in which the non-head (or 'non-syllabic element') gains more 'colour' (i.e. it gradually moves towards a maximally palatal position (i.e. /ɪ/) or a maximally labial position (i.e. /ʊ/).

6.2 Shifts in long vowels and diphthongs

Whereas context-free lowering of the highest short vowels to their lax counterparts is widely attested, context-free lowering of the highest long vowels (i.e. /iː, uː/) is hardly ever found. In contrast, the process of raising the lowest long vowel in a system seems to be fairly common. Consider in this respect that the raising of late PIE /ɒː/ was accompanied by rounding, so that the vowel merged with /ɔː/ in early PGmc. Also, in the early history of Old Icelandic, long /aː/ was spontaneously rounded and fell together with /ɔː/. I assume that raising of /aː/ resulted in a back round rather than a back spread vowel, given that rounding seems to be the unmarked state for back vowels. Hence, spread back vowels tend to round spontaneously, whereas spread front vowels do not, i.e. context-free changes /iː/ > /yː/ and /eː/ > /øː/ are unlikely. Another spontaneous shift that short and long low vowels may undergo is fronting: a spread back vowel tends to become a spread front vowel. For low vowels, then, we see that rounding, fronting and/or raising is common. I have not come across any language in which /aː/ was diphthongized. If it is true that the incentive for diphthongization is the difficulty of maintaining steady air pressure throughout the length of the vowel, then this is apparently not the case for the lowest vowel; therefore, there does not seem to be an incentive for spontaneous diphthongization of /aː/. Conversely, the diphthongs /ai/ and /au/ often monophthongize to /aː/.

The high-mid vowels /eː, oː/ may be raised to fill in the position of high vowels once the latter have undergone a change, or they may push away the high vowels when they are themselves 'pushed' by the raising of low-mid vowels. Consider in this respect the fact that raising of non-high tense vowels occurred in English, Dutch, and German (cf. the cognates *book, boek, Buch*, with PGmc */oː/ > /uː/), albeit at different periods. Low-mid /ɛː, ɔː/ may be raised when 'pulled' or 'pushed' (e.g. after the introduction of a front or back low vowel). There appear to be no cases where high-mid and low-mid vowels undergo spontaneous rounding or unrounding, or spontaneous fronting or retraction. Hence, whereas low vowels may undergo a change in colour (i.e. they frequently undergo rounding or fronting), mid vowels tend to retain their colour, but may shift in height or become diphthongs. The most common diphthongization processes involve on- and offgliding. In Old Frisian, for example, /eː/ came to be realized as /ie/ (cf. also the change /eː/ > /ie/-/je/ in Old Icelandic), and /oː/ turned into /ue/. In Early Modern English, /eː/ became /ei/, and /oː/ gradually developed into /ou/.

The kinds of diphthongizations of a monophthong that are described in the literature seem to permit the generalization that diphthongization always results in a structure in which either the initial or the second portion (or both) is characterized by a single element. Thus, |I| appears as the initial element in diphthongs like /je, iu, io/ and as the final element in diphthongs like /ei, ui, œi/, |U| is initial in /uo/ and final in /ou/, and |A| is initial in /ai, au/ and final in /ea, oa, ua/. Diphthongization of lax vowels often involves lengthening, to such a degree that it encroaches on the duration of its tense counterpart, and subsequently comes to be realized as a diphthong with a centralizing component (Andersen 1972: 31), i.e. |@| is initial in /əu/ and final in /iə/.

Diphthongization therefore does not seem to result in such diphthongs as /oy, øɔ, eœ/, at least not directly.

Once a diphthong has emerged, its two portions may develop further: the non-syllabic part becomes more palatal or labial, while the head (or 'syllabic') portion becomes more sonorous (as is reflected, for example, by the PGmc merger of the PIE falling diphthongs /ai, oi/ to /ai/, and /au, ou/ to /au/). The change of falling diphthongs whose first portion is a mid vowel may be attributed to a general tendency of 'polarization' of height, so that e.g. /eɪ/ eventually becomes /aɪ/, whereas /oʊ/ develops into /aʊ/ (e.g. Stampe 1972; Labov 1994). Another change that may affect diphthongs is monophthongization: /ai/ and /au/ may turn into /aː/ (loss of colour component), /ai/ often changes to front /æː/, and /au/ may change to back /ɔː/. In the latter two changes, the components that specify the two portions of the diphthong are merged in the representation of the resulting monophthong.

7 Conclusion

This paper has discussed a number of unconditioned diachronic changes affecting short and long vowels in a number of Germanic languages. An attempt was made to account for these changes in terms of DP representations: lowering and raising of non-high vowels was interpreted as the gradual promotion/demotion of |A|, fronting of short and long /a/ and long /uː/ as the introduction of |I|, rounding of /a/ as the insertion of |U|, unrounding of /yː, øː/ as the deletion of |U|, and centralization of non-low short vowels as the addition of dependent |@|). In addition, we considered a number of cases which involve lengthening of short vowels followed by a quantity shift, diphthongization of non-low monophthongs, and monophthongization of diphthongs.

References

Andersen, Henning (1972): "Diphthongization." – In: *Language* 48, 11–50.
Anderson, John M. (1980): "On the internal structure of phonological segments: evidence from English and its history." – In: *Folia Linguistica Historica I*, 185–212.

Anderson, John M. & Colin J. Ewen (1987): *Principles of Dependency Phonology.* – Cambridge University Press: Cambridge.

Anderson, John M. & Charles Jones (1977): *Phonological Structure and the History of English.* – Amsterdam: Elsevier North Holland.

Antonsen, Elmer H. (1972): "The Proto-Germanic Syllabics (Vowels)." – In: Coetsem, Frans van & Herbert L. Kufner (eds.): *Towards a Grammar of Proto-Germanic*, 117–140. Tübingen: Niemeyer.

Árnason, Kristján (1980): *Quantity in Historical Phonology: Icelandic and Related Cases.* – Cambridge University Press: Cambridge.

Árnason, Kristján (2005): *Hljóð.* – Reykjavík: Almenna Bókafélagið.

Awedyk, Wieslaw & Camiel Hamans (1989): "Vowel Shifts in English and Dutch: formal or genetic relation?" – In: *Folia Linguistica Historica VII*, 99–114.

Benediktsson, Hrein (1959): "The vowel system of Icelandic: a survey of its history." – In: *Word* 15, 282–312.

Bremmer, Rolf H. Jr. (2009): *An Introduction to Old Frisian: History, Grammar, Reader, Glossary.* – Amsterdam/Philadelphia: John Benjamins.

Campbell, A. (1983): *Old English Grammar.* – Oxford: Clarendon Press.

Donegan, Patricia J. (1985): *On the Natural Phonology of Vowels.* – New York: Garland.

Durand, Jacques (2002): "The vowel system of Danish and phonological theory." – Ms., Université de Toulouse II & CNRS/ERSS.

Ewen, Colin J. (1995): "Dependency relations in phonology." – In: Goldsmith, John (ed.): *Handbook of Phonological Theory*, 570–585. Oxford: Blackwell.

Harris, John (1994): *English Sound Structure.* – Oxford: Blackwell.

Haugen, Einar (1958): "The phonemics of Modern Icelandic." – In: *Language* 34, 55–88.

– (1972): *First Grammatical Treatise: The Earliest Germanic Phonology. An Edition, Translation and Commentary* (2nd edn.). – London: Longman.

Hulst, Harry van der & Norval S.H. Smith (eds.) (1988): *Features, Segmental Structure and Harmony Processes.* Vol. 1. – Dordrecht: Foris.

Jespersen, Otto (1965): *A Modern English Grammar on Historical Principles.* Vol. 1: Sounds and Spellings, 231–247. London: Allen & Unwin.

Jones, Charles (1980): "Rounding and fronting in Old English phonology: a dependency approach." – In: *Folia Linguistica Historia I*, 125–138.

Labov, William (1994): *Principles of Linguistic Change.* Vol. 1: Internal Factors. – Oxford/Cambridge, MA: Blackwell.

Lass, Roger (1984): "Vowel system universals and typology: prologue to theory." – In: *Phonology Yearbook* 1, 75–111.

Lehmann, Winfred P. (1993): *The Theoretical Bases of Indo-European Linguistics.* – London/New York: Routledge.

Luick, Karl (1940): *Historische Grammatik der englischen Sprache.* Bd. 1, Abt. 1–2. – Leipzig: Bernhard Tauchnitz.

Martinet, André (1952): "Function, structure, and sound change." – In: *Word* 8, 1–32.

– (1955) : *Economie des Changements Phonétiques.* – Bern : Francke Verlag.

Penny, Ralph (2002): *A History of the Spanish Language* (2nd edn.). – Cambridge: Cambridge University Press.

Pétursson, Magnus (2005): "The development of Icelandic from the mid-16th century to 1800." – In: Bandle, Oskar, Kurt Braunmüller, Ernst Hakon Jahr, Allan Karker, Hans-Peter Naumann & Ulf Teleman (eds.): *The Nordic Languages: An International Handbook of the History of the North Germanic Languages.* Vol. 2, 1258–1269. Berlin/New York: De Gruyter.

Smith, Norval S.H. (2000): "Dependency phonology meets OT: a proposal for a new approach to segmental structure." – In: Dekkers, Joost, Frank van der Leeuw & Jeroen M. van de Weijer (eds.): *Optimality Theory: Phonology, Syntax, and Acquisition,* 234–276. Oxford: Oxford University Press.

Stampe, David (1972): "On the natural history of diphthongs." – In: *Papers from the Eighth Regional Meeting of the Chicago Linguistic Society,* 578–590.

Krisztina Polgárdi

The distribution of vowels in English and trochaic proper government*

1 Introduction

The distribution of stressed vowels in English shows that short lax and tense vowels are in complementary distribution: the former cannot occur in open syllables, the latter in closed syllables. Long lax vowels belong to an in-between category: they do not occur in closed syllables and before vowels. The absence of pre-vocalic lax vowels (whether short or long, stressed or unstressed) is confirmed by the distribution and realisation of reduced vowels. A number of proposals have been made to account for parts of this pattern. For example, with regard to the restriction on short vowels, Hammond (1997) proposes that stressed syllables in English are required to be heavy, and that the apparently open stressed syllable in words like *city* is closed by the first part of a virtual geminate.

The aim of this paper is to provide an analysis of the complete pattern. I propose an analysis in a loose CV framework, where representations are made up of strictly alternating C and V positions, but where words can start with a V position and end in a C position (cf. Lowenstamm 1996; Polgárdi 1998, 2002). The analysis also uses trochaic (i.e. left-to-right) proper government, following Rowicka (1999a,b). The requirement on stressed positions in English is then that such positions must properly govern an empty nucleus to their right. Long vowels and diphthongs satisfy this requirement by themselves; these vowels cannot be followed by a consonant cluster, because the empty nucleus inside the cluster would have no proper governor. Short lax vowels, in contrast, must be followed by a cluster, either of the coda-onset type (including virtual geminates) or of the 'bogus' type. Diphthongs and closed syllables have the same structure word-internally, but the latter end in a C position word-finally. This accounts for their different behaviour in stress assignment. As we will see, this analysis is supported by

* Previous versions of this paper were presented at OCP7 in Nice, 2010, and at the Research Institute for Linguistics of the Hungarian Academy of Sciences, 2010. I would like to thank the participants of these meetings, and the two anonymous reviewers for their helpful comments. I also gratefully acknowledge the travel support of the University of Szeged.

accents such as Welsh English, where the virtual geminates of standard English are in fact audible.

The paper is organized as follows. Section 2 presents the English data and outlines Hammond's partial analysis. Section 3 discusses the phenomenon of tonic lengthening in Italian (which is similar to the English pattern, except that in Italian vowels lengthen in stressed open syllables). I will examine Larsen's (1998) strict CV account of tonic lengthening, which assumes iambic proper government and analyzes stress in terms of an extra empty CV unit. Section 4 provides a loose CV analysis of stressed vowels in English. Section 5 examines unstressed vowels, which are analyzed as being either completely empty, or as containing a single element, **I** or **U**. Since schwa can also occur in positions where it could be properly governed (and therefore remain silent), a solution in terms of lexical marking is proposed. Section 6 discusses Ségéral & Scheer's (2008) analysis of English aspiration in terms of gemination (i.e., as involving an empty CV unit *preceding* the stressed vowel), and shows why such an account is inadequate. Finally, section 7 summarises the main points of the paper.

2 Data

The system of English (Received Pronuncation, RP) full vowels is given in (1), with the vowels in the second row occurring before (an underlying) /r/. (The data in this paper are based on Burzio 2007; Chomsky & Halle 1968; Gimson 1980; Harris 1994; Jones 1966; Kreidler 1989; Nádasdy 2006; Wells 1982, 1990.)

(1) RP English vowel system

	short									long							
Pre-R	ɪ	ɛ	æ	ɒ	ʌ	ʊ	ɔːₗ	ɑːₗ	(ɜːₗ)	iː	uː	eɪ	əʊ	aɪ	aʊ	ɔɪ	
							ɔː₂	ɑː₂	ɜː₂	ɪə	ʊə	ɛə	ɔː₃	aɪə	aʊə	ɔɪə	
				lax									tense				

a. *short lax*	b. *long lax*		c. *long lax pre-R*	d. *tense*		e. *tense pre-R*	
/ɪ/ pit	/ɔːₗ/	paw	/ɔː₂/ port	/iː/	bee	/ɪə/	beer
/ɛ/ pet	/ɑːₗ/	spa	/ɑː₂/ part	/uː/	boo	/ʊə/	boor
/æ/ pat	(/ɜːₗ/	colonel)	/ɜː₂/ pert	/eɪ/	bay	/ɛə/	bear
/ɒ/ pot				/əʊ/	bow	/ɔː₃/	bore
/ʌ/ putt				/aɪ/	buy	/aɪə/	tire
/ʊ/ put				/aʊ/	bough	/aʊə/	tower
				/ɔɪ/	boy	/ɔɪə/	Moir

(1) shows three relevant dimensions: length, tenseness (vs. laxness), and whether a vowel must be followed by (an underlying) /r/. The tense-lax classification is based on the phonological behaviour of the vowels, for example in vowel shift phenomena and in how they are influenced by a following /r/. Short vowels are always lax (1a), and they do not need to be followed by /r/.[1] Tense vowels are always long (1d,e), and are realised as monophthongs or diphthongs. In pre-R position, they are obligatorily 'broken' into a centring diphthong or triphthong (or the monophthong /ɔːɟ/) (1e), with the /r/ itself being realised only when followed by a vowel. Long lax vowels either result from pre -R 'broadening' (1c) (typically accompanied by loss of the triggering /r/)[2], or they are underlying (1b). The example of *colonel* appears in parentheses, because it is the sole example containing underlying /ɜːₗ/. Subscript numbers are added to distinguish vowels which sound the same in RP but behave differently.[3]

The table in (2) shows the distribution of stressed vowels in different syllabic positions ('$' denotes a syllable boundary, '#' a word boundary). In (2), I restrict my attention to monomorphemic forms; pre-R vowels have not been included, as these are by definition followed by (an underlying) /r/.

(2)   Distribution of stressed vowels in syllable structure

		(i) short lax	(ii) long lax	(iii) tense
internal	(a) _ $CV	ˈsɪti 'city'	ˈɔːtəm 'autumn'	ˈmiːtə 'metre'
	(b) _ $CCV	ˈmækrəʊ 'macro'	ˈɔːdri 'Audrey'	ˈmaɪkrəʊ 'micro'
	(c) _ C$CV	ˈvɛktə 'vector'	*	*
	(d) _ $V	*	*	ˈruːɪn 'ruin'
final	(e) _ #	*	brɑː 'bra'	braʊ 'brow'
	(f) _ C#	hʊk 'hook'	hɔːk 'hawk'	hɔɪk 'hoick'
	(g) _ CC#	gʌlp 'gulp'	*	*

---

[1] However, they can be followed by /r/ if this /r/ is not separated from the following vowel by a word(-level) boundary, as in *carrot* /æ/ or *occurr+ence* /ʌ/.

[2] /r/ is retained in the context of a following vowel across a word(-level) boundary, as in *occurr#ing* or *occur#* in /ɜːₖ/, when we find both broadening and the presence of /r/.

[3] In fact, the three /ɔː/s are kept distinct by some speakers of General American (GA), as [pɒː], [pɔrt], and [bor], respectively. Similarly, some of the /ɑːₗ/s are pronounced as /æ/ in GA, as in b<u>a</u>th.

A comparison of columns (i) and (iii) shows that the distribution of short lax and tense vowels is almost complementary. Short lax vowels do not occur before a vowel (2i.d) and word-finally (2i.e); that is, they cannot occur at the end of a syllable, except in (2i.a-b). Tense vowels, in contrast, cannot occur in a closed syllable (2iii.c, 2iii.g), except in (2iii.f). Long lax vowels form an in-between category: like tense vowels they are ruled out in closed syllables (2ii.c, 2ii.g); like short lax vowels they are ruled out pre-vocalically (2ii.d). These generalisations are summarised in (3).

(3) Generalisations

   a. Short lax vowels must be followed by a tautosyllabic consonant (but (2i.a-b))
   b. Tense vowels cannot be followed by a tautosyllabic consonant (but (2iii.f))
   c. Long lax vowels are ruled out in closed syllables and pre-vocalically

Note that the restrictions in (2c) and (2g) do not apply to coronal clusters and to *s*-clusters, e.g. ['ʃəʊldə] 'shoulder', ['iːstə] 'easter', [peɪnt] 'paint', [ɑːsk] 'ask'. (Words with a long vowel followed by a cluster of /s/ and a non-coronal consonant are found only in accents like RP that lengthened the historically short vowel in this environment.) I will not deal with these cases further here.

The pattern in (2i) can be accounted for by requiring stressed syllables to be heavy in English (i.e. 'Stress-to-Weight'), as is proposed by Hammond (1997). In Hammond's analysis, non-reduced syllables must be minimally bimoraic. Long vowels and diphthongs satisfy this requirement underlyingly, while in a closed syllable containing a short lax vowel, the second mora is provided by the coda consonant ('Weight-by-Position'). (2i.d-e), like *['rʊm] and *[bræ], are then excluded, because a short lax vowel in an open syllable is light, i.e. monomoraic. To account for the existence of examples like ['sɪti] and ['mækrəʊ] (2i.a-b), Hammond assumes that the stressed syllables in these forms are in fact closed by a 'virtual consonant', or a 'covert geminate', which provides the second mora.

However, Hammond does not discuss the restriction in (2ii-iii.c,g), viz. that English also rules out long vowels in closed syllables (e.g. *['viːktə], *[guːlp]). To account for this, we must also pose an *upper* limit on stressed rhymes, in effect restricting them to contain *exactly two* moras (or positions). In addition, we need to make a distinction between the status of different word-final consonants. Since certain types of 'superheavy' rhymes, i.e. those in (2ii-iii.f) and (2i.g), are well-formed, but only word-finally, their final consonant must be assumed to be extrasyllabic (i.e. [hɔːk] (VV$C), [gʌlp] (VC$C)), so that their rhymes are also bimoraic. (This does not help forms like *[guːlp], which are still trimoraic under this analysis.) But if a word-final consonant directly follows a short lax vowel, as in [hʊk] (2i.f), then it must be moraic, to satisfy the bimoraic requirement. In an analysis like this, short and long stressed vowels are in fact in proper complementary distribution in English (the only exception being (2ii.d)).

The absence of long lax vowels in pre-vocalic position (2ii.d) must then be the result of a separate constraint. This is confirmed by inspection of the distribution of reduced vowels, given in (4).

(4)   Distribution and realisation of reduced vowels according to syllable position

		(i) [ə]	(ii) [ɪ/i/j]	(iii) [ʊ/u/uː/w]
internal	(a) _ $CV	ə'fɛkt 'affect'	ɪ'fɛkt 'effect'	ju'naɪt 'unite' 'rɛɡjʊlə 'regular'
	(b) _ $CCV	ə'kleɪm 'acclaim'	ɪ'klɪps 'eclipse'	nju'trɪʃn 'nutrition'
	(c) _ C$CV	'kɒntəmpleɪt 'contemplate'	'ænɪkdəʊt 'anecdote'	*
	(d) _ $V	*	kri'eɪt 'create' 'hɪd{i/j}əs 'hideous'	ˌsɪtʃu'eɪʃn 'situation' 'vɪʒ{u/w}əl 'visual'
final	(e) _ #	'səʊfə 'sofa'	'səʊfi 'Sophie'	'menjuː 'menu'
	(f) _ C#	'mætək 'mattock'	'ætɪk 'attic'	*
	(g) _ CC#	*	*	*

Columns (ii) and (iii) show that [ɪ] and [ʊ] have different realisations depending on their context. Simplifying somewhat, we can say that they are tensed word-finally (4ii-iii.e) and tensed or glided pre-vocalically (4ii-iii.d). [ə], which has no tense (or glide) counterpart, cannot occur before another vowel (4i.d). Thus, there seems to be a general ban on pre-vocalic lax vowels, whether these are short or long, stressed or unstressed.

3 Italian tonic lengthening

Before turning to the analysis of the English data, let me first discuss Italian. The Italian data are similar to the English data, but differ from them in interesting ways. Moreover, the Italian data have been analyzed by Larsen

(1998), in a framework that is similar to the one that I use for the analysis of English.

In Italian, consonant length is contrastive but vowel length is not. The examples in (5) show that the distribution of short and long vowels is predictable.

(5) Italian: distribution of long vowels

    a. ['faːto]   'destiny'

    b. ['piːgro] 'lazy'

    c. ['parko] 'park'

    d. ['fatːo]   'fact'

A stressed vowel is long if it precedes a single intervocalic consonant (5a) or a cluster of the type which is analysed as a branching onset (5b) in 'standard' Government Phonology (GP; see e.g. Kaye et al. 1990). Stressed vowels are therefore lengthened in open syllables.[4] If a stressed vowel is followed by a cluster of the coda-onset type (5c) or by a geminate (5d), then it remains short. That is, in a closed syllable, tonic lengthening does not apply. In other words, a stressed syllable must be heavy in Italian, either by virtue of being closed, or by containing a long vowel. This is an illustration of 'Stress-to-Weight'.

Larsen (1998) analyses the Italian data in the framework of strict CV phonology (see Lowenstamm 1996). In this framework, 'syllable structure' consists of strictly alternating C and V positions. As a consequence, the representation of closed syllables, geminate consonants and long vowels involves an empty position, as shown in (6a-c).

(6)   Strict CV (Lowenstamm 1996)

    a. Closed syllable   b. Geminate consonant   c. Long vowel

Geminates and long vowels consist of two CV units. In a geminate, the consonantal melody straddles an empty V position; in a long vowel, the vocalic melody straddles an empty C position.

---

[4] This discussion ignores some complicating issues, in particular that word-final stressed vowels do not lengthen. See Larsen (1998) for an account of this, and for an analysis of *Raddoppiamento Sintattico*, which applies when a word-final stressed vowel is followed by a consonant-initial word.

Larsen proposes that in languages with tonic lengthening, stress always creates an extra CV unit. In addition, an empty CV unit must be properly governed in order to remain in the representation, and at least one of its positions must eventually be filled. In other words, a CV unit cannot remain completely empty.[5] Proper government, applying on the nuclear projection, is defined in (7).

(7) Iambic (right-to-left) Proper Government (Kaye 1990)

   A nuclear position A properly governs a nuclear position B iff

a. A governs B (adjacent on its projection) from right to left
b. A is not properly governed

The application of Italian tonic lengthening is illustrated in (8).

(8) Long vowel

   a. Before a non-branching onset   b. Before a 'branching onset'

In (8a), the stressed (underlined) vowel precedes a single intervocalic consonant. The second CV unit is created by stress, and its V position is properly governed by V_3. The melody of the stressed vowel spreads to V_2 in order to license it segmentally. (8b) represents the same scenario before a 'branching onset'. The empty nucleus inside the internal cluster (V_3) does not need to be properly governed because it is trapped inside a closed domain of consonantal interaction (as indicated by the square brackets). This 'infrasegmental government' (Scheer 1999) licenses V_3 to remain silent. V_4 is therefore free to properly govern V_2, and spreading from V_1 ensues.

In (9) we see the contexts where tonic lengthening cannot apply.

---

[5] This restriction does not apply to the initial empty CV unit which replaces the boundary symbol '#', traditionally used to identify the beginning of the word (see Lowenstamm 1999). This site normally remains silent. In this paper I assume trochaic proper government, and so do not adhere to the idea of an initial empty CV unit.

(9) Short vowel

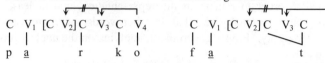

a. Before a coda-onset cluster   b. Before a geminate

When the stressed vowel is followed by a coda-onset cluster (9a) or a geminate (9b), the V_2 position of the inserted empty CV unit cannot be properly governed by V_3, because the latter is itself properly governed by V_4. The ungoverned empty CV unit is therefore removed from the representation and the stressed vowel remains short.

In my view, Larsen's analysis faces two problems. First, if the manifestation of stress in languages with tonic lengthening is the extra CV unit, then words of the type in (9) contain no stressed position, because the empty CV unit is ultimately deleted from their representation. Another problem is that although, according to Larsen, tonic lenghtening is controlled by proper government, the latter — operating from right-to-left, (i.e. between V_3 and V_2 in (8a)) — is not related to the stressed position (i.e. V_1) in any way.

4 A loose CV analysis with trochaic proper government

We have seen so far that the relationship between stress and length is similar in English and Italian, but that these languages also differ in interesting ways. In both languages, the domain of stress comprises two CV units (Stress-to-Weight). However, while the requirement that stressed syllables be heavy causes dynamic alternations in Italian (e.g. [ka'deːre] 'fall-INF' vs. ['kaːde] 'fall-3SG'), it is a distributional generalization in English. (The reason for this is that consonant length is not manifested on the surface in English; consonants are phonetically short both following and preceding short stressed vowels, as in *atom* ['ætəm] and *atomic* [ə'tɒmɪk]). Further, vowel length is contrastive in English, whereas in Italian consonant length is contrastive. In both languages, lengthening is observed in sounds for which length is non-contrastive (even if only virtually).[6]

In this paper, I propose to analyse the restriction on English stressed rhymes by requiring the stressed position to properly govern an empty

---

[6] I see no reason to expect that this is universal. However, Hayes (1995) also observes that stress-induced lengthening tends to be non-neutralising.

nucleus to its right, thus avoiding the problems of Larsen's analysis. Since lax vowels are represented as headless and tense vowels as headed in GP (e.g. Harris 1994), this requirement ensures that all stressed vowels are heads in some sense. I further propose that short vowels in seemingly open rhymes satisfy this requirement by being followed by a virtual geminate, similarly to Hammond's (1997) analysis.

To achieve this, I follow Rowicka (1999a,b) and assume trochaic (left-to-right) proper government instead of the more usual right-to-left type, as defined in (10).

(10) Trochaic (left-to-right) Proper Government (Rowicka 1999a,b)

A nuclear position A properly governs a nuclear position B iff

a. A governs B (adjacent on its projection) from left to right

b. A is not properly governed

Finally, I will assume a 'loose' CV skeleton instead of the 'strict' CV skeleton as argued for in Polgárdi (1998, 2002). These approaches are not radically different: word-medially they are the same; they differ (potentially) at word edges only. More specifically, the loose CV approach dispenses with domain-final empty nuclei that are always inaudible. This means that words do not need to end in a V position: C-final words are allowed (just like V-initial words, when there is no initial phonetic consonant). However, word-medially a strict alternation of C and V positions is still required.

Domain-final empty nuclei present a number of serious problems (see Polgárdi 1998 for discussion). One of these is illustrated in (11), where the adjectival root-level suffix *-al* is added to the noun *órigin*, resulting in the stress-shifted form *original*. In a strict CV approach, the root ends in the empty V_4 while the suffix starts with the empty C_5. This empty sequence is then customarily deleted, as is indicated by the angle brackets (this is what Gussmann & Kaye 1993 call 'reduction').

(11)   Strict CV: reduction

$$\text{CVCVC V}_3\ \text{C}_4<\text{V}_4\,\text{C}_5>\ \text{V}_5\ \text{CV} \qquad \text{CVCV}\ \text{C}\ \text{V}_3\ \text{C}_4\,\text{V}_5\ \text{C}\ \text{V}$$

$$\text{'ɒr ɪ dʒ ə n} \quad + \quad \text{ə l} \quad \rightarrow \quad \text{ə 'rɪ dʒ ə n ə l}$$

However, this analysis is problematic since it violates the Projection Principle (given in (12)) in that it also removes the proper governing relation between V_3 and V_4.

(12) Projection Principle (Kaye et al. 1990: 221)

> Governing relations are defined at the level of lexical representation and
> remain constant throughout a phonological derivation.

In a loose CV approach, no reduction is necessary, since a consonant-final
root and a vowel-initial suffix can simply be concatenated. As a result, no
governing relationship has been deleted. This is shown in (13).

(13) Loose CV: no reduction

$$
\begin{array}{cccccc}
\text{V} & \text{C} & \text{V} & \text{C} & \text{V} & \text{C} \\
| & | & | & | & | & | \\
\end{array}
\quad
\begin{array}{cc}
\text{V} & \text{C} \\
| & | \\
\end{array}
\quad
\begin{array}{cccccccc}
\text{V} & \text{C} & \text{V} & \text{C} & \text{V} & \text{C} & \text{V} & \text{C} \\
| & | & | & | & | & | & | & | \\
\end{array}
$$

ˈɒ r ɪ dʒ ə n + ə l → ə ˈr ɪ dʒ ə n ə l

Let us now see how the data in (2) can be analysed in this approach. (14)
shows the representation of a stressed vowel (the initial vowels of *city*,
cinema and *metre*) preceding a single intervocalic consonant, i.e. in a word-
internal 'open syllable'.

(14) (=2a)   _$CV

a. short lax: virtual geminate   b. long lax/tense

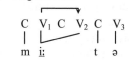

The representation of a long lax or tense vowel involves two CV units (14b),
just like in Larsen's analysis. However, according to Rowicka (1999a,b), the
relationship between the two halves of a long vowel is one of proper
government. Since the C position between V_1 and V_2 is unfilled, this
governing relationship is manifested by spreading the melodic content of V_1
into V_2. (In those cases where the intervening C position is filled, as in e.g.
vector in (16) below, there is of course no possibility for spreading.) In this
analysis, the V_2 position is properly governed by V_1 and not by V_3. In this
way, the requirement on stressed positions (in English) to properly govern an
empty nucleus to their right is satisfied. As Italian [ˈfaːto] would have the
same representation (apart from having derived instead of underlying length),
lengthening of the vowel in that case would be directly connected to it being
stressed, via proper government. This then obviates the second problem of
Larsen's analysis.

The stressed short lax vowel in (14a) is also required to properly govern an
empty nucleus to its right; for this reason, an extra CV unit is created. As this
CV unit cannot remain completely empty, at least one of its positions must be
filled. In English, just like in Italian, the sound for which length is non-

contrastive undergoes lengthening; in English, this is the following consonant, which spreads its melody into C_2. However, since RP English lacks phonetic geminates, the resulting geminate is merely 'virtual' (for earlier use of this device in strict CV phonology, see e.g. Lowenstamm 1996).[7] The example of *cinema* in (14a) demonstrates that gemination occurs following stressed vowels only, and that this gemination is not a word-minimality effect, since it also applies in longer words. (14a,b) thus show that the superficially similar surface forms in (2i.a) and (2ii-iii.a) in fact have different representations.

Finally, one further difference between the representations in (14a) and (14b) must be noted, viz. that the long vowel in (14b) is represented by a solid line connecting the melody of V_1 to V_2, while in the geminate in (14a) the melody of C_3 is connected to C_2 by a dashed line. This difference is meant to show that the long vowel is underlying while the geminate is derived. If both were derived, then there would be no way of telling which melody is supposed to spread.

To preserve the insight that in both cases the melody is distinctively located in the head position (V_1 and C_3) only, and is phonologically unspecified in the dependent position, I use Harris' (1994) notion of spreading as interpretation. The solid or dashed line which connects the melody to the dependent position then simply indicates the domain over which the melody should be phonetically interpreted, underlyingly or as a result of derivation. (As it happens, in virtual geminates the melody is *not* interpreted phonetically in C_2, but the domain is nevertheless demarcated phonologically.)

Examples of a stressed vowel preceding a word-internal 'branching onset' are provided in (15).

(15) (=2b)   _$CCV

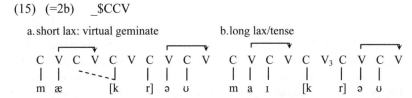

Here we find the same scenario as preceding a word-internal non-branching onset, in (14). A long lax or tense vowel can occur here (15b), because the

---

[7] English has phonetic 'fake' geminates, e.g. [nː] in *un#natural*, but these are split by an intervening word-level boundary. Their phonological representation is quite different from that of true (though virtual) geminates. The melody of 'fake' geminates is lodged distinctively in both C positions separately and so does not result from spreading to an empty position.

empty V_3 inside the 'branching onset' does not need to be properly governed; it is already licensed to remain silent by infrasegmental government (Scheer 1999), as was discussed in section 3. In the case of a short lax vowel (15a), a virtual geminate is again created to satisfy the requirement on stressed vowels to properly govern.

As was shown in (2), tense vowels behave alike, regardless of whether they are realised as diphthongs or as long monophthongs. The representations in (15) are in line with the analysis of German diphthongs in Ségéral & Scheer (1998), which is also supported by Dutch, where diphthongs behave like closed syllables (Van der Hulst 1984, 1985). However, in English the situation is more complicated. With regard to stress assignment in verbs, word-internal closed syllables and syllables with a long vowel or diphthong behave alike, in that they count as heavy. Word-finally, however, diphthongs form a natural class with long vowels in attracting stress (e.g. *dený*, *agrée*), as opposed to syllables closed by a single consonant, which are normally unstressed (e.g. *fínish*). (The pattern found in nouns is more varied; here not all final diphthongs and long vowels attract stress, and we find forms like *Julý* alongside forms like *féllow*.) As we will see below, the analysis proposed here is in fact capable of accounting for the different behaviour of word-internal and word-final closed syllables.

Examples of a stressed vowel in a word-internal 'closed syllable' are given in (16).

(16) (=2c)   _C\$CV

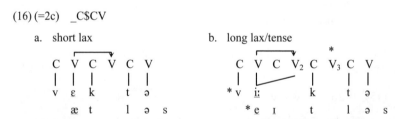

A stressed short lax vowel can occur here, because it can properly govern the empty nucleus to its right (16a). (In Italian, words like ['parko] would have the same structure, and thus contain a representation of stress, unlike in Larsen's analysis; compare (9a).) However, a long lax or tense vowel cannot occur in this position (16b), because the governed V_2 position cannot properly govern V_3. An ungoverned position such as V_3 cannot remain silent; it is for this reason that a long vowel cannot be followed by an inaudible nucleus.

The contrast between (16a) and (16b) in fact provides an additional argument for a CV representation: the restriction concerning short vs. long vowels that we observe in (16) does not apply just to coda-onset clusters but also to 'bogus' clusters (e.g. ['ætləs] 'atlas' vs. *['eɪtləs]), where the consonants can form neither a coda-onset cluster nor a branching onset in any version of GP, and so must be separated by an empty nucleus; cf. e.g. Kaye et al. 1990).[8] An analysis in which short vowels are restricted to closed syllables cannot account for these cases.

Consider next the representation of forms with hiatus, i.e. the context before a vowel.

(17) (=2d)   _$V

    a. short lax: b. tense (but no long lax)
        CV unit cannot remain empty

A stressed short lax vowel cannot occur in this position, because it needs to properly govern. In (17a) the inserted (underlined) CV unit cannot be filled, as there is no consonantal melody on the right from which spreading can take place; since CV units cannot remain completely empty, (17a) is therefore ill-formed. A tense vowel, in contrast, can occur in this position without further provisions (17b). However, a long lax vowel cannot, on account of the general ban on pre-vocalic lax vowels; compare in this respect the lack of unstressed lax vowels in this context (e.g. *[krɪˈeɪt]), which are not subject to the requirement of proper government.

Having examined all the word-internal possibilities, we now turn to the word-final cases. (18) provides examples of the absolute word-final position.

(18)   (=2e)   _#

    a. short lax: b. long lax/tense
        CV unit cannot remain empty

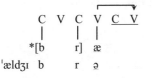 

---

[8] In 'standard' GP, consonant clusters come in three types. In complex onsets and coda-onset clusters, the consonants are assumed to be adjacent, which is supported by the observation that we find phonotactic constraints holding between them. (The former are by and large restricted to non-homorganic obstruent-liquid sequences, the latter to clusters of falling sonority.) Any other type of consonant cluster is considered to be 'bogus', i.e. separated by an inaudible nucleus. Of course, in a strict/loose CV framework, all clusters are by definition bogus clusters.

As (18b) shows, a stressed long lax or tense vowel can occur in this context. However, a short lax vowel cannot (18a), since it also needs to properly govern — but the inserted (underlined) CV unit cannot be filled, as there is nothing to spread to it. Since a CV unit cannot remain empty, the form in (18a) is ungrammatical. The example of *algebra* shows that if a word-final short vowel is unstressed, then there is no extra final empty CV unit (whose presence is required by stress only), and the representation is well-formed.

Examples involving single word-final consonants are given in (19).

(19) (=2f)   _C#

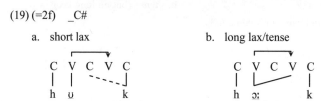

a.   short lax   b.   long lax/tense

These representations are entirely parallel to the ones given in (14), except that there are no final vowels in (19). In strict CV, there would in fact not be any difference, since in this approach (19a,b) would both contain a final empty V position. However, this would result in ill-formed representations, since these empty nuclei would be ungoverned and so could not remain silent, as was shown in (16b). This could be remedied by reintroducing the parameter of domain-final licensing (which has been made superfluous by assuming trochaic proper government), to account for just these cases. The problem with this solution is that words like *finish* would then have two possible analyses: one where the final empty nucleus is governed by the preceding pronounced vowel, and one where it is licensed parametrically. In loose CV, these problems can be avoided, since in this approach words do not need to end in a V position.

In a longer example, e.g. *dévélop*, the empty CV unit is, of course, not inserted after the last vowel, but after the penultimate one, as this is the vowel that is stressed. This is shown in (20a).

(20) Stress in verbs

a.   final CVC   b.   final diphthong

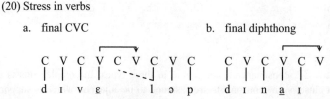

If English word-final consonants are uniformly represented by a final C position (without a following empty V), as proposed in (19), whereas diphthongs always constitute a governing domain (to capture the natural class they form with long vowels), we can explain the pattern of stress assignment

described above. A 'heavy syllable' is then equivalent to a proper governing domain, which can be found underlyingly in long vowels, diphthongs and word-internal 'closed syllables' (as in (16a)). These attract stress, which explains why a verb like *deny* in (20b) has final stress. A word-final 'syllable' that is closed by a single consonant, however, does not contain a governing domain (i.e. it is light), and therefore stress moves to the left if the word is long enough, as in (20a).[9]

Finally, consider the context before two word-final consonants, in (21).

(21) (=2g)　_CC#

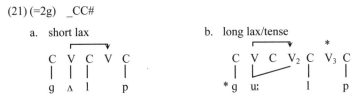

a.　short lax

b.　long lax/tense

Again, these representations are parallel to those in (16a,b). A stressed short lax vowel can occur in this environment (21a), since it can properly govern the empty nucleus inside the final cluster; a long lax or tense vowel is illicit in this position (21b), since the ungoverned V_3 cannot remain silent. Note also that it no longer needs to be stipulated that 'superheavy rhymes' such as (19b) and (21a) occur word-finally only, because the 'bachelor' Cs (i.e. Cs without a following V) that such rhymes contain are restricted to word edges. One further question arises in relation to (21a), viz. whether bogus clusters are allowed to follow short lax vowels word-finally, as is the case word-internally (16a). I tentatively suggest that they are, but that the final consonant must in such cases be realised as syllabic, as in e.g. *bottle* [ˈbɒtl̩]. An account of the behaviour of English syllabic consonants is beyond the scope of this paper, however.

In summary, we have seen that stressed short and long vowels are in complementary distribution in English. The analysis of the distribution of English vowels presented in this paper has a number of advantages over previous approaches. As opposed to an analysis along the lines of Hammond (1997), where stressed 'rhymes' were required to contain *exactly two* positions, here the restriction is no longer arbitrary: a stressed position must properly govern an empty nucleus in order to be a head in some sense. In addition, only a CV analysis is capable of unifying the representations of

---

[9] The representation of diphthongs in its present form cannot account for the phonotactic restrictions holding between their component parts (not present in 'closed syllables' proper), and so requires further refinement. Further research on the difference between glides and other consonants should also make the difference between the representation of final sequences like those in (20a,b) less stipulative.

coda-onset clusters and bogus clusters, both of which can provide a following context for lax vowels. Another advantage of a CV analysis is that there is no need (or even a possibility) for extrasyllabicity, and that final consonants are treated in a uniform manner. The final bachelor C is not equivalent to extrasyllabicity, and neither is it invented for the sake of 'superheavy syllables'. As opposed to Larsen (1998), in the present analysis, stress manifests itself in every word, since all words must contain a proper governing domain at the end of the derivation.[10] Also, lengthening is indeed controlled by the stressed position — via proper government.

An additional advantage of the analysis presented here is that it is supported by accents such as Welsh English, where virtual geminates in fact become audible. Inspection of the literature reveals that there is no consensus as to the precise context of lengthening. Thomas (1984: 185) observes that "single consonants in medial position following a short stressed vowel are phonetically long", as in (22a).

(22) Welsh English

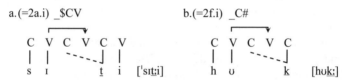

a.(=2a.i) _$CV

C V C V C V
| | ⌐---⌐ | |
s ɪ   t i   ['sɪt̬i]

b.(=2f.i) _C#

C V C V C
| | ⌐---⌐
h ʊ   k   [hʊkː]

Connolly (1981) also reports lengthening in word-final context, as in (22b). In his description, lengthening also applies after /iː, uː/ and diphthongs, when these are fully shortened before a fortis consonant, as well as to certain, not precisely specified, types of clusters (the latter of which I will not attempt to account for here).

---

[10] Note that the implication is unidirectional: if there is stress, then there is also a proper governing domain, but not vice versa. This allows the possibility of unstressed 'closed syllables' in pre-tonic, antepenultimate position in Italian. English is somewhat more complicated in that it has more degrees of stress, and heavy syllables typically attract stress, suggesting that the Weight-to-Stress principle is active as well (in addition to Stress-to-Weight, which is the focus of this paper).

5 Unstressed vowels

Turning to unstressed vowels, we have seen in (4) that these are reduced to [ə], [ɪ/i/j], or [ʊ/u/uː/w]. This reduction could be analysed as involving the loss of all the elements of a full vowel, resulting in a schwa, or as involving the loss of all elements except **I** or **U**. The latter typically results in the headless, i.e. lax, vowels [ɪ,ʊ] (being unstressed), although these can be required to become headed, i.e. tense [i,u/uː], in certain positions (4ii-iii.d,e), or to appear in a C position and surface as a glide [j,w] (4ii-iii.d).

In this account, schwa could be represented as an empty nucleus which surfaces when it is ungoverned. This is shown in (23); in both (23a) and (23b), the final empty nucleus V_3 must surface, because V_2 cannot govern it.

(23) Schwa as an ungoverned empty nucleus

a. after a cluster

b. after a long lax/tense vowel

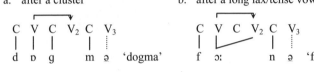

However, schwa is also found in environments where it could be properly governed, as is shown by such pairs as *vector* ['vɛktə] vs. *rickety* ['rɪkəti], and *chimney* ['tʃɪmni] vs. *Romany* ['rɒmənɪ].

(24) Governable vs. non-governable empty nucleus: word-internal context

a. (16a=2c.i) _C$CV

b. (14a=2a.i') $Cə

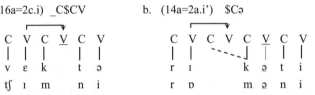

The underlined empty nucleus is properly governed in (24a) but not in (24b), where, as a result, a virtual geminate must appear to satisfy the requirement on stressed positions.

The difference becomes clearer if we compare the underlying representation of *rickety* and *Romany*, given in (25), with (24a).

(25) Underlying representation of *rickety* and *Romany*

C V C <u>V</u> C V
| | | | |
r ɪ k   t i
r ɒ m   n i

In (25), stress has not yet been assigned. Hence, the virtual geminate is not yet present, and the only difference between (24a) and (25) lies in whether or not the underlined empty nucleus is governable. As can be seen in (24), the consonants flanking the empty nucleus can form either a coda-onset or a bogus cluster. Bogus clusters provide the most acute problem; these are separated by an empty nucleus in all versions of GP, but a distinction must somehow be made between those empty nuclei that are properly governable and those that are not. (Near-minimal pairs like [gʌlp] *gulp* vs. [ˈgæləp] *gallop* illustrate the same phenomenon; the only difference is that these forms lack the final V positions present in (24).)

Turning now to word-final context, in minimal pairs like [hɛn] *hen* vs. [ˈhɛnə] *henna* we find a different type of contrast. It seems to be the case that in English a final empty nucleus (underlined in (26b)) following a short lax vowel and a single consonant can never be properly governed.

(26) Word-final empty nucleus: non-governable

    a. (19a=2f.i) _C#   b. (14a=2a.i') _$Cə

```
     C  V  C  V  C              C  V  C  V  C  V
     |  |    ˋ---ˏ              |  |    ˋ---ˏ    ⋮
     h  ε       n              h  ε       n  ə
```

The difference with respect to the pairs in (24) stems from the fact that (26a) ends in a C position rather than in an empty nucleus. Again, this can be seen more easily if we consider the underlying representations of *hen* and *henna*, without the virtual geminates.

(27) Underlying representations

    a. C V C   b. C V C V

```
       C  V  C              C  V  C  V
       |  |  |              |  |  |
       h  ε  n              h  ε  n
```

Here one option would be to assume that the underlying representation of *hen* also ends in an empty nucleus, as in (28), to make the contrast parallel to the one between (24a) and (25).

(28) Alternative underlying representation of *hen*

```
     C  V  C  V
     |  |  |
     h  ε  n
```

However, the problem with this is that we would then expect final CVC sequences to attract stress. As we have seen in (20), this is contrary to fact. A further problem with (28) is that we would predict no word-final gemination in Welsh English, which is again contradicted by the evidence in (22b). Hence, we must conclude that English word-final consonants occupy a final C position, as was proposed above, and that final empty nuclei following a short lax vowel and a consonant are not properly governable.

Returning to the issue raised in (24), we have the following options for representing the contrast between properly governable and non-governable empty nuclei. The first is to use lexical marking. This is not elegant, but it has been employed in a comparable situation in Turkish (see Polgárdi 2009). In Turkish, the high vowel /ɨ/ and its harmonic counterparts alternate with zero, the vowel that is also traditionally regarded as lacking any distinctive features (or elements). However, not all segmentally empty nuclei do in fact alternate. There are even minimal pairs like *koyun* 'chest-NOM', *koynu* 'chest-ACC' vs. *koyun* 'sheep-NOM', *koyunu* 'sheep-ACC', suggesting that the two types must be distinguished lexically. In Turkish, there is evidence to lexically mark the alternating group, i.e. the properly governable empty nuclei, as the stems in question form a closed class consisting mainly of nouns denoting body parts, or are loanwords. However, the question of which type of nucleus should be lexically marked in English is rather less clear.

A second option would be to assume that schwa is not empty. This raises the obvious question as to what its representation should be. And how should we then represent reduction (i.e. the alternation between a stressed full vowel and unstressed schwa, as in ['ætəm] *atom* vs. [ə'tɒmɪk] *atomic*)? Representing schwa as a headless (or empty-headed) **A**, as suggested by Kaye et al. (1985), would work for this example, since both full vowels in the root contain **A**. However, it is problematic for examples like *credulity* [krə'dju:ləti] vs. *credulous* ['kredjələs] and *proximity* [prɒk'sɪməti] vs. *proximate* ['prɒksəmət], where the underlined alternating full vowels contain **U** and **I** respectively, but not **A**. This would mean that reduction, in some cases at least, involves element substitution. Harris (1994) attempts to solve this problem by proposing an extra melodic prime, viz. the 'neutral element'. This element is assumed to be present in every melodic expression as a dependent, and surfaces automatically as a head when all other elements have been lost by reduction, providing a non-empty representation for schwa. However, the neutral element is problematic since, unlike all other elements, it does not characterise a natural class and it fails to take part in phonological processes such as spreading. For these reasons, I reject this option.

A third possibility is not to assume any underlying schwas, but to try to derive all schwas from full vowels by reduction. The problem with this approach is that not all schwas are alternating. Consider forms such as *salad* ['sæləd], *toilet* ['tɔɪlət], *oppress* [ə'pres] and *volunteer* [ˌvɒlən'tɪə]; on what basis could we decide about the underlying full vowel?

Finally, we could assume that virtual geminates are underlying. However, the problem with this is that their occurrence is totally predictable from stress (which is itself largely predictable from syllable structure and from certain other factors). Moreover, this solution would not be of any help for words with sequences of schwas, e.g. *tetanus* ['tɛtənəs], where nothing would force the second schwa to surface (given that words like *balance* ['bæləns] are also well formed). Notice also that we would not want to posit an underlying virtual geminate after the first schwa, since this would incorrectly attract stress to the penultimate position.

I conclude that the first option, viz. that of lexical marking, is the least problematic. Further research is necessary to determine which nuclei should be lexically marked.

6 Aspiration as gemination?

To conclude this paper, I consider briefly an analysis of English aspiration by Ségéral & Scheer (2008). Although aspiration is not germane to the present discussion, Ségéral & Scheer's analysis is interesting because it claims the exact opposite of what I have proposed above. Ségéral & Scheer assume a strict CV framework with iambic proper government. Following Lowenstamm (1999), they further identify the beginning of the word (#) with an empty CV unit, to make it accessible to the phonology, as in (29b). Analysing lenition and fortition, in addition to a number of other phenomena, Ségéral & Scheer define a strong C position as a position which follows an empty nucleus. The reason for this is that in this context the following vowel must govern the empty V position but it can also license its own onset. This provides the most favourable conditions for the latter (as government destroys the melodic content of its target, while licensing supports it). The subtypes of strong positions (underlined) are illustrated in (29), for *vector* ['vɛktə], *today* [t̪ʰə'deɪ], (Italian) *fato* ['faːto] 'destiny', and *become* [bɪ'kʰʌm].

(29) Strong C-positions: following an empty V-position

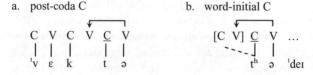

    a. post-coda C   b. word-initial C

c. C following a stressed vowel: d. C preceding a stressed vowel:
     Italian   English

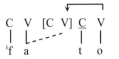   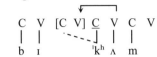

There are three relevant cases: post-coda consonants (29a), word-initial consonants (29b), and consonants next to a stressed vowel (29c-d). Ségéral & Scheer adopt Larsen's idea that stress is manifested as an extra CV unit, although they regard the position of this unit with respect to the stressed vowel as parametric. In a language with tonic lengthening, such as Italian, the CV unit follows the stressed vowel (29c) and the *following* consonant is predicted to be strong. In a language like English, on the other hand, the CV unit precedes the stressed vowel (29d), and so the *preceding* consonant is expected to be strong.

Support for this analysis comes from aspiration in voiceless stops, which is found before stressed vowels (29d) and word-initially (29b). By inserting the CV unit before the stressed vowel, these two contexts can now be unified. Aspiration is then analyzed as a case of fortition (more specifically, as gemination) to prevent it from applying in unstressed post-coda context, e.g. to the /t/ in *vector*, in (29a).

There is a serious problem with Ségéral & Scheer's account, however. In English, coda-onset clusters also occur before a stressed vowel. In this context voiceless stop onsets do become aspirated, as is shown by the first /t/ of *dictate* in (30).

(30) Stressed vowel following a coda-onset cluster

$$\text{?}$$
$$\text{C} \quad \text{V} \quad \text{C} \quad \text{V}_2 \quad [\text{C}_3 \text{ V}] \quad \underline{\text{C}_4} \quad \text{V} \quad \text{C} \quad \text{V} \quad \text{C} \quad \text{V}$$
$$\text{d} \quad \text{ɪ} \quad \text{k} \qquad\qquad {}^{'}\text{t}^{\text{h}} \quad \text{e} \quad \text{ɪ} \qquad \text{t}$$

If C_4 must spread to C_3 to aspirate the stop, then it is not clear how the V_2 position becomes licensed — but without such licensing the representation is ungrammatical, and such forms should be non-existent.[11] This prediction is incorrect.

---

[11] The representations in (29d) and (30) show that in a strict CV analysis with iambic proper government, words have to end in a V position, and if this position is empty, it must be licensed to remain silent by the domain-final parameter. In fact, such licensed final empty nuclei need to be allowed to properly govern a preceding empty nucleus, as can be seen in (30).

It is also surprising that the accent that actually exhibits phonetic geminates, i.e. Welsh English, has them on the opposite side of (short) stressed vowels. In addition, Ségéral & Scheer's analysis cannot account for the distribution of vowels, the topic of the present paper. In fact, I am not convinced that aspiration should be regarded as fortition, or that it should be treated at the same level as the phonotactic generalizations considered in this paper. An in-depth analysis of aspiration is beyond the scope of this paper, however.

7 Summary and conclusion

This paper has shown that a loose CV analysis that assumes trochaic proper government can account for the distribution of both stressed and unstressed English vowels with a minimum of theoretical machinery. By requiring a stressed position to properly govern an empty nucleus, we ensure that all stressed vowels are heads in some sense. In addition, assuming left-to-right proper government makes it possible for the stressed position to control lengthening.

Questions left for further research include the following: understanding the general ban on pre-vocalic lax vowels, working out the representation of syllabic consonants, refining the account of schwa and the representation of diphthongs, and determining the status of aspiration vis-à-vis a loose CV approach.

References

Burzio, Luigi (2007): "Phonology and phonetics of English stress and vowel reduction." – In: *Language Sciences* 29, 154–176.

Chomsky, Noam & Morris Halle (1968): *The Sound Pattern of English.* – New York: Harper & Row.

Connolly, John H. (1981): "On the segmental phonology of a South Welsh accent of English." – In: *Journal of the International Phonetic Association* 11, 51–61.

Gimson, A.C. (1980): *An Introduction to the Pronunciation of English* (3rd edn.). – London: Edward Arnold.

Gussmann, Edmund & Jonathan Kaye (1993): "Polish notes from a Dubrovnik cafe I: the yers. – In: *SOAS Working Papers in Linguistics and Phonetics* 3, 427–462.

Hammond, Michael (1997): "Vowel quantity and syllabification in English." – In: *Language* 73, 1–17.

Harris, John (1994): *English Sound Structure.* – Oxford: Blackwell

Hayes, Bruce (1995): *Metrical Stress Theory. Principles and Case Studies.* – Chicago: The University of Chicago Press.

Hulst, Harry van der (1984): *Syllable Structure and Stress in Dutch.* – Dordrecht: Foris.

– (1985): "Ambisyllabicity in Dutch." – In: Bennis, Hans & Frits Beukema (eds.): *Linguistics in the Netherlands 1985*, 57–66. Dordrecht: Foris.

Jones, Daniel (1966): *The Pronunciation of English* (4th edn.). – Cambridge: Cambridge University Press.

Kaye, Jonathan (1990): "'Coda' Licensing." – In: *Phonology* 7, 301–330.

Kaye, Jonathan, Jean Lowenstamm & Jean-Roger Vergnaud (1985): "The internal structure of phonological elements: a theory of Charm and Government." – In: *Phonology Yearbook* 2, 305–328.

– (1990): "Constituent structure and government in phonology." – In: *Phonology* 7, 193–231.

Kreidler, Charles W. (1989): *The Pronunciation of English. A Course Book in Phonology.* – Oxford: Basil Blackwell.

Larsen, Uffe Bergeton (1998): "Vowel length, *Raddoppiamento Sintattico* and the selection of the definite article in Modern Italian." – In: Sauzet, Patric (ed.): *Langues et Grammaire II-III: phonologie*, 87–102. Université Paris 8, Paris.

Lowenstamm, Jean (1996): "CV as the only syllable type." – In: Durand, Jacques & Bernard Laks (eds.): *Current Trends in Phonology: Models and Methods*, 419–441. CNRS/ESRI, Paris X.

– (1999): "The beginning of the word." – In: Rennison, John & Klaus Kühnhammer (eds.): *Phonologica 1996. Syllables!?*, 153–166. The Hague: Holland Academic Graphics.

Nádasdy, Ádám (2006): *Background to English Pronunciation.* – Budapest: Nemzeti Tankönyvkiadó.

Polgárdi, Krisztina (1998): *Vowel Harmony. An Account in Terms of Government and Optimality.* – PhD dissertation, University of Leiden. The Hague: Holland Academic Graphics

– (2002): "Hungarian superheavy syllables and the strict CV approach." – In: Kenesei, István & Péter Siptár (eds.): *Approaches to Hungarian.* (Vol. 8, Papers from the Budapest Conference), 263–282. Budapest: Akadémiai Kiadó.

– (2009): "Trochaic proper government, loose CV, and vowel-zero alternation in Hungarian." – In: Dikken, Marcel den & Robert M. Vago (eds.): *Approaches to Hungarian.* (Vol. 11, Papers from the 2007 New York Conference), 143–165. Amsterdam/Philadelphia: John Benjamins.

Rowicka, Grażyna (1999a): "On trochaic Proper Government." – In: Rennison, John & Klaus Kühnhammer (eds.): *Phonologica 1996. Syllables!?*, 273–288. The Hague: Holland Academic Graphics.

– (1999b): *On Ghost Vowels. A Strict CV Approach.* – PhD dissertation, University of Leiden. The Hague: Holland Academic Graphics.

Scheer, Tobias (1999): "A theory of consonantal interaction." – *Folia Linguistica* 32, 201–237.

Ségéral, Philippe & Tobias Scheer (1998): "A generalized theory of ablaut: the case of Modern German Strong Verbs." In: Fabri, Ray, Albert Ortmann & Teresa Parodi (eds.): *Models of Inflection*, 28–59. Tübingen: Niemeyer.

Ségéral, Philippe & Tobias Scheer (2008): "The Coda Mirror, stress and positional parameters." – In: Carvalho, Joaquim Brandão de, Tobias Scheer & Philippe Ségéral (eds.): *Lenition and Fortition*, 483–518. Berlin: Mouton de Gruyter.

Thomas, Alan R. (1984): "Welsh English." – In: Trudgill, Peter (ed.): *Language in the British Isles*, 178–194. Cambridge: Cambridge University Press.

Wells, John C. (1982): *Accents of English* (Vols. 1-3). – Cambridge: Cambridge University Press.

– (1990): *Longman Pronunciation Dictionary*. – Harlow: Longman.

Bert Botma & Marc van Oostendorp

A propos of the Dutch vowel system 21 years on, 22 years on*

1 Introduction

When this paper appears, it will be almost exactly 22 years since Norval
Smith, together with a group of students, presented a paper at the annual
conference of the Dutch Linguistics Association, entitled ''A propos of the
Dutch vowel system' 21 years on'. The title of the talk, and of the article
which appeared later that year (Smith et al. 1989), referred to an unpublished
manuscript written by Rudolf de Rijk in 1967, during a stay at MIT.[1] De
Rijk's study of the Dutch vowel system was the first in the then emerging
framework of generative phonology — though the problems posed by the
phonological classification of Dutch vowels had been a concern of linguists
for a much longer time, dating back at least as far as the end of the 19th
century (see e.g. Van Helten 1887).

As for other West Germanic languages, the main challenge facing an
analysis of the Dutch vowel system is how the phonological difference
between two sets of vowels — one typically transcribed as /aː, eː, øː, oː, i, y,
u/, the other as /ɑ, ɛ, ɪ, ɔ, ʏ/ — should be characterized.[2] Phonetically, there
appear to be two differences between these sets. First, all members of the
second set are short, while all but the high vowels in the first set are long.
Second, the two sets differ in terms of quality, with (for want of more
specific terms) the former usually described as 'tense' and the latter as 'lax'.

For the purposes of phonology, a more important observation is that the
two sets show different phonological behaviour. This concerns first and

---

* The authors would like to thank Norval Smith for his inspiration, his insights, and
his many contributions to phonology in the Netherlands and the phonology of
Dutch. Thanks are also due to Colin Ewen, Ben Hermans, and Björn Köhnlein for
useful comments, and to Koen Sebregts for sharing his data on Dutch bunched /r/.
The first author acknowledges the assistance of the Netherlands Organization of
Scientific Research (NWO) for funding project no. 2008/01214/GW.
[1] This originally unpublished manuscript was published many decades later, in an
Internet collection of 100 influential articles on Dutch linguistics (see de Rijk
1967).
[2] The native Dutch vowel system also contains schwa, as well as the diphthongs /ɑu,
ɛi, œy/.

foremost their phonotactic distribution. The most prominent difference is that long/tense vowels can be followed by *at most* one consonant, whereas short/lax vowels must be followed by *at least* one consonant — or alternatively, that short/lax vowels necessarily occur in a closed syllable. This is illustrated in (1), where /ɑ/ in (1a) represents the short/lax vowels and /aː/ in (1b) the long/tense ones:

(1) a.   */rɑ/   /rɑm/   /rɑp/   /rɑmp/
          ram   rap   ramp
          'ram'   'quick'   'disaster'

    b.   /raː/   /raːm/   /raːp/   */raːmp/
          ra   raam   raap
          'yard'   'window'   'turnip'

Some exceptions to this generalization should be noted. First, short/lax vowels are found at the end of interjections, as in *bah* [bɑ], *goh* [xɔ]. Second, long/tense vowels can be followed by a cluster if the consonants involved are coronal (e.g. *paars* 'purple', *haard* 'hearth'), as well as in a handful of exceptional words (e.g. *twaalf* 'twelve', *hielp* 'help-PAST-SG'). These exceptions are usually relegated to specific parts of the lexicon, as are interjections, while coronal consonants are usually assigned a special phonotactic status (e.g. Paradis & Prunet 1991).

With these qualifications in mind, we now turn to the ways in which the two sets of Dutch vowels have been analyzed. Broadly speaking, three approaches can be distinguished in the phonological literature. These are summarized in (2).

(2) Approaches to the phonological classification of Dutch vowels

     a. The phonetic property of length is basic; the other properties are derived from this.

     b. The phonetic property of tenseness is basic; the other properties are derived from this.

     c. The (phonological) distinction between open and closed syllables is basic; the other (phonetic) properties are derived from this.

In recent years, the Dutch phonological community seems to have converged on (2b), which is the approach advocated by Smith et al. (1989), among others. However, approach (2a) still enjoys considerable support, e.g. in phonological descriptions of Dutch (Booij 1995) and in textbooks (Kooij & Van Oostendorp 2003). Approach (2c) was favoured by such linguists as Sievers (1901) and Trubetzkoy (1939), and is also reflected by the descriptive terms 'checked vowel' and 'free vowel', used in (mostly) the British tradition (e.g. Cohen 1952) — but it has not, as far as we are aware, figured in any recent analyses of the Dutch vowel system.

In this chapter, we review the arguments put forward in the literature for each of the three approaches described above. This will lead us to return to approach (2c), a perspective which has long been out of the limelight but fits in well with what we believe is a promising trend in recent work, viz. the idea that certain phonological contrasts are more appropriately encoded in representational terms rather than in terms of phonetically based features (e.g. Golston & Van der Hulst 1999; Pöchtrager & Kaye 2010).

The chapter is structured as follows. First, in section 2, we provide a brief historical overview of previous analyses of the Dutch vowel system. In section 3, we note two problems that are faced by an approach in which the basic distinction is taken to be one of 'tense' vs. 'lax'. The first of these is that in such an approach the distributional restrictions on short/lax vowels must be stated twice: once in the form of a feature and once in the form of a constraint on the syllable in which these vowels appear. The second problem is that the phonetic correlates of the labels 'tense' and 'lax' on which this approach is based are unclear. In view of these problems, we go on to offer a re-appraisal of approach (2c) in section 4, where we argue that the basic distinction between the two sets of vowels is made at the syllabic level. More specifically, our claim is that tense and lax vowels are identical at the segmental level, but differ in terms of the structure of the syllable rhymes which contain them. Section 5 examines briefly some consequences of this proposal, viz. the idea that syllable structure forms part of the underlying representation, the status of schwa (which can occur in both open and closed syllables), and the way in which the structures we propose are implemented by the phonetics.

2 Phonological approaches to the Dutch vowel system

The question of the proper classification of the Dutch vowel system is one of the oldest problems in Dutch phonology. Pre-structuralist linguists (who did not call themselves phonologists) such as Van Helten (1887) and Verdam (1923) referred to a distinction between 'long' and 'short' vowels, in line with approach (2a). Their focus was primarily on earlier stages of Dutch, for which a length distinction is reasonably well supported. Historically, the long/tense vowels of Dutch derive from vowels which were either already long in earlier stages of (West) Germanic, or were the result of lengthening processes (e.g. open syllable lengthening).

The early structuralists tended to take a different point of view. For example, De Groot (1931) distinguished between 'bright' (for 'long') and 'dull' (for 'short') vowels, but this impressionistic classification was not accepted by many of his contemporaries (see e.g. Moulton 1962). More typically, structuralist authors would adopt approach (2c) and refer to the contrast as one of 'strongly cut' vs. 'weakly cut', a terminology which had originally been introduced by Sievers (1901) and further developed in the work of Trubetzkoy (e.g. 1939: 196). In this view, the greater length of vowels in a weakly cut position was taken to be a by-product of a more basic distinction between open and closed syllables, viz. 'the syllable cut'. As far as we can see, no theoretical or empirical arguments were provided for taking the syllable cut, rather than length, to be primary in this approach. For Trubetzkoy, vowel length certainly was a possible dimension of contrast, for example in his analysis of Hopi.

Post-war (late-structuralist, pre-generative) phonologists took an entirely different perspective. For example, Cohen et al. (1959) objected to the syllable cut and a length contrast on the grounds that the phonetic basis for both was unclear. In particular, they observed that the high vowels /i, y, u/ pattern with the non-high vowels /aː, eː, øː, oː/ phonologically, despite the fact that the former are short phonetically. For this reason, Cohen et al. preferred the term 'tense' to describe this set. This term was also adopted by early generative phonologists. For example, De Rijk's (1967) choice for 'tense' is explicitly based on the work of Cohen et al., although he argues that the distinction between 'tense/lax' and 'long/short' is merely a terminological matter, which does not affect the phonological analysis. A large part of De Rijk's paper is devoted to the formalization of a system of rules that tense vowels in contexts which could be called 'open syllables' and lax them in 'closed syllables' — though the notion of the syllable was absent from the (pre-) SPE framework in which De Rijk presented his ideas.

The advent of Autosegmental Phonology (Goldsmith 1976) gave a new impetus to approach (2a). In autosegmental terms, length is not represented by a feature, as it was in SPE, but by the association of a bundle of phonological features to two 'skeletal' or 'x'-positions. Zonneveld (1978) was the first to point out that such a representation, when incorporated in a model that recognizes the syllable, goes a long way towards explaining the distribution of Dutch long/tense vowels. In such a model, the distributional restrictions that were given in (1) can be understood as follows:

(3) a.   Dutch rhymes contain at least two positions and at most three.

    b.   Short vowels occupy one position and long vowels two.

An autosegmental approach to vowel length is therefore capable of describing an important aspect of Dutch phonotactics, and does so in a way that is much more natural and straightforward than the rather complex and arbitrary set of rules of, for example, De Rijk. As a result, this version of the length-based approach became part of the generative mainstream in the 1980s and 90s, figuring in, among others, Van der Hulst (1984), Trommelen & Zonneveld (1989), Kager (1989), Fikkert (1994), and Booij (1995).

The autosegmental length theory is not without problems, however. For one thing, Van Oostendorp (1995, 2000) observes that such a theory must stipulate that schwa is long phonologically (despite being short phonetically), because, like long vowels, it can occur word-finally (e.g. *mode* /moːdə/ 'fashion') but not before two non-coronal consonants (e.g. *arend* /aːrənd/ 'eagle' vs. */aːrəmp/). Van Oostendorp further observes that a length-based approach is problematic from the point of view of markedness. First, with regard to stress, it would imply that Dutch is a weight-sensitive language in which only closed syllables count as heavy — a typologically highly marked state of affairs. Second, with regard to syllable structure, the implication would be that Dutch lacks the universally unmarked CV syllable type (at least, in stressed position).

Observations like these led some phonologists to return to approach (2b), viz. one in which the basic contrast is one of quality rather than quantity. The main proponents of this approach are Smith et al. (1989), Van Oostendorp (1995, 2000), and, more recently, Gussenhoven (2009).[3] Assuming a version of Dependency Phonology, Smith et al. argue that long/tense vowels are distinguished from their short/lax counterparts in having an additional privative feature (or 'element') |I|, which they equate with tenseness, or [ATR].[4] Smith et al. further propose a set of three 'Syllabification Principles', given in (4):

(4) Syllabification Principles (Smith et al. 1989: 138, 141)

    a. A syllable with a specified vowel must have a rhyme with at least two slots.

    b. A lax (specified) vowel may not be the final sound in a syllable.

    c. Syllables containing specified vowels must if possible fill unoccupied slots, from a rhyme-external source.

We will not go into the rather complicated way in which these principles interact, except to say that (4a,b) cover similar ground as (3a,b), but are more arbitrary. For example, no reason is provided why it should be the absence of |I| which makes a segment unable to occur at the end of a syllable.

Principle (4c) serves to distinguish between short and long high tense vowels. Dutch has a marginal contrast between these, with the latter occurring in loanwords, e.g. native *kiem* /kim/ 'germ' vs. non-native *team*

---

[3] For a Government Phonology perspective of this approach, see Van der Hulst (2003); Polgárdi (2008).

[4] The same feature in head position denotes palatal constriction and is a property of front vowels.

/tiːm/ 'team', but neither can occur in syllables closed by more than one non-coronal consonant (e.g. */kimp/, */tiːmp/). It will be clear that this difference is difficult to represent in a purely length-based account, although it is not impossible. For example, Hermans (1992) represents long tense vowels as having two x-positions that are both linked to segmental material, while in short tense vowels only the first of the two x-positions is linked. Smith et al. employ the same surface representations for this contrast, except that in their approach the extra x-position of short high tense vowels is filled by material from the following consonant. However, there seems to be no empirical difference between the two representations, since Dutch lacks geminate consonants, at least within prosodic words (e.g. Booij 1995).[5]

Smith et al., then, present a hybrid approach between tenseness and length in which the former is underlying and the latter derived in the phonology. The special status of schwa is captured by the proviso that the principles in (4) apply to 'specified' vowels only. The invisibility of vowel length to stress is treated derivationally, by assuming that stress assignment applies before lengthening of tense vowels.

Van Oostendorp (1995, 2000) proposes a more radical version of the tense/lax approach. His claim is that length does not play a role in the phonology of Dutch at all.[6] Rather, length is taken to be a phonetic derivative of a phonological contrast that is represented by an underlying, monovalent feature [lax] (or [RTR]). Van Oostendorp expresses the correlation between lax vowels and their phonotactic distribution in terms of an Optimality-theoretic constraint, which we give here in a slightly simplified form:

(5) CONNECT(rhyme, [lax])

    A vowel is the head of a branching rhyme *iff* it has the feature [lax].

The constraint in (5) forces lax vowels to be heads of closed syllables and tense ones to be heads of open syllables. Such an analysis has two immediate advantages. First, it accounts for the distribution of schwa, which, like tense vowels, lacks [lax] and therefore must occur in open syllables. Second, since length is absent from the phonology, syllables containing tense vowels function as light, making Dutch a regular weight-sensitive language.

One objection that could be raised against (5) is that like Smith et al.'s approach, it establishes an arbitrary relation between a segmental property (viz. the feature [lax]) and a syllabic structure (viz. a branching rhyme). Van Oostendorp attempts to remedy this in two different ways. First, he argues

---

[5] However, Nooteboom (1971) shows that consonants following short vowels are significantly longer than those following long vowels (see also Ernestus 2000).

[6] Except in loan phonemes, i.e. the vowels which Smith et al. (1989: 135) call "French tense" (/iː, yː, uː/) and "French lax" (/ɛː, Yː, ɔː /).

that CONNECT(rhyme, [lax]) is a member of a more general family of constraints that links aperture features to prosodic complexity. For example, CONNECT constraints also regulate the phonotactics of schwa, which has no aperture features at all and so can occur in an extremely limited subset of syllable templates only (basically, CV syllables).[7] Second, Van Oostendorp argues that there are languages in which the relation between laxness and a branching rhyme holds independently. For example, in Eastern Javanese, all vowels in a word are RTR if the final syllable is closed, and are ATR otherwise. This suggests that in this language final syllables must satisfy CONNECT(rhyme, [lax]), with RTR spreading leftwards. Notice that an analysis of this pattern in terms of autosegmental length is much less straightforward, since bi-positionality cannot spread.

The most recent contribution to the debate is Gussenhoven (2009), who follows the main tenets of Van Oostendorp's approach, but argues that the presence of length in the (native) phonology of Dutch is independently required. One of Gussenhoven's arguments concerns the observation that high tense vowels undergo lengthening before /r/, except when this /r/ is part of a cluster (e.g. *vier* [viːr] 'four' vs. *wierp* [ʋirp] 'throw-SG-PAST').[8] We return to this issue below, in section 5. Gussenhoven further observes that all tense vowels are long when they occur in a stressed syllable, which he attributes to an Optimality-theoretic constraint STRESSTOWEIGHT. However, in Gussenhoven's approach, too, length is absent underlyingly, and so does not influence the stress system.

3 The tense/lax approach: two problems

In the preceding section, we have seen that there are good arguments for taking the underlying contrast in the Dutch vowel system to be one of quality rather than quantity, e.g. between a series of tense and lax vowels. However, while such an analysis seems in general to be preferable to a length-based analysis, we believe that it faces two problems. We examine these problems in this section, setting the stage for the alternative, syllabic approach that we present in section 4.

---

[7] Except in word-final position, where schwa can be followed by a single consonant. For discussion, see Kager & Zonneveld (1986) and Van Oostendorp (1995, 2000).

[8] Gussenhoven further observes that the [i] in *wierpen* [ʋirpən] 'throw-PL-PAST' is short, which suggests that the lengthening process is restricted to stems.

The first problem is one of duplication. In the tense/lax analyses of both Smith et al. and Van Oostendorp, the phonological properties of the lax vowels are stated twice: once at the level of segmental structure (in terms of the absence of a dependent |I|, or the presence of [lax]), and once at the level of syllabic structure (in terms of an obligatorily branching rhyme). This dual specification is not only unparsimonious, but also requires a relation between segmental and syllabic structure that is essentially arbitrary — recall (4b) and (5). Clearly, it would be preferable to state the contrast between tense and lax vowels just once.

The second problem facing a tense/lax account concerns the phonetic correlates of tenseness, which have so far proved elusive. Here the first question that should be asked is whether this is a serious problem. On the one hand, it is widely accepted that the features used to account for phonological phenomena must be grounded in phonetics (though see e.g. Hjelmslev 1953; Hale & Reiss 2008). On the other, the question of how tense and lax vowels should be defined phonetically is perhaps not a strictly phonological question, but one which concerns the phonetics–phonology interface. From this perspective, the main observation is that Dutch has two sets of vowels with phonologically distinct behaviour — something which holds irrespective of the phonetic exponence of these sets. Recent tense/lax approaches have tended to take a somewhat agnostic view on this issue, as is reflected by Van Oostendorp's (1995, 2000) use of the terms 'A' and 'B' vowels, for example. Nevertheless, it is clear that a tense/lax analysis of the Dutch vowel system would gain considerable support if the labels 'tense' and 'lax' could be shown to have consistent correlates. Convincing phonetic support for these labels has not been forthcoming, however.

Smith et al. and Van Oostendorp both implicate the tongue root in the phonetic feature definition of tenseness, in line with earlier studies on other, non-Germanic languages (see in particular Stewart 1967; Halle & Stevens 1967). Smith et al. (1989: 134) assume that dependent |I|, which specifies tense vowels, correlates with "pharyngeal expansion", i.e. tongue-root advancement (ATR). Van Oostendorp (1995: 43) represents lax vowels in terms of the feature [lax], which he notes has "a straightforward articulatory definition" in terms of tongue-root retraction, or RTR. However, closer inspection reveals that there are good grounds to be suspicious of these accounts. First of all, Dutch does not provide any consistent evidence for what is considered to be the main correlate of tongue-root advancement, viz. a lowered F_1. In a recent experiment in which the formant values (F_1, F_2) of tense and lax mid-vowel pairs were measured, /e, o/ were seen to have a lower F_1 than their lax congeners /ɪ, ɔ/, but the F_1 of lax /ʏ/ was higher than that of tense /ø/ (Botma et al. 2012). Cross-linguistic evidence also suggests that tenseness does not correlate with tongue-root advancement in any straightforward way. For example, MacKay (1977) shows that English tense vowels do not necessarily involve tongue-root advancement; on the basis of his data, the best that can be said is that tense vowels show tongue-root advancement compared to lax vowels with the same height and frontness. MacKay further observes that /o/ involves tongue-root retraction, despite patterning as tense. The relation between tongue-root advancement and tenseness is also tenuous in German, where /ɪ/ has a greater degree of tongue-root advancement than /i/ (Ladefoged & Maddieson 1996), even though /ɪ/ patterns as lax and /i/ as tense. More generally, Ladefoged & Maddieson observe that the nature of tongue-root advancement in English and German differs from that in West African languages like Akan and Igbo, for which [ATR] was originally proposed. Tongue-root position is a separately controlled variable in Akan and Igbo, which have ATR-harmony, but correlates with tongue height in English and German, leading Ladefoged & Maddieson to conclude that tenseness is not an independent parameter in vowel description.

It has also been proposed that the tense/lax contrast can be defined in terms of relative peripherality, with the lax vowels being more centralized than their tense congeners (e.g. Lindau 1979; Harris & Lindsey 1995; Botma et al. 2012). Such an account has been criticized on the grounds that it would make tenseness the only feature whose exponence is defined in relative terms (e.g. Lass 1984; Van Oostendorp 1995, 2000). However, as Botma et al. note, this does not seem to be a problem in the approach of Harris & Lindsey, where the representation of vowels includes a 'centrality' element that is more prominent in lax vowels than in tense ones, with relative prominence formalized in terms of dependency relations, in much the same way as in Smith et al.'s approach. Compare in this respect the mean formant frequencies (F_1, F_2) of the Dutch tense and lax vowels as measured by Van Nierop et al. (1973) and Pols et al. (1973), in (6). (Lax vowels are represented in boxes).

(6) The Dutch tense and lax vowels (adapted from Van Nierop et al. 1973 and Pols et al. 1973)

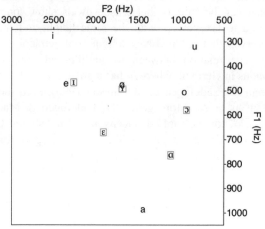

On the basis of (6), Botma et al. conjecture that the lax vowels are closer to the 'neutral position of the vocal tract' — a position which is characterized acoustically by the vowel space in the region of around 650Hz (F_1) and 1500Hz (F_2). They observe that this characterization corresponds reasonably well to part of the articulatory definition of tense vowels in Chomsky & Halle (1968: 324–325), as having "a greater deviation from the neutral or rest position of the vocal tract" (see Jakobson et al. 1952 for an acoustic definition). However, this account of the Dutch tense/lax contrast requires a more precise characterization of the notion of 'neutral position of the vocal tract'. Botma et al. do not discuss this issue, except to note that this position is unlikely to correlate with schwa.

These problems notwithstanding, it is worth noting that both approaches described above offer some potentially interesting insights. For example, an approach which equates laxness with [RTR] can attribute the lack of high lax vowels in Dutch to the marked feature combination [RTR, high] (Archangeli & Pulleyblank 1994; see also Van Oostendorp 1995, 2000). An approach which equates tenseness with relative peripherality, on the other hand, offers what seems to be a straightforward explanation for the predictable length of the non-high tense vowels: if such vowels involve a greater magnitude of their articulatory gestures, then their greater duration would follow from this. However, as there seems to be insufficient evidence for relative peripherality, and sufficient evidence against tongue-root involvement, we conclude that to date no consistent phonetic correlate of tenseness has been found.

In view of the problems noted above, we will suggest an alternative approach which by-passes the featural level altogether and encodes the relevant contrast exclusively at the syllabic level. We develop a preliminary outline of this approach in section 4.

4 A prosodic alternative: the return of the syllable cut

We believe that the problems noted in section 3 are avoided if we make the contrast between the two sets of vowels in the Dutch vowel system exclusively at the prosodic level. More specifically, we suggest that the difference between long/tense and short/lax vowels is made in terms of a branching vs. a non-branching rhyme structure. This is illustrated in (7) for the low vowels [aː] and [ɑ], in the words *ra* [raː] 'yard' (7a) and *ram* [rɑm] 'ram' (7b) respectively.

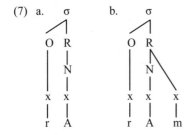

In (7a,b), 'A' denotes the set of features which the vowels in *ra* and *ram* have in common. These features, it will be noted, are identical, because the contrast between the vowels is not made at the segmental level, but at the level of the rhyme: (7a) has a non-branching rhyme while (7b) has a branching rhyme. We assume that the phonetic differences between long/tense [aː] and short/lax [ɑ] are the result of this structural difference. We will offer some speculations as to how structures of the kind in (7) are implemented by the phonetics in section 5.

Our account crucially relies on the assumption that the syllable rhyme is restricted to a maximum of two segments. More concretely, following Van Oostendorp (1995, 2000) we assume that consonants which cannot be syllabified under the rhyme occupy the onset position of a following empty-headed syllable. This is the case, for example, for /p/ in words like *raap* [raːp] 'turnip' (8a) and *ramp* [rɑmp] 'disaster' (8b):

(8) a.

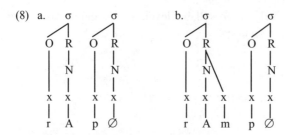

As was already intimated, the essence of this approach goes back to Sievers (1901), who distinguished between *stark geschnitten* and *swach geschnitten* syllables, and to Trubetzkoy's (1939) *Silbenschnittkorrelation*. Notice that an approach which allocates the phonological contrast at the syllabic level obviates the two problems observed in section 3. First, the contrast between the two sets of vowels is stated just once (at the level of the syllable rhyme), and so does not involve an ad hoc relation between segmental composition and syllabic structure. Second, since the contrast is not specified at the segmental level, no recourse is required to features whose phonetic exponence is unclear. Finally, notice that in a syllabic approach, just as in a tense/lax approach, the long/tense vowels are phonologically short, i.e. dominate just one *x*-position, which makes them light for the purposes of stress assignment.

5 Some implications of the syllabic approach

The decision to specify the contrast between long/tense and short/lax vowels at the level of the syllable rhyme raises a number of questions. The most important of these concern the implication that syllable structure is underlying, the status of schwa (which can occur in both open and closed syllables), and the question of how the structures we propose are implemented by the phonetics. Finally, we consider briefly how our approach can deal with Gussenhoven's arguments for recognizing phonologically relevant length.

First, the syllabic approach outlined in section 4 can be maintained only if syllable structure is posited as underlying. As such, our proposal is in line with the ideas put forward in Golston & Van der Hulst (1999), who claim that certain phonological features — stricture features, in their case — can be dispensed with if they are construed of instead as forming part of the phonological structure. Our proposal is also in line with ideas developed in Pöchtrager & Kaye (2010), who argue that a contrast which is realized as voicing phonetically (the |L| element of Government Phonology) can be formalized phonologically in terms of the presence or absence of prosodic positions.

Traditionally, the main argument against underlying syllable structure is that it is predictable from underlying precedence relations between segments. Golston & Van der Hulst point out that this argument can also be reversed: if syllable structure is underlying, then the linear order of segments can be derived from this. (For instance, if a complex onset consists of /p/ and /r/, then the order [pr] is predictable.) Golston & Van der Hulst also adduce various types of phonological evidence for underlying syllables. For example, they observe that lexical templates and word minimality requirements are often sensitive to syllable structure. In addition, they note that the presence of underlying syllables is well motivated on psycholinguistic grounds, among other things by tip-of-the-tongue phenomena.

A potential drawback of positing underlying syllable structure is that differences in syllabification never appear to be distinctive: there are no languages with minimal pairs such as /o.ma/ vs. /om.a/, for example. It is worth noting that this observation concerns onsets and not rhymes, and that it is a problem not just for our approach. As far as we know, all existing theories of syllable structure must stipulate that a consonant in a CVC sequence will, all things being equal, form a syllable with the following vowel. In our approach, a requirement is needed to the effect that underlying syllabic configurations are maintained, as otherwise the contrast between tense and lax vowels will be neutralized.

Another question that is raised by a syllabic approach concerns the status of schwa, which occurs in both open and closed syllables (e.g. *mode* /modə/ 'fashion', *moeder* /mudər/ 'mother'). This means that schwa is found in the structural configurations in in (9a,b), the final syllables of *mode* and *moeder* respectively.

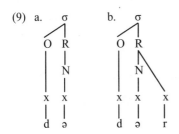

The fact that the phonetic implementation distinguishes between (7a) and (7b), i.e. between /rA/ and /rAm/, but not (apparently) between (9a) and (9b), is interesting, but not necessarily a strong argument against our approach. Indeed, it has often been suggested that schwa is a 'targetless' vowel (e.g.

Browman & Goldstein 1992), or that it lacks featural content (Van Oostendorp 1995, 2000; see also Koopmans-Van Beinum 1993). If so, it seems reasonable to assume that the phonetic implementation treats schwa different from other, specified vowels.

A more problematic observation is that Dutch schwa syllables cannot end in more than one non-coronal consonant — recall *arend* vs. **aremp*. This has been taken as an indication, e.g. by Zonneveld (1978), that schwa forms a natural class with the long/tense vowels, despite the fact that it is neither tense nor long. This is not the only possible conclusion, however. Given our assumptions about syllable structure, we can rephrase the ban on əCC sequences as a ban on sequences of a (closed) schwa-headed syllable and a following empty-headed syllable.[9] Similarly, the observation that tense vowels cannot be followed by two consonants can be rephrased as a ban on two consecutive empty-headed syllables — a restriction which figures prominently in the Government Phonology literature. We can generalize over these two observations as follows:

(10) Schwa-syllables and empty-headed syllables cannot be followed by an empty-headed syllable.

The generalization in (10) makes sense for the following reasons. First, if it is indeed the case that schwa lacks a feature specification, then we expect it to display similar behaviour as empty heads. A syllable headed by schwa differs minimally from one whose head is completely empty. This is illustrated in (11) for the second syllable of the words *tante* /tɑntə/ 'aunt' and *kant* /kɑnt/ 'lace' respectively. The schwa in (11a) has a root node (represented as 'RT') but lacks any further segmental specification, such as place or aperture features. The nucleus of the empty-headed syllable in (11b) lacks any segmental specification whatsoever:

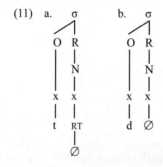

---

[9] Modulo coronal clusters, as in *arend*, which require a different analysis. We could assume, for example, that they are dominated directly by the Prosodic Word, similar to what is proposed in Van Oostendorp (2002).

A second argument for (10) concerns the observation that both schwa-headed and empty-headed syllables avoid stress. In fact, these syllables do not just resist stress, but require the immediately preceding syllable to be stressed. This suggests that both schwa-headed and empty-headed syllables prefer to be in the weak position of a foot (in Dutch, a trochee), which in turn suggests the following principle:

(12)   Syllables whose heads lack (sufficient) features appear in the weak position of a trochaic foot.

Since a trochaic foot has just one weak position, (10) follows from this as a lemma.

To conclude this section, we offer some speculative thoughts on how we envisage the phonetic implementation of the contrast between branching and non-branching rhymes. Let us suppose first of all that rhymes — which in our approach are limited to a maximum of two x-positions — have a roughly fixed duration.[10] (This may be true for stressed vowels in particular.) If this is the case, then we may expect vowels in non-branching rhymes to be longer than those in branching ones; the latter contain two segments, which must be squeezed in the same temporal domain as a single segment in a non-branching rhyme. We might further conjecture that the 'tenseness' of vowels in non-branching rhymes is an automatic consequence of their greater length, which permits a greater magnitude of the vowels' articulatory gestures. However, in the absence of compelling phonetic support for 'tenseness', such an account remains highly tentative — and it is in any case not strictly required in our approach.

Finally, let us briefly return to Gussenhoven's reasons for representing length in the (native) Dutch vowel system. As was already noted in section 2, one reason concerned the observation that stressed vowels are phonetically long. This argument does not strike us as very compelling, however. If the length of stressed vowels is predictable, then it would seem reasonable to attribute this to the phonetic implementation, in much the same way as we suggest for the comparatively greater length of vowels in non-branching rhymes.

We also believe that there is some reason to be skeptical of Gussenhoven's second argument, viz. the observation that high vowels lengthen before stem-final /r/ (as in *vier* [viːr] 'four'). Lengthening of vowels before /r/ is not limited to high vowels but affects all vowels (e.g. 't Hart 1969; Collins & Mees 1999). In addition, depending on the type of /r/ allophone involved, the

---

[10] We could refer to this as 'rhyme-timing', on analogy with the notions of 'stress-timing' and 'syllable-timing' from Pike (1945) — though whether there is empirical evidence for rhyme-timing is an open question.

effect on the preceding vowel may be characterized as lengthening, or as a kind of diphthongization (or breaking). The latter effect appears to be typical for speakers who have a 'bunched' approximant /r/, a realization that is increasingly found in modern Standard Dutch (e.g. Van Bezooijen 2005). It seems to us that the greater length of the preceding vowel can in such cases be attributed to the transition from the (pre-)dorsal gestures of the high vowel to the gestures of /r/, in line with the Articulatory Phonology approach in Gick & Wilson (2006). The data in Scobbie & Sebregts (2011) show that bunched /r/ in Dutch is consistently characterized by pharyngeal constriction, effected by retraction of the tongue root. This suggests that if pre-/r/ breaking is accounted for in terms of a constraint, a feasible candidate would be a markedness constraint that militates against the combination of [RTR] and [high] — the same constraint that was mooted in section 3 to account for the absence of lax high vowels. (See also Hall & Hamann 2010 for an articulatory account of the dispreference of sequences of /r/ and a high front vocoid.)

If it is indeed the case, as Gussenhoven claims, that high vowels are lengthened before /r/ (and more so than non-high vowels), then pre-/r/ lengthening apparently suspends the marginal contrast between short and long high vowels found in pairs like *kiem* /kim/ vs. (non-native) *team* /tiːm/. In our approach, a form like *vier* would then consist of an initial open syllable with a long vowel, with the /r/ forming part of a following empty-headed syllable. This analysis ties in rather well with Lavoie & Cohn's (1999) observation that English words such as *feel* and *fail* (and in rhotic varieties, *fear* and *fire*) are perceived by speakers as being somewhere between one and two syllables, in particular when the liquid is 'dark', i.e. vocalized. Botma et al. (2008) offer a Government Phonology account of such forms in which dark liquids occupy the rhymal adjunct position of the second, empty-headed syllable. Such a representation also seems feasible for words like *vier*, as in (13).

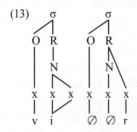

In realizations such as [viːər] and [viːjər], the syllabic positions between the vowel and /r/ are filled with transitional, non-distinctive material.

If the claim that length is absent from the phonology is to be maintained, then the lengthening of high vowels before /r/ must be a property of surface representations. This suggests that the syllabification in (13) is enforced by a constraint such as in (14).

(14)   No high vowel in a syllable closed by /r/.

The motivation for this constraint is likely to be the articulatory conflict between high vowels and bunched/RTR [r], as outlined above. Notice also that (14) seems to be violable, since it does not appear to be satisfied in exceptional forms such as *wierp* 'throw-SG-PAST'. Following Gussenhoven, we may assume that this decision is made at the stem level, and that later levels of the phonology respect the length established there. This would also account for the short vowel in the form *wierpen* 'throw-PL-PAST'.

6 Conclusion

Are we going round in circles? Do phonologists merely write papers every twenty-odd years to solve old problems with old analyses? As we have seen, it has been recognized for quite some time that Dutch has two sets of vowels which differ from each other in length, tenseness, and syllable structure. Each of these three properties has at some point been argued to be central, basic, or 'underlying'. The analysis we offer in this paper can in some sense be seen as going back to one of the earliest analyses, Sievers' and Trubetzkoy's distinction in terms of two types of syllables.

However, we believe that there is no reason for pessimism, as the circles seem to us to be spiralling inwards. Just as Smith et al.'s proposal made use of the insights of length theory, ours builds on the insights of both the length and the tense/lax approach. The optimal theory may ultimately be one in which we can plausibly say that length, tenseness, and syllable structure comprise the same formal object. In fact, our speculations on the phonetic implementation of branching and non-branching rhymes already hint in this direction: a vowel in an open syllable has more 'space' and so a more 'pronounced' articulation, which is manifested phonetically by a greater length and tenseness. We believe that phonological theory is advancing in the right direction, and are confident that it will have made even more progress 23 years on.

References

Archangeli, Diana & Douglas Pulleyblank (1994): *Grounded Phonology.* – Cambridge, MA: MIT Press.

Booij, Geert (1995): *The Phonology of Dutch.* – Oxford: Oxford University Press.

Botma, Bert, Colin J. Ewen & Erik Jan van der Torre (2008): "The syllabification of postvocalic liquids: an onset specifier approach." – In: *Lingua* 118, 1250–1270.

Botma, Bert, Koen Sebregts & Dick Smakman (2012): "The phonetics and phonology of Dutch mid vowels before /l/." To appear in *Journal of Laboratory Phonology* 3(2).

Browman, Catherine P. & Louis Goldstein (1992): "Articulatory phonology: an overview." – In: *Phonetica* 49, 155–180.

Chomsky, Noam & Morris Halle (1968): *The Sound Pattern of English.* – New York: Harper and Row.

Cohen, Antonie (1952): *The Phonemes of English: A Phonemic Study of the Vowels and Consonants of Standard English.* – The Hague: Martinus Nijhoff.

Cohen, Antonie, C.L. Ebeling, K. Fokkema & A.G.F. van Holk (1959): *Fonologie van het Nederlands en het Fries.* – Den Haag: Martinus Nijhoff.

Lavoie, Lisa & Abigail Cohn (1999): "Sesquisyllables of English: the structure of vowel-liquid syllables." – In: Ohala, John J., Yoko Hasegawa, Manjari Ohala, Daniel Granville & Ashlee C. Bailey (eds.): *Proceedings of the 14th International Congress of Phonetic Sciences.* Vol. 1, 109–112. University of California, Berkeley.

Collins, Beverley & Inger M. Mees (1999): *The Phonetics of English and Dutch* (4th edn.). – Leiden: Brill.

De Groot, Albert W. (1931): "De wetten der phonologie en hun betekenis voor de studie van het Nederlands." – In: *Nieuwe Taalgids* 25, 225–239.

De Rijk, Rudolf (1967): "Apropos of the Dutch vowel system." Ms., MIT (electronic edition at http://dbnl.nl/tekst/rijk004apro01_01/).

Durand, Jacques (2005): "Tense/lax and the vowel system of English." – In: Carr, Philip, Jacques Durand & Colin J. Ewen (eds.): *Headhood, Elements, Specification and Contrastivity,* 77–97. Amsterdam/Philadelphia: John Benjamins.

Ernestus, Mirjam (2000): *Voice Assimilation and Segment Reduction in Casual Dutch. A Corpus-based Study of the Phonology-Phonetics Interface.* PhD dissertation, Free University Amsterdam. – Utrecht: LOT.

Fikkert, Paula (1994): *The Acquisition of Prosodic Structure.* PhD dissertation, Leiden University. – The Hague: Holland Academic Graphics.

Gick, Bryan & Ian Wilson (2006): "Excrescent schwa and vowel laxing: cross-linguistic responses to conflicting articulatory targets." – In: Goldstein, Louis, Doug H. Whalen & Catherine T. Best (eds.): *Papers in Laboratory Phonology 8: Varieties of Phonological Competence,* 635–659. Berlin/New York: Mouton de Gruyter.

Goldsmith, John (1976): *Autosegmental Phonology.* PhD dissertation, MIT.

Golston, Chris & Harry van der Hulst (1999): "Stricture is structure." – In: Hermans, Ben & Marc van Oostendorp (eds.): *The Derivational Residue*, 153–174. Amsterdam/Philadelphia: John Benjamins.

Gussenhoven, Carlos (2009): "Vowel duration, syllable quantity, and stress in Dutch." – In: Hanson, Kristin & Sharon Inkelas (eds.): *The Nature of the Word. Essays in Honor of Paul Kiparsky*, 181–198. Cambridge, MA: MIT Press.

Hale, Mark & Charles Reiss (2008): *The Phonological Enterprise*. – Oxford: Oxford University Press.

Hall, T.A. & Silke Hamann (2010): "On the cross-linguistic avoidance of rhotic plus high front vocoid sequences." – In: *Lingua* 120, 1821–1840.

Halle, Morris & Kenneth N. Stevens (1967): "On the feature 'advanced tongue root'". – In: *Quarterly Progress Report* 94, 209–215. Cambridge, MA: Research Laboratory of Electronics.

Harris, John & Geoff Lindsey (1995): "The elements of phonological representation." – In: Durand, Jacques & Francis Katamba (eds.): *Frontiers in Phonology: Atoms, Structures, Derivations*, 34–79. London/New York: Longman.

Hermans, Ben (1992): "On the representation of quasi-long vowels in Dutch and Limburgian." – In: Bok-Bennema, Reineke & Roeland van Hout (eds.): *Linguistics in the Netherlands 1992*, 75–86. Amsterdam: John Benjamins.

Hjelmslev, Louis (1953): *Prolegomena to a Theory of Language* (IJAL Memoir 7). – Baltimore: Indiana University Publications in Anthropology and Linguistics.

Jakobson, Roman, C. Gunnar M. Fant & Morris Halle (1952): *Preliminaries to Speech Analysis*. – Cambridge, MA: MIT Press.

Kager, René (1989): *A Metrical Theory of Stress and Destressing in Dutch and English*. – Dordrecht: Foris.

Kager, René & Wim Zonneveld (1986): "Schwa, syllables and extrametricality in Dutch." – In: *The Linguistic Review* 5, 197–221.

Kooij, Jan & Marc van Oostendorp (2003): *Fonologie. Uitnodiging tot de Klankleer van het Nederlands*. – Amsterdam: Amsterdam University Press.

Koopmans-van Beinum, Florina J. (1993): "What's in a schwa?" – In: *IFA Proceedings 1992*, 53–62.

Ladefoged, Peter & Ian Maddieson (1996): *The Sounds of the World's Languages*. – Oxford: Blackwell.

Lass, Roger (1984): *Phonology*. – Cambridge: Cambridge University Press.

Lindau, Mona (1979): "The feature Expanded." – In: *Journal of Phonetics* 7, 163–167.

MacKay, Ian (1977): "Tenseness in vowels: an ultrasonic study." – In: *Phonetica* 34, 325–352.

Moulton, William G. (1962): "The vowels of Dutch: phonetic and distributional classes." – In: *Lingua* 11, 294–312.

Nooteboom, S.G. (1972): *Production and Perception of Vowel Duration. A Study of Durational Properties of Vowels in Dutch*. – PhD dissertation, Utrecht University.

Paradis, Carole & Jean-François Prunet (eds.) (1991): *The Special Status of Coronals*. – San Diego: Academic Press.

Pike, Kenneth (1945): *The Intonation of American English*. – Ann Arbor: University of Michigan Press.

Polgárdi, Krisztina (2008): "The representation of lax vowels in Dutch: a loose CV approach." – In: *Lingua* 118, 1375–1392.

Pols, Louis C.W., Herman R.C. Tromp & Reinier Plomp (1973): "Frequency analysis of Dutch vowels from 50 male speakers." – In: *Journal of the Acoustical Society of America* 53, 1093–1101.

Pöchtrager, Markus & Jonathan Kaye (2010): "GP 2.0." – Ms., Boğaziçi Üniversitesi, Istanbul.

Rietveld, A.C.M. & Vincent J. van Heuven (1997): *Algemene Fonetiek.* – Bussum: Coutinho.

Scobbie, James M. & Koen Sebregts (2011): "Acoustic, articulatory, and phonological perspectives on allophonic variation of /r/ in Dutch." – In: Folli, Raffaela & Christiane Ulbrich (eds.): *Interfaces in Linguistics: New Research Perspectives*, 257– 277. Oxford: Oxford University Press.

Sievers, Eduard (1901): *Grundzüge der Phonetik.* – Wiesbaden: Breitkopf und Kärtel.

Smith, Norval S.H., Roberto Bolognesi, Frank van der Leeuw, Jean Rutten & Heleen de Wit (1989): "Apropos of the Dutch vowel system 21 years on." – In: Bennis, Hans & Ans van Kemenade (eds.): *Linguistics in the Netherlands 1989*, 133–142. Dordrecht: Foris.

Stewart, John (1967): "Tongue-root position in Akan vowel harmony." – In: *Phonetica* 16, 185–204.

't Hart, Johan (1969): "Fonetische steunpunten." – In: *De Nieuwe Taalgids* 62, 168– 174.

Trommelen, Mieke & Wim Zonneveld (1989): "Stress, diphthongs, *r* in Dutch." – In: Bennis, Hans & Ans van Kemenade (eds.): *Linguistics in the Netherlands 1989*, 143–152. Dordrecht: Foris.

Trubetzkoy, Nikolaj S. (1939): *Grundzüge der Phonologie.* – Prague: Jednota Československých Matematiků a Fysiků.

Van Bezooijen, Renée (2005): "Approximant /r/ in Dutch: routes and feelings." – In: *Speech Communication* 47, 15–31.

Van der Hulst, Harry (1984): *Syllable Structure ůShosuke Haraguchi on the Occasion of his Sixtieth Birthday*, 313–343. Tokyo: Kaitakusha.

Van Helten, Willem L. (1887): *Middelnederlandsche Spraakkunst.* – Groningen.

Van Nierop, Dick J.P.J., Louis C.W. Pols & Reinier Plomp (1973): "Frequency analysis of Dutch vowels from 25 female speakers." – In: *Acustica* 29, 110–118.

Van Oostendorp, Marc (1995): *Vowel Quality and Syllable Projection.* – PhD dissertation, Tilburg University.

– (2000): *Phonological Projection.* – Tübingen: Niemeyer.

– (2002): "The phonological and morphological status of the Prosodic Word adjunct." – In: *Linguistische Berichte* 11, 209–235.

Verdam, J. (1923): *Uit de Geschiedenis der Nederlandsche Taal.* – Zutphen: Thieme.

Zonneveld, Wim (1978): *A Formal Theory of Exceptions in Generative Phonology.* – Lisse: Peter de Ridder Press.

Harry van der Hulst

A minimal framework for vowel harmony

1 Introduction

In this article, I will discuss the bare minimum of theory needed to account for vowel harmony patterns.[1] The proposed model, 'Radical cv Phonology' (RcvP), finds its origin in the framework of Dependency Phonology (Anderson & Ewen 1987; DP) and shares three fundamental aspects with this framework:

(1) a. Phonological primes are unary ('monovalent') elements
    b. Elements, when combined, enter into head–dependency relations
    c. Elements are grouped into units ('gestures')

The details of my theory differ from those in Anderson & Ewen in a number of respects. First, RcvP uses a smaller set of elements, grouped in a slightly different set of gestures. The idea of gestures is similar to that of 'class nodes' as used in Feature Geometry (see Clements 1985; Sagey 1986). Second, I adopt certain ideas that were first presented in the Government Phonology (GP) approach of Kaye et al. (1985), who offer a theory of segmental structure which shares important insights with DP, notably regarding (1a,b). The present approach shares with Kaye et al. a notational system in which elements are represented on 'lines' (which are similar to the 'autosegmental tiers' of Goldsmith 1976), as well as the idea that vowel harmony is the result of a lateral licensing relation between syllable heads, as suggested in Dienes (1997) and Ritter (1999).

Another important aspect of my approach is the adoption of Trubetzkoy's (1939) notion of 'morphophoneme' (or 'morphoneme'), which involves a disjunctive representation of alternants. For example, in Finnish, the vowels /u/ and /y/ alternate as the result of palatal harmony. I will represent the alternating vowels as |U(I)|, and adopt the convention that the element |I| can be phonetically interpreted if and only if it is laterally licensed by a local and

---

[1] For an extensive discussion of the general model within which the present discussion is couched, see Van der Hulst (2005, 2012a). This paper is a direct continuation of the work on vowel harmony that Norval Smith and I carried out in the 1980s and 1990s — a long and fruitful period of collaboration, which we can hopefully pick up and continue in the coming years.

non-variable (i.e. licensed) instance of another element |I|.[2] Thus, the present approach does *not* view vowel harmony as a feature filling or feature copying procedure.[3] In Trubetzkoy's view, 'archisegmental' representations capture instances of automatic, exceptionless neutralization, i.e. cases where a potential contrast is altogether absent from the phoneme inventory (paradigmatic neutralization), and cases where a potential contrast is absent in a particular position (syntagmatic neutralization). Morphophonemes, on the other hand, capture alternations that are subject to lexical irregularity. Although it is not necessarily the case that instances of vowel harmony display lexical irregularity (i.e. that they are 'lexical' in the sense of Kiparsky 1981, 1985), this seems to be the typical situation. We will see that the model proposed here can predict whether neutral vowels behave as *transparent* or *opaque* to the harmony process, following the original insight of Van der Hulst & Smith (1986). In addition, in a morphophonemic approach there is no need to invoke underspecification (or non-specification) for the purpose of representing vowel harmony, nor do we need recourse to Van der Hulst & Smith's *ad hoc* idea of 'segmental brackets' to deal with disharmonic roots.

The structure of this paper is as follows. In section 2, I will explain the basic ideas of the RcvP approach, with special reference to vowel structures. In sections 3 and 4, I make some remarks about the phonetic interpretation of elements and underspecification of phonological structures. I also illustrate the constraints that govern these structures. Section 5 discusses (and rejects) a proposal to use the presence (vs. the absence) of head-marking contrastively. In section 6, I apply the RcvP model to vowel harmony, using data from Finnish vowel harmony to illustrate the model. Section 7 deals with transparency and opacity, and defends the idea that these two types of behaviour of non-harmonic vowels can be predicted. I further discuss some potential counterexamples and problems for the model proposed here, and some possible ways to resolve these.

2 Gestures, elements and headedness

In RcvP, each segment has a tripartite structure consisting of a Laryngeal, Manner and Place gesture, as in (2). Within each gesture, we find precisely two elements.

---

[2] As in Dependency Phonology, elements are placed between vertical lines.
[3] My approach resembles the 'activation model' of Backley & Takahashi (1996), which is discussed in Van der Hulst (2012b).

(2)

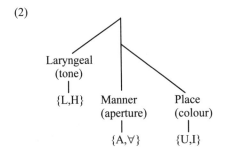

Laryngeal
(tone)
|
{L,H}   Manner   Place
        (aperture) (colour)
         | |
        {A,∀}   {U,I}

In this paper, I focus on vocalic structures and ignore the 'tonal' elements |L| and |H| (for discussion of these, see Van der Hulst 2005, 2012a). The six elements in (2) can in fact be replaced by just two, viz. |C| and |V|, as in (3) (hence the name *Radical* cv Phonology).

(3)   Elements   RcvP coding

Manner	A	∀	V	C
Place	U	I	V	C
Laryngeal	L	H	V	C

This reduction is possible because each gesture contains exactly two elements. This allows us to say that the element labels |A|, |U| and |L|, because they occur under different gestures, are paradigmatically speaking in complementary distribution, and so can be reduced to one and the same element, viz. |V|. The same holds for |∀|, |I| and |H|, which can be reduced to |C|. Complementary distribution is a familiar criterion that is used to reduce allophones to phonemes (where allophones are in complementary distribution in a syntagmatic sense). However, the same criterion can be applied to elements, provided that the elements that we reduce to |C| or |V| have something in common. In RcvP, the claim is that in each gesture |A|, |U| and |L| represent vowel- or rhyme-oriented choices (and so reduce to |V|) while |∀|, |I| and |H| represent consonant- or onset-oriented choices (and so reduce to |C|). However, for practical purposes I will here use the element labels |A, U, L, ∀, I, H| in this paper, so as to avoid cumbersome expressions such as '|Place: V|' (instead of '|A|').

It is important to note that |V| and |C| can occur in both onset and rhyme positions. For example, in the manner gesture, |A| is a vowel-oriented element because it is preferred in the syllable nucleus (i.e. the head of the rhyme), and because it denotes maximal openness and sonority. On the other hand, |∀| is a consonant-oriented element because it is preferred in the syllable onset, and because it denotes closure and hence minimal sonority. In vowels, |A| denotes [open] or [low], and |∀| [closed] or [high] (and [ATR]; cf. below). In (obstruent) consonants, |A| and |∀| denote [fricative] and [stop], respectively.[4] For the place and laryngeal gestures we see the same difference, with |U| and |L| representing vowel-oriented choices and |I| and |H| consonant-oriented ones. Reasons of space preclude a more detailed discussion of the interpretation of elements; for this, see Van der Hulst (2012a). However, it should be stressed that two opposing elements cannot be viewed as two *values* of a single feature, e.g. '[+open]' (for |A|) and '[−open]' (for |∀|). The reason for this, as we will see, is that in RcvP two opposing elements can be combined within a single gesture. This is impossible for two values of a binary feature, as this would entail a contradiction.

It seems reasonable to assume that the elements |I| and |U| are relevant in the representation of both vowels and consonants (as in Anderson & Ewen 1987, and, with a different set of feature labels, in Clements 1991), with |I| denoting 'coronal/front' and |U| 'labial/round'. What is perhaps less clear is that the same is true for the laryngeal elements |L| and |H|. In the spirit of Halle & Stevens (1971), I propose that |L| and |H| denote phonation distinctions in consonants (voiced, voiceless, etc.) and (primarily) tonal distinctions in vowels; see Van der Hulst (2012a) for further details. The idea that there is, in addition to this, a set of primes denoting manner in consonants *and* aperture in vowels is, I believe, unique to RcvP. The upshot is that RcvP does not have any elements which are exclusive to either consonants or vowels, in line with the program of Jakobson et al. (1952).

In the remainder of this paper I will limit my attention to vowel structures, ignoring the elements |L| and |H|. Of the remaining four elements, three are the place elements |A, I, U|, familiar from DP and GP. In addition to these, I assume a fourth element, viz. |∀|. Notice that a fourth element is also assumed in both DP (the 'schwa' element) and GP (the 'cold vowel' or ATR element; cf. Kaye et al. 1985, 1990). Both these elements are similar to |∀|.[5]

Gestures may contain a single element or a combination of elements. In the latter case, the elements enter into a head–dependency relation, such that

---

[4] The labels between square brackets represent phonetic properties that correspond to the phonological elements. I have used articulatory properties here, but elements obviously also have corresponding acoustic properties. I will remain neutral as to which of these two types of properties should be regarded as more basic.

[5] Later versions of GP have abandoned a fourth element in the description of vowels (see e.g. Kaye 2001). The removal of the ATR element has come with a price, in that the notion of headedness has been extended in such a way that the presence (vs. the absence) of headedness is a distinctive option. See Van der Hulst (2012a) for detailed discussion and criticism of this idea (see also section 5).

one element is the head and the other the dependent.[6] As was suggested in (1), I assume that variable dependency relations hold *within* gestures. This means for example that within Manner either |A| or |∀| can be the head if both elements are combined. It would seem that dependency relations *between* the gestures themselves are universally fixed, with Manner being the head. In this respect, RcvP departs from standard DP and arguably offers a more restrictive approach to segment-internal structure. For arguments in favour of the general dependency relation in (1), see Van der Hulst (2005, 2012a).[7]

Headedness can be represented in a number of ways. DP uses representations of the kind in (4a), where a head, when combined with a dependent, graphically dominates it. Other notations have also been used, such as a difference in linear order (head first, dependent second) or capitalization. In this paper I will represent heads by means of underlining (which is common in GP), as in (4b):

(4) a. X   X   Y   Y
         | |
         Y   X

    b. X̲   X̲Y   Y̲X   Y̲   (or X̲   YX̲   XY̲   Y̲)[8]

    c. X̲[X] X̲Y   Y̲X   Y̲[Y]

The structures in (4c) show that a head, when it occurs without a dependent, can be interpreted *as if* it has itself as a dependent. Such predictable dependents will not be indicated. Their virtual presence can be viewed as the result of a 'universal redundancy rule' X ⇒ X, which leads to 'enhancement' (in the sense of Stevens & Keyser 1989) of the head. I will refer to the four structures in (4a-c) as 'basic structures' (regardless of the way headedness is represented), while 'bare' X and Y will be called 'simple structures'.

Following Kaye et al. (1985), I assume that an element in dependent position corresponds to a single phonetic attribute while an element in head position (without an accompanying dependent) denotes a complete segment

---

[6] Schane (1984), who also uses unary elements, does not use head–dependency relations. Instead, he assumes the possibility of multiple occurrences of elements, e.g. for representing different degrees of aperture.

[7] For related work that is also based on the notion of dependency and unary elements, see Smith (2000) and Botma (2004).

[8] Underlining is critical in combinations, since here it must be made explicit which element is the head. Strictly speaking, an element which occurs without a dependent is always a head, so that here underlining could be considered redundant (and will in fact be omitted below); I return to this issue in section 4.

— an idea that is also implicit in DP.[9] For example, in isolation, the head element |U| denotes back rounded /u/, while dependent |U| denotes labiality (i.e. rounding), as in /y/.[10] If the element |U| occurs with a dependent |I|, the result is a 'fronted /u/', i.e. a kind of 'central' rounded vowel. I will return to the interpretation of such structures shortly.

The idea of having different (but related) phonetic interpretations for elements is referred to as the 'dual interpretation' of elements (cf. Van der Hulst 1988a). Consider for example (5):

(5) The dual interpretation of |A| and |∀|

	Head	Dependent
A	/a/	'low (or retracted)'
∀	/i/	'high' (or rather ATR; cf. below)

Combinations of |A| and |∀| denote intermediate aperture degrees and correspond to intermediate central vowels, as in (6):

(6) A A∀ ∀A ∀

 /a/ /ɜ/ /ə/ /ɨ/ (central)
   /ʌ/ /ɤ/ /ɯ/ (back unrounded)

In the case of a three-way distinction in aperture there is a choice of IPA symbols, provided we make the (not uncommon) assumption that languages never employ a phonological contrast between central and back unrounded vowels.

---

[9] The (implicit) assumption in DP is that the dependent interpretation differs from the head interpretation. One specific interpretation of this idea is offered in Van der Hulst (1988a), where it was proposed that the dependent interpretation of |I| is ATR. This proposal is not adopted in the present model, which is closer to standard DP and to Kaye et al. (1985). More specifically, the C/V coding of elements used here is reminiscent of the 'charm values' used by Kaye et al., an idea which was subsequently abandoned in GP. Kaye et al. derive the dual interpretation of elements by interpreting a head as a full matrix of phonetic properties (corresponding to the traditional binary features), while dependents add 'hot' features only. This idea, too, was abandoned. For a more detailed discussion of these issues, see Van der Hulst (2012a).

[10] For ease of exposition I refer to phonemic entities (hence the use of slant lines), although it is important to bear in mind that IPA symbols represent approximate phonetic values. A notation such as /u/ is shorthand for the corresponding elemental structure, which represents a cognitive phonological entity that plays a contrastive role in a particular language.

All vowels considered so far are 'manner-only' or 'colourless' vowels. Let us therefore now consider the 'colour' elements, viz. |U| and |I|. These have the dual interpretations in (7):

(7)   Interpretation of |U| and |I|

	Head	Dependent
U	/u/	'round'
I	/i/	'front'

Adopting the 'autosegmental line-notation' of Kaye et al. (1985) yields the following representations for the four front unrounded vowels (headedness is indicated by means of underlining):

(8)   /æ/   /ɛ/   /e/   /i/
              ∀   ∀̲   ∀
       A   A̲   A
       I   I   I   I

A convenient 'flat' notation for e.g. /e/ would be $\{\underline{\forall}AI\}$.[11]

The next question that must be addressed concerns the interpretation of combinations of |U| and |I|. Consider (9), where |U| and |I| are combined with the aperture element |∀|:

(9)   /u/   /ʉ/   /y/   /i/
       ∀   ∀   ∀   ∀
       U   U̲   U   I
             I   I̲

Both Anderson & Ewen (1987) and Kaye et al. (1985) stipulate that there is no difference between |U̲I| and |UI̲|, which both yield a rounded front vowel.[12] However, I assume that these combinations in fact denote two distinct vowels, which are sometimes referred to as 'outrounded' /y/, i.e. a rounded front vowel', and 'inrounded' /ʉ/, a fronted back-round vowel. These vowels are sometimes contrastive, for example in Swedish.

Cross-classifying aperture and colour, and allowing for both colourless and mannerless vowels, yields 25 different vowels, given in (10):

---

[11] Further bracketing could be added for clarity, i.e. $\{(\underline{\forall}A)(I)\}$. This would be required in the corresponding RcvP notation , where {CVC} would be ambiguous between {(CV)(C)} and {(C)(VC)}.

[12] Kaye et al. attempt to derive this using an elegant 'fusion calculus', but this idea was later abandoned (see Kaye 2000).

(10)   I   IU   Colourless   U̠I   U

	I	IU	Colourless	U̠I	U
∀	i	ʏ	ɨ ~ ɯ	ʉ	u
Mannerless	ɪ	ʏ	ə (~ schwa)		ʊ
∀̠A	e	ø	ɘ ~ ɤ ~ ɐ	θ	o
A∀̠	ɛ	œ	ɜ ~ ʌ	ɞ	ɔ
A	æ	ɶ	a ~ ɑ		ɒ

Note in (10) that headedness is specified for each gesture separately.

It is interesting to compare the chart in (10) to the IPA chart for vowels, in (11):

(11)

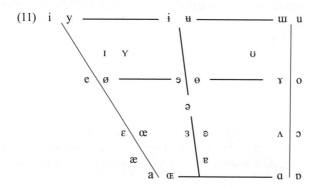

Clearly, the goal of a phonological theory should not be to characterize each and every IPA symbol in terms of a unique element structure. What matters is rather which sound types can occur contrastively in languages. Thus, by lumping different phonetic symbols in one cell, I make the claim that these vowels cannot occur contrastively in any language. Another possible mismatch between the phonology and the IPA is that certain IPA-symbols might correspond to different phonological structures in different languages.

A couple of comments are in order regarding the relation between (10) and (11). First, the IPA chart represents /a/ as front and /æ/ as slightly higher, while in my approach /a/ is analyzed as colourless, with /æ/ being its front counterpart, as in (8). Second, /ə/, i.e. schwa, is represented as a vowel that has neither colour nor aperture. (The symbol /ə/ is sometimes also used to represent the ATR counterpart of the low vowel; I will use the symbol /ɐ/ for this.). As can be seen in (10), schwa is not the only mannerless vowel; in particular, high RTR vowels are also treated as mannerless. This suggests that the presence (vs. the absence) of a head |∀| encodes the ATR distinction among high and low vowels, while among mid vowels this distinction depends on whether ∀ is a head or dependent.

3 The phonetic interpretation of elements

The two elements occupying each gesture are phonological concepts that cover an infinite array of phonetic distinctions within a certain phonetic space. Thus, in the aperture space, |A| groups together an infinite set of aperture degrees, ranging from maximally open to more closed articulations, while |∀| groups articulations ranging from the most close to more open configurations. Somewhere 'in the middle' there is a critical point which divides the two categories, and aperture degrees that straddle this dividing line might be closer to each other than apertures that push the boundaries of a single category. It is well-known from the literature on categorical perception that humans (as well as other animals) have the ability to categorize perceptual spaces into two distinct categories along the lines described here. In this sense we can say that the two elements within each gesture divide a phonetic space into two categories, as in (12):

(12)   aperture

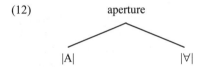

If divisions of the perceptual space are recursive, (12) can be further divided as in (13):

(13)   a.   Manner

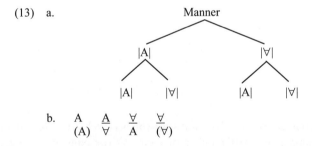

b.   A   A   ∀   ∀
      (A)   ∀   A   (∀)

Van der Hulst (2005: 195) shows that (13a) and (13b) can be seen as notational variants of the same idea.[13]

If the phonetic space is construed of as multidimensional, then each split arguably correlates with some fixed phonetic dimension. For example, in the case of vowel manner it could be argued that the manner space results from

---

[13] The 'nested subregister model' of Salting (2005) also represents phonological categories in terms of a double split. Salting applies this model to vowel height and place categories, and discusses the parallels between his model and RcvP.

both jaw aperture and from tongue root position. This raises the question
whether the phonological representation in (13a) correlates with the phonetic
interpretation in (14a) or in (14b):

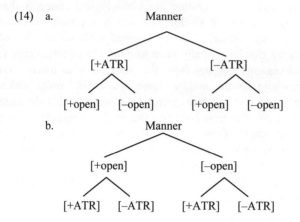

(14) a.   Manner

          [+ATR]   [−ATR]

    [+open]   [−open]   [+open]   [−open]

      b.   Manner

          [+open]   [−open]

    [+ATR]   [−ATR]   [+ATR]   [−ATR]

Work in RcvP has thus far assumed that the aperture division is more 'basic'
than the ATR division. Following Dresher (2009), it might be suggested that
the choice between these two phonetic interpretations of the double
categorical split is language-dependent, however. The potential consequences
of this kind of variability are discussed in Van der Hulst (2012a), as are the
correlations between RcvP and Dresher's model.

4 Underspecification and intrasegmental phonotactic constraints

4.1 Underspecification

In this section, I consider some of the ways in which vowel structures *could*
be represented using a minimal number of elements (or equivalent units)
combined with head–dependency relations. In particular, I will argue against
the use of underspecification in RcvP representations. This sets the stage for
the discussion of vowel harmony in sections 5 and 6, where we will see that
underspecified representations are not helpful in accounting for vowel
harmony patterns.

Generally speaking, there are two grounds for underspecification. First,
predictable specifications can be left out of the structural description of
sounds; let us call this 'non-contrastive underspecification'. Second, in any
system of opposing units, it is logically possible to replace one member in the

opposition by zero, thus replacing a contrast between A and B by A and $\varnothing$ (or $\varnothing$ and B). Let us call this 'contrastive underspecification' (for this term, see also Steriade 1995). (15) fleshes out both arguments in relation to RcvP.

(15) Grounds for underspecification

    a. Non-contrastive underspecification:

       i. Non-distinctive elements need not be specified
      ii. Non-distinctive headedness need not be specified
     iii. Headedness need not be specified if there is only one element in a gesture

    b. Contrastive underspecification:

       i. In each gesture, one element can be designated as the default option (and so be left unspecified)
      ii. If headedness among two elements is contrastive, the headedness specification of one of the two combinations can be left unspecified (i.e. the default option)

Note that (15aiii) was assumed in e.g. (6) (cf. also fn. 8). The type of underspecification in (15b) has been called 'radical underspecification' in Archangeli (1984) (see also Kiparsky 1985).[14] The idea of contrastive (or radical) underspecification is perhaps crucial in a traditional binary feature model, where it essentially encodes the monovalency hypothesis of DP and GP. That is, the claim that '–' is the default value of the feature [round], and is thus omitted even when there is a contrast between /i/ and /y/, is a 'weaker' way of saying that roundness is (acting as) monovalent. In a monovalent approach, on the other hand, we could say that contrastive underspecification is directly encoded in the system of phonological primes, rather than a derivational option or a language-specific matter. However, this should not be taken to mean that the 'zero-option' cannot be used in a monovalent system; as was already noted, the zero-option is potentially present in any system of elements (for this issue, see Ewen & Van der Hulst 1986).

Applying contrastive underspecification to RcvP-type representations would mean that the full specification of the contrast between /e/ and /ɛ/ can be reduced (as per (15bii)) to either (16b) or (16c):

(16)   /e/   /ɛ/

    a. $\underline{\lor}A$ $\forall\underline{A}$ (full specification)
    b. $\underline{\lor}A$ $\forall A$
    c. $\forall A$ $\forall\underline{A}$

---

[14] There is no connection between this use of the word 'radical' and its use in 'Radical' cv Phonology. Indeed, the issue of non-contrastive or radical underspecification is orthogonal to the basic tenets of RcvP.

As far as the elements themselves are concerned, there is less need for contrastive underspecification in a monovalent approach simply because such approaches use fewer primes. For example, the fact that roundness and backness are encoded by one and the same element obviates the need for redundancy rules which capture the relation between these two properties. However, notice that some elements may be (partially) redundant even in a monovalent system. For example, according to (15ai), the element |∀| can be eliminated in all systems where vowels with either |I| or |U| are non-low; and according to (15aii), systems with a single row of mid vowels would not require a specification of head-dependency relations between |A| and |∀|. Both these situations are illustrated below, in section 4.2.

Despite this, we should not automatically take either type of underspecification as a goal that is worth pursuing. It has been argued that redundant elements (left out based on non-contrastive underspecification) and default elements (left out based on contrastive underspecification) tend to be phonologically inert. This is an interesting hypothesis which needs to be re-examined in the context of a monovalent system like RcvP. However, note that in RcvP there is no need to explain the inertness of '[–back]', '[–round]', '[–low]' and '[–ATR]', since these properties simply do not exist.

Finally, it is worth noting another kind of underspecification, which will play an important role in my discussion of vowel harmony below. This underspecification arises if we specify the common core of alternating vowels only, but leave the alternating part underspecified. Consider for example a suffix vowel that is targeted by root-controlled palatal vowel harmony. In a binary approach, it is common to represent such a vowel as [Øback]. In a unary approach, this kind of underspecification is impossible, as we have seen. Here the vowel in question would simply be represented without the element |I| (the equivalent of [–back]), which amounts to saying that in this type of harmony, it is the back vowel that is basic. Given this, it could be objected that a monovalent approach is unable to represent the contrast between alternating (i.e. [Øback]) and non-alternating (i.e. [–back] or [+back]) vowels. I will return to this issue in section 6, where I argue that this problem is avoided if we make use of the concept of the 'morphophoneme'. Specifically, I will claim that alternating vowels contain the element |I| as a 'variable' element which must be licensed in order to receive a phonetic interpretation. Non-alternating back vowels, on the other hand, simply lack this |I|.

4.2 Intrasegmental constraints

Given the idea of free combination of elements, any actual vowel system represents a subset of the set of possible vowels. This subset can be characterized in terms of a set of constraints (or wellformedness conditions). Constraints are propositions that are true of the system, and they can often be formulated in different but logically equivalent ways (cf. Melis 1976). For example '$\neg (A \wedge B)$' is logically equivalent to '$A \rightarrow \neg B$' or '$B \rightarrow \neg A$'. It is important to note here that the use of a negative operator in constraints does not change the system of unary elements into a binary one. This is because the negative operator occurs *in constraints only*, and not in the representation of morphemes. Constraints that are said to be true of the system characterize the set of structures that can be submitted to the phonetic implementation module.

The full specification of a 2-vowel system with just /ɨ/ and /a/ (as has been claimed for Kabardian) is as in (17a); this system is subject to the constraints in (17b):

(17)   a.   A two-vowel system, fully specified

/ɨ/   /a/
∀
‾
         A
         ‾

b.   Constraints for a 2-vowel system

Aperture: i. $\neg \varnothing$ ("cannot be empty")
            ii. $\neg (A \wedge \forall)$ ("no mid vowels")
Colour: $\varnothing$ ("I and U do not occur")

As per (15aiii) this means that headedness specifications could be omitted:

(18)   A two-vowel system, underspecified as per (15aiii)

/ɨ/   /a/
∀
         A

Headedness information can then be 'restored' if we assume the following principle:

(19)   A sole element in a gesture is the head of that gesture.

Also, as per (15bi), one of the two elements can be omitted, with the omitted element being the default option:

(20)   A two-vowel system, underspecified as per (15aiii) and (15bi)

   /ɨ/   /a/
   ∀

In RcvP, the element |A| would be the most likely default manner element for vowels, given the fundamental principle in (21):[15]

(21)   In a syllabic C-position, the C-element is default; in a syllabic V-position, the V-element is default.

As was already mentioned in section 1, this follows from a universal redundancy rule, given in (22):

(22)   The unmarked dependent is identical in terms of C/V labeling.

From this, it follows that for rhymal heads the unmarked aperture element is |A| (i.e. [Manner: V]).[16] To 'restore' the element |A|, we can rely on a default rule which follows automatically from the principle that an element that is filled in must be the opposite of the specified element.[17] In the case at hand:

(23)   In the syllabic 'nucleus' (= V) position, the unmarked aperture is |A| (= V).

Let us now turn to more complex vowel systems. Consider first the 3-vowel system in (24):

(24)   A 3-vowel system, fully specified

   /i/   /u/   /a/
   ∀   ∀
                 A
   I
          U

This system is subject to the following constraints.

---

[15] In RcvP, the C/V notation is also applied at the syllable level. Thus the 'onset' is a C unit and the 'rhyme' is a V unit; see Van der Hulst (2005, 2012a).

[16] An idea that could be worth exploring is that in certain specific cases |∀| rather than |A| is left out; this would then trigger a default rule filling in |∀|. Here I leave open the question of whether such 'markedness reversal' (as it is called in radical underspecification theory) is necessary.

[17] In radical underspecification theory this is called a 'complement rule' (Archangeli 1984).

(25)   Constraints (for a three-vowel system)[18]

    a. Aperture: i. $\neg\varnothing$ ("cannot be empty")
                  ii. $\neg(A \wedge \forall)$ ("no mid vowels")

    b. Colour: $\neg(I \wedge U)$ ("|I| and |U| do not combine")[19]

    c. Cross-gestural: $I \vee U \leftrightarrow \forall$ ("|∀| and colour must co-occur")

In order to determine the relevant constraints, we must determine which possible vowels (of the full set of options in (10)) are missing, and how these can be ruled out on the basis of predictable or impossible element combinations.

(26)   A 3-vowel system, underspecified as per (15aiii)

      /i/   /u/   /a/
                    A
     I
           U

We can further leave out either one colour element or the aperture element for /a/:

(27) a.   A 3-vowel system, underspecified as per (15aiii, bi), with default |U|

      /i/   /u/   /a/
                    A
     I

    b.   A 3-vowel system, underspecified as per (15aiii, bi), with default |I|

      /i/   /u/   /a/
                    A
          U

RcvP predicts that (27a), where the default for colour is |U|, is the preferred option, given that |U| is a V-type element (see (3)). In Radical Underspecification Theory (Archangeli 1984), it has been argued that it is /i/ that is more likely to be unspecified, as in (27b). Finally, Van der Hulst (2012a) suggests that (27a) is more likely to occur in prominent (i.e. accented) positions and (27b) in non-prominent ones. This is tantamount to

---

[18] From (25aii) and (25c) it follows that |A| does not occur with colour elements.

[19] Kaye et al. (1985) suggest that certain combinations of elements can be excluded using 'line conflation'. However, given that constraints are needed anyway, there seems to be no need to use a different mechanism for |I| and |U|.

saying that epenthetic vowels are non-optimal vowels: speakers do not use the 'best', i.e. the most sonorous, vowels in such non-prominent contexts.[20]

A third possibility in a 3-vowel system is to leave /a/ unspecified, as in (28):

(28)   A three vowel system, underspecified as per (15aiii, bi), with default |A|

        /i/   /u/   /a/
                 U
         I

Future work should explore the question of whether these options correlate with different phonological behaviours of /i/, /u/ and /a/ in different languages.

In Van der Hulst (2012a) I discuss vowel systems of increasing complexity, the results of which, for reasons of space, cannot be discussed here in full. As was mentioned, it is in fact unclear whether underspecified representations play any other role than saving storage space. Of primary importance are the constraints that characterize a specific vowel system as a subset of the set of all possible vowel structures. These constraints need to be stated. However, it is possible that impoverished representations have an explanatory role to play, for example when it could be shown that redundant information plays no role in the phonology of languages. I refer to both Clements (2002) and Dresher (2009) for discussion of this issue. Meanwhile, I will assume that there seems no harm in representing phonological structure in the most minimal fashion.

It is important to point out that impoverished structures should be mapped onto full representations *monotonically*, i.e. by adding rather than by deleting information. Given this, no separate rules are required to fill in the underspecified structures, since for each impoverished structure there will be only one unique fully specified structure that is compatible with that structure and the constraints. Notice in this respect that the constraints as such do not act as filling-up rules. The fact that some constraints take the form of implicational statements does not make them rules, since a statement like A $\rightarrow$ B is logically equivalent to $\neg(A \wedge \neg B)$.

---

[20] This suggests that languages may use different vowel inventories in accented and non-accented positions. This option is explored in Van der Hulst (2012a).

5 Contrastive head marking

Some versions of GP, e.g. Walker (1995), suggest that ATR distinctions can be made in terms of what I will call 'contrastive headedness'. The idea is that a combination of elements can be contrastively headed or non-headed, with the former adding a phonetic specification that corresponds to [ATR] (or its acoustic result). In this type of approach, a 10-vowel system can be represented as in (29). (Notice that GP does not distinguish between an aperture and colour gesture.)

(29) A 10-vowel system with ATR

/i/	/u/	/ɪ/	/ʊ/	/e/	/o/	/ɛ/	/ɔ/	/ɐ/	/a/
				A	A	A	A	A̲	A
I̲		I		I̲		I			
	U̲		U		U̲		U		

In this view, ATR-harmony involves the requirement that all vowels in the domain are either headed (ATR) or non-headed (non-ATR).

In the model proposed here, a 10-vowel system would be represented as follows:

(30) A 10-vowel system, fully specified[21]

/i/	/u/	/ɪ/	/ʊ/	/e/	/o/	/ɛ/	/ɔ/	/ɐ/	/a/
∀̲	∀̲			∀̲	∀̲	∀	∀	∀̲	
				A	A	A̲	A̲	A	A̲
I̲		I		I̲		I̲			
	U̲		U̲		U̲		U̲		

This system is subject to the constraints in (31):

(31) Constraints

    a. Aperture: –

    b. Colour: $\neg(I \wedge U)$ ("|I| and |U| do not combine")

    c. Cross-gestural: i. $(I \vee U) \wedge A \rightarrow \forall$
                    ii. $\neg(I \vee U) \wedge A \rightarrow \underline{\forall}$

The minimally specified version of (30) is given in (32):

---

[21] Recall that in RcvP headedness is specified for each gesture.

(32)   A 10-vowel system, minimally specified

/i/	/u/	/ɪ/	/ʊ/	/e/	/o/	/ɛ/	/ɔ/	/ɐ/	/a/
∀	∀			∀̲	∀̲	∀	∀	∀̲	
				A	A	A̲	A̲	A	A
I		I		I		I			
	U		U		U		U		

The difference is that that the headed structures in (29) correspond exactly to the structures in (30) and (32) which have the element |∀| as a head. In order to see this, we must consult the fully specified structures.[22] I prefer my approach over that proposed in GP because the presence of |∀| as the antagonist of |A| better fits the overall architecture of RcvP, where each gesture has two elements. This argument, then, follows the logic of 'structural analogy' (cf. Anderson 1992, 2006). In addition, the use of contrastive head-marking undermines a central principle of DP, namely that all structures are headed.[23] I conclude, therefore, that contrastive headedness is in conflict with the fundamental architecture of RcvP.

6 Vowel harmony

Assuming the four primitives |I, U, A, ∀|, let us now consider the issue of vowel harmony. With four elements, four types of vowel harmony are predicted:

(33)   Vowel Harmony types

Palatal harmony involves |I|
Labial harmony involves |U|
ATR harmony involves |∀|
Lowering harmony involves |A|

---

[22] This brings out the important point that phonological 'processes' need access to information that could be left unspecified in the most minimal representation. I will leave open the question of whether this applies to all information that can be left out. For example, it has been claimed, in e.g. Dresher (2009), that only contrastive elements (features, in other frameworks) can be phonologically active.

[23] I also reject Anderson and Ewen's option of 'mutual dependency' (or 'double-headedness'), which I believe also loosens the system, and is, in a sense, comparable to the use of 'non-headedness' (i.e. absence of head-marking) in GP.

In this paper I will focus briefly on palatal harmony in Finnish as a showcase for how RcvP can account for the behaviour of non-alternating vowels (which usually lack a harmonic counterpart).

6.1 The vowel harmony relation

How should vowel harmony be represented? In a unary system, it is impossible to say that vowel harmony is the result of 'needy', i.e. underspecified, vowels (cf. Nevins 2010), since there is no underspecification to express this 'neediness'. Nevertheless, the idea of 'neediness' is similar in spirit to the GP approach, where 'emptiness' (more specifically, empty nuclei) requires licensing (cf. Kaye et al. 1990). I suggest that a vowel which undergoes harmony possesses the harmonizing element as a *variable element*, i.e. as an element which can be present only if it is licensed by a non-variable, i.e. licensed, occurrence of that same element.[24] Thus, alternating vowels contain the harmonic element as a 'variable'; variable elements will be represented between parentheses.[25] Segmental structures that contain a variable element will be called 'morphophonemes'. For example in Finnish, all vowels that are front (in stems) or *can* be front (in suffixes) are represented as morphophonemes:

(34) /u/ ~ /y/   {U(I)}
      /o/ ~ /ø/   {AU(I)}
      /a/ ~ /æ/   {A(I)}

While a complete theory of licensing remains to be developed (see Van der Hulst 2012b), for the purpose of this article it suffices to say that variable elements can be licensed in two ways:

(35) a. Positional licensing

   A variable element X is licensed in position P (where P is the first/last syllable in domain D, where D is a Word or Stem/Root).

   b. Lateral licensing

   A variable element X is licensed by a preceding/following occurrence of X.

---

[24] Scheer (2004) argues on independent grounds that vowel-zero alternations require the specification of the alternating element as 'variable', particularly in cases where zero alternates with two types of vowels, e.g. in Polish yer-alternations.

[25] This notation can in fact be interpreted as a form of underspecification, as in Declarative Phonology, where (x) denotes "either x or nothing" (see e.g. Scobbie et al. 1996).

At this point it is important to make a distinction between the notions of morphophoneme and archiphoneme. Archiphonemes express the idea of underspecification while morphophonemes capture the idea of the lexical listing of alternants, a notion that was revived in Hudson (1974) and Hooper (1976). An archiphoneme can be used in cases where there is neutralization of contrast (which corresponds to non-contrastive underspecification). For Trubetzkoy, a typical example was final devoicing, where the contrast between, say, /d/ and /t/ is contextually neutralized, yielding an archisegment /T/ which has all the properties that /d/ and /t/ have in common. If we extend this concept to those cases in which the neutralization is context-free, we could say that neutral vowels are archisegments. In the neutral vowels of Finnish, for example, the variable element (I) *can* be left unspecified. However, as I will show, neutral vowels are more appropriately viewed as containing the variable element *at all times*, because they actually participate in the harmony process.

6.2. Palatal harmony in Finnish

Finnish has the following vowel inventory:

(36)	[–back]		[+back]		
	[–round]	[+round]	[–round]	[+round]	
	/i/	/y/	–	/u/	[+high,–low]
	/e/	/ø/	–	/o/	[–high,–low]
	/æ/	–	/a/	–	[–high,+low]

Each vowel occurs as short and long. The four traditional features constitute the minimal set that is needed to express the relevant contrasts in the Finnish vowel system. In RcvP, the fully specified unary representation of the Finnish vowel system is as follows:

(37)   The Finnish vowel system, fully specified

/i/	/y/	/u/	/e/	/ø/	/o/	/æ/	/a/
Ɐ	Ɐ	Ɐ	Ɐ	Ɐ	Ɐ		
			A	A	A	A	A
I	I	I	I	I	I	I	
	U	U		U	U		

This system is subject to the following constraints:

(31)   Constraints on the Finnish vowel system

 a. Aperture: $\neg\varnothing$
        $A \rightarrow \underline{\forall}$

 b. Colour: $I \rightarrow \underline{I}$

 c. Cross-gestural: i. $\neg A \rightarrow \forall$
         ii. $\forall \rightarrow (I \vee U)$

Since Finnish has palatal harmony, |I| is represented as being variable (barring certain exceptions which are discussed below). This means that we have the following set of morphophonemes:

(39) Finnish morphophonemes (preliminary)

/i/	/y~u/	/e/	/ø~o/	/æ~a/
$\underline{\forall}$	$\underline{\forall}$	$\underline{\forall}$	$\underline{\forall}$	
		A	A	$\underline{A}$
(I)	(I)	(I)	(I)	(I)
	U		U	

The shorthand notation for morphophonemes is /x~y/. This raises the question to what extent the non-low non-round front vowels are morphophonemes. If 'x' and 'y' represent the two possible structures for each morphophoneme, then (39) should actually be replaced by (40):

(40) Finnish morphophonemes (revised)

/i~ɨ/	/y~u/	/e~ə/	/ø~o/	/æ~a/
$\underline{\forall}$	$\underline{\forall}$	$\underline{\forall}$	$\underline{\forall}$	
		A	A	$\underline{A}$
(I)	(I)	(I)	(I)	(I)
	U		U	

After all, if the variable |I| is not licensed for the first and third morphophoneme, then it will not be there, in which case the first morphophoneme would contain $\underline{\forall}$ only. At the risk of releasing the 'abstractness genie' I will accept that, phonologically speaking, Finnish never lost the back counterparts of /i/ and /e/, viz. /ɨ/ and /ə/. This means that the constraint in (38c) is not in fact valid. The surface reality of Finnish is that /i/ and /ɨ/ are mapped onto the same phonetic event, and likewise for /e/ and /ə/.

 Let us consider some straightforward examples (taken from Kiparsky 1981 and Ringen & Heinämäki 1999), which I will first describe in the way that is customary in the vowel harmony literature:

(41) a. Front words   b. Back words

vækkæræ	'pinwheel'	makkara	'sausage'
pöytæ	'table'	pouta	'fine weather'
kæyræ	'curve'	kaura	'oats'
tyhmæ	'stupid'	tuhma	'naughty'

Suffixes have front and back alternants depending on the quality of the stem:

(42) a. tyhmæ-stæ 'stupid-ILL' b. tuhma-sta 'naughty-ILL'

One of the most interesting aspects of the Finnish harmony system is the presence of two 'neutral vowels' /i/ and /e/. The data in (43) show that these vowels occur with both front and back harmonic vowels:

(43) a. Front words   b. Back words

værttinæ	'spinning wheel'	palttina	'linen cloth'
isæ	'father'	iso	'big'
kesy	'tame'	verho	'curtain'

Interestingly, if the neutral vowel is preceded by a back vowel, the suffix alternant is back. This suggests that neutral vowels in Finnish are transparent, since they act as though they are invisible to the harmony process:

(44) a. Front words

værttinæ-llæ-ni-hæn   'with spinning wheel, as you know'
lyø-dæ-kse-ni-kø   'for me to hit'

    b. Back words

palttina-lla-ni-han   'with linen cloth, as you know'
lyo-da-kse-ni-ko   'for me to create'
tuoli-lla   'on the chair'

As the example *tuoli-lla* shows, neutral vowels do not condition front alternants, even when they are the last vowel of the stem. Notice also that suffix alternants are not always determined by the first vowel of the stem, as is evidenced by disharmonic stems of the type in (45):

(45) afææri - æ   'business-PART'
      tyranni - ko   'tyran'

Here it is clearly the last non-neutral stem-vowel which determines the suffix alternant.

Consider next the forms in (46), which show that roots containing neutral vowels only take front suffixes.

(46) velje-llæ   'brother-ADESS'
      tie-llæ   'road-ADESS'

Let us see how we can account for these standard facts in RcvP. Adopting the representations in (40), all vowels in front roots and all suffix vowels contain the variable element (I). In roots, this (I) is licensed in the first syllable (indicated in boldface); this element in turn licenses each subsequent occurrence of (I), including those in suffixes (as is indicated by '>'):[26]

(47) a. tyh mæ - stæ 'stupid-ILL'
    (I) > (I) > (I)

  b. tuhma - sta 'naughty-ILL'
       (I)

Note that in roots containing back vowels only, nothing happens. In such roots, agreement between vowels results from the complete absence of the harmonic element. The suffix that is added to a back vowel root will find its variable element unlicensed; as a result, this suffix will also be back.

If a neutral vowel occurs in a back vowel root, it will, like all other vowels in that root, lack the variable element. Effectively, we do not have /i/ or /e/, but /ɨ/ or /ɘ/ in those roots. However, if the neutral vowel occurs in a front vowel root it does contain the variable element. Turning now to suffixes, I will argue that here the variable element is *always* present, even when the suffix contains a so-called neutral vowel. The latter part of this proposal is perhaps the most controversial. (The first part may be empirically wrong if there are suffixes that are invariantly back, which is at least a theoretical possibility.) But why insist that the so-called neutral vowels in suffixes always contain the variable element? The reason for this claim is that only by making this assumption can we maintain that the licensing relation is strictly local (i.e. cannot skip vowels). Consider the two following forms (cf. also (44)):

(48) a. værttinæ - llæ - ni - hæn 'with spinning wheel, as you know'
    (I)>(I)>(I)>(I)>(I)>(I)

  b. palttina - lla-ni-han 'with linen cloth, as you know'
      (I)(I) (I)

In (48a) we have a front vowel root. The variable element in the initial vowel is positionally licensed; each of the subsequent vowels is laterally licensed by

---

[26] It could be suggested that all occurrences of |I| within roots are licensed, instead of attributing the licensing of non-initial syllables to licensed |I|'s in preceding syllables. Nevins (2010) discusses some facts from Turkish which suggest that within roots only the first vowel is specified for the harmonic feature and that subsequent vowels acquire their feature through copying. This suggests that a distinction must be made between positional initial licensing and lateral licensing.

the licensed |I| of the immediately preceding vowel. Clearly, if we were to specify [i] without |I|, as in (49), licensing would not be local:

(49)   vært ti næ - llæ-ni-hæn   'with spinning wheel, as you know'
       (I)>>>>(I) > (I)>>>(I)

If licensing is not local we cannot explain the phenomenon of opacity; I will discuss this below.

In (48b), suffix vowels will be back because their variable element cannot be licensed. Of course, in the case of /ɨ/ phonetic interpretation will realize this structure as [i].

It is important to note that the term 'transparent' is a complete misnomer in this analysis. A so-called neutral vowel that is preceded by a back vowel is not transparent to anything, since there is no 'backness' that 'spreads' through it; a neutral vowel that is preceded by a front vowel, on the other hand, passes on the 'frontness' itself.

As we have seen, front vowel roots that contain neutral vowels only, as in (46), always take front suffixes. This is shown in (50) for the form [tiellæ]:

(50)   ti   e -   llæ   'road-ADESS'
       (I) > (I) > (I)

How can we account for this? Given what has been proposed thus far it does not follow that roots with phonetic [i] and [e] must be phonologically front. In fact, if we consider Hungarian (whose vowel harmony system is very similar to that of Finnish), we observe that here a subclass of the so-called 'neutral vowel roots' take back suffixes (cf. Törkenczy 2011, who refers to these roots as 'anti-harmonic'):

(51)   a. víz-nek   'water-DAT'   b. híd - nak   'bridge-DAT'
           (I) >(I)   (I)

Why does Finnish lack anti-harmonic roots? And why, for that matter, is the class of anti-harmonic roots in Hungarian a fairly small, closed set of roots? To explain these patterns, we must again refer to an old principle, viz. the Naturalness Condition of Postal (1968), which I here interpret as a condition which bears on the relationship between phonological structures and phonetic events, rather than on two *phonological* levels:[27]

(52)   Naturalness Condition
       Every phonological object has a unique phonetic interpretation.

---

[27] Indeed, the model proposed here does not recognize more than one phonological level. It attributes phenomena such as phonetic merger to the phonetic interpretation module, rather than to phonological rules that create derived phonological levels.

We can regard this condition as a guideline for the language learner, i.e. "assume that each phonetic event has a unique phonological representation". Since roots in Finnish and Hungarian do not alternate, the learner will be biased to assume that the phonetically front vowels have a unique and invariable phonological representation in which the frontness corresponds to a phonological element, namely |I|. However, we must assume that the Natural Condition is a guideline only. If we interpret the phonetic merger of two vowels as a historical development, then it is apparently not the case that the phonology must follow suit.

Let us next consider the representation of Hungarian 'disharmonic' roots. Here the key insight is that vowels are disharmonic either by virtue of containing a *non*-variable element or by lacking a variable element altogether. Thus, using the examples in (53), the disharmonic sequences /o-y/ and /y-o/ would be represented as follows (note that /y/ is reflected as <ü> in Hungarian orthography).

(53) a.   k o szt y m - n ek

           A   A
        U   U
           I > (I)   (A non-variable instance of |I| in /y/)

    b.   b y r o - n ak
               A
        U U
       (I)   (I)   (Absence of variable (I) in /o/)

In (53a) we expect a following harmonic suffix vowel to be front, since the invariable |I| will license the variable |I| in the suffix vowel. I will refer to invariable elements as being 'lexically licensed'. In section 7, I will account for the observation that the invariant /o/ in (53b) behaves as opaque. It should be clear at this point that this is because licensing relations are strictly local; this means that the |I| element in the first vowel of the stem in (53b) cannot license the variable element in the suffix.[28]

---

[28] An important question is how suffixes that fail to alternate should be represented. If such suffixes invariably contained a back vowel, they would lack the variable element; and if they contain a non-variable (i.e. lexically licensed) element, they would be invariably front. My impression is that the former case is more widely attested, which might mean that lexical licensing is limited to (or is more common for) roots. This issue needs further exploration.

7 Predicting the behaviour of neutral vowels

7.1 The Van der Hulst & Smith (1986) theory

The question arises whether the behaviour of so-called neutral vowels, which can be either transparent or opaque, can be predicted.[29] Van der Hulst & Smith (1986) argue that it can, and I maintain that their proposal is still valid. Van der Hulst & Smith's theory can be summarized as in (54) (see also Van der Hulst 1988):[30]

(54) Opacity and Transparency

    a. A vowel that is *incompatible* with the harmonic element is *opaque*

    b. A vowel that is *compatible* with the harmonic element is *transparent*

The great advantage of this theory is that it is eminently simple. We have seen that (54b) applies to Finnish, where /i/ and /e/ are clearly compatible with the harmonic element since they contain it. (Van der Hulst & Smith used the term 'compatible' because they assumed that neutral vowels are underspecified for the harmonic element; I have shown in this paper that this is not desirable because it undermines a strictly local conception of licensing.)

Let us next consider a case of opacity, as is illustrated by ATR harmony in Tangale (see Van der Hulst & Van de Weijer 1995). This language has a 9-vowel system of the type in (55):

(55) The Tangale vowel system, fully specified

/i/	/u/	/ɪ/	/ʊ/	/e/	/o/	/ɛ/	/ɔ/	/a/
∀	∀	∀	∀	∀	∀	∀	∀	
				A	A	A	A	A
I		I		I		I		
	U		U		U		U	

The Tangale system is subject to the constraints in (56):

---

[29] For general discussion on neutral (or non-participating) vowels, see Van der Hulst & Van de Weijer (1995), Krämer (2003) and Archangeli & Pulleyblank (1994, 2007).

[30] Krämer (2003) raises a number of valid objections against Van der Hulst & Smith's theory, which the current formalization pre-empts; see Van der Hulst (2012b) for discussion.

(56) Constraints on the Tangale vowel system

   a. Aperture: –

   b. Colour: ¬(I ∧ U)   "|I| and |U| do not combine"

   c. Cross-gestural: i. ∀ → (I ∨ U)   "no central vowel except /a/"
                        ii. (I ∨ U) ∧ A → ∀

To account for the harmony, the following morphophonemes must be postulated:

(57) /i~ɪ/   /u~ʊ/   /e~ɛ/   /o~ɔ/   /a/
      (∀)   (∀)   (∀)   (∀)
                        A   A   A
       I   I
               U   U

Against this background, consider next a sequence consisting of a neutral low vowel that is preceded by an ATR vowel:

(58) /u/   /a/   /e/
      (∀̲)   ∀̲
             A   A
                    I
       U

Here an explanation is required for the observation that the initial |∀|, which is positionally licensed, cannot itself license an |∀| in the suffix vowel. Van der Hulst & Smith accounted for this in terms of a restriction on spreading, arguing that since the low vowel cannot be linked to ATR (on account of the language lacking low ATR vowels), it cannot also be linked to the suffix, as this would result in discontinuous spreading. That is, spreading of the harmonic element must be local, and so cannot skip vowels. This 'spreading metaphor' (cf. Anderson 1980) has not been adopted in the present analysis; rather, the fact that the initial, licensed |∀| cannot license the variable |∀| in the suffix across the /a/ is attributed to the condition that licensing relations must be local, i.e. hold between adjacent syllable heads.

It is now clear why, in the present analysis, neutral vowels of the type found in Finnish *must* contain the variable element when they occur in front vowel roots and in suffixes, rather than be underspecified for it. Recall that if /i/ and /e/ were underspecified for |I|, then we would have to assume that a preceding front vowel can license a following suffix vowel *across* an intervening /i/ or /e/ (see (49)). In such an approach, licensing is not a strictly local phenomenon. But to account for Tangale-type opacity, on the other hand, licensing *must* be regarded as local, as we have just seen.

A further comment is in order regarding the licensing of the element |∀|. In an ATR system, [–ATR] mid vowels contain |∀| as a dependent.

(59)   /ɛ/   /ɛ/
       ∀   (∀̲)

Clearly, the dependent |∀| cannot license a variable occurrence of the same element in a suffix: a dependent element cannot license a head element. This can be interpreted as an instance of a head–dependent asymmetry in the sense of Dresher & Van der Hulst (1998). The question of whether the reverse is possible (i.e. a head element licensing a dependent element) remains to be established.

The astute reader will have detected a potential problem for the claim that the present model predicts that in an ATR system low retracted vowels *must* be opaque. A system in which such low vowels act transparently can be derived if we say that in such a case the low vowels would actually be low vowels with the variable element |∀̲|, on the assumption that the phonetic interpretation can simply leave an element uninterpreted. In other words, if the phonetic interpretation can produce (60a), why can it not also produce (60b)?

(60)   a. /i/   /ɨ/   b.   /a/   /ɐ/

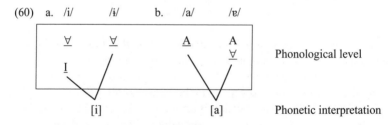

Phonological level

[i]   [a]   Phonetic interpretation

Van der Hulst & Smith did not face this problem. The reason for this is that they had in fact not released the 'abstractness genie', so that for them (60a) was not necessary. For reasons provided earlier, I now believe that the abstractness genie must come out of the bottle. This means that the present model must account for the opacity of the low vowel in Tangale in a different fashion. My suggestion is that (60b) is excluded because of the following interface condition:

(61)   Naturalness Condition (revised)
       Every licensed phonological object has a unique phonetic interpretation.

The principle in (61) states that while not every property of a phonetic event is rooted in phonology (although this can still be the null hypothesis), phonetics cannot freely *ignore* phonological elements. That a phonological object can 'understate' phonetics is of course hardly controversial (there are many properties in the phonetic signal that are not phonologically relevant). The revised Naturalness Condition puts a limit on abstractness, and thus keeps the abstractness genie in check. It effectively disallows the *diacritic specification* of phonological elements, allowing (60a) but barring (60b). From the learner's perspective this means that we cannot postulate an element for which there is no phonetic evidence (as in 60b), while we can fail to postulate an element for which the phonetics suggests that it should be present in the phonology (as in 60a). In other words, the phonetic interpretation can 'add', but not 'delete' (or 'ignore'). Needless to say, the hypothesis embodied in (61) needs further testing. As it stands, it explains the asymmetry that we find in vowel harmony systems, viz. that neutralization towards the harmonic element leads to 'transparency' (in the case of Finnish front vowels) while neutralization away from the harmonic element leads to opacity (as in Tangale).

It is perhaps useful to point out why Van der Hulst & Smith did not release the abstractness genie in their analysis of ATR harmony, and why, in Finnish palatal harmony, they did not posit underlying back vowels in those cases where surface front vowels fail to impose their frontness on following vowels.[31] In such cases, Van der Hulst & Smith assumed that /i/ and /e/ are underspecified for the element |I|, which is then filled in before phonetic interpretation. However, this approach must stipulate that in *initial* syllables /i/'s *are* apparently fully specified, in order to account for the fact that roots consisting of neutral vowels condition front vowel suffixes only. If this were universally true, then we could attribute this to the requirement that vowels in stressed syllables vowels be fully specified (Finnish has initial stress). But, as we have seen, it is not universally true that front vowel roots take front suffixes. In Hungarian we have a set of roots that take back suffixes (see (51)). This means that for those roots we would have to stipulate that the element |I| is not specified in the stressed syllable, which effectively means that we have a contrast between /i/ and /ɨ/ after all, thus unleashing the abstractness genie.

7.2 An alternative to transparency

Demirdache (1988) and Ritter (1995) propose a different account of transparency, which makes use of the head or dependent status of an element.

---

[31] I have been skeptical of this kind of abstractness ever after reading Kiparsky (1968), even though he considers the kind of use made of it here rather well motivated. Discussion with David Michaels has made me more receptive to abstractness, however.

For Finnish or Hungarian they propose that |I| in neutral vowels is a head element, while in other cases it is a dependent. I will refer to this use of headedness as 'diacritic headmarking', since headedness here is used to explain phonological behaviour rather than phonetic properties:[32]

(62) /i/   /y/   /u/   /e/   /ø/   /o/   /ö/   /a/
                           A   A   A   A̲   A
      I̲   I   I̲   I   I
            U̲   U   U̲   U̲

Representing the neutral vowels as in (62) allows the generalization that vowels with a head |I| do not trigger palatal harmony. To account for the fact that /i/ and /e/ in neutral vowel roots do trigger harmony of suffix vowels, it must be stipulated that non-initial /i/ and /e/ are not |I|-headed.

Demirdache also discusses the fact that Finnish /y/ and /ö/ are optionally transparent, as has been claimed in Campbell (1980). According to Demirdache, this is possible because in these vowels |I| *can* be specified as the head. Indeed, since GP argues that differences in headedness of |I| and |U| never result in phonemic contrasts (see section 2), headedness of |I| can be used diacritically to encode a difference in behaviour. Notice, too, that this approach predicts that /æ/ cannot be transparent, since marking |I| as head would neutralize the contrast between /æ/ and /e/. The data in Campbell suggest that this prediction is borne out.[33]

How can the alleged transparency of /ø/ and /y/ be accounted for in the present analysis? At first sight, it seems reasonable to suggest that front vowels in disharmonic roots can be represented with a variable rather than an invariable (I), as in (63):

(63) a. m a rt tyy ri   -a
              A̲   A̲
                    U
                   (I) (I) (I)

      b. m a rt tyy ri   -æ
              A̲   A
                    U
                  I̲>>(I)>> (I)

However, this account fails because in (63a) /y/'s variable (I) remains unlicensed, so that the structure would be interpreted as [u] rather than [y]. It would seem that in this case we cannot simply say that the frontness is added

---

[32] Notice that diacritic headmarking is similar to contrastive head-marking (as discussed in section 5). The crucial difference is that the former has no phonetic correlates but is a purely diacritic device.

[33] Nevins (2010: 177) attributes this to the low vowel being a "sonority hurdle".

by the phonetic interpretation, because structures containing {∀̶ U} are interpreted as [u] in other cases. We do not want to assume that phonetic interpretation is 'erratic'. It would seem, therefore, that in the present approach there is no way in which the non-harmonic behaviour of /y/ and /ø/ can be accounted for. The non-harmonic behaviour of these vowels would seem to be due to the fact that the words in question fail the harmony system altogether.

7.3 Unexpected behaviour of neutral vowels

Van der Hulst (1988b) examines a variety of cases in which vowels that are incompatible with the harmonic element appear to be transparent, as well as cases in which vowels that are compatible with the harmonic element fail to be transparent. Here I discuss briefly how such cases can be handled in the present approach.

Given locality of licensing, we expect that one specific situation should not be able to occur, viz. a Tangale-type case in which the low vowel is transparent. For a while it was believed that this was the case in Kinande (see Schlindwein 1987). However, it has subsequently been shown that the low vowel does in fact undergo ATR harmony (see Gick et al. 2006; Kenstowicz 2008). Hence, there is no constraint against a low ATR vowel in this language.

The most interesting challenge to Van der Hulst & Smith's approach to opacity comes from Mongolian rounding harmony, in which /u/ and /ʊ/ do not act as harmonic triggers, whereas /i/ is skipped (cf. Van der Hulst & Smith 1988).[34] Both facts are seemingly at odds with Van der Hulst & Smith's approach. The Mongolian vowel system is given in (64):

$$(64) \quad \begin{array}{ll} i & u \\ & ʊ \\ e & o \\ a & ɔ \end{array}$$

If rounding harmony is triggered exclusively by /o, ɔ/, and targets low vowel suffixes only, then we may conclude that it is dependent on both licensor and licensee having the element |A|. This is also the reason why /i/ can be skipped, and /u/ and /ʊ/ are opaque. In Van der Hulst & Smith's approach, the explanation for this pattern would involve establishing a licensing relation between low vowels for the element |U|. An intervening non-low vowel that

---

[34] Mongolian also has ATR harmony, which is ignored here.

lacks |U|, viz. /i/, does not block this licensing relation, but a non-low rounded vowel (i.e. /u/ or /ʊ/) does. This is illustrated in (65):

(65) a. m ɔ r i -tɔ i   'horse-COMP'
          A   A
         (U)>>>(U)
          I   I

      b. ɔr ʊ: l a:d   'enter-CAUS-PERF'
          A   A
         (U) U   (U)

The only solution that seems possible here would be to take Steriade's (1981) notion of 'parasitic harmony' literally, and to assume that the licensing relation in (65) is *relative* to the |A|-tier. This would mean that the relation in (65a) is local, in that it holds between two adjacent |A| elements; the intervening /i/ is simply invisible. In (65b), on the other hand, the licensing relation between the initial |U| and the |U| in the suffix is blocked on account of an intervening |U| specification, which blocks the licensing relation. Notice also that there is no licensing relation between this intervening |U| and the variable |U| in the suffix, since these do not share an |A| element.[35]

On a final note, Paul Kiparsky (p.c.) suggests that there are Finno-Ugric languages where neutral /i/ and /e/ consistently impose frontness on a following suffix vowel, even when they are preceded by a back vowel. The present model does not exclude this possibility; it can be accounted for by assuming that such neutral vowels contain an invariant rather than a variable instance of |I|. This issue is discussed in more detail in Van der Hulst (2012b).

8 Conclusion

The RcvP model proposed in this article is minimal in the sense that it uses a set of just four monovalent elements (and dependency), and does not require any form of underspecification. Vowel harmony is accounted for in terms of a licensing relation between elements. Variable elements propagate the harmony if they are licensed; if they are not, they remain 'mute', i.e. phonetically uninterpreted. The behaviour of neutral vowels as either transparent or opaque falls out naturally from the fact that licensing relations

---

[35] Other cases of this sort are reported in Li (1996); I suspect that these can be analyzed in a similar fashion (see Van der Hulst 2012b).

are local. The present paper has sketched the general outline of this approach, which originates in joint work with Norval Smith; it is examined in more detail, and applied to a more extensive set of empirical data in Van der Hulst (2012b).

References

Anderson, Stephen R. (1974): *The Organization of Phonology.* – New York: Academic Press.

Aronoff, Mark (1994): *Morphology by Itself: Stems and Inflectional Classes.* – Cambridge, MA: MIT Press.

Anderson, John M. (1992): *Linguistic Representation: Structural Analogy and Stratification.* – Berlin: Mouton de Gruyter.

Anderson, John M. & Colin J. Ewen (1987): *Principles of Dependency Phonology.* – Cambridge: Cambridge University Press.

Anderson, John M. & Jacques Durand (1988): "Vowel harmony and non-specification in Nez Perce." – In: Hulst, Harry van der & Norval S.H. Smith (eds.): *Features, Segmental Structure and Harmony Processes.* Vol. 2, 1–18. Dordrecht: Foris.

Anderson, John M. (2006): "Structural analogy and universal grammar." – In: Bemúdez-Otero, Ricardo & Patrick Honeybone (eds.): *Phonology and Syntax – The Same or Different? Lingua* 116, 601–633.

Anderson, Stephen R. (1980): "Problems and perspectives in the description of vowel harmony." – In: Vago, Robert M. (ed.): *Issues in Vowel Harmony*, 1–48. Amsterdam: John Benjamins.

Archangeli, Diana (1984): *Underspecification in Yawelmani Phonology and Morphology.* – PhD dissertation. Cambridge, MA: MIT.

Archangeli, Diana & Douglas Pulleyblank (1994): *Grounded Phonology.* – Cambridge, MA: MIT Press.

– (2007): "Harmony." – In: de Lacy, Paul (ed.): *The Cambridge Handbook of Phonology.* 353–378. Cambridge: Cambridge University Press.

Backley, Phillip & Toyomi Takahashi (1996): "Activate α: harmony without spreading." – In: *UCL Working Papers in Linguistics* 8, 487–518.

Botma, Bert (2004): *Phonological Aspects of Nasality: An Element-based Dependency Approach.* – PhD dissertation, University of Amsterdam. Utrecht: LOT Publications.

Campbell, Lyle (1980): "The psychological and sociological reality of Finnish vowel harmony." – In: Vago, Robert M. (ed.): *Issues in Vowel Harmony*, 245-70. Amsterdam: John Benjamins.

Clements, George N. (1985): "The geometry of phonological features." – *Phonology Yearbook* 2, 225–252.

– (1991): "Place of articulation in consonants and vowels: a unified theory." – In: *Working Papers of the Cornell Phonetics Laboratory* 5, 37–76. Ithaka, NY: Cornell University.

Demirdache, Hamida (1988): "Transparent vowels." – In: Hulst, Harry van der & Norval S.H. Smith (eds.): *Features, Segmental Structure and Harmony Processes.* Vol. 2, 39–76. Dordrecht: Foris Publications.

Dienes, Peter (1997): "Hungarian neutral vowels." – In: *The Odd Yearbook 1997,* 151–180.

Dresher, B. Elan (2009): *The Contrastive Hierarchy in Phonology.* – Cambridge: Cambridge University Press.

Dresher, B. Elan & Harry van der Hulst (1998): "Head–dependency in phonology: complexity and visibility." – In: *Phonology* 15, 317–52.

Ewen, Colin J. & Harry van der Hulst (1986): "Single-valued features and the nonlinear analysis of vowel harmony." – In: Bennis, Hans & Frits Beukema (eds.): *Linguistics in the Netherlands 1985,* 39–48. Dordrecht: Foris Publications.

Gick, Bryan, Douglas Pulleyblank, Fiona Campbell & Ngessimo Mutaka (2006): "Low vowels and transparency in Kinande vowel harmony." – *Phonology* 23, 1–20.

Goldsmith, John (1976): *Autosegmental Phonology.* PhD dissertation, MIT.

Halle, Morris & Kenneth N. Stevens (1971): "A note on laryngeal features." – In: *Quarterly Progress Report* 101, 198–213. Research Laboratory of Electronics, MIT.

Hooper, Joan B. (1976): *Introduction to Natural Generative Phonology.* – New York: Academic Press.

Hudson, Grover M. (1974): "The representation of non-productive alternations." – In: Anderson, John M. & Charles Jones (eds.): *Proceedings of the First International Conference on Historical Linguistics.* Vol. 2, 203–229. Amsterdam: North-Holland.

Hulst, Harry van der (1988a): "The dual interpretation of |i|, |u| and |a|." – In: *NELS* 18, 208–222.

– (1988b): "The geometry of vocalic features." – In: Hulst, Harry van der & Norval S.H. Smith (eds.): *Features, Segmental Structure and Harmony Processes.* Dordrecht: Foris. 77-126.

– (2005): "The molecular structure of phonological segments." – In: Carr, Philip, Jacques Durand & Colin J. Ewen (eds.): *Headhood, Elements, Specification and Contrastivity,* 193–234. Amsterdam/Philadelphia: John Benjamins.

– (2012a): "An outline of Radical cv Phonology." – Ms., University of Connecticut.

– (2012b): "Asymmetries in vowel harmony." – Ms., University of Connecticut.

Hulst, Harry van der & Norval S.H. Smith (1986): "On neutral vowels." – In: Bogers, Koen, Harry van der Hulst & Maarten Mous (eds.): *The Phonological Representation of Suprasegmentals,* 233–279. Dordrecht: Foris.

Hulst, Harry van der & Norval S.H. Smith. (1988): "Tungusic and Mongolian vowel harmony: a minimal pair." – In: Coopmans, Peter & Aafke Hulk (eds.): *Linguistics in the Netherlands 1988,* 79–88. Dordrecht: Foris.

Hulst, Harry van der & Jeroen M. van de Weijer (1995): "Vowel harmony." – In: Goldsmith, John (ed.): *The Handbook of Phonological Theory,* 495–534. Oxford: Blackwell.

Jakobson, Roman, Gunnar M. Fant & Morris Halle (1952): *Preliminaries to Speech Analysis: The Distinctive Features and their Correlates* (2nd edn.). – Cambridge, MA: MIT Press.

Ka, Omar (1994): *Wolof Phonology and Morphology*. – Lanham, MD: University Press of America.

Kaye, Jonathan (2000): "A user's guide to Government Phonology (GP)." – Ms., University of Ulster.

Kaye, Jonathan, Jean Lowenstamm & Jean-Roger Vergnaud (1985): "The internal structure of phonological elements: a theory of charm and government." – In: *Phonological Yearbook* 2, 305–328.

– (1990): "Constituent structure and government in phonology." – In: *Phonology* 7, 193–232.

Kenstowicz, Michael (2008): "Two notes on Kinande vowel harmony." – Paper presented at the annual meeting of the Linguistic Society of America, Chicago.

Kiparsky, Paul (1981): "Vowel harmony." – Ms., MIT.

– (1985): "Some Consequences of Lexical Phonology." – In: *Phonology Yearbook* 2, 83–138.

Krämer, Martin (2003): *Vowel Harmony and Correspondence Theory*. – Berlin: Mouton de Gruyter.

Li, Bing (1996): *Tungusic Vowel Harmony: Description and Analysis*. – PhD dissertation, University of Amsterdam. The Hague: Holland Academic Graphics.

Melis, Ed. (1976): "Fonologische verschijnselen in onderlinge samenhang: een hypothese." – In: Koefoed, Geert & Arnold Evers (eds.): *Lijnen van Taaltheoretisch Onderzoek*, 367–380. Groningen: H.D. Tjeenk Willink.

Nevins, Andrew (2010): *Locality in Vowel Harmony*. – Cambridge, MA: MIT Press

Postal, Paul (1968): *Aspects of Phonological Theory*. – New York: Harper and Row.

Pulleyblank, Douglas (1996): "Neutral vowels in Optimality Theory: A comparison of Yoruba and Wolof." – In: *Canadian Journal of Linguistics* 41, 295–347.

Ringen, Catherine & Orvokki Heinämäki (1999): "Variation in Finnish vowel harmony: An OT account." – In: *Natural Language and Linguistic Theory* 17, 303–337.

Ritter, Nancy A. (1999): "The effect of intrasegmental licensing conditions on elemental spreading." – In: Hannahs, S.J. & Michael Davenport (eds.): *Issues in Phonological Structure*. Amsterdam: John Benjamins. 55–74.

Ritter, Nancy A. (1995): *The Role of Universal Grammar in Phonology: A Government Phonology Approach to Hungarian*. – PhD dissertation, New York University.

Sagey, Elizabeth (1986): *The Representation of Features and Relations in Nonlinear Phonology*. – PhD dissertation, MIT.

Salting, Don (2005): "The geometry of harmony." – In: Oostendorp, Marc van & Jeroen M. van de Weijer (eds.): *The Internal Organization of Phonological Segments*. Berlin: Mouton de Gruyter. 93–120.

Schane, Sanford (1984): "The fundamentals of particle phonology." – In: *Phonological Yearbook* 1, 129–55.

Scheer, Tobias (2004): *A Lateral Theory of Phonology*. – Berlin/New York: Mouton de Gruyter.

Schlindwein, Deborah (1987): "P-bearing units: a study of Kinande vowel harmony."
  – In: McDonough, Joyce & Bernadette Plunkett (eds.): *Proceedings of NELS 17*,
  551–567. Amherst, MA: University of Massachusetts, GLSA.
Scobbie, James M., John S. Coleman & Steven Bird (1996): "Key aspects of
  Declarative Phonology." – In: Durand, Jacques & Bernard Laks (eds.): *Current
  Trends in Phonology: Models and Methods*. Vol. 2, 685–710. ESRI/Manchester:
  University of Salford.
Smith, Norval S.H. (2000): "Dependency Phonology meets OT: a proposal for a new
  approach to segmental structure." – In: Dekkers, Joost, F. van der Leeuw & Jeroen
  M. van de Weijer (eds.): *Optimality Theory: Phonology, Syntax, and Acquisition*,
  234–276. Oxford: Oxford University Press.
Steriade, Donca (1981): "Parameters of metrical harmony rules." – Ms., MIT.
  – (1995): "Underspecification and markedness." – In: Goldsmith, John (ed.): *The
  Handbook of Phonological Theory*, 114–174. Cambridge, MA: Blackwell.
Stevens, Kenneth N. & Samuel J. Keyser (1989): "Primary features and their
  enhancement in consonants." – *Language* 65, 81–106.
Törkenczy, Miklós (2011): "Hungarian vowel harmony." – In: Oostendorp, Marc van,
  Colin J. Ewen & Keren D. Rice (eds.): *The Blackwell Companion to Phonology*
  (Vol. 5), 2963–2990. Malden, MA/Oxford: Wiley-Blackwell.
Trubetzkoy, Nikolaj S. (1939[1977]): *Grundzüge der Phonologie* (6th edn.). –
  Göttingen: Vandenhoeck and Ruprecht.
Walker, Caitlin (1995): "ATR-harmony as H-Licensing." – In: *SOAS Working Papers
  in Linguistics and Phonetics* 5, 107–120.

Diana Archangeli, Jeff Mielke & Douglas Pulleyblank

Greater than noise: frequency effects in Bantu height harmony*

1 Introduction

A major concern of phonological theory is how complex phonological patterns can be acquired simply through exposure to imperfect language data. Central to this topic is the nature of the cognitive apparatus brought to bear on this problem of acquisition. The 'nativist' extreme in this regard is to postulate a highly articulated Universal Grammar (UG), with a rich set of structures that are specific to language, hard-wired into the language-learning infant. The 'nurture' extreme is to assume that there is very little cognitive infrastructure that is specific to language. Instead, general purpose learning mechanisms are applied to language data, resulting in an Emergent Grammar (EG) that develops from exposure to the patterns of an adult grammar. These two proposals make different predictions about the nature of sound patterns. In this study, our basic question is whether the distribution of sounds within languages with vowel harmony exhibits the patterns predicted by UG or those predicted by EG. To do so, we explore the frequency of words that violate height harmony rules, and as we will see, in several languages they are less frequent than would be expected by chance, but more frequent than would be expected on the basis of a categorical phonological rule, i.e., the robustness of the patterns is greater than the noise in the data, but less than exceptionless.

We pose this question against the backdrop of Optimality Theory (OT), a model in which the phonological challenge to the language learner is to figure out the ranking of a set of universal constraints (Prince & Smolensky 1993; McCarthy & Prince 1993, 1994). Recent research has seriously challenged the universality of phonological distinctive features (Mielke 2005, 2008) and phonological constraints (Pulleyblank 2006; Hayes & Wilson 2008). Mielke's work, for example, argues against universally-defined distinctive

* Thanks to Larry Hyman for detailed comments on an earlier draft, to Beth Rogers for preparation of the files taken from CBOLD, and to Michael McAuliffe for library research. Thanks also to *freelang.net* for providing word lists for the control languages, and to Robin Dodsworth for statistics help. This paper was supported in part by a Standard Research Grant from the Social Sciences and Humanities Research Council of Canada to Douglas Pulleyblank.

features, suggesting instead that as a language is learned, the learner figures out the necessary features. If such work is correct, it undermines the UG/OT proposal that all constraints are universal: Since many constraints refer to specific features, if features are not universal, then particular constraints involving features cannot be universal either — and consequently, if the type of constraint interaction postulated by OT is on the right track, the theory is nonetheless on the wrong track in assuming a universal, innate set of phonological constraints.

We begin with a brief discussion of what we mean by Emergent Grammar. We then move into the core of the paper, a consideration of certain ways in which UG and EG make different predictions about the patterns we expect to find in phonological systems. We test these predictions by examining the frequencies of vowel co-occurrence patterns in a number of Bantu languages with 5-vowel systems, /i, e, a, o, u/. Conducting a test based on patterns observed in a set of lexical databases, we demonstrate that the attested co-occurrence patterns are consistent with the EG predictions but contradict the UG predictions. Our conclusion supports phonological analysis in Emergentist terms, rather than in Universalist terms.

2 Background: Emergent Grammar

Under the strongest form of Emergence, there is no built-in knowledge of the nature of language. Consequently, when language sound is perceived, there is no prior organization to fit those sounds into. This contrasts with UG, where acquisition would include interpreting sounds and sound sequences in terms of innate distinctive features and innate constraints governing feature co-occurrence. Consequently, under EG we hypothesize that acquisition involves myriad hypotheses about the items being acquired — how the sounds are made and what the sequence of sounds is, as well as hypotheses based on the various contexts in which the sounds were perceived, etc. Similarity between the hypotheses made by an individual speaker about independent utterances results in connections drawn between those hypotheses, connections that are defined by the similarities.

There are several effects of such connection via similarities; we consider a few here. First, connection via similarities results in distinct tokens ultimately being perceived as instances of the same type of sound, leading to the identification of segments. It also results in separate highly similar utterances being connected and ultimately identified as morphemes and words. Additionally, it results in the recognition of similar sound sequences across multiple lexical items, i.e., the identification of sound patterns. Furthermore, connections become increasingly abstract, as second-order similarities are identified and additional connections are drawn. We speculate that these higher-order similarities culminate in the sophisticated phonological and lexical systems of adult grammars; for some preliminary work of this type on the same phenomena examined here, see Archangeli et al. (2011); Archangeli & Pulleyblank (in prep.).

Importantly for our purposes here, these connections serve as attractors (Mohanan 1993). The effect of an attractor is that the more frequently a pattern is found, the more readily new items will be interpreted as fitting that pattern, even in cases where fitting the pattern might require misperception. This is comparable to a priming effect in that the occurrence of a pattern primes a speaker/learner for other occurrences of that same pattern. Attractors facilitate learning because lexical items conforming to an established pattern require less attention than lexical items not conforming to the generalization. Hence the larger the class of conforming lexical items, the less the learner needs to pay attention to individual lexical items (in that respect) during acquisition, during perception, and during production. As such, errors/ changes are expected to be in the direction of a pattern both in the specific environments where a pattern has been grammaticized, as well as in environments where there is no effect of sufficient magnitude to be considered grammatical. As we explore and compare the predictions of EG and UG, we will see that this point plays an important role in distinguishing the two models.

3 The predictions of UG and EG

We outline here two broad types of predictions concerning possible/ impossible data patterns, goodness of fit and domain extension. We discuss two important respects in which UG and EG differ in their predictions about the ways that phonological patterns will be manifested in a language's frequency data.

(1)   Prediction types

    a.**Goodness of fit**: how close do the data fit to the canonical ideal of ungrammatical patterns being completely unattested and grammatical patterns being randomly distributed?

    b.**Domain extension**: to what extent does a pattern in one domain extend to another domain, whether phonological or morphosyntactic?

3.1 Goodness of fit

Goodness of fit refers to whether attested language data diverge to a marked degree from the expectations imposed by the phonological grammar, namely that ungrammatical patterns are unattested and that grammatical patterns are randomly distributed. The fit would be perfect if ungrammatical forms were completely unattested, i.e. observed with a frequency of zero. Grammatical forms, in contrast, might be observed exactly as frequently as expected, or might in some cases be over-represented in some context if rules pushed representations towards particular values. That is, if we compare observed values (*O*) and expected values (*E*), then perfect fit would result in ungrammatical forms having an *O/E* value of 0 (i.e., zero forms), while grammatical forms would have an *O/E* value of ≥ 1.

While both UG and EG predict the same type of asymmetrical differences between the *O/E* values of grammatical and ungrammatical forms, the extent to which the data might deviate from perfect distribution differs in the two theories. UG, in and of itself, predicts exceptionless behaviour (perfection) while EG predicts non-absolute tendencies.[1]

The presence of non-absolute phonological regularities does not in itself invalidate UG-style phonological analysis. Lexicons are full of over- and under-represented structures that are residues of once-productive sound patterns, language contact, and other historical facts. If these patterns are not recognized by the language learner, then they are not part of phonology, and phonological theory does not require an account for them. It is problematic if non-absolute patterns (such as the harmony pattern established below for verbs in our test languages) are recognized by the learner. A UG-style formalism that deals in absolute sound patterns provides no indication of how such non-absolute data patterns are converted by the learner into the absolute patterns encoded in a UG grammar. We return to this issue below in discussing evidence that the non-absolute harmony patterns we observe are in fact part of the phonology and not strictly 'unnoticed' or 'insignificant' regularities in the lexicon, in sections 5.2-5.4.

3.1.1 UG goodness of fit: tight adherence to predictions

In OT, some type of harmony-inducing markedness constraint *FG serving to rule out a disharmonic sequence will either outrank relevant constraints on

---

[1] Note that a model predicting identical *O/E* values for grammatical and ungrammatical forms simply fails as an adequate model of language grammar. Thus, it is no surprise that UG and EG both predict the same type of asymmetry between *O/E* values of grammatical and ungrammatical forms. The difference between the two models lies in the goodness of fit.

faithfulness (*FG >> FAITH) or be outranked by the relevant faithfulness constraints (FAITH >> *FG).

(2)   OT ranking possibilities
   a. disharmonic sequence prevented: *FG >> FAITH
   b. disharmonic sequence allowed: FAITH >> *FG

In the former case (2a), all else being equal, the sequence under consideration should be completely absent from the language; in the latter case (2b), the sequence FG should be attested, with its frequency determined by independent factors governing the probability of each member of the sequence occurring. Thus, an OT grammar is categorically 'either/or': a pattern is either sanctioned by the grammar or prohibited. With the grammar *FG >> FAITH, (2a), the relevant *O/E* values of prohibited sequences should be 0. On the other hand, with the grammar of (2b), FAITH >> *FG, the *O/E* values for the same sequences should be $\geq$ 1, all else being equal. As mentioned above, patterns of alternation could cause particular patterns to be over-represented relative to others; furthermore, since the prohibited sequences are severely under-represented, other sequences will be somewhat over-represented, hence *O/E* $\geq$1 rather than *O/E* = 1.[2]

Note that systematic sub-patterns are predicted to be possible and are not exceptions in the sense being discussed here. For example, if F must be followed by G in some context Q (FG/Q) then the ranking FG/Q >> *FG would result in a restricted subclass of FG sequences in the context Q, in spite of the general prohibition against FG sequences. Such patterns are systematic sub-patterns, not exceptions. True exceptions in UG models are predicted not to occur. Exceptions to either general patterns or more specific sub-patterns should be nonexistent according to the phonological grammar per se. Rare exceptions are possible only as a kind of extra-grammatical 'noise'. As such, exceptional behaviour constitutes a softening of the strict categorical picture otherwise predicted, but such softening is restricted to whatever magnitude can plausibly be attributed to extra-grammatical effects. Factoring in such exceptional 'noise', cross-linguistic data may not be fully 'either/or', but should nevertheless have *O/E* values for ungrammatical forms that are tightly clustered near zero.[3]

---

[2] While we frame this point here in terms of OT, a rule-based approach achieves the same categorical effect by the application of rules to ill-formed sequences.

[3] Clements & Sezer (1982) on Turkish vowel harmony illustrate this point. Assuming a grammar for Turkish with vowel harmony in derived contexts, Clements & Sezer address the problem of accounting for what is apparently a very large class of exceptions in underived forms. Based on what we would interpret as the categorical behaviour hypothesis, they argue that harmony must be restricted to derived

Note that both rule-based and constraint-based UG accounts get around the expectation that there be absolutely no exceptions by postulating otherwise ad hoc devices such as exception features and parochial language-specific constraints. (An approach to phonological encoding such as Direct OT (Golston 1996) is an exception to this point.) Such postulations might slightly soften the prediction that ungrammatical values be zero, but values very close to zero are clearly the expectation.[4]

3.1.2 EG goodness of fit: loose adherence to predictions

Under EG, grammatical expressions emerge from the discovery of patterns in the data. There are no a priori restrictions on what a data set must look like, hence no absolute restrictions on the range of data types that may be attested. This is true for an individual language, and is therefore predicted to be true cross-linguistically.

Given the theory of EG laid out in section 2, whereby similarities are represented via connections (and are ultimately grammaticized), the stronger the connection, the more likely it is to function as an attractor. This means that errors would be expected to be in the direction of conforming to the generalization: more data will come to conform with a pattern than will not. There is no expectation, however, of perfection. Generalizations are not expected to be perfect; learners do not wait for perfection in establishing patterns. While the EG approach is similar to the UG model in predicting cross-linguistic results to have O/E values clustered around 0 and 1, it differs from the UG model in that EG does not predict that individual languages will necessarily or always exhibit extreme behaviour. Though the extremes may constitute the best attractors, languages are expected to vary significantly, with a much looser, gradient adherence to the two extremes. In short, EG expects patterns to be imperfect.[5]

---

contexts. That is, the existence of a large set of exceptions is not possible according to the theory, so Clements & Sezer's conclusion for Turkish is that there is no grammar of harmony governing any underived forms. This provides no explanation of the very large set of underived lexical items that are harmonic. In such a case, the EG approach predicts a bifurcation of the lexicon, into those items that obey the harmony generalization and those that are exempt from it.

[4] Some types of 'exceptions' are better thought of as systematic sub-patterns because they are dealt with grammatically, e.g. by the interaction of full vs. underspecification and rules/constraints. For recent discussion, see Kim & Pulleyblank (2009).

[5] One consequence is that under EG there must be a formal mechanism to represent gradient behaviour, but such a mechanism is inherent to the model, not a post hoc add-on. See Hayes & Wilson (2008); Archangeli et al. (2011); Archangeli & Pulleyblank (in prep.).

3.2 Domain Extension

By the 'domain' for a phonological pattern, we mean the restriction of applicability to some defined phonological or morphosyntactic class. For example, a constraint might be restricted in its applicability to the class of verbs, or to the class of nouns; it might be restricted to the class of phonological words, to the class of nonlow vowels, and so on. (See Archangeli & Pulleyblank 2002 for exemplification of domains in the ATR harmony system of Kinande.) All such domains constitute restrictions that are in some sense 'external' to the phonological material actually addressed by the condition. As we show here, UG and EG theories make strikingly different predictions about whether the domain of a pattern is expected to extend beyond what is specified by the grammar. UG predicts the absence of gradual domain extension; EG predicts gradual domain extension.

3.2.1 UG: Absence of Gradual Domain Extension

There is no grammatical reason to expect a constraint or rule governing a particular class Q to have an effect on a distinct class R. For example, the constraint *FG/Q (F must not be followed by G in the context Q) would be predicted to have no effect in context R, where Q and R are disjoint environments. Relating this to the Bantu patterns under examination, imagine that a *FG constraint were restricted to the morphosyntactic domain of verb. A UG analysis would predict a complete absence of effect in some other morphosyntactic domain, for example, noun, or else a complete, categorical extension of the pattern to include the new domain. Similarly, imagine that the same constraint were restricted to the phonological class of rounded vowels: A UG account would predict a complete lack of effect on the phonological class of unrounded vowels, or else a complete extension to include the unrounded class.

    The prediction of a lack of extension beyond the domain to which a constraint is restricted is not limited to an optimality theoretic UG. For example, all else being equal, the simplicity metric of Chomsky & Halle (1968) would prefer a rule expressed in terms of fewer features to a rule expressed in terms of more features. Hence a rule schematically expressed as F→G/P would be preferred to the rule F→G/PQ. We might therefore expect a change from a grammar with the 'PQ' environment to one with the more general 'P' environment. The point of importance here is that given the means of rule expression, such a shift would be expected to be categorical, not gradual.

    Overall, grammatical theory of a UG type makes no predictions of asymmetric feature distribution in any class other than that defined by rule/constraint. All else being equal, random distribution ($O/E = 1$) is expected.

3.2.2 EG: Gradient Domain Extension

EG predicts the gradual generalization of an effect to broader classes. As noted above, generalizations constitute data attractors, and such attraction could be relevant for items within a narrowly defined class as well as for items outside that class. Such extension of an effect could therefore involve extension to a different morphosyntactic class or to a different phonological class. It would of course be expected that the strength of an effect within the defined domain would be greater than outside of the defined domain. It would also be expected that there might be interacting pressures constituting pressure against wanton extension. But the basic expectation is that there would be an effect in domains not identified in the characterization of the pattern itself.

3.3 Summary and discussion

To summarize, UG and EG make quite different predictions about the nature of phonological patterns. Under UG, the predictions are categorical: a phonological pattern exists or it does not exist. This predicts tight statistical adherence to postulated patterns (either a pattern holds almost without exception in a language or it is not a phonological pattern) coupled with the absence of gradual extensions of a pattern into new morphosyntactic or phonological domains.

By contrast, EG's attractor effect predicts looser statistical adherence to postulated patterns, expecting that patterns will hold largely within a lexicon but that there may be reasonably large numbers of 'exceptions'. More specifically, EG predicts that a pattern holding in some domain is expected to appear as a tendency in other domains, whether morphosyntactic or phonological. This extension would provide evidence that the patterns are internalized by speakers, and therefore that they are phonological and not unanalyzed historical residues (for relevant discussion, see Blevins 2006).

	UG	EG
Goodness of fit	tight	loose
Gradient extension of morphosyntactic domain	no	yes
Gradient extension of phonological domain	no	yes

Table 1. Predictions

It is worth pointing out that this highly categorical, all-or-nothing interpretation of UG is rarely if ever observed in practice — it is abundantly clear from even a small amount of data that language is messy, and phonologists have worked to account both for the tidy patterns and for the messiness. The strategy, regardless of the theory, is to determine whether any of the principles already existing within the theory can account for the pattern; if not, then a new principle is proposed. From a UG perspective, the performance/ competence contrast provides one mechanism, by relegating the messiness to performance and the orderly behaviour to competence. The challenge, of course, is to provide a good theory of what constitutes performance, what constitutes competence, and how to navigate between the two. Other principles can, and have, been proposed in UG to account for vagaries of the data. By contrast, EG assumes that speakers form a grammar hypothesis based directly on the language data in its full, complex, and messy glory, the basic raw material from which an analysis emerges. Under EG, accounting for the messiness is intrinsic to hypothesizing a grammar; under UG, the messiness is often viewed as an uninteresting residue.

We turn now to a discussion of the data with which we test these hypotheses and our methodology for making these tests.

4 Data and methodology

Our test case here is height harmony in Bantu. It is well documented that Bantu languages exhibit a variety of patterns of vowel harmony (Hyman 1999). Our particular focus is height harmony in systems with five vowels: /i, e, a, o, u/. Height harmony in Bantu is an interesting test case because (i) it is found in languages with only five vowels, so the tests themselves are very manageable; (ii) height harmony is typically restricted to verbs, giving a morphosyntactically restricted domain; (iii) in some languages it is asymmetric (not holding in *e. . .u* sequences), a phonologically restricted domain: we restrict our study to asymmetric cases. Of particular importance to the discussion here is the tremendous resource of the Comparative Bantu OnLine Dictionary (CBOLD).[6] This resource provides searchable databases of a large number of Bantu languages, allowing for the detailed examination of lexical patterns. The data sets in CBOLD make it possible to compare the frequency of occurrence of various vowel sequences in a fairly large number of lexical items drawn from a fairly large number of related languages. This

---

[6] http://www.cbold.ish-lyon.cnrs.fr.

methodology, of considering the statistical distributions of segment sequences, fits into a growing body of literature, such as Coleman & Pierrehumbert (1997); Frisch et al. (2000); Pozdniakov & Segerer (2007); Hammond (2011).[7] The investigation of the frequency of disharmonic stems has clear parallels with work on backness and rounding harmony in Turkic languages by Harrison and colleagues (Harrison 1999; Harrison et al. 2002).

4.1 Height harmony

The canonical pattern of Bantu height harmony, the one we consider here, is illustrated by the following data from Ciyao (Ngunga 2000: 45–47).[8]

	'-il' applicative			'-ul' reversive		
a.	dim-	dim-il-	'cultivate'	siv-	siw-ul-	'close/open up'
b.	wut-	wut-il-	'pull'	uuv-	uuw-ul	'hide/reveal'
c.	saam-	saam-il-	'move'	mat-	mat-ul-	'adhere/peel off'
d.	pet-	pet-el-	'ornament'	sweek-	sweek-ul-	'insert/pull out'
e.	soom-	soom-el-	'read/study'	som-	som-ol-	'pierce/extract'

Table 2. Bantu Height Harmony in Ciyao

The Ciyao data is typical of the pattern of interest here. Harmony is restricted to stems; that is, it applies between roots and suffixes, excluding prefixes from the domain of harmony. Front high vowels in suffixes surface as high after both root vowels that are high (Table 2a,b) and root vowels that are low (Table 2c). However, a front vowel does not surface as high after a mid vowel, surfacing only as mid in that environment (Table 2d,e). Featurally, the pattern is asymmetric in that back vowels behave slightly differently. After high and low vowels, the behaviour of back vowels is comparable (Table 2a-c); after a mid back vowel, the pattern is also similar, with only a mid vowel possible (Table 2e); after a front mid vowel, however, a back high vowel surfaces unchanged (Table 2d). Expressing this asymmetric behaviour

---

[7] We thank Larry Hyman for drawing Pozdniakov & Segerer (2007) to our attention. That work examines the frequencies of consonant place in CVC sequences, using a methodology similar to the methodology used here.

[8] The examples here do not include the final vowel, because it is not included in the examples in Ngunga (2000) on which Table 2 is based. However, all of our analyses are based on the stem-field in CBOLD, a field that includes the final vowel.

processually, a high front vowel lowers after any mid vowel; a high back vowel lowers after a mid back vowel.[9] Table 3 summarizes this pattern.

	i	u
i	√	√
e	–	√
a	√	√
o	–	–
u	√	√

Table 3. Basic asymmetric height harmony in suffixes with high vowels

As seen in Table 3, three cells are crucial in defining a pattern of Bantu asymmetric height harmony, namely those for *e. . .i, o. . .i,* and *o. . .u.* The frequency of occurrence of these three vowel sequences will form the cornerstone of our tests below for harmonic behaviour. The categorical UG approach expects virtually no items with these sequences while the gradient EG approach expects they will be under-represented but not necessarily completely absent.

4.2 Language selection

The criteria below were used to select test and control languages, based on their vowel inventories and reported harmony patterns.

All languages

The languages examined were all required to have only the 5 vowels /i, e, a, o, u/. All languages had to have data in an accessible format (or allowing for reorganization where necessary) so that searches would be comparable across languages.

Test languages

Test languages were required to exhibit Bantu asymmetric height harmony, exhibiting morphological alternations involving suffixes which are high after both high and low vowels and mid after mid vowels, as per the pattern shown in Table 3. Given our criteria, we identified six test languages in the

---

[9] Within OT, we might adopt an analysis along the lines of Beckman (1997), though nothing in our present discussion hinges on the precise nature of the formal analysis. Moreover, if Hyman (1999) is correct that the historical account of vowel height harmony is one of peripheralization, not lowering (see section 5.1, below), then it would certainly be appropriate to consider a formal 'raising' analysis.

Comparative Bantu OnLine Database (CBOLD): Bukusu, Chichewa, Ciyao, Ikalanga, Jita, and Nkore-Kiga.

Control languages

Control languages were required to have no indication of vowel harmony in their vowel distribution. Six non-Bantu control languages were drawn from dictionaries provided by *freelang.net*[10] because the CBOLD data did not provide relevant controls.[11] The control languages are Ainu, Fulfulde[12], Hebrew, Japanese, Kiribati, and Maori.

Details on the six test languages are given in (3). Our analysis was restricted to single words, excluding any multiword phrases in the word lists. The number of lexical items listed for each language below is the number of words remaining after exclusion of multiword phrases. However, we did not exclude any words on the basis of having a morpheme in common. Thus, our data may include multiple words with the same root (but does not include multiple phrases with the same word, because it does not include multiword phrases).

---

[10] http://www.freelang.net/

[11] We considered using control languages from CBOLD but ran into difficulties. For example, we considered Punu (Niger-Congo, Bantu; Gabon & Congo; B43 in Guthrie 1967-71; CBOLD: Blanchon 1994), but rejected it because Punu disallows mid vowels except in the root-initial syllable, giving a highly skewed distribution. We also considered Ndebele (Ndebele: Niger-Congo, Bantu; Lesotho, South Africa, & Swaziland; S44 in Guthrie 1967-71; CBOLD: Pelling 1971), but rejected it as a control because it has a partial harmony system. (See Hyman (1999) for discussion of the many different harmony patterns found in Bantu.) To avoid these difficulties, we include control languages from outside Bantu.

[12] Fula, of which Fulfulde is one of the names, is a language spoken in dispersed communities throughout much of West Africa, with multiple dialects. Descriptions differ as to the precise characterization of the vowel system. For example, Paradis (1989) discusses a dialect of Fula spoken in Mauritania and Senegal, analyzing the vowel system as consisting of seven vowels, with a largely predictable contrast between the mid vowels /e, o/ and /ɛ, ɔ/; see also Archangeli & Pulleyblank (1994), Krämer (2003). Arnott (1969, 1970), focussing on the Gombe dialect of Nigeria, describes a five-vowel system cross-cut by length. Arnott notes quality distinctions in the vowels but considers such differences predictable from a basic quantity distinction. The data in Freelang represents the variety spoken in Guinea, and presents the language with 5 vowels cross-cut by length.

(3) The test cases[13]

- Bukusu: Niger-Congo, Bantu; Kenya; E31C in Guthrie (1967-71); CBOLD: KWL (1998); morphological alternations demonstrated in Mutonyi (2000); 808 verbs, 1361 nouns, 2502 lexical items in total (.fm)

- Chichewa: Niger-Congo, Bantu; Malawi; N31B in Guthrie (1967-71); CBOLD: Mtenje (2001); morphological alternations demonstrated in CBOLD; 2007 verbs, 2104 nouns, 4598 lexical items in total (.txt)

- Ciyao: Niger-Congo, Bantu; Malawi, Mozambique & Tanzania; P21 in Guthrie (1967-71); CBOLD: Ngunga (2001); morphological alternations demonstrated in Ngunga (2000); 2583 verbs, 2969 nouns, 6444 lexical items in total (.txt)

- Ikalanga: Niger-Congo, Bantu; Botswana & Zimbabwe; S16 in Guthrie (1967-71); CBOLD: Mathangwane (1994); morphological alternations demonstrated in Mathangwane (1999) (though asymmetric nature of harmony not discussed there); 1149 verbs, 1640 nouns, 2899 lexical items in total (.fm)

- Jita: Niger-Congo, Bantu; Tanzania; J25 in Guthrie (1967-71); CBOLD: Downing (1999); morphological alternations demonstrated in Downing (1999) (though asymmetric nature of harmony not discussed there); 865 verbs, 998 nouns, 1888 lexical items in total (.txt)

- Nkore-Kiga: Niger-Congo, Bantu; Kenya; J13 in Guthrie (1967-71); CBOLD: Taylor (1959); morphological alternations demonstrated in Taylor (1985); 2994 verbs, 3827 nouns, 6696 lexical items in total (.txt)

Details on the six control languages are given in (4).

(4) The control cases
- Ainu: language isolate; Japan; 1636 lexical items
- Fulfulde: Niger-Congo, Atlantic; Senegal to Cameroon; 194 lexical items
- Hebrew: Afroasiatic, Semitic; Israel; 1038 lexical items
- Japanese: Japonic; Japan; 49,027 lexical items
- Kiribati: Austronesian, Oceanic; Kiribati; 5118 lexical items
- Maori; Austronesian, Oceanic; New Zealand; 769 lexical items

Before describing our methodology, two caveats are in order. First, while the CBOLD data organization made it possible to search nouns and verbs in two separate classes, the freelang.net data structure did not allow us to easily separate nouns from verbs. Consequently all control comparisons are against

---

[13] CBOLD includes references as indicated here, but without complete bibliographical information. For each test language, there is a .txt data set version (.txt) and a FileMakerPro™ version (.fm) of the data set in CBOLD. We used the .txt version unless the data was more accessible through the .fm version.

a set including both nouns and verbs, as well as other word classes. Since the expected noun-verb differences are a special property of the Bantu languages in question, and we are aware of no effect of lexical category on vowel distribution in the control languages, we do not expect this to be problematic. Second, both data sources make it possible to get data concerning type frequency, but not token frequency. We found no sources providing information about the frequency of particular lexical items in connected discourse in the languages of interest in this study.

4.3 Methodology

For each language examined, we established the frequency of all two-vowel sequences in CBOLD 'stems'.[14] We did not include morphological boundaries within stems, so all V_1. . .V_2 sequences within stems were included in the frequency counts, that is, all stem-internal cases of a V_1. . .V_2 sequence, where '. . .' may represent any number of consonants. Vowel sequences in the 'stem' field were counted, subject to the following exclusions. First, items with empty 'stem' fields, no vowels in the stem (e.g. a stem like 'lw-'), or a single vowel in the stem (e.g. a stem like 'ku') were effectively excluded from the count. Second, stems including spaces were not counted, e.g. stems like 'i- ka', 'nye- nye', 'cema -xo'. Fourth, homophones were excluded. The data collected therefore bear on sequence types, not numbers of tokens of particular sequences. Since the languages considered all have 5 vowels, a total of 25 vowel sequences must be considered for each language. The basic approach is to establish how many examples of a given type would be expected (E) , and to compare this expected value with the actual number of observed (O) sequences. The resulting O/E values for particular vowel sequences in the test languages can be compared with the corresponding values in the control languages.

To give a flavour of the data extraction process, we illustrate the process with Ciyao, one of the test languages in (3). A sample of the Ciyao data available in CBOLD is given to the left of the vertical line in Table 4. The columns 'Stem', 'Tone', Part of Speech ('POS'), 'Class', and 'Gloss' represent the kinds of fields available in CBOLD. From the 'Stem' field, all two-vowel sequences are extracted, as indicated in the rightmost column of

---

[14] We used the 'stem' field for all languages except for Ikalanga, where the comparable information was labeled 'root' in the FileMakerPro™ file. The items in that field correspond to items in the field labeled 'stem' in the .txt file for Ikalanga.

Table 4, headed 'Observations'. (Note that a long vowel, e.g. in the first item, *-n'weesula*, is classed as a single vowel, not as a sequence of two vowels.)[15]

Stem	CBOLD data categorization				data extraction
	Tone	POS	Class	Gloss	Observations
-n'weesula	HHLL	V	15	'abrase the skin'	*e...u, u...a*
-loongana	HHLL	V	15	'accompany'	*o...a, a...a*
-soonjela	HHLL	V	15	'accuse'	*o...e, e...a*
-pokolanya	HHLL	V	15	'arbitrate'	*o...o, o...a, a...a*
-tumika	HHL	V	15	'act as a servant'	*u...i, i...a*
-paambika	HHLL	V	15	'add to a load'	*a...i, i...a*
-paambicila	HHLLL	V	15	'add to, increase'	*a...i, i...i, i...a*
-oonjecesya	LLHLL	V	15	'add to, increase'	*o...e, e...e, e...a*
-mata	HH	V	15	'adhere'	*a...a*
-maambatila	HHLLL	V	15	'adhere, stick'	*a...a, a...i, i...a*
-nyaambatila	HHLLL	V	15	'adhere, stick to'	*a...a, a...i, i...a*
...	...	...	...	...	...

Table 4. CBOLD word list (Ciyao verbs)

Counting the number of occurrences of each $V_1...V_2$ pair gives the observed frequencies. For example, a verb such as *-pokolanya* 'arbitrate' would be counted as having one *o...o* sequence, one *o...a* sequence, and one *a...a* sequence. (As noted in footnote 8, the final vowel is included in all analyses.) For Ciyao verb stems, the observed values are as shown in Table 5. The column and row headed 'T' give the total number of items. Thus, there are 1455 *a...V₂* pairs and 3296 $V_1...a$ pairs; there are 5758 verbs in all; etc.

		V_2					
		i	e	a	o	u	T
	i	361	0	815	8	93	1277
	e	3	269	395	0	111	778
V_1	a	271	6	933	4	241	1455
	o	10	117	360	355	0	842
	u	423	3	793	4	183	1406
	T	828	395	3296	371	868	5758

Table 5. Observed frequencies: Ciyao verbs

If all vowels were equally frequent and randomly distributed, the frequency of each $V_1...V_2$ sequence would be 230 ($\frac{1}{25}$ of 5758, the total number of

---

[15] All the observations about vowel sequences abstract away from tone, as shown in this table. Whether a vowel is low or high toned does not change its status with respect to the analysis here.

sequences), and significant deviations from this would indicate a non-random distribution. However, since the five vowels are not equally frequent, the expected frequencies of the V_1. . .V_2 sequences depend on the frequency of each vowel. For instance, in Bantu, verbs typically end with the vowel /a/, resulting in a preponderance of V_1. . .V_2 pairs with /a/ as the second vowel (this is seen in Table 5 where the 3296 V_1. . .*a* pairs outnumber all other sequences with a different V_2). To account for such asymmetries, expected frequencies have therefore been calculated based on the number of occurrences of the specific vowels in V_1. . .V_2 sequences:

(5)   Calculation of expected frequencies

Expected frequency of V_1...V_2: (V_1 freq * V_2 freq) / total

For example, given the 5758 vowel pairs of the Ciyao database, the expected frequency of an an *a*. . .*a* sequence is (3296*1455)/5758, which rounds to 833; the expected frequency of an *a*. . .*e* is (395*1455)/5758, which rounds to 100; and so on. The expected values for all V_1. . .V_2 sequences are as in Table 6.

Dividing the Observed values by the Expected values (the ratio *O/E*) allows us to determine whether the actual recorded number of tokens of a specific V_1...V_2 sequence is as expected (close to 1), under-represented (less than 1), or over-represented (greater than 1). For example, as shown in Table 7, *u*. . .*a* and *e*. . .*u* occur very close to as expected, *e*. . .*o*, *i*. . .*e*, and *o*. . .*u* are unattested (*O/E* = 0), *u*. . .*e*, *u*. . .*o*, and *a*. . .*o* are strongly under-represented (*O/E* of 0.03 and 0.04), while *e*. . .*e*, *o*. . .*o*, *o*. . .*e* and *u*. . .*u* are strongly over-represented (*O/E* > 2).

While an *O/E* value of 1 for all sequences indicates that the segments are randomly distributed, if some sequences have very low *O/E* values (e.g., because they are prohibited), we expect the nominal *O/E* value for other sequences to be somewhat above 1, since the total of observed values across sequences is the same as the total of expected vowels: fewer observations of a prohibited sequence means more observations of other sequences. If there is a recurrent repair strategy for prohibited vowel sequences, then we expect the output of the repair to be over-represented. For example, if Ciyao historically had verbs with the sequence *o*. . .*u* (which has a frequency of 0 in our data set), and these were repaired by lowering /u/ to [o], there would be more observed *o*. . .*o* sequences than expected, which is what is observed in Table 7.

		i	e	a	o	u	T
				V_2			
	i	$^{361}/_{184}=1.97$	$^{0}/_{88}=0.00$	$^{815}/_{731}=1.11$	$^{8}/_{82}=0.10$	$^{93}/_{193}=0.48$	1277
	e	$^{3}/_{112}=0.03$	$^{269}/_{53}=5.04$	$^{395}/_{445}=0.89$	$^{0}/_{50}=0.00$	$^{111}/_{117}=0.95$	778
V_1	a	$^{271}/_{209}=1.30$	$^{6}/_{100}=0.06$	$^{933}/_{833}=1.12$	$^{4}/_{94}=0.04$	$^{241}/_{219}=1.10$	1455
	o	$^{10}/_{121}=0.08$	$^{117}/_{58}=2.03$	$^{360}/_{482}=0.75$	$^{355}/_{54}=6.54$	$^{0}/_{127}=0.00$	842
	u	$^{183}/_{202}=0.91$	$^{3}/_{96}=0.03$	$^{793}/_{804}=0.99$	$^{4}/_{91}=0.04$	$^{423}/_{212}=2.00$	1406
	T	828	395	3296	371	868	5758

Table 7. Observed/Expected ratios: Ciyao verbs

In evaluating the key sequences, *e. . .i, o. . .i,* and *o. . .u,* we use the *O/E* values to determine whether the occurrence is as expected or is under- or over-represented. The criterion for significance of under- or over-representation is whether the *O/E* values of particular $V_1...V_2$ sequences are significantly different from the same sequences in the control languages.

(6) Interpretation of *O/E* results

    a. as expected: 1

    b. non-occurring: 0

    c. over-represented: > 1

    d. under-represented: < 1

An issue with interpreting raw *O/E* ratios is that ratios for under-represented sequences span the range [0, 1) and ratios for over-represented sequences span the range (1, +∞). Under- and over-representation are made directly comparable by taking the base-2 log of the *O/E* ratio ($\log_2 O/E$). For example, under the assumption that being twice as frequent or three times as frequent as expected is comparable in magnitude to being half or one third as frequent as expected, the raw *O/E* values (2.0 and 3.0 vs. 0.5 and 0.3 respectively) are unrevealing but the $\log_2$ values allow straightforward comparison:

(7) *O/E* ratios and $\log_2 O/E$ values

O/E	$\log_2 O/E$	
4.00	2.00	four times as frequent as expected
3.00	1.58	three times as frequent as expected
2.00	1.00	twice as frequent as expected
1.00	0.00	as frequent as expected
0.50	− 1.00	half as frequent as expected
0.33	− 1.58	one third as frequent as expected
0.25	− 2.00	one fourth as frequent as expected

Converted into log values, over-representation is indicated by a positive number, while under-representation is indicated by a negative number. The $\log_2 O/E$ values for vowel sequences in Ciyao verbs are given in Table 8.[16]

		V_2					
		i	e	a	o	u	T
	i	0.98	n/a	0.16	−3.36	−1.05	1277
	e	−5.22	2.33	−0.17	n/a	−0.08	778
V_1	a	0.37	−4.06	0.16	−4.55	0.14	1455
	o	−3.60	1.02	−0.42	2.71	n/a	842
	u	−0.14	−5.01	−0.02	−4.50	1.00	1406
	T	828	395	3296	371	868	5758

Table 8. $\log_2$ of Observed/Expected ratios: Ciyao verbs

For our analysis, we use the log values.

5 Results

There are three tests to consider: (i) goodness of fit, (ii) extension to morphosyntactic domains, and (iii) extension to phonological domains. Before presenting our results for these tests, we first provide necessary background by establishing that Bantu height harmony holds in verbs in our test languages, but not in nouns.

5.1 Bantu height harmony in verbs

Although it is clear that Bantu height harmony applies within verbs, it is often less clear from descriptions whether (the same type of) harmony also holds of nouns. Greenberg (1951) suggests that harmony held of both nouns and verbs in Proto-Bantu; Hyman (1999), on the other hand, argues that Proto-Bantu did not have height harmony in either verbs or nouns. We adopt Hyman's proposal here (resolving, indeed even discussing, the various issues involved in the development of Bantu height harmony goes well beyond the scope of this paper). Hyman's basic argument involves a mapping of the range of patterns observed in synchronic Bantu grammars, arguing that the

---

[16] The $\log_2$ O/E is undefined for the three unattested sequences, because the log of zero is undefined. It can be thought of as infinitely negative.

simplest historical analysis involves a proto-language with seven vowels (the standard assumption), where harmony developed by a peripheralization of historical mid vowels, where the peripheralization was blocked in cases where a mid vowel was protected by a preceding mid vowel. Hence 'harmony' resulted from mid vowels raising to high, with such raising blocked adjacent to mid vowels. This resulted in mid-mid sequences (and low-high or high-high in derived cases). The force of Hyman's argument lies in his account of why this analysis derives asymmetric harmony, differences in patterns with five vs. seven vowels, and so on. If this proposal for harmony as an innovation is correct, and harmony in nouns is innovative where it occurs, this would mean that harmony is actively spreading from verbs to nouns, providing evidence that harmony at least in verbs is part of speakers' phonological knowledge. If, on the other hand, it turns out that harmony in nouns is conservative and receding, it could be the case that it is a historical remnant that speakers may or may not encode in their repository of phonological knowledge. Evidence that would bear on this issue might be the extent to which properties of synchronic verb harmony show themselves to be in the pattern of 'retreat'. The questions involved are important, because residual vowel harmony in nouns (as opposed to active extension) could provide weaker evidence for gradient phonological knowledge in Bantu height harmony. Though beyond the scope of the work reported on here, we hope to address some of the relevant issues through lexical examination of various additional systems of Bantu height harmony involving languages with seven vowels, and differing patterns of harmony, both symmetric and asymmetric. See Hyman (1999) for relevant background.

Note that even in specific language descriptions, the noun/verb harmony situation is often unclear. For example, Mathangwane (1999: 57) claims that "vowel harmony in Ikalanga is found in both verb and noun roots," but in her discussion of noun roots it appears that the harmony there is quite different from the harmony observed in verbs. While verbs in Ikalanga exhibit precisely the asymmetric pattern of height harmony under consideration here, harmony in nouns is more restricted. For disyllabic forms, Mathangwane (1999: 52) notes that "noun roots in Ikalanga allow all the possible vowel patterns." In particular, she cites numerous examples of *e. . .i* nouns, *o. . .i* nouns, and *o. . .u* nouns. Where harmony is attested, it is "in trisyllabic nouns where the first two vowels agree in harmonic height" (1999: 56). Such cases, while interesting, seem clearly different from harmony in verbs. Although the first two vowels are consistent with the prohibition on mid-high sequences, the second and third vowels need not be. Mathangwane (1999: 57) cites examples like [ɲéɲédzí] 'star' where *e...i* is possible in nouns.

Thus, there are two issues to consider. First, we demonstrate that there is height harmony in the verbs of the test languages but not in the control languages. We then compare the distribution of *e. . .i, o. . .i,* and *o. . .u* in nouns and verbs in the test languages, and demonstrate that there are markedly different distributions in the two morphosyntactic classes, with fewer instances of the key sequences in verbs than in nouns. In this way we establish the morphosyntactic domain restriction, to verbs, on Bantu height harmony in the test languages.

5.1.1 Verbs in test languages vs. control languages

We now compare the occurrence of *e. . .i, o. . .i,* and *o. . .u* in the test language verbs vs. in the control languages (recall that the control data is not separated into verb and noun classes). The results show a significant difference, supporting the analysis of height harmony in the verbs of the test languages. As Figure 1 demonstrates, each sequence is less frequent in the test languages (the six Bantu languages with height harmony) than in the three control languages.

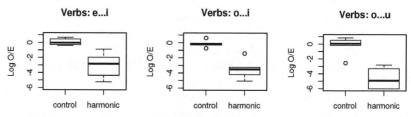

Figure 1: Harmonic vs. control languages (verbs)

Linear regressions were performed for each of the three vowel sequences, with $\log_2 O/E$ as the dependent variable and Language Type (harmonic vs. control) as a factor.[17] Language Type is significant for all three vowel sequences (*e. . .i*: Estimate = -3.07084, $\bar{R}^2 = 0.6448$, p = 0.00101; *o. . .i*: Estimate = -3.6658, $\bar{R}^2 = 0.7787$, p = 0.000089; *o. . .u*: Estimate = -3.9985, $\bar{R}^2 = 0.7075$, p = 0.000371). Each of the three Estimates is between -3 and -4, indicating that the harmony languages have $\log_2 O/E$ values that are between 3 and 4 less than the $\log_2 O/E$ values for control languages. In O/E terms, this means that the sequences are between 8 and 16 times more under-represented for harmony languages than for control languages.[18] The Adjusted R^2 ($\bar{R}^2$) values of 0.6448 and higher indicate that the majority of the between-language variation in $\log_2 O/E$ can be accounted for by whether the

---

[17] Undefined $\log_2 O/E$ values (for unattested sequences) are replaced by -6 for all of the statistical tests and plots. This is less than the most negative $\log_2 O/E$ value for unattested sequences in all of the tests.

[18] This is because $2^3 = 8$ and $2^4 = 16$.

language is classified as harmonic or control. Our conclusion, not unexpected, is that there is height harmony in the verbs of our test languages.

5.1.2 Comparing nouns and verbs in test languages

Next, the same three sequences, *e. . .i, o. . .i,* and *o. . .u,* are compared in nouns vs. verbs in the test languages. We find a significant difference in the distribution of each of these sequences in the two morphosyntactic classes: as seen by the boxplots in Figure 2, the prohibited forms are more frequent in nouns than in verbs, supporting the analysis of Bantu height harmony in the class of verbs but not in nouns.

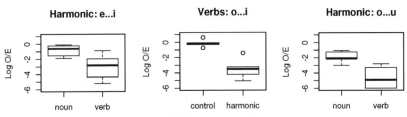

Figure 2: Nouns vs. verbs (harmonic languages only)

Morphosyntactic Class (verb vs. noun) is a significant factor for all three sequences (*e. . .i:* Estimate = −2.1825, $\bar{R}^2$ = 0.4333, p = 0.0119; *o. . .i:* Estimate = −3.1215, $\bar{R}^2$ = 0.7303, p = 0.000244; *o. . .u:* Estimate = −2.2730, $\bar{R}^2$ = 0.5059, p = 0.00571). The difference in the expected direction indicates that height harmony is greater in verbs in these languages: there are significantly fewer instances of the key sequences in verbs than there are in nouns. The differences between test language nouns vs. control language words (see Figure 4 in section 5.3) are nevertheless significant, though the differences between nouns and controls are smaller than the differences between test language verb and nouns. Overall, the key sequences in nouns are under-represented, but to a much less extent than in verbs. In addition, though these three sequences are under-represented in nouns, the $\log_2$ *O/E* values are close enough to zero (at least for *e...i* and *o...i*) that height harmony in nouns could only be postulated if the learner was willing to accept very large numbers of examples inconsistent with the harmonic requirement.

5.1.3 Summary

The results above demonstrate that the expected pattern of Bantu height harmony obtains in the test languages, and that it is found in the verbs, but not to the same extent in the nouns. We are now in a position to consider the results of the three tests.

5.2 Goodness of fit

UG predicts a tight fit between the expected patterns and the attested patterns: $\log_2 O/E$ values will be substantial and negative (or undefined, as in the case where the O/E ratio is zero) for disallowed sequences and will be 0 or greater than 0 for allowed sequences. EG predicts a loose fit, with negative $\log_2 O/E$ values for disallowed sequences and tending to be 0 or greater for allowed sequences. Furthermore, for EG, individual languages are expected to show a fair amount of variation in these patterns while with UG, individual language values are expected to be fairly similar, since *degree* of vowel harmony is not a parameter for sound patterns represented in that model.

Recall from section 4.1 that languages with Bantu height harmony and languages without such harmony can be distinguished by their values for the three sequences *e. . .i*, *o. . .i*, and *o. . .u*. These sequences are ungrammatical in height harmony languages but, all else being equal, grammatical in languages without Bantu height harmony. The goodness-of-fit test is therefore to compare the $\log_2 O/E$ values for these three crucial sequences in test and control languages. Under UG we expect large negative or undefined values in the test languages while under EG we expect a looser clustering. We express this by using a variable *t*, for 'threshold': In test languages, the $\log_2 O/E$ values for *e. . .i*, *o. . .i*, and *o. . .u* should be under threshold, or $\log_2 O/E < t < 0$.

	Test languages	Control languages
UG	$\log_2 O/E \rightarrow -\infty$	$\log_2 O/E \approx 0$
EG	$\log_2 O/E < t < 0$	$t < \log_2 O/E \approx 0$

Table 9. Goodness of fit predictions: *e…i, o…i, o…u*

The $\log_2 O/E$ values for the three sequences are shown in Figure 3. For each of the test languages, values for verbs and nouns are indicated with filled and unfilled circles, respectively. Dotted lines show the range in which the threshold *t* could occur, if there is a phonological pattern involving verbs but not nouns. Only three $\log_2 O/E$ values are undefined, meaning the sequences are completely unattested. These are *o. . .u* in Chichewa, Ciyao, and Nkore-Kiga.[19]

The pattern here is consistent with the predicted loose fit of EG; it is inconsistent with the predicted tight fit of UG. The two exceptions are

---

[19] Recall that in these cases, the other values, which are negative but not undefined, are contrary to the UG prediction. Setting aside two outliers (Nkore-Kiga *e. . .i* and Hebrew *o. . .u*), the $\log_2 O/E$ values for verbs in test languages range from undefined to −1.42, and the $\log_2 O/E$ values for words in control languages range from −0.73 to 0.84.

Hebrew *o. . .u*, which appears to be an unexpected pattern in that language, and *e. . .i* in Nkore-Kiga. Examination of the Nkore-Kiga data reveals that the preponderance of *e. . .i* sequences occurs in vowel-initial stems; Larry Hyman (p.c.) points out that many of the relevant stems involve a reflexive prefix 'e-', e.g. /ku-búza/ *kubúza* 'to cause loss, be lost to', /ku-é-búza/ *kwébuza* 'to hide oneself' (with the infinitival prefix /ku-/). If we consider the initial vowel of vowel-initial forms not to be part of the stem (i.e. the stem in [kwébuza] would be {buza}), thereby excluding such vowels from the domain of harmony, the $\log_2$ *O/E* value for Nkore-Kiga *e. . .i* is −2.66, which is in line with the other test languages. The numbers for the other two sequences that do not include /e/ as V_1 are not substantially affected by this change.

The chart in Figure 3 vividly illustrates the differences. While the overall picture is of low values in the harmonic cases and high values in the nonharmonic cases, there is no tight clustering of values. Furthermore, there are no general patterns across the languages vis-à-vis the distribution of these sequences. However, as both models predict, in the control languages virtually all sequences cluster around 0 (the sole exception is *o. . .u* in Hebrew).

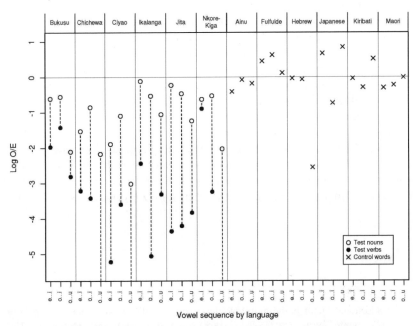

Figure 3: Goodness-of-fit $\log_2$ *O/E* values for test and control languages

Two issues remain that cannot be adequately addressed in this paper. First, if the harmonic $\log_2 O/E$ values were to be considered consistent with UG, it would mean that the theory tolerates a fairly high amount of extra-grammatical 'noise'. For such a theory to be falsifiable would require a quantitative determination of how much of this kind of noise is acceptable before grammaticality is lost. Without such a determination, the facts of Bantu vowel distribution constitute a counter-example to the expectations of UG. Second, we have assumed that some notion of threshold would be needed with EG. Determining (i) whether a threshold is the right way to consider such cases, and (ii) what the quantitative nature of such a threshold must be, are both necessary for EG to be considered successful in this regard; see Archangeli et al. (2011) for discussion. Thus qualified, it appears that the goodness-of-fit results are at least more suggestive of the EG account than the UG account.[20]

5.3 Extension of the morphosyntactic domain

In this section, we investigate whether harmony extends from the domain of verbs into a different morphosyntactic domain, nouns. UG predicts an absence of extension while EG predicts extension due to the attractor effect.

As seen in section 5.2, UG predicts that ungrammatical patterns should have undefined $\log_2 O/E$ values (i.e., Observed = 0), while grammatical patterns should have $\log_2 O/E$ values close to 0 or greater ($O/E \geq 1$). Since harmony is not grammatically imposed in nouns, $\log_2 O/E$ values in both test and control languages are therefore expected to be close to 0. In contrast, the attractor effect within EG makes the prediction that $\log_2 O/E$ values for the relevant patterns in test languages will be less than 0, even though a categorical harmony pattern is not grammatically imposed in nouns. That is, the $\log_2 O/E$ values in nouns should be greater than threshold (since the patterns are not excluded by the grammar) but less than predicted by chance. For control languages, EG, like UG, predicts $\log_2 O/E$ values to be close to 0.

---

[20] An additional factor is the morphological structure: disyllabic nouns are typically CVCV while verbs are CVC-VC. For some discussion, see section 6. The frequency counts in this paper are based on undifferentiated stems, with noun/verb as the only distinction beyond the sequence of sounds. A full EG analysis of these languages would address word-internal morphological structure.

	Test languages	Control languages
UG	$\log_2 O/E \approx 0$	$\log_2 O/E \approx 0$
EG	$t < \log_2 O/E < 0$	$t < \log_2 O/E \approx 0$

Table 10. Morphosyntactic domain extension predictions: *e...i, o...i, o...u* in nouns

These predictions involve two separate comparisons. On the one hand, according to EG, the sequences *e. . .i, o. . .i, o. . .u* in nouns in test languages should have higher *O/E* values than the verbs in test languages (since verbs must have values below threshold and nouns must have values above threshold). On the other hand, EG predicts that these three sequences in nouns will have *O/E* values in test languages below those of the control languages. UG shares the first prediction but differs in the latter prediction, where no differences are predicted between the values for *e. . .i, o. . .i, o. . .u* in nouns in test languages and the corresponding sequences in control languages.

Verbs vs. nouns in test languages

We have already seen that within test languages, the $\log_2 O/E$ values for the sequences *e. . .i, o. . .i,* and *o. . .u* in verbs are significantly lower than in nouns (compare nouns and verbs in test languages in Figure 3). Thus EG is consistent with the first prediction. In some languages such as Chichewa and Ciyao, there is a fairly strong bias against *e...i, o...i, o. . .u* even in nouns while in other languages, such as Jita and Ikalanga, the tendency is less marked. (The one anomalous case is the sequence *e...i* in Nkore-Kiga; see discussion in section 5.2 above.)

Nouns in test languages vs. controls

The second prediction of EG is that the attractor effect of harmony will result in the $\log_2 O/E$ values for the three sequences *e...i, o...i,* and *o...u* in test language nouns being lower than the corresponding values in the control languages, even though in both test language nouns and in controls, these sequences are grammatical. Indeed, all three vowel sequences are less frequent in harmony languages than in control languages, as seen in Figure 4.

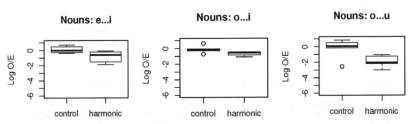

Figure 4: Harmonic nouns vs. control languages

These differences are smaller than the differences in verbs, but all three are significant (*e. . .i*: Estimate = −0.88839, $\bar{R}^2$ = 0.3464, p = 0.0259; *o. . .i*: Estimate = −0.5443, $\bar{R}^2$ = 0.35, p = 0.0251; *o. . .u*: Estimate = −1.7255, $\bar{R}^2$ = 0.425, p = 0.0129).

Important for the comparison between UG and EG, we see significant under-representation of all three vowel sequences. Since UG predicts no differences between grammatical patterns in control languages and grammatical patterns in test language nouns, these results are inconsistent with the UG predictions. Overall, the $\log_2$ *O/E* values for nouns in the test languages show a tendency towards the harmonic pattern, results that are consistent with the predictions of EG. Evidence from Bantu height harmony shows that the pattern extends gradiently beyond verbs into nouns, a broader morphosyntactic domain.[21]

5.4 Extension of phonological domain

In this section, we explore extension of the phonological domain. Standard Bantu asymmetric height harmony prohibits the high front /i/ preceded by either mid vowel, and prohibits the high back/round /u/ preceded by back/round /o/. A phonological extension of this pattern would be to prohibit any mid-high sequence. As seen for morphosyntactic extension in section 5.3, the attractor effect of EG predicts phonological extension while the all-or-nothing effect of UG predicts an absence of extension.

The differing predictions of UG and EG for these cases are similar to the predictions for morphosyntactic extension in Table 10; we give them in Table 11. First, EG predicts a lower-than-expected incidence of *e. . .u* in test languages compared to controls. Second, EG predicts that the incidence of *e. . .u* in verbs is lower than in nouns in the test languages. Both predictions are due to the attractor effect. UG on the other hand predicts $\log_2$ *O/E* will be close to 0 in all cases, whether test or control.

	Test languages	Control languages
UG	$\log_2$ *O/E* ≈ 0	$\log_2$ *O/E* ≈ 0
EG	$t < \log_2$ *O/E* < 0	$t < \log_2$ *O/E* ≈ 0

Table 11. Phonological domain extension predictions: grammatical *e...u*

---

[21] Larry Hyman (p.c.) points out that other morphosyntactic extensions are possible, such as extending height harmony into prefixes (often limited to one prefix, often optional); see Leitch (1996). This requires recognition of morpheme boundaries, which is beyond the scope of our current discussion. See Archangeli & Pulleyblank (in prep.).

To test this, we examine the $\log_2 O/E$ values of the sequence *e. . .u*. Height harmony restricts the sequences *e. . .i, o. . .i*, and *o. . .u* in verbs. To see whether there is a phonological domain extension, we made two comparisons. First, we looked at $\log_2 O/E$ values for *e. . .u* in test language verbs, comparing those values to *e. . .u* controls. Second, we looked at *O/E* values for *e. . .u* in test language nouns, comparing those values too to *e. . .u* controls.

Extension to *e. . .u* sequences within verbs

Considering first the case of verbs, we predict exactly the same pattern between test languages and control languages. As seen in Figure 5 (left), however, although *e. . .u* sequences in verbs appear to be slightly less frequent than in controls, the difference is not significant (Estimate = -0.3240, $\overline{R}^2 = 0.1027$, p = 0.164).

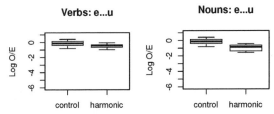

Figure 5: *e...u* in verbs and nouns vs. control languages

It appears, therefore, that the results with verbs are incompatible with the EG predictions. We discuss this in section 6 below.

Extension to *e. . .u* sequences within nouns

Consider next the case of nouns. We have seen that harmony does not hold in nouns. That is, the sequences *e. . .i, o. . .i*, and *o. . .u* are grammatical in nouns, unlike in verbs. Nevertheless, we have seen that these sequences are also under-represented in nouns. What then of the sequence *e. . .u*? This sequence is grammatical both in verbs and nouns. At issue is whether the grammatical effect seen in other mid-high sequences extends to the sequence *e. . .u* in nouns.

As seen above in Figure 5 (right), there are fewer *e. . .u* sequences in nouns in test languages than in the control languages, a significant effect (Estimate = -0.7898, $\overline{R}^2 = 0.4475$, p = 0.0104). A third linear regression comparing verbs and nouns in test languages shows that the trend in the unexpected direction is nearly significant (Estimate = 0.4658, $\overline{R}^2 = 0.2402$, p = 0.060436). A difference between verbs and nouns would be surprising, but the under-representation of the grammatical *e. . .u* sequence, significant in nouns, is predicted by the EG account, but unexplained by the UG account.

6 Discussion

A review of the tests examined here shows that all observed patterns are consistent with EG except for the failure of harmonic under-representation to extend to *e. . .u* sequences in verbs (Figure 5). The failure to phonologically extend in verbs may seem particularly surprising given the observation of phonological extension in nouns. Since height harmony is observed in verbs, not nouns, we would expect a priori that the attractor effect should be stronger in verbs, not nouns – yet clearly, this is not the case. Inspection of individual language $\log_2 O/E$ values (Figure 6) shows the nearly significant trend of phonological extension to *e. . .u* sequences being stronger in nouns, observed in all languages except Jita and Nkore-Kiga.

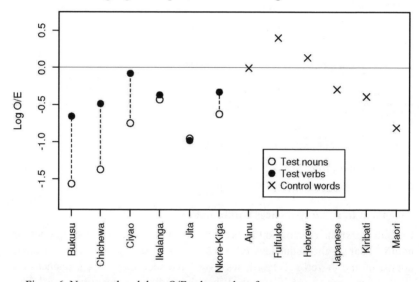

Figure 6: Nouns and verb $\log_2 O/E$ values values for *e…u*

The source of this apparent anomaly, we suspect, lies in properties of Bantu verbal and nominal morphology. Typical Bantu roots are disyllabic for nouns and monosyllabic for verbs. As a result, a vowel sequence such as *e. . .u* can readily be found within a morpheme for nouns, but only in a morpheme sequence for verbs. Consider the case of Ciyao. An examination of the database in CBOLD shows 113 examples of the sequence *e. . .u* in verbs and 75 examples of the same sequence in nouns. If we consider what follows the *e. . .u* sequence, we find that the largest classes in the verbs consist of cases where *e. . .u* is followed by one of the sequences [la] or [ka] (47 and 36 examples respectively; 73% of *e. . .u* in verbs). Some examples with [la] are given in (8).

(8)   The sequence *e. . .u* in Ciyao verbs

      a.   -eejékula   'remove what has been placed against or on'
      b.   -swéékula   'pull out; unsheathe'
      c.   -vélékula   'swing a child round from the back to hip. . .'

Nouns, in contrast, exhibit the majority of the *e. . .u* sequences word-finally (44 examples; 59%), as in the examples in (9).

(9)   The sequence *e...u* in Ciyao nouns

      a.   -teéngu   'wooden stool'
      b.   -kwéésú   'fruit of the tamarind'
      c.   -tewu   'beard'

Were the learner to allow the attractor effect of the verbal prohibition on the sequences *e. . .i, o. . .i,* and *o. . .u* to cause examples such as those in (8) and (9) to be reanalyzed as [e. . .o], the effect would be very different in the two types of cases. For nouns, most of the [e. . .u] sequences would be morpheme-internal; a change in the phonological form would result in a change for a single morpheme. As such, the only pressure to not change to a more harmonic form would be faithfulness to the specific lexical item that would be affected by the change.

For verbs, however, a change would have more far-reaching effects. The reason that the [e. . .u] sequence is so frequently followed by sequences like [la] and [ka] is that these forms involve root-suffix-final vowel sequences, involving suffixes such as *-ul* 'reversive-transitive' and *-uk* 'reversive-intransitive' (Ngunga 2000: 192). Assuming that the learner has identified verbal morphemes, cases such as (8) would all be recognized to be polymorphemic, as in (10); see Ngunga (2000: 193).

(10)   Polymorphemic analysis of the sequence *e...u* in Ciyao verbs

      -root-reversive-final vowel

      a.   -eejék-ul-a   'remove what has been placed against or on'
      b.   -swéék-ul-a   'pull out, unsheathe'
      c.   -vélék-ul-a   'swing a child from the back to the hip...'

This means that if a particular example such as *-vélékula* were to be reanalyzed as *-vélékola*, consistent with extended harmony, then we would have an instance of the reversive allomorph *-ol* after /e/ where the *-ol* allomorph normally occurs only after /o/; see Table 2 above. Given the systematic pattern of morphophonemic alternation exhibited by *-ul/-ol*, to change the morpheme in one word would either create an exception to the pattern or require changes in every word containing the reversive morpheme. The result is that every reversive form with the sequence *e. . .u* constitutes pressure against reanalyzing any single instance of the *e. . .u* sequence. Given the extent to which polymorphemic sequences constitute the source of *e. . .u* sequences in verbs, this morphology results in pressure for verbs not to change, and therefore not to extend the general harmonic prohibition to the sequence *e. . .u*.

Before concluding, we note that there are other types of extensions possible, both morphosyntactic and phonological. In addition to extending harmony to the /e. . .u/ sequence, another example would be to include all nonhigh vowels as triggers, i.e. including /a/ as a trigger. On the morpho-syntactic side, harmony could, for example, extend from the stem domain to the word domain (Leitch 1996; Hyman 1999). We leave the investigation of such cases for the future. See also footnote 21.

6. Conclusion

We have considered two classes of predictions of Emergent and Universal Grammar approaches to language: goodness of fit and domain extension. We tested these predictions by comparing the distribution of specific vowel sequences in 6 Bantu languages with height harmony against 6 control languages without harmony. All languages had 5-vowel systems, /i, e, a, o, u/. Results for both goodness of fit and domain extension are consistent with EG, and pose problems for UG: The harmony pattern within verbs is not categorical; it appears to extend both phonologically and morphologically.

These results are an early step in a much larger research program, that sketched in Mohanan et al. (2009); the evidence in favour of EG (and against UG) supports continued exploration of the emergent nature of phonology. Important directions for such research are indicated by this work. Perhaps the most obvious is the interaction of harmony with vowel-initial forms in Nkore-Kiga and with the general Bantu *-uC* verbal suffixes: these interactions demonstrate the need to integrate the phonological system with an Emergent morphology. Precursor to understanding the interaction of phonology and morphology are (i) the demonstration that statistical patterns of the sort discussed here can transform into phonological generalizations (the focus of Archangeli et al. 2011) and (ii) the general issue of the formal representation of a phonological system and lexicon for a language which has less-than-perfect adherence to patterns. While the treatment of 'exceptions' is nothing new in phonological research, exceptions are fully expected in the

Emergent approach. Thus, the treatment of exceptions is a necessary element in a full model of Emergent phonology.

References

Archangeli, Diana, Jeff Mielke & Douglas Pulleyblank (2011): "From sequence frequencies to conditions in Bantu vowel harmony." – Paper presented at Phonology in the 21st Century, McGill University.

Archangeli, Diana & Douglas Pulleyblank (1994): *Grounded Phonology.* – Cambridge, MA: MIT Press.

– (2002). "Kinande vowel harmony: domains, grounded conditions, and one-sided alignment." – In: *Phonology* 19, 139–188.

– (in prep.): *Emergent Phonology.* Ms., University of Arizona and University of British Columbia.

Arnott, D.W. (1969): "Fula." – In: Dunstan, Elizabeth (ed.): *Twelve Nigerian Languages*, 57–71. New York: Africana Publishing Corporation.

– (1970): *The Nominal and Verbal System of Fula.* Oxford: Clarendon.

Beckman, Jill. (1997): "Positional faithfulness, positional neutralisation and Shona vowel harmony." – In: *Phonology* 14, 1–46.

Blevins, Juliette (2006): "A theoretical synopsis of Evolutionary Phonology." – In: *Theoretical Linguistics* 32. 117–165.

Chomsky, Noam & Morris Halle (1968): *The Sound Pattern of English.* – New York: Harper & Row.

Clements, George N. & Engin Sezer (1982): "Vowel and consonant disharmony in Turkish." – In: Hulst, Harry van der & Norval S.H. Smith (eds.): *The Structure of Phonological Representations* (Part II), 213–256. Dordrecht: Foris.

Coleman, John & Janet Pierrehumbert (1997): "Stochastic phonological grammars and acceptability." – In: *Computational Phonology: Third meeting of the ACL Special Interest Group in Computational Phonology*, 49–56. Somerset: Association for Computational Linguistics.

Downing, Laura (1999): "Jita electronic dictionary provided to CBOLD." (http://www.cbold.ish-lyon.cnrs.fr/; includes data from the Tanzania Language Survey).

Frisch, Stefan, Nathan R. Large & David B. Pisoni (2000): "Perception of wordlikeness: effects of segment probability and length on the processing of nonwords." – In: *Journal of Memory and Language* 42, 481–496.

Golston, Chris (1996): "Direct Optimality Theory: representation as pure markedness." – In: *Language* 72, 713–748.

Greenberg, Joseph H. (1951): "Vowel and nasal harmony in Bantu languages." – In: *Zaire* 5.8, 813–820.

Guthrie, Malcolm (1967-71): *Comparative Bantu: An Introduction to the Comparative Linguistics and Prehistory of the Bantu Languages* (Vols. I-IV). London: Gregg.

Hammond, Michael (2011): "Welsh mutations and statistical phonotactics." – In: Carnie, Andrew (ed.): *Formal Approaches to Celtic Linguistics*, 337–358. Newcastle upon Tyne: Cambridge Scholars Publishing.

Harrison, K. David (1999): "Vowel harmony and disharmony in Tuvan and Tofa." – In: Saito, M., Y. Abe, H. Aoyagi, M. Arimoto, K. Murasugi & T. Suzuki (eds.): *Proceedings of 2nd Asian GLOW*, 115–130. Tokyo: TUFS.

Harrison, K. David, Mark Dras & Berk Kapicioglu (2002): "Agent-based modeling of the evolution of vowel harmony." – In: Hirotani, Mako (ed.): *Proceedings of NELS* 32 , 217–236. Amherst, MA: GLSA Publications.

Hayes, Bruce & Colin Wilson (2008): "A maximum entropy model of phonotactics and phonotactic learning." – In: *Linguistic Inquiry* 39, 379–440.

Hyman, Larry M. (1999): "The historical interpretation of vowel harmony in Bantu." – In: Hombert, Jean-Marie & Larry M. Hyman (eds.): *Bantu Historical Linguistics: Theoretical and Empirical Perspectives*, 235–295. Stanford: CSLI.

Kim, Eun-Sook & Douglas Pulleyblank (2009): "Glottalization and lenition in Nuu-chah-nulth." – In: *Linguistic Inquiry* 40, 567–617.

Krämer, Martin (2003): *Vowel Harmony and Correspondence Theory*. Berlin: Mouton de Gruyter.

Leitch, Myles (1996): *Vowel Harmonies of the Congo Basin: An Optimality Theory Analysis of Variation in the Bantu Zone C.* – PhD dissertation, University of British Columbia.

Mathangwane, Joyce (1999): *Ikalanga Phonetics and Phonology: A Synchronic and Diachronic Study*. Stanford, CA: Stanford Monographs in African Languages.

McCarthy, John J. & Alan Prince (1993): "Prosodic morphology I: constraint interaction and satisfaction." Ms., Rutgers University: Rutgers University Center for Cognitive Science.

– (1994): "The emergence of the unmarked: optimality in prosodic morphology." – In: Gonzàlez, Mercè (ed.): *Proceedings of NELS 24*, 333–379. Amherst, MA: GLSA Publications.

Mielke, Jeff (2005): "Ambivalence and ambiguity in laterals and nasals." – In: *Phonology* 22, 169–203.

– (2008): *The Emergence of Distinctive Features*. Oxford: Oxford University Press.

Mohanan, K.P. (1993): "Fields of attraction in phonology." – In: Goldsmith, John (ed.): *The Last Phonological Rule: Reflections on Constraints and Derivations*, 61–116. Chicago: Chicago University Press.

Mohanan, K. P., Diana Archangeli & Douglas Pulleyblank (2009): "The emergence of Optimality Theory." – In: Uyechi, Linda & Lian-Hee Wee (eds.): *Reality Exploration and Discovery: Pattern Interaction in Language and Life*, 143–158. Stanford University: Center for the Study of Language and Information.

Mutonyi, Nasiombe (2000): *Aspects of Bukusu Morphology and Phonology*. PhD dissertation, Ohio State University.

Ngunga, Armindo (2000): *Phonology and Morphology of the Ciyao Verb*. Stanford: CSLI.

Paradis, Carole (1989): *Phonologie et morphologie lexicales: les classes nominales en peul (Fula)*. PhD dissertation, Université de Montréal.

Pozdniakov, Konstantin & Guillaume Segerer (2007): "Similar place avoidance: a statistical universal." – *Linguistic Typology* 11, 307–348.

Prince, Alan & Paul Smolensky. (1993[2004]): *Optimality Theory: Constraint Interaction in Generative Grammar*. – London: Blackwell.

Pulleyblank, Douglas (2006): "Minimizing UG: constraints upon constraints." – In: Baumer, Donald, David Montero & Michael Scanlon (eds.): *WCCFL* 25, 15–39. Somerville, MA: Cascadilla Proceedings Project (http://lingref.com/, document 1430).

Taylor, Charles (1985): *Nkore-Kiga*. Beckenham: Croom Helm Ltd.

Ben Hermans

The phonological representation of the Limburgian tonal accents

1 Introduction

The dialects of Limburg and the adjacent Ripuarian and Moselle Franconian dialects have two tonal accents, Accent 1 and Accent 2. In the generative tradition it is taken for granted that these accents are to be represented tonally. In this article I want to take issue with this approach. I will show that there is an array of facts that cannot be explained with lexical tones. These facts rather suggest that the tonal contrast should be expressed by prosodic constituency. Specifically, I will argue that Accent 2 is a trochee dominating two syllables, whereas Accent 1 is a monosyllabic trochee. This has also been suggested in a recent manuscript by Wolfgang Kehrein (Kehrein 2010). The facts I will put forward are all polysyllabic borrowings. I show that, in borrowings, the quality of the tonal accents depends on the quality of the posttonic vowel. Facts of this type are very problematic for a tonal approach. My data are taken from the dialect of Maasbracht, in the middle of the Dutch part of Limburg.

With the exception of Wolfgang Kehrein (2010), these facts have so far not been taken into consideration in the literature. With this study I hope to fill this gap.

It should be noted that my article is only concerned with borrowings. Native, truly Germanic, items are not taken into consideration. Although the question how the accents are distributed in native items is very important, it is a different issue, one I cannot go into due to lack of space.

I have structured this article in the following way. In the next section I define what I mean by a tonal account. In the second section I show that the quality of the tonal accents can be determined by the quality of the vowel in the following syllable. In the third section I show that it is possible to explain these correlations in terms of prosodic constituents. This leads me to the conclusion that the most economic way to represent the tonal accents is in terms of prosodic constituents, not in terms of lexical tone.

2 The classical generative representation of the tonal accents

Since the publication of Schmidt's doctoral thesis (Schmidt 1986) the tonal accents in Limburg and the neighboring dialect areas in Germany regained the attention they used to have in the thirties of the 20th century. Also generative phonology discovered it as an interesting topic, in particular due to the efforts of Gussenhoven. In his work Gussenhoven develops detailed analyses of the realizations of the two accents in various positions in the sentence. According to Gussenhoven and his coworkers the contrast between the two accents is to be expressed in terms of lexical tones. Important publications defending this hypothesis are: Gussenhoven & Van der Vliet (1999), Gussenhoven (2004 & 2008), Heijmans & Gussenhoven (1998), Peters (2006, 2008) and Fournier (2008). Consider the two words [ha:²s] 'glove' and [ha:¹s] 'hare', taken from the dialect of Roermond. Writing about this dialect Gussenhoven (2000) argues that the lexical contrast is tonal; whereas the word with Accent 1 does not have a tone at the underlying level, the word with Accent 2 has a high tone on its second mora. Thus, at the underlying level the contrast between Accent 1 and Accent 2 looks as follows:

(1)

The asterisks represent moras. Long vowels are attached to two moras. An onset consonant is attached to the same mora as the vowel to its right; after a long vowel a coda consonant is linked to the second mora.

The realizations of the accents are determined by the interaction between the lexical tones and the intonational melodies. The declarative melody, for instance, has the structure HL, where H is the focus tone and L the boundary tone. The focus H-tone is inserted in the stressed syllable, where it fills the first mora. The boundary tone, occupying the final position of the intonational unit, spreads to the second mora. This only happens if that mora does not have a lexical tone. The focus syllables, in non-final position, receive the following representations in declaratives:

(2)

In (2) the bracket indicates the boundary of the intonational phrase, to which the boundary L is attached. In the representation on the left this L spreads to the second mora, creating a falling tone. In the representation on the right it does not spread. The resulting tonal structure is phonetically realized as a level high tone.

The representations in (2) account for the realizations of the two accents if they are located in the non-final position in a sentence. If they occupy the final position, Accent 2 is realized with a falling-rising tone. Gussenhoven (2000) accounts for this with a metathesis rule, switching around the final H and boundary tone. In final position, then, the representation of the two accents is as in (3).

(3)

Gussenhoven's approach has led to important insights with respect to the realization of the tonal accents in various positions in the sentence. Without denying the importance of this work, we want to have a look at the typological predictions this approach makes and see whether they can be tested.

If it is true that the tonal accents are lexical tones, then certain predictions are made with respect to the interaction between segmental structure and tonal structure. In particular it should be the case that these interactions should resemble the kind of interactions that are typical of tonal languages. Let me give one schematic example of the type of phenomenon I am interested in. Suppose we have a word with two syllables, the first of which has a high tone. In the schematic representation below consonants and vowels are indicated with C and V.

(4)   H
       |
    $C V_1 \ C V_2$

The simple question I want to raise is the following. Are there any relations between the high tone in V_1 position, and the properties of the second syllable? For instance, are there any rules requiring the presence of H in the first syllable if the vowel in the second syllable is high? Or, are there any rules requiring the absence of H if the vowel of the second syllable is non-high? Relations of this type are not expected if the tonal accents are tones. The reason is that tones in real tone languages do not behave in this way. It just does not happen that the quality of a vowel determines the quality of a tone in a preceding syllable. To the extent that we do find phenomena of this type in the Limburgian dialects, there is reason to believe that the tonal accents in these dialects are not lexical tones, but something else. In this article we will systematically explore the relations that exist between the quality of a vowel and the tonal properties of the syllable preceding that vowel.

To this end I have compiled a list of borrowings in the dialect of Maasbracht. We have worked with three informants, two males and one female. All three are between 55 and 60 years old. They have lived their whole life in Maasbracht. They speak their dialect at home, and, in non-formal circumstances, also at work. All three have a high school education, but they are not academics.

I have obtained the judgments of the three informants in the following way. As a native speaker of Maasbracht, I read out the list of borrowings in random order, asking: 'which pronunciation is correct: X Accent 1' (pronouncing form X with Accent 1) 'or X Accent 2' (pronouncing form X with Accent 2).

Due to lack of space I cannot develop a detailed account of all types of borrowings. I therefore restrict myself to words with penult stress. In the next section we present an overview of the results.

3 Correlations between tonic and posttonic syllables

In this section I investigate the correlations that exist between a vowel's quality and the tonal quality of the preceding syllable. As explained in the previous section this is an important matter. If these relations do exist, there is reason to believe that the tonal accents should not be represented with lexical tones only, because tones do not directly interact with properties of a vowel in the next syllable.

The first regularity is the following: if a syllable contains a high vowel, then the preceding syllable almost always has Accent 2. I was able to compile 63 forms with this structure. Of these, 61 have Accent 2, and only 1 has Accent 1. Here are 10 examples illustrating this regularity.

(5)   *If a vowel is high, then the preceding syllable has Accent 2*

[braː²ni]	'swank'	[koloː²ni]	'colony'
[baː²li]	'railing'	[ɪmploː²zi]	'implosion'
[baː²mi]	'noodle'	[fidyː²si]	'confidence'
[ɔː²li]	'oil'	[dæn²di]	'dandy'
[troː²ni]	'mug'	[pæn²ti]	'panty'

These examples show that a high vowel favours Accent 2 in the preceding syllable, irrespective of the structure of that syllable. Low, mid and high vowels and also closed syllables behave identically; they have Accent 2 if a high vowel follows. I found just one exception to this pattern, the word [ækskʏr¹zi] 'excursion'.

If a syllable has a non-high vowel, then the preceding syllable favours Accent 1. I was able to find 74 forms with posttonic [a]. The great majority of these forms, viz. 62, has Accent 1. Below 10 forms illustrating this pattern are listed.

(6)   a.   *If a vowel is non-high, then the preceding syllable has Accent 1*

      [draː¹ma] 'drama'   [stoː¹ma]   'stoma'
      [sahaː¹ra] 'Sahara'   [oː¹ma]   'grandma'
      [hijeː¹na] 'hyena'   [jamɑi¹ka]   'Jamaica'
      [zoː¹da] 'soda'   [aɣæn¹da]   'agenda'
      [soː¹fa] 'sofa'   [værɑn¹da]   'verandah'

12 words contradict this tendency. All these forms have a closed, stressed syllable, and the great majority has a voiceless obstruent in the onset of the posttonic syllable. I have listed them in (6b), under the heading 'apparent exceptions'. The reason for this will become clear as I go on. There are only two forms with a closed stressed syllable, followed by a posttonic low vowel which is preceded by a voiced consonant. They are listed in (6c).

(6)   b.   *Apparent exceptions*

      [ɑl²fa]   'alfa'   [sɪr²ka]   'circa'
      [mɑl²ta] 'Malta'   [kɔn²tra]   'contra'
      [dæl²ta] 'delta'   [pɑm²pa]   'pampas'
      [aɔr²ta] 'aorta   [ɪŋ²ka]   'Inca'

   c.   *True exceptions*

      [pɑn²da] 'panda'
      [pɪn²da] 'peanut'

If a vowel is mid, then the immediately preceding syllable has a strong preference for Accent 1. I was able to compile 37 forms with this structure. Of these, 30 obey the generalization; 10 of them are listed below. Seven forms do not obey the regularity. Again, the great majority of them has a closed stressed syllable, and a voiceless consonant in the onset of the following syllable. I have listed them under the heading 'apparent exceptions'. There is only one example that has to be listed as a true exception.

(7) a. *If the posttonic vowel is mid, then the stressed syllable has Accent 1*

[kaː'no]   'canoe'   [poː'lo]   'polo'
[piaː'no]   'piano'   [ɣiː'ro]   'giro'
[meː'tro]   'metro'   [pɔr'no]   'porno'
[veː'to]   'veto'   [tʏr'bo]   'turbo'
[miː'ra]   girl's name   [sɑl'vo]   'salvo'

b. *Apparent exceptions*

[sɑl²to]   'somersault' [mɑŋ²ko]   'shortcoming'
[kɔn²to]   'account'   [ʃɑm²po]   'shampoo'
[frɑŋ²ko]   'Franco'   [tæm²po]   'tempo'

c. *True exceptions*

[sɑl²do]   'balance'

Let us now move on to the words with penult stress ending in closed
syllables. I managed to compile 67 forms with this structure. The majority of
these forms, viz. 54, have Accent 1 on the penult syllable. In (8a) we present
10 instances of this pattern. There are 13 forms with Accent 2. Eleven of
these are apparent exceptions, in the sense that the stressed syllable is closed,
and the onset consonant of the next syllable is voiceless. I have listed them in
(8b). There are therefore 2 forms with a really exceptional Accent 2 followed
by a closed syllable in final position. They are listed as exceptions in (8c).

(8) a. *If the final syllable is closed, then the penult syllable favors Accent 1*

[jaː'nʏs]   'Janus'   [nøː'trɔn]   'neutron'
[eː'pɔs]   'epic'   [juː'das]   'Judas'
[liseː'jʏm]   'kind of high school'   [hʊnduː'ras]   'Honduras'
[loː'tʏs]   'lotus'   [kʏr'zɔr]   'cursor'
[moː'tɔr]   'motor'   [kʏr'zʏs]   'course'

b. *Apparent exceptions*

[abɔr²tʏs]   'abortion'   [mɑŋ²ko]   'shortcoming'
[kɔr²pʏs]   'corpus'   [kɑm²pʏs]   'campus'
[sɪr²kʏs]   'circus'   [sæn²trʏm]   'center'
[hær²pæs]   'herpes'   [pɑm²pʏs]   'Pampus'
[hɔr²tʏs]   'hortus'   [ɣibrɑl²tɑr] 'Gibraltar'
[bɑl²kɑn]   'Balkans'

c. *True exceptions*

[klitoː²rɪs]   'clitoris'   [smeː²rɪs]   'policeman'

Clearly, words ending in a closed syllable tend to have Accent 1 in the
stressed syllable immediately preceding it. Again there seems to be a rather
large class of systematic exceptions; words with a stressed closed syllable

followed by a voiceless consonant in onset position always have Accent 2.

It seems clear, then, that there are four important regularities. These are listed in (9).

(9) a. A non-high vowel requires Accent 1 in the preceding syllable;
   b. A high vowel requires Accent 2 in the preceding syllable;
   c. A final closed syllable requires Accent 1 in the preceding syllable;
   d. A closed syllable followed by a voiceless consonant in onset position requires Accent 2.

We can legitimately conclude, then, that the tonal quality of the preceding syllable is determined by the quality of the vowel and the closed nature of the syllable. In my view this is problematic for a purely lexical tonal approach. By this I mean any theory that is based on the premise that the tonal accents are to be represented with tones *only*. These are theories of the type described in section 1; theories that posit underlying tones to represent the lexical contrast, and that combine these lexical tones with intonational tones. Theories of this type have difficulties with the regularities formulated in (9), because in these theories it is not possible to relate the quality of a vowel and the structure of a syllable *directly* to the tonal properties of the preceding syllable.

Normally, in generative phonology, relations between adjacent syllables are expressed in terms of prosodic constituents. This means that the facts presented in this section ought to be explained in terms of prosodic constituency. If we succeed in this enterprise, then we can claim that prosodic constituency determines the distribution of tones. But, if that is the case, we can claim that the lexical contrast between the two accents can also be described in terms of prosodic constituency. This again entails that the Limburgian tonal accents are not really tonal, in the sense that they emerge out of the interaction between lexical tones and intonational tones. Instead of this, they are intonational tones whose distribution is determined by a word's prosodic structure.

In the next section I will show that it is possible to explain the generalizations in (9) in terms of prosodic constituents.

4 A foot-based generative analysis of the tonal accents

In this section I propose an analysis of the tonal accents in terms of foot structure. My claim is that Accent 1 is a monosyllabic trochee, whereas Accent 2 is a bisyllabic trochee. Before I start my analysis I will have to say a few words about the representations I will be working with.

Basically, I assume the theory of stress proposed in Halle & Vergnaud (1987). In this theory, prosodic structure is expressed by asterisks that are assigned metrical structure (that is, each asterisk constitutes a constituent with a head, and, if it branches, also a dependent). There is one important difference between Halle and Vergnaud's representations and the ones I will be working with. Halle and Vergnaud assume that syllables are located in a separate dimension. I assume that they are integrated in the same dimension where feet are located. Also, moras participate in this dimension, where they constitute the lowest level. Let me make this clear with a schematic example.

(10)

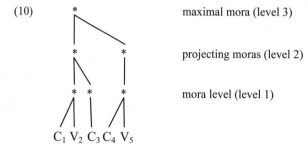

        maximal mora (level 3)

        projecting moras (level 2)

        mora level (level 1)

The root nodes, which I represent by C and V, have to be dominated by moras. These are right-headed constituents, and they are located at the basic level, or the mora level.

The second level is the level with the 'projecting' moras. In the representation in (10) the postvocalic consonant does not project to level 2. It therefore occupies a dependent position in the constituent whose head is the mora dominating the first two root nodes. The constituents of the projecting level are right-headed. At the next level, it is decided where the stresses, or the feet, are located. In (10), the constituent dominating the first three root nodes is the head of the constituent in which the constituent containing C_4 and C_5 is located. This is the structure of a bisyllabic trochee. It is a foot containing three moras, and the first two moras are located in the head position of the foot.

Compare this with another parsing that is theoretically possible. Suppose that the postvocalic consonant does project higher up, to the second level. I propose that in that case our hypothetical example receives the following representation:

(11)

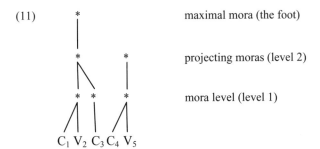

Here the postvocalic consonant occupies a mora that is the head of a constituent that is located at level 2. The constituent immediately dominating the
consonant is a dependent at level 2, not a head. At level 3 a trochee is built.
Now, the trochee dominates two positions at level 2. It cannot incorporate the
final level 2 constituent because feet are maximally binary; they can
maximally contain two positions at the level immediately below. Essentially,
then, the configuration in (11) is an even trochee.

For the Limburgian dialects we need both feet. In fact, the bisyllabic
trochee will phonetically be realized as Accent 2, whereas the monosyllabic
trochee will be realized as Accent 1.

When exactly will these two feet be used? My main hypothesis is that the
shorter trochee is used when it is not possible to parse an unstressed syllable
in the foot. This is a consequence of the high sonority of the unstressed
syllable, or the fact that the syllable is closed. The longer trochee is used
when it *is* possible to parse the unstressed syllable in the foot. This foot can
therefore become bisyllabic. Let us now see how this works.

In the generative literature on stress it is well documented that vowels of
low sonority, e.g. high vowels and central vowels, avoid stress. Conversely,
vowels of relatively high sonority tend to attract stress. Sources where these
phenomena are put into a theoretical perspective are De Lacy (2002, 2004,
2006) and Kenstowicz (1997, 2004). One of the constraints formulated in the
generative theory of stress is the following (cf. in particular De Lacy's work):

(12) *Non-Head/High-Son
      A segment of high sonority should not be exclusively linked to a mora that
      is dominated by a foot's dependent.

We define a segment of high sonority as any segment with greater sonority
than a high vowel. Thus, high vowels, sonorant consonants and obstruents are
irrelevant for the constraint *Non-Head/High-Son.

Let us look at the form [kaːˈno] 'canoe'. This word is one of the forms
listed in (7), all showing the same tendency: non-high vowels prefer Accent 1
in the preceding syllable. This is the tendency formulated in (9a). Suppose
that this word had a bisyllabic foot. It would then look as follows:

(13) *(incorrect) representation of* [kaːˈno]

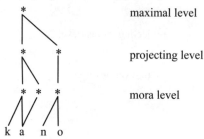

In this form the final syllable contains a vowel of relatively high sonority. Due to *NON-HEAD/HIGH-SON (12), this vowel cannot occupy a dependent syllable in a foot, so the structure in (13) violates *NON-HEAD/HIGH-SON. Now the preceding syllable receives *two* asterisks at the intermediate level. It receives two constituents of this type because the foot is subject to the Minimal Size constraint. This constraint requires that a foot have two daughters. In this way a second, projecting mora must be created, in order to carry the daughter asterisk required by Mimimal Size. The representation in (14) satisfies all relevant constraints.

(14) *(correct) representation of* [kaːˈno]

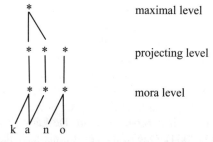

Although the long vowel *a* occupies a position in the dependent of the foot, it also occupies a position that is a head at all levels of the foot. This is a simple consequence of the fact that, as a long vowel, it is doubly linked to the two moras at the lowest level, and one of these moras is not a dependent at any level. In sum, the stressed vowel is not *exclusively* linked to a foot's dependent.

I have explained Accent 1 in words ending in a highly sonorant vowel in the following way. Vowels of high sonority avoid a position in which they are linked to a foot's dependent position. They are therefore not parsed in a foot. The remaining part of the foot becomes bipositional, due to the constraint Mimimal Size. Let us now turn to the words ending in a high vowel.

Consider a form like [baː²mi] 'noodle, which is one of the forms listed in (5). These forms illustrate the generalization in (9b). I propose that this word has the following representation:

(15) *representation of* [baː²mi]

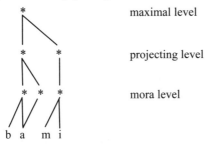

This representation satisfies *NON-HEAD/HIGH-SON, for the simple reason that it does not apply to a segment of relatively low sonority. Therefore, even though the high vowel occupies a dependent position, this does not lead to a violation of *NON-HEAD/HIGH-SON. Our explanation of the regularity in (9b), then, is as follows. High vowels prefer Accent 2 in the preceding syllable, because a high vowel can occupy a dependent position.

I have shown that closed syllables favour Accent 1 in the preceding syllable. I have formulated this tendency in (9c). A form like [jaː¹nʏs] 'Janus', appearing in (8), instantiates this tendency. One of the oldest constraints of the generative theory of stress is a constraint excluding branching constituents from a dependent position. It is one of the cornerstones of the theory of stress developed in Hayes (1980).

(16) QUANTITYSENSITIVIY (QS)
      If a constituent at the projecting level branches, then it may not occupy a dependent position in the foot.

Now consider the representation of the word 'Janus', given in (17).

(17) *representation of* [jaː¹nʏs]

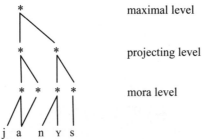

The vowel [ʏ] is a high, lax vowel. As far as *Non-Head/High-Son* is concerned, this vowel could therefore be located in a dependent position. And yet, in the representation in (17) it does not. This is a consequence of the constraint QS. The final consonant requires a mora, creating a branching constituent. Due to QS, this branching constituent should not occupy a dependent position in the foot. Not being allowed in a dependent position, the branching constituent cannot be parsed at the level of the foot. It can therefore only be parsed at the two lower levels. The preceding syllable receives *two* asterisks above the moras, because of Minimal Size.

I now have explained the regularities formulated in (9a-c). The central hypothesis is that in the Limburgian dialects two constraints are very important: *Non-Head/High-Son*, which excludes vowels of relatively high sonority from a dependent position, and QS, which excludes branching constituents from a dependent position in the foot. In the case of the posttonic high vowels *one branching* projecting constituent is created to the left of the stressed syllable, as shown in (15). In the case of posttonic mid and low vowels, and also in the case of posttonic closed syllables, *two non-branching* constituents are created to the left of the stressed syllable, as shown in (14) and (17).

This leaves us with the tendency we have formulated in (9d). I have shown that words with a stressed closed syllable which is followed by a voiceless onset always have Accent 2. A representative example is [ɑl²fa] 'alpha', appearing in (6a). This tendency is so strong that it overrules any other tendency. Stated differently, in closed syllables that are followed by an onset, Accent 1 is only allowed if the onset contains a voiced consonant, as in [kʏr¹zɔr] 'cursor' (8), for instance.

Words like [ɑl²fa], with Accent 2 in a closed penult position, must have a representation similar to [baː²mi] (15), and they exclude a representation similar to the one of [kaː¹no] (14). The latter representation is the one we expect, because the final vowel in [ɑl²fa] is highly sonorous.

Suppose [ɑl²fa] were to have Accent 1. It would then have the following representation:

(18) *(incorrect) phonological representation of* [ɑl²fa]

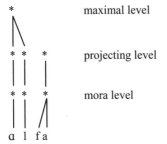

Apparently, a sonorant consonant in the coda position only allows a mora in the head position at the projecting level if it is followed by a voiced onset (Van Oostendorp 2005). Let us assume that sonorant consonants at the head level must have the feature Voice. We know that the feature Voice is only possible if it is linked to the onset position. If it is not linked to an onset, it is erased (Lombardi 1995). These requirements explain the widespread phenomenon of final devoicing.

We can now analyze the tendency of (9d) in the following way. In forms where a sonorant consonant is followed by a voiceless consonant in the onset, the requirement that Voice be licensed by the onset cannot be met. If Voice cannot be licensed by the onset, then the requirement that a sonorant consonant in a head mora be specified for Voice cannot be met either. If that requirement cannot be met, then a sonorant consonant cannot be allowed in a head mora. This implies that Accent 1 is not possible. The representation of [ɑl²fa], then, must be as follows:

(19) *(correct) representation of* [ɑl²fa]

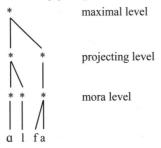

The foot now dominates the highly sonorous vowel in the unstressed position. The vowel must be dominated by the foot because of Minimal Size, which means that the foot must have two daughters. Since the sonorant consonant cannot constitute a daughter of the foot, the vowel [a] must function as a daughter. In order to ensure that a foot dominates a highly sonorous vowel in unstressed position we have to rank the constraint *NON-HEAD/ HIGH-SON below two other constraints: the constraint which requires that a sonorant consonant in head position be licensed by Voice, and the constraint which requires that a foot be minimally binary.

Having explained the difference between Accent 1 (two non-branching constituents at the projecting level) and Accent 2 (one branching constituent at the projecting level) we have to answer the question why these representations are realized as Accent 1 and Accent 2, respectively.

Recall from the first section (cf. (2)), that in declaratives a focus syllable with Accent 1 is realized as a falling tone, whereas a focus syllable with Accent 2 has a level high lexical tone. To account for this difference we just have to say that the declarative melody HL is carried by the asterisks at the projecting level. This yields the tonal difference between Accent 1 and Accent 2. We illustrate this with the representations in (20).

(20)   *tonal difference between Accent 1 and Accent 2 in declaratives*

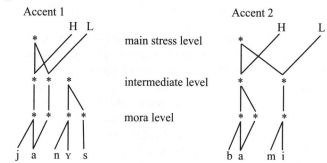

In [jaːˈnʏs] the two tones of the declarative melody are both assigned to the long vowel, creating a falling pitch phonetically. In the case of [baː²mi], however, the two tones of the declarative melody are assigned to two different vowels, located in separate syllables. The first vowel carries the high tone, creating a level high tone phonetically. The second vowel carries the low tone of the declarative melody.

I have now explained all the facts of the preceding section in terms of prosodic constituents. An important conclusion is that Accent 1 contains two non-branching constituents at the projecting level, whereas Accent 2 contains one branching constituent at the projecting level. To explain the facts of the preceding section it is not necessary to refer to tone. In fact, the most important tendencies formulated in (9a–c) cannot possibly be explained in terms of tones only, because tones cannot directly refer to properties of the preceding syllable. Only prosodic constituents can relate properties of two consecutive syllables to each other.

If the analysis of borrowings forces us to account for the difference between Accent 1 and Accent 2 in terms of prosodic constituents, then the lexical contrast should also be expressed in this way. It is certainly preferable to express the contrast in terms of the representations that are necessary anyway. At the level of underlying contrast we therefore also posit the following representations:

(21)   *Accent 1 and Accent 2 at the underlying level, expressing lexical contrasts*

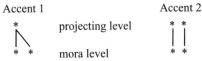

In the phonology of borrowings we need these representations to account for the rather rare exceptions to the general patterns. In the phonology of native items, which I haven't explored due to lack of space, we need them to express the contrast between Accent 1 and Accent 2 before a schwa, and in monosyllabic words.

5 Conclusion

I have shown that the distribution of the tonal accents is often predictable. If a stressed syllable is followed by a high vowel, then it favors Accent 2. If a stressed syllable is followed by a vowel of high sonority then it strongly prefers Accent 1. Furthermore, if a stressed syllable is followed by a closed syllable, then it clearly prefers Accent 1. Regularities of this type cannot be expressed in terms of tones only. They can only be explained with prosodic constituents. Concretely I have proposed that Accent 1 is a (phonetic) syllable containing two non-branching constituents at the projecting level, whereas Accent 2 is a (phonetic) syllable containing one branching constituent at the projecting level. These representations are necessary to account for the regularities we can observe. If they are needed on independent grounds it is also possible to use them to express the lexical contrast. Lexical tones are therefore superfluous.

References

De Lacy, Paul (2002): *The Formal Expression of Markedness.* – PhD dissertation, University of Massachusetts, Amherst.
– (2004): "Markedness conflation in Optimality Theory." – In: *Phonology* 21, 145–199.
– (2006): *Markedness: Reduction and Preservation in Phonology.* – Cambridge: Cambridge University Press.
Fournier, Rachel (2008): *Perception of the Tone Contrast in East Limburgian dialects.* PhD dissertation, Radboud University Nijmegen. – Utrecht: LOT publications.
Gussenhoven, Carlos (2000): "The lexical tone contrast of Roermond Dutch in Optimality Theory." – In: Horne, Merle (ed.): *Prosody: Theory and Experiment. studies presented to Gösta Bruce*, 129-167. Dordrecht: Kluwer.
– (2004): *The phonology of tone and intonation.* – Cambridge: Cambridge University Press.
Gussenhoven, Carlos & Jörg Peters (2004): "A tonal analysis of Cologne Schärfung." – In: *Phonology* 21, 251–285.
– (2009): "De tonen van het Limburgs." – In: *Nederlandse Taalkunde* 13, 87–114.
Gussenhoven, Carlos & Peter van der Vliet (1999): "The phonology of tone and intonation in the dialect of Venlo." – In: *Journal of Linguistics* 35, 99–135.
Halle, Morris & Jean-Rorger Vergnaud (1987): *An Essay on Stress.* – Cambridge: MIT Press.
Hayes, Bruce (1980): *A Metrical Theory of Stress Rules.* – PhD dissertation, MIT. [Revised version distributed by Indiana Linguistics Club, Bloomington].
– (1995): *Metrical Stress Theory: Principles and Case Studies.* – Chicago: University of Chicago Press.
Heijmans Linda & Carlos Gussenhoven (1998): "The Dutch dialect of Weert." – In: *Journal of the International Phonetic Assocation* 28, 107–112.
Kehrein, Wolfgang (2010): "There is no tone in Cologne." – Unpublished Manuscript, University of Amsterdam.
Kenstowicz, Michael (1997): "Quality-driven stress." – In: *Rivista di Linguistica* 9, 157–188.
– (2004): "Quality-sensitive stress" [abridged]. – In: McCarthy, John (ed.): *Optimality Theory in Phonology: A reader*, 191–201. Malden, MA/Oxford,: Blackwell.
Lombardi, Linda (1995): "Laryngeal neutralization and syllable wellformedness." – In: *Natural Language and Linguistic Theory* 13, 39–74.
Peters, Jörg (2006): "The dialect of Hasselt." – In: *Journal of the International Phonetic Association* 36, 117–125.
– (2008): "Tone and intonation in Hasselt." – In: *Linguistics* 46, 983–1018.
Prince, Alan & Paul Smolensky (1993): *Optimality Theory: Constraint Interaction in Generative Grammar.* – Rutgers NJ: Rutgers University Center for Cognitive Science. [Published in 2004, Oxford: Blackwell].

Riad, Tomas (1992): *Structures in Germanic Prosody. A diachronic study with special reference to the Nordic languages.* – PhD Dissertation, Stockholm University.

Schmidt, Jürgen Erich (1986): *Die mittelfränkischen Tonakzente (Rheinische Akzentuierung).* – Stuttgart: Franz Steiner Verlag.

Van Oostendorp, Marc (2005): "Expressing inflection tonally." – In: *Catalan Journal of Linguistics* 4, 107–126.

Carlos Gussenhoven

Quantity or durational enhancement of tone: the case of Maastricht Limburgian high vowels*

1. Introduction

When asked what the difference is between the Maastricht Dutch words [zi] 'sea' and [ziː] 'she; they', [brytʃə] 'bread-DIM' and [bryːtʃə] 'bride-DIM', or [brut] 'bread' and [bruːt] 'bride', speakers of that dialect will say that the short-voweled words have *stoottoon*, while the long-voweled words have *sleeptoon*. These are the popular terms for the two members of a tone contrast known as TA1 (*TonAkzent* 1) or Accent 1 (for *stoottoon*) and TA2 or Accent 2 (for *sleeptoon*). Their characterization of these contrasts as tonal agrees with the older literature (Houben 1905), but not with the claim in Gussenhoven & Aarts (1999) that the difference between the longer and the shorter high vowels is due to a quantity contrast.

The reason why this analytical difference has come about is that the tonal contrast, which does exist on non-high vowels, is generally realized through a difference in duration, while the difference between the pitch contours for Accent 1 and Accent 2 is often not very salient, to the extent that its tonal character has been denied (van Buuren 1991). In Figure 1, we compare the two tones in sentence-final syllables, with declarative (panels a and b), interrogative (panels c and d) and continuative intonation (panels e and f). In each case, there is a substantial duration difference, the syllable with Accent 2 being longer than that with Accent 1. In the case of the declarative intonation (panels a and b), the Accent 1 contour is a fall, while the Accent 2 contour is a rising-falling shape with narrowed pitch range, from mid to lowered high to mid-low. Despite the difference in pitch, the greater duration

* A shortened version of this chapter appeared as 'Quantity vs durational enhancement of the tone contrast in the Maastricht vowel system' in the *Proceedings of the 17th International Conference of Phonetic Sciences* (Hong Kong 2011). This chapter owes its existence to the congenial and fruitful collaboration with Flor Aarts. Renske Teeuw helped with the duration measurements, while Frans van der Slik and Bert Cranen helped with the statistics and graphics. I thank two anonymous reviewers for their critical questions, which have helped improve a pre-final version.

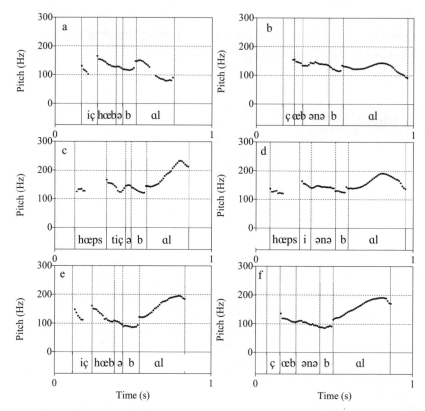

Figure 1. Intonation-phrase-final pronunciations of [bɑl¹] 'dance party' (panels a, c, e) and [bɑl²] 'ball' (panels b, d, f) in a declarative carrier sentence *Iech höb e/ene X* 'I have a X' (panels a,b), an interrogative carrier sentence *Höpstiech e/ene X* 'Do you have a X?' (panels c, d) and a continuative carrier sentence *Iech höb e/ene X, meh iech …* 'I have an X, but I … ' (panels e, f).

of the Accent 2 declarative contour makes it sound like a drawn out version of the falling contour of Accent 1. In the interrogative intonation (panels c and d), there would at first sight seem to be no difference between the pitch contours for the two tone categories, both being rises followed by a narrow fall. However, the fall at the end of the contour for Accent 1 has no perceptual effect and occurs in the final part of the utterance with low intensity, while Accent 2 is a steep rise which is audibly checked by a weak fall. The realization of the tone contrast in the continuative intonation (panels e and f)) is purely a matter of duration, there being no pitch differences. As in the case of the interrogative contour in panel (c), the contours in panels (e) and (f) end in a visible mini-fall, but this has no auditory effect.

These monosyllabic contours, therefore, largely rely on of the role of duration in the maintenance of the tone contrast. Other contexts allow the tonal character of the contrast to be more apparent. For instance, post-focal speech, which has no intonational pitch accent, reveals the tonal nature of the contrast quite readily. While words with Accent 1 are largely treated as in the standard language in that context, those with Accent 2 show a pitch peak, attributable to a lexical H-tone (Gussenhoven & Aarts 1999).

Maastricht is not the only dialect that presents a confusing picture as to what durational differences are to be attributed to, quantity or tone. Gussenhoven & Peters (2004) argue for a tonal analysis of the dialect of Cologne, which like the Maastricht dialect heavily relies on duration as a cue to the tone contrast, on the basis of distributional criteria. However, that dialect is comparatively well behaved, and combines an orthogonal quantity contrast with an orthogonal tone contrast, and thus all vowels contrast for quantity and tone. In the Maastricht case, a tonal analysis and a quantity analysis are in competition for the contrasts between the shorter and longer high vowels.

The Maastricht vowel system is given in (2), following Gussenhoven & Aarts (1999). As in the standard language, high vowels before /r/ are categorically long if they occur in the same foot, making */ir, yr, ur/ ungrammatical. One vowel, /ə/, is not listed, and only appears in unstressed syllables.

(2)　　*Short*　　*(V)*　　　　　　*Long (V_iV_i) and diphthong (V_iV_j)*

i	y	u	iː	yː	uː
ɪ	ʏ	ʊ	eː	øː	oː
ɛ	œ	ɔ	ɛː	œː	ɔː
æ	ɑ			aː	
			ɛi	œy	ɔu

The aim of this contribution is to support the claim by Gussenhoven & Aarts (1999) that high vowels contrast for quantity, not tone, by comparing the duration differences between tonal minimal pairs and minimal pairs with high vowels. If the duration differences between the two classes of high vowels are phonetically and distributionally comparable to those between the non-high vowels, the phonological origin of the durational differences is likely to be the same. However, if the durational difference between the two classes of high vowels does not pattern like that between members of the tonal minimal pairs, the difference between them must be taken to have a different phonological origin, viz. that of quantity.

2 A production experiment

2.1 Method

Scripted speech was recorded on the basis of a corpus of sentences containing five tonal minimal pairs and two minimal pairs with high vowels by a middle class, male speaker in his mid-sixties. Three of the tonal pairs had the stressed syllable in word-final position: /bɑl^1/ 'dancing party' - /bɑl^2/ '(playing) ball', /bɛi^1/ 'bee' - /bɛi^2/ 'near, at', and /ɣə'beːt^1/ 'territory' - /ɣə'beːt^2/ 'set of teeth'. They represented the three possible long rimes VN, V_iV_j and V_iV_i. Two minimal pairs had penultimate stress: /'spøː^{1}lə/ 'rinse' - /'spøː^{2}lə/ 'play' and /'ɛi^{1}kə/ 'egg+DIM' - /'ɛi^{2}kə/ 'oaken'. The minimal pairs contrasting long and short high vowels were /zi/ 'sea' - /ziː/ 'she' and /'butə/ 'penalty' - /'buːtə/ 'outside'. These 14 experimental words were embedded in a number of sentences which were chosen so that they appeared in three positions in the sentence, final with sentence accentuation, final without sentence accentuation and medial with sentence accentuation. Each of these occurred in four discourse contexts. These were the declarative condition, the polar interrogative intonation, the surprised polar interrogative condition and the continuative condition. The first two were elicited with simple syntactic statement and question sentences, the third with the help of preceding sentences or words expressing surprise, like *Wat?* 'What?', and the fourth with sentences like *Heer wèlt neet speule (meh heer wèlt wandele)* 'He doesn't want to play (but he wants to go for a walk)', where *speule* is the target word. This corpus was recorded several times. Additionally, a smaller corpus of sentences was recorded in which words appeared in sentence medial position without intonational pitch accent, as well as a corpus of compounds in which the tone class of both constituent words was varied. Before the recordings, there was no hypothesis about the number of phonological intonation contours there were in the dialect. The identification of the intonation contours and their interaction with the tone contrast is reported in Gussenhoven (2012).

The investigation reported here was based on the minimal pairs with all-sonorant rimes (i.e. the ones mentioned in the text above with the exception of /ɣə'beːt^1/ 'territory' - /ɣə'beːt^2/ 'set of teeth'), and comprised 96 utterances with tonal minimal pairs and 60 with high-vowel minimal pairs. Intonation was controlled for by only including recordings of members of minimal pairs that were available in all three sentential positions spoken with the same intonation. Segment durations in the target words were determined with the help of Praat (Boersma & Weenink 1999-2009). Boundaries between the vowel and sonorant coda in the case of the words for 'ball' and 'dance party' were often hard to determine. Since the lengthening for Accent 2 words is spread over the entire sonorant rhyme, we decided to report rhyme durations rather than vowel durations (meaning that [l] in those two words was included in the reported values). Because the number of intonation contours in each of the three discourse conditions was unequal and we had no interest in any duration differences between intonation contours, we merged the data across intonation conditions.

2.2 Results

The interest is in the different patterning of the durational variation across contexts for the two sets of syllable rhymes rather than in any duration differences between the sets as such. For this reason, I report the results for the two datasets separately.

2.2.1 Tonal minimal pairs

The durations of the tonally different rimes were analyzed by means of a repeated measures analysis of variance, with WORDTYPE (monosyllabic, disyllabic), TONE (Acc 1, Acc 2) and POSITION (non-final, final accented, final unaccented) as factors. Main effects were found for WORDTYPE [$F(1)=192.2$; $p<.001$; $\eta^2=.965$], TONE [$F(1)=85.4$, $p<.001$; $\eta^2=.924$] and POSITION [$F(2)=535.5$, $p<.001$; $\eta^2=.994$], while all two-way interactions were significant: WORDTYPE and TONE [$F=47.9$, $df=2$; $p<.001$; $\eta^2=.873$], WORDTYPE and POSITION [$F(2)=30.1$, $p<.001$; $\eta^2=.909$] and TONE and POSITION [$F(2)=19.4$, $p<.01$; $\eta^2=.866$]. Pairwise comparisons showed that the phrase-internal condition is significantly different from both phrase-final conditions ($p<.001$), but that the latter two did not differ significantly. Panel (a) of Fig. 2 gives rime durations for Accent 1, pooled over /bɑl^1/ 'ball, party' and /bɛi^1/ 'bee', and Accent 2, pooled over /bɑl^2/ 'ball, toy' and /bɛi^2/ 'near, by', in non-final accented position as well as final accented and unaccented positions, averaged over eight repetitions. Panel (b) gives the equivalent data for the rimes of the penultimate syllables in /'spøː^{1}lə/ 'rinse' and /'ɛi^{1}kə/ 'egg-DIM' (Accent 1) as compared with those of /'spøː^{2}lə/ 'play' and /'ɛi^{2}kə/ 'oaken'.

The interaction between WORDTYPE and TONE is due to the greater differentiation of Accent 1 and Accent 2 in the case of the word-ultimate stressed syllables, where Accent 2 is 34% longer than Accent 1 in phrase-final position and 22% longer than Accent 1 in phrase-internal position, but much smaller in word-penultimate syllables, where the lengthening reaches only 10%, both finally and non-finally in the phrase. The interaction between WORDTYPE and POSITION is due to the greater difference between the

final and non-final positions for vowels in word-ultimate stressed syllables
than for the vowels in the word-penultimate stressed syllables. This reflects
the fact that final lengthening is most effective in phrase-final syllables,
affecting penultimate syllables much less or not at all. The interaction
between TONE and POSITION reflects the fact that Accent 1 and Accent 2
are differentiated most in phrase-final position. This would appear to be
especially true for the word-ultimate vowels (cf. Fig. 2), but there was no
three-way interaction in the data.

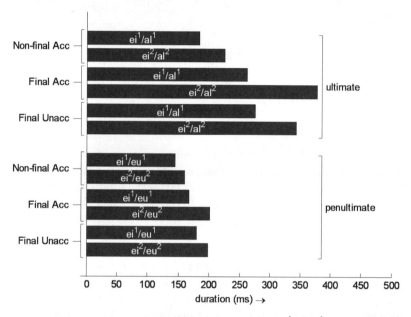

Figure 2. Durations (ms) of the word-ultimate rimes in /bɛi¹/, /bɑl¹/ compared with
those in /bɑl²/, /bɛi²/ in accented phrase-internal position (NonFinal Acc), phrase-
final accented position (Final Acc), and phrase-final unaccented position (Final
Unacc) (above) as well as of the word-penultimate rimes in /spøː¹lə/, /ɛi¹kə/
compared with those in /spøː²lə/, /ɛi²kə/ in the same positions (below).

2.2.2 Minimal pairs with high vowels

Fig. 3 presents corresponding data for the high vowels. The data in panel (a)
are based on vowel durations in /zi/ 'sea' and /ziː/ 'she', while those in panel
(b) are based on /'butə/ 'penalty' and /'buːtə/ 'outside', averaged over five
repetitions. An analysis of variance was performed on the duration of the
vowel, with WORDTYPE (monosyllabic, disyllabic), QUANTITY (short,

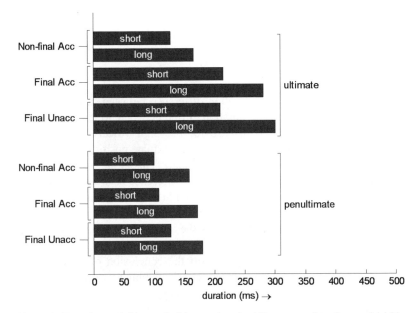

Figure 3. Durations of the word-ultimate rime in /zi/ compared to those of /ziː/ in accented phrase-internal position (Nonfinal Acc), phrase-final accented position (Final Acc), and phrase-final unaccented position (Final Unacc) (above) as well as of the word-penultimate rime in /ˈbutə/ compared to those in /ˈbuːtə/ in the same positions (below).

long) and POSITION (non-final, final accented, final unaccented) as factors. Main effects were found for WORDTYPE [F(1)=376, p<.001; η²=.989], QUANTITY [F(1)=941.2, p<.001; η²=.996] and POSITION [F(2)=135.1, p<.01; η²=.971], while there was a significant interaction between WORDTYPE and POSITION [F(2)=243.8, p<.001]. Pairwise comparisons showed that the non-final condition is significantly different from both phrase-final conditions (p<.001), but that the latter two did not differ significantly. The interaction is due to the greater differentiation between phrase-final and phrase-internal positions for the monosyllabic words than for the disyllabic words, as is evident in Fig. 3. Final lengthening is most effective in phrase-final syllables: the longer duration in monosyllables than in (trochaic) disyllables reflects the fact that word-final stressed syllables are longer than otherwise identical non-final syllables.

3 Discussion

3.1 General conclusion

These results show that the duration difference between /i, u/ and /iː, uː/ is treated differently from the duration difference due to the tone contrast. Word-finally, the duration increase for the high vowels is 34% (phrase-internal 31%, phrase-final 36%), and in penultimate position in the word it is 54% (58% phrase-internal, 50% phrase-final). This is the opposite pattern to that found for the tone contrast, where the difference between Accent-1 rimes and Accent 2-rimes is considerably reduced in the word-penultimate position, relative to the word-ultimate position. In line with this difference, we see that the effect size (η^2) for QUANTITY is the largest of the three factors, while that for TONE is the smallest.

This difference in patterning support the conclusion of Gussenhoven & Aarts (1999) that there is quantity contrast for the high vowels, but durational enhancement of the tone contrast for the long non-high vowels. Durational enhancement of the tone contrast appears to be an exaggeration of word-final and phrase-final lengthening for Accent 2. The pattern found for tonal enhancement is thus typologically akin to phrase-final lengthening, as found in a large number of languages (e.g. Cambier-Langeveld & Turk 1997). By contrast, the durational realization of the quantity distinction is much less influenced by position in the sentence, and doesn't rely on phrase-final lengthening in the way the durational enhancement of the tone contrast does.

I have resorted to durational data to argue for the position that high vowels contrast for quantity rather than tone. However, a reviewer raised the sensible question what the pitch data are for words with high vowels in stressed syllables. The answer is that they present a confusing picture, for which reason I had excluded any discussion from an earlier version of this chapter. In most cases, repetitions of sentences with the same discourse conditions have the same intonation contour, but rarely are these the ones that would be predicted on the basis of the data for the tonal minimal pairs, if it is assumed that the long high vowels have Accent 2 and the short high vowels have Accent 1. In some cases, novel contours are used, as in panel (a) of Fig. 4 (next page). Here, /ˈbutə/ 'fine, penalty' has a falling contour, which in this position is used as an interrogative intonation in Accent 1 words. An Accent 1 declarative contour would have a low accented syllable followed by a (rise-) fall in the last. In panel (b), /ˈbuːtə/ 'outside, in the country' is pronounced with a perfect Accent 2 contour, a rise in the stressed syllable and a mid level final unstressed syllable. In panel (c), /zi/ 'sea' would appear to have a time-compressed Accent 2 contour, a version of the contour in panel (b) of Fig. 1, but one that doesn't at all sound like an Accent 2 contour. In panel (d), /ziː/ 'she' is pronounced with a lengthened fall, a stretched version of the Accent 1 contour shown in panel (a) of Fig 2. It is clear that the pitch contours used for the high vowels are not those used for the tonal words, all of which behave as predicted by the grammar outlined in Gussenhoven (2012).

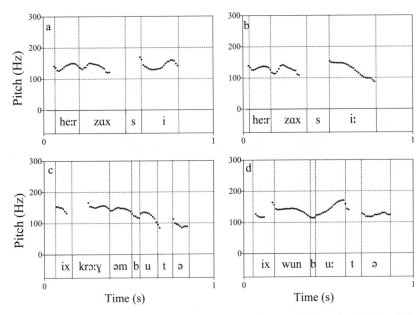

Figure 4. Declarative intonation contours for *Iech zag 'zie'* 'I say "sea"' (panel a) and *Iech zag 'zie'* 'I say "she"' (panel b), *Iech kroag 'n boete* 'I'll be fined' (panel c), *Iech woon boete* 'I live in the country' (panel d).

3.2 Durational enhancement as one of many enhancing features

The considerable durational enhancement of the tone contrast reflects the fact that the pitch distinction between Accent 1 and Accent 2 is not salient, at least not in intonation-phrase final position. There is a further set of facts that suggests that the tone contrast is hard to maintain: its uneven distribution over the vowels of the dialect. To begin with, short vowels require a second sonorant mora in the stressed syllable, meaning that syllable rimes with V_iV_i, V_iV_j and VN (where N is a nasal or liquid) can have the contrast, but rimes with VT (where T is an obstruent) cannot. Further, no contrast is possible on any rime with /β/ or /j/ in the coda, regardless of whether a long or a short vowel precedes, e.g. /høːj/ 'hats' and /iβ/ 'century'. Next, a rime with a lax long vowel, like /tɛːt/ 'tête de veau', /vœːl/ 'much', /plɔːts/ 'place', cannot have the contrast.

The explanation for these gaps in the distribution of the lexical tone is due to conflicts with enhancement strategies in other segmental contexts. First, in addition to being shorter, the three diphthongs /ɛi, œy, ɔu/ end in close second elements when combining with Accent 1, while partly monophthongizing when combining with Accent 2. The monophthongization of diphthongs with Accent 2 causes them to be acoustically close to the mid-open monophthongs. That is, the vocoid in [bɛːʲ] (/bɛi²/ 'near, at') is similar to that in [tɛːt] /tɛːt/ ('tête de veau'). If the mid long vowels were to have realizations with Accent 2, causing them to be lengthened, they would be hard to keep distinct from the diphthongs with Accent 2. Second, the tense mid vowels /eː, øː, oː/ are pure monophthongs when co-occurring with Accent 2, but are narrow rising diphthongs [ei, øy, ou] when co-occurring with Accent 1. Because of the diphthongal realization with Accent 1 for the mid vowels and diphthongs, there is no phonetic space for an instantiation of Accent 2 on rimes ending in glides. If by the side of the contrast between /ɣə'beːt¹/ 'territory' and /ɣə'beːt²/ 'set of teeth' there were also an Accent 2 version of the vowel-plus-glide /eːj/, which occurs in /ɣə'beːjt/ 'repeated acts of offering', the subtlety of the contrasts would be too great: [ej] in 'territory' vs. [eː] in 'set of teeth' vs. [eːj] in 'continued acts of offering' hardly allow for a fourth option [eːːj] for non-existent */eːj²/. A phonetic implementation of a hypothetical word like */beːj²/ would incongruously need to reduce the pronunciation of the final /j/ in order to distinguish it from Accent 1. However, reduction of the glide would make it similar to an Accent 1 pronunciation of the monophthong /eː/, which is [ej], and if it is deleted altogether, it would be similar to the Accent 2 pronunciation of /eː/, which is [eː].

Equally understandably, combining the tone contrast with the quantity contrast in the high vowel series would force the lengthening of syllable rimes with Accent 2 to compete with the lengthening for phonological quantity, jeopardizing the quantity contrast. Significantly, the tone contrast *does* exist in rimes with high vowels before /r/. This reinforces the explanation, since before /r/ the high tense vowels have no quantity contrast, and are consistently long. Here, the tone contrast is illustrated by the Accent 1 word /kiːr¹/ 'time' (as in 'three times') and the Accent 2 word /kiːr²/ 'chink'. Every high-voweled syllable before coda [r] in fact either has Accent 1 or Accent 2.

The distribution of the tone contrast over rime types is summarized in (3).

(3)

			iːr	yːr		uːr
ɪN	ʏN	ʊN	eː	øː		oː
ɛN	œN	ɔN				
æN		ɑN			aː	
			ɛi	œy		ɔu

where N = /m, n, ŋ, l, ʀ/ in the coda

Because of the durational enhancement of Accent 2 rimes in phrase-final position, /bɛl¹/ 'bell' is shorter than /vɛl²/ 'skin'. Because of vowel quantity, each of them is shorter than /keːl¹/ 'throat' and /deːl²/ 'barn, farmyard', respectively. Since the lengthening due to long quantity in word-ultimate position is in fact less than that due to Accent 2, /vɛl²/ is longer than /deːl¹/. When an obstruent follows the vowel in the coda, this four-way quantity-tone contrast is reduced to a three-way contrast, because no tone contrast is possible on VT-rimes: /βɛx/ 'gone' (a predicative adjective), /βeːx¹/ 'roads', /βeːx²/ 'road'.

3.3 Outlook

From a synchronic perspective, the co-occurrence restrictions between tones and vowels reveal how the dialect manages to maintain its vocalic quality and quantity oppositions in the presence of a lexical tone contrast whose phonetic realization encroaches on the same phonetic space as is used by the quality and quantity contrasts. Effectively, the dialect maintains the tone contrast where this can be achieved without seriously jeopardizing the other vocalic contrasts. It is conceivable that the lexical tone contrast was once orthogonally combined with all vowels, as it still is in the dialects of Cologne (Gussenhoven & Peters 2005) and Hamont (Verhoeven 2007). If so, the situation we encounter today in Maastricht is a stage in an ongoing process of distributional restriction of the tone contrast. The dialect of nearby Weert shows where this process is likely to be going. It no longer *has* a tone contrast (Heijmans 2003, Heijmans & Gussenhoven 1998). While in some cases the lexical distinctions have been lost, in other cases the Weert dialect has segment structures in the rime of former words with Accent 2 which cause that syllable to be longer than the syllable with which it contrasted tonally in an earlier stage of the language. Weert thus gave up the tone contrast, but partly salvaged it by reinterpreting the tonal contrast in terms of an already existing quantity contrast, and in part by expanding the phonotactic structure of the rime with short vowel-plus-glide combinations like [æj], which are phonetically shorter than diphthongs like [ɛi], to be used for former Accent 1 words.

A reviewer raised the point that my account does not explain why, in situations of conflict, the tone contrast is sacrificed rather than the vowel contrast. In general, this question has been seen in the light of contrast perceivability, with non-salient contrasts being particularly liable to disappear. However, it also touches on an underresearched issue, that of *functional load* and its possible implications for the expendability of phonological contrasts. Interestingly, the intonation system of the dialect, too, shows many gaps (Gussenhoven 2012). Specifically, there are two contours for intonation-phrase final nuclear syllables with Accent 1, three for penultimate nuclear syllables with Accent 1 and four for pre-penultimate nuclear syllables with Accent 1, while the number of contours for nuclear syllables with Accent 2 is three, regardless of position. In all cases, there is a declarative as well as an interrogative intonation contour available for either tone class. The dialect has apparently reduced its intonation system selectively, rather than giving up the tone contrast, and the balance between lexical tone and intonation was therefore in favour of lexical tone. The phonology of Maastricht Limburgian is a textbook case of enhancement. It raises many analytical questions, and their resolution in turn raises new ones. Work on language change no doubt would benefit from considering cases like these, in which a phonological system has come under strain due to the introduction of a novel contrast, the Franconian tone.

References

Boersma, Paul & David Weenink (1992-2009): Praat: Doing phonetics by computer. Versions 14 and 15. – http://www.praat.org

Cambier-Langeveld, Tina & Alice Turk (1997): "A cross-linguistic study of accentual lengthening: Dutch *vs.* English." – In: *Journal of Phonetics* 27, 255–280.

Gussenhoven, Carlos (2012): "Asymmetries in the intonation system of Maastricht Limburgish." - In: *Phonology* 29, 39–79.

Gussenhoven, Carlos & Flor Aarts (1999): "The dialect of Maastricht." – In: *Journal of the International Phonetic Association* 29, 55–66.

Gussenhoven, Carlos & Jörg Peters (2004): "A tonal analysis of Cologne *Schärfung*." – In: *Phonology* 21, 251–285.

Heijmans, Linda (2003): "The relationship between tone and vowel length in two neighboring Dutch Limburgian dialects." – In: Fikkert, Paula & Haike Jacobs (eds.): *Development in Prosodic Systems*, 7–45. Berlin/New York: Mouton de Gruyter.

Heijmans, Linda & Carlos Gussenhoven (1998): "The dialect of Weert." – In: *Journal of the International Phonetic Association* 28, 101–112.

Houben, Johan H.H. (1905): *Het Dialect der Stad Maastricht.* – Maastricht: Leiter-Nypels.

van Buuren, Luc (1991): "A study of quantity in Mestreechs." – In: *York Papers in Linguistics* 15, 251–280.

Verhoeven, Jo (2007): "The Belgian Limburg dialect of Hamont." – In: *Journal of the International Phonetic Association* 37, 219–225.

Jeroen M. van de Weijer

Using local constraint conjunction to discover constraints: the case of Mandarin Chinese*

1 Introduction

This paper, inspired by the collection of papers in Wang & Smith (1997), discusses a restriction in synchronic Mandarin Chinese which involves voiced stops, rising tone and nasal codas. The paper argues that this restriction can be described only as the result of the combined action of two constraints, i.e. a 'local constraint conjunction'. We discuss the exact formulation of this conjunction and note that, in Optimality Theory, the two constraints in a conjunction should also be instantiated separately. In this way, local constraint conjunctions provide a novel way of discovering constraints.

The paper is organized as follows. Section 2 will give some brief background information on the relevant phonology of Mandarin Chinese, illustrate the basic facts and describe the generalization. Section 3 will introduce local constraint conjunction, and show how the relevant generalization can be captured in Optimality Theory (Prince & Smolensky 1993 [2004]; OT). Section 4 discusses the implications of this strategy and concludes by identifying areas for further research.

2 Background on Mandarin Chinese

2.1 Segments, tones and syllable structure

The exact consonantal and vocalic inventory of Mandarin Chinese (MC) is a matter of some dispute (see contributions to Wang & Smith (1997), Li (2002)

---

* This paper is dedicated to Norval Smith, with fond memories of the happy hours we spent in many contexts, in the early days of the Holland Institute of Generative Linguistics, on many a TIN-dag, and in many other places. For me, Norval's monumental knowledge, as well as deep understanding of all things phonological has set a standard that is always worth striving for, but can never be attained.

and Duanmu (2007) and many other sources for discussion). Here we will focus on those aspects that are uncontroversial and that are relevant to the main point to be made. As is well known, MC has a contrast between voiced and voiceless stops (including affricates) in the onset. Alternatively and more accurate phonetically, the relevant contrast is between voiceless unaspirated and voiceless aspirated stops, see e.g. Xu & Xu (2004). The standard pinyin transcription of Chinese characters uses voiced stop symbols like *b*, *d*, *g*, which we will also adopt here.

There is a four-way tone contrast in MC: high level (tone 1), rising (tone 2), a dipping contour (tone 3) and falling (tone 4). Figure 1 gives a graphic display of the various tone contours:

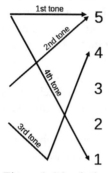

Figure 1: Mandarin tone chart

The four tones contrast in many lexical items. The examples in (1) are intended to illustrate this fact, as well as the fact that codas are limited to alveolar or velar nasals (the examples also show that characters that sound alike sometimes have a 'sound radical' in common):

(1) 帆 fan1 'sail'   芳 fang1 'perfume'
    凡 fan2 'ordinary'   房 fang2 'room'
    反 fan3 'turn over'   纺 fang3 'spin, weave'
    饭 fan4 'rice, food' 放 fang4 'put'

There are no complex onsets, although a glide may follow the initial consonant:

(2) 票 piao4 'ticket'
    牛 niu2   'ox, cow'
    快 kuai4 'fast, sharp'
    元 yuan2 'dollar' (phonetically [jw])

These glides have been analysed in different ways — either as secondary articulations on the onset, or as the initial part of diphthongs (see e.g. Duanmu 1999, 2007, 2008; Yip 2003, and references cited there), among other possibilities. In Van de Weijer & Zhang (2008) we analyse the syllable structure of Chinese as an X-bar-structure, in which the glide occupies the specifier position of the nuclear vowel:

(3)

$$N^{max}$$

C $\quad$ N″

G $\quad$ C′

N^0 $\quad$ C

|

V

Particularly in combination with OT, this structure makes it possible to capture a number of generalizations with respect to Chinese syllable structure. For one, it makes it possible to distinguish between obligatory and optional positions. Only the N^0 position, as the head of the syllable, is obligatory (it is also the only position that can be complex, since diphthongs such as /ai/ are allowed, illustrating a head–dependent asymmetry in the sense of Dresher & Van der Hulst (1998)).[1] All other (non-head) positions are optional and subject to high-ranked *COMPLEX: the initial C-position is limited to one consonant, the position marked "G" is limited to one glide, and the final C-position is limited to a nasal (though see below for a discussion of final [-r] in diminutive formation). Furthermore, different domains in this structure can be identified with different phonological functions: the N″ position can be identified with the 'Final', a part of the syllable which is well-supported in traditional accounts of Chinese phonology (see Wang & Smith (1997), Van de Weijer & Zhang (2008) for discussion). The nucleus of the syllable itself (N′) is the domain for tone assignment.

2.2 A restriction on tone 2

Not all combinations of tones and all syllable structures are permitted in MC. In particular, if a syllable begins with a voiced stop (as pointed out above: more accurate phonetically these are voiceless unaspirated stops) in the onset and is closed by a nasal, the rising tone (tone 2) is not permitted: syllables such as *bán, *dán, *gán, *jín, or *bíng, *dóng, *zháng are not found or very

---

[1] Note that if the nucleus is complex, then there cannot be a coda (*-ain, *-aoŋ), a constraint on N′.

infrequent.[2] The prohibition is rooted in a complicated set of changes in Mandarin around a thousand years ago, in which, among other things, voiced stops became voiceless unaspirated stops. Also, syllables with tone 2 in the high register (so-called *yangshang* tones, which were basically allotones of tone 1) became tone 4 after voiced stops. The full set of changes is controversial and cannot be done justice to here; see e.g. Wang (1985) for an overview. Informal observation suggests that the prohibition is synchronically active psycholinguistically, since native speakers reject putative names such as *Béng* for putative foreign products as possible words. As a reviewer rightly points out, this needs to be checked more carefully in further investigation, especially in comparison to other unattested patterns.

If any other type of consonant apart from voiceless unaspirated stop appears in the onset (including nasals or glides), then the rising tone is permitted on the vowel. If there is no nasal coda, tone 2 is also permitted. These two possibilities are illustrated in (4):

(4) a. Tone 2 is permitted after consonants other than voiced stops before a nasal coda:

糖	tang2	'sugar'	王	wang2	'king'
燃	ran2	'to burn, ignite'	盘	pan2	'disk, tray'
平	ping2	'level, even'	蒙	meng2	'to cover'
人	ren2	'person'	寻	xun2	'to seek'
羊	yang2	'sheep'	零	ling2	'zero'

   b. Tone 2 is permitted after voiced stops if there is no nasal coda:

拔	ba2	'raise, pull'	达	da2	'reach, arrive'
隔	ge2	'to separate'	打	da2	'hit, get, play'
鼻	bi2	'nose'	敌	di2	'enemy'
极	ji2	'extreme'	轴	zhou2	'axis, spool'

The words in (4b) had various tones in Middle Chinese — we will not be concerned here with their historical development, but focus on the synchronic situation.

Note that there are very few — if any — good examples of onsetless words which have tone 2 and a final nasal (cf. 昂 *ang2* in 昂首 *ang2shou3* 'hold one's head high; high, soaring'). Perhaps this is a subregularity that will need to be looked into in the future.

---

[2] An interesting exception is 甭 [béng], 'there's no need to', which is a contraction (orthographically as well as phonologically) of the characters 不 (*bu2/4*) 'no' and 用 (*yong4*) 'need' (thanks to Zhu Lei for pointing this out to me). A reviewer additionally notes the colloquial forms 哏 (*gen2*) 'comical' and 咱 (*zan2*) as in 咱们 (*zan2men*) 'we'.

The condition against tone 2 illustrated by the examples in (4) can be formalized as in (5):

(5)　　*[$\begin{array}{c}-\text{son} \\ +\text{voice}\end{array}$] $\begin{array}{c}\text{V} \\ \text{Tone 2}\end{array}$ [$\begin{array}{c}+\text{cons} \\ +\text{nasal}\end{array}$]] σ

The phonetic motivation for a condition such as (5) is relatively well understood. Voiced obstruents are well-known to be associated with relatively lower tonal registers (Hombert 1978; Bradshaw 1999). This is seen particularly well in processes of tonogenesis (e.g. Haudricourt 1954; Hyslop 2009). Thus, voiced stops and high (or here: rising) tone are natural antagonists. See below for further discussion.

A number of comments on (5) are in order. First of all, since MC does not permit voiced fricatives in the onset, it is not necessary to specify [–cont] in the left-hand side of the condition. Note that Duanmu (2007: 24) regards initial [r] as a (voiced) fricative, transcribed [ʐ], on the basis of (one of) the phonetic realizations of this sound. However, since /r/ seems to pattern with the sonorants, at least for the process discussed here (and also because it is the only other sound permitted in the coda in morphologically complex words, involving the diminutive suffix 儿 (pinyin: *er2*)), we will assume that phonologically it is a sonorant. Secondly, we have used "Tone 2" specifically in the condition, to underscore the fact that other tones, in particular tone 1 (level-high) and tone 3 (dipping), which also involve a high component, are not subject to the condition. Third, recall that voiced stops are phonetically voiceless unaspirated stops; we might therefore have to read [–voice, –spread glottis] for [+voice] in this constraint. Fourth and most important, we need to discuss whether the right-hand side of the constraint is properly characterized. Since the only closed syllables in MC are those closed with a nasal, it would be possible to leave out the [+nasal] specification. Why should tone 2 be forbidden in syllables ending with a nasal? The effect of nasals, and sonorants in general, on tone in tonogenesis is not so well understood as that of obstruents on tone (but see, recently, Hyslop (2009) for discussion). Since nasals are voiced, they might also be regarded as antagonistic to high tone. Alternatively, the relevant interaction here is not between nasality and tone, but between syllable structure and tone. On this account, tone 2 is not permitted after voiced obstruents in a closed syllable and the condition in (5) could be simplified, as shown in (6):

(6)　　*[$\begin{array}{c}-\text{son} \\ +\text{voice}\end{array}$] $\begin{array}{c}\text{V} \\ \text{Tone 2}\end{array}$ [+cons]] σ

If characterized in this way, the question would be why tone 2 is forbidden in closed syllables. There are some parallels in other (Chinese) languages where a particular tone does not occur in particular syllable types (see Gordon

(2002) for a discussion of restrictions on contour tones in particular syllable types). A case in point is Shanghainese, where tones 4 and 5 occur in 'checked' syllables only, i.e. syllables closed by a glottal stop (see e.g. Zee & Maddieson (1979)) and tones 1-3, therefore, are not permitted. A similar situation obtains in Cantonese, where only three of the seven tones occur in syllables closed by a stop (Yip 2002: 174), all of them level tones.

One further source of data that bears on this question comes from (Beijing) MC diminutive formation, which causes syllables to become closed in the morphology by a final [-r] (see Duanmu (2007: Chapter 9)).[3] Duanmu (2007: 223) explicitly discusses the interaction between suffixation and tone, but notes only that in some pairs of words the contrast between tones 3 and 4 is lost. So, tone 2 is preserved in syllables closed by a diminutive [-r]. This is also confirmed by the following examples (collected with kind help from the Friday Linguistics Salon at Shanghai International Studies University):

(7) Root   Diminutive

角   jue2   'actor, role'   角儿   juer2   'id-DIM.'
侄   zhi2   'nephew'   侄儿   zhir2   'id-DIM.'
拔   ba2   'raise, pull'   拔儿   bar2   'id-DIM.'
葱白 cong1bái2 'onion'   葱白儿 cong1bair2   'id-DIM.'
嗝   ge2   'hiccup'   打嗝儿 da3 ger2   'have the hiccups'

This indicates that if we wish to interpret the condition in (5) above strictly as an output condition, as in standard OT, it must include the specification of nasality, and cannot just refer to the fact that the syllable must be closed.

We will therefore continue to adopt the definition of the constraint in (5) for the discussion below.

3 Local constraint conjunction

The constraint on the occurrence of tone 2 (rising tone) in MC can be understood as two conditions: the first is a condition against tone 2 after voiced obstruents and the second is a prohibition of the same tone in syllables closed by a nasal. Separately, these constraints are not strong enough to prevent rising tone in MC words that either start with a voiced stop (recall the data in (4a)) or in words that end in a nasal (see the data in (4b)). However, when

---

[3] Alternatively, the final [r] can be analysed as part of the nucleus, rhotacizing the vowel.

both conditions are violated at the same time, high tone (or rather rising tone) is ruled out.

A situation like this can be elegantly captured by using constraint conjunction (Smolensky 1993, 1995, 2006; Kirchner 1996; Moreton & Smolensky 2002): the condition in (5) is the result of combining the two constraints in (8):

(8) a. *Voice/Rising: "No rising tone (tone 2) after a voiced onset"
    b. *Nasal/Rising: "No rising tone (tone 2) in a syllable closed by a nasal"

The reasoning behind local constraint conjunction is that violating the combination of two markedness constraints is worse than violating either of them alone. High tone in a voiced-onset syllable is marked, but it is still permitted. A high tone in a syllable closed by a nasal is marked but also permitted. However, a high tone in a voiced onset syllable which is *also* closed by a nasal combines the 'worst of two worlds', and is not permitted. The combined constraint, already stated informally in (5) above, is stated as a conjoined constraint in (9):

(9) *Voice/Rising ∩ *Nasal/Rising (*VRNR)

    "No rising tone in a syllable with a voiced onset and a nasal coda"

Both separate constraints are relatively low-ranked in MC, and at any rate lower than a tone faithfulness constraint which allows Tone 2 to surface, even in words with a voiced onset or a coda nasal. This is shown in the tableaux in (10):

(10) a. The conjoined constraint permits codaless words with voiced onsets

/dá/ 'reach'	*VRNR	Faith(Tone)	*Voice/Rising	*Nasal/Rising
☞ [dá]			*	
[dā]		*!		

    b. The conjoined constraint rules out words with a voiced onset in a closed syllable

/dán/	*VRNR	Faith(Tone)	*Voice/Rising	*Nasal/Rising
[dán]	*!		*	*
☞ [dān]		*		

Other constraints (not discussed here) might determine the choice for another tone to surface in (10b). What remains to be shown is that in other languages a constraint like *Voice/Rising is highly ranked; this a topic for further research.

A second point that must be noted with respect to the constraint hierarchy of MC is that the combined constraint *VRNR is not inviolable, especially when tone sandhi is taken into account: the well-known tone 3 sandhi role changes the first of a tone-3 syllable into tone 2 before another tone 3 syllable, which applies, for instance, in 管理 *guan3 li3* 'to manage' and will result in a phonetic syllable [guan2]. The tone sandhi constraint must therefore dominate VRNR.

Local constraint conjunction has been the topic of some controversy, since it adds considerable power to (OT) grammars. It has been a matter of debate, for instance, whether only two markedness constraints can be combined in this way (as in the case at hand) or if markedness and faithfulness can be similarly combined; see e.g. Moreton & Smolensky (2002) and references cited there. For the case of MC, however, it seems that the idea of local constraint conjunction is exactly right.

In this way, local constraint conjunction can even be said to serve a function in the discovery of the nature of the (putatively universal) constraint set: whenever a constraint conjunction is found of two constraints A ∩ B, then the separate constraints A and B must be part of the constraint set CON. Thus, cases like those in Mandarin force us to look for languages that instantiate either of the constraints in (8), instead of the more usual situation in which two well-established constraints are combined to result in a constraint conjunction.

6 Conclusion

The case of 'tonotactics' discussed here raises a number of questions. Why is the high level tone (tone 1) permitted in the environment in which the rising tone is ruled out? This might be related to the fact that rising tones take a longer time than level tones to pronounce, as suggested by Yip (2002) for Cantonese, and are therefore more difficult to "fit into" a closed syllable. However, for Mandarin this begs the question why tones 3 and 4, which also involve contours, are permitted in this environment, and why tone 2 is permitted in syllables closed by diminutive [-r]. Further phonetic investigation is necessary here, for instance with respect to the question whether there is a vowel length difference between vowels in closed syllables and in open syllables in this variety of Chinese.

From a theoretical perspective, the case of MC is interesting, because it illustrates a way of finding and arguing for Optimality constraints that is different than usual. The usual discussion in local constraint conjunction revolves around the question whether two separate, individually motivated constraints can be seen in action as a locally conjoined constraint. The tonotactics of Mandarin clearly call for the combined action of two constraints; in such a situation both separate constraints also need to be valid constraints in OT.

References

Bradshaw, Mary (1999): *A Cross-linguistic Study of Consonant-Tone Interaction.* – PhD dissertation, Ohio State University.

Dresher, B. Elan & Harry van der Hulst (1998): "Head-dependent asymmetries in phonology: complexity and visibility." – In: *Phonology* 15, 317–352.

Duanmu, San (1999): "The syllable in Chinese." – In: Hulst, Harry van der & Nancy A. Ritter (eds.): *The Syllable: Views and Facts*, 477–500. Berlin, Mouton de Gruyter.

– (2007): *The Phonology of Standard Chinese* (2nd edn.). – Oxford: Oxford University Press.

– (2008): *Syllable Structure. The Limits of Variation.* – Oxford: Oxford University Press.

Gordon, Matthew (2002): "A typology of contour tone restrictions." – In: *Studies in Language* 25, 423–462.

Haudricourt, André G. (1954): "De l'origine des tons en vietnamien." – In: *Journal Asiatique* 242, 68–82.

Hombert, Jean-Marie (1978): "Consonant types, vowel quality, and tone." – In: Fromkin, Victoria (ed.): *Tone: A Linguistic Survey*, 77–111. New York: Academic Press.

Hyslop, Gwendolyn (2009): "Kurtöp tone: a tonogenetic case study." – In: *Lingua* 119, 827–845.

Kirchner, Robert (1996): "Synchronic chain shifts in Optimality Theory." – In: *Linguistic Inquiry* 27, 341–350.

Li, Chris Wen-Chao (2002): "X-slots, feature trees, and the Chinese sound inventory: a twenty-first century take on Mandarin phonological structure." – In: *Journal of the American Oriental Society* 122, 553–561.

Moreton, Elliot & Paul Smolensky (2002): "Typological consequences of local constraint conjunction." – In: *WCCFL* 21, 306–319.

Prince, Alan & Paul Smolensky (1993 [2004]): *Optimality Theory – Constraint Interaction in Generative Grammar.* – London: Blackwell.

Smolensky, Paul (1993): "Harmony, markedness and phonological activity." – Ms., Johns Hopkins University. ROA-87.

– (1995): "On the internal structure of the constraint component Con of UG." – Paper presented at University of California, Los Angeles.

– (2006): "Optimality in phonology II: harmonic completeness, local constraint conjunction, and feature domain markedness." – In: Smolensky, Paul & Géraldine

Legendre (eds.): *The Harmonic Mind: From Neural Computation to Optimality-Theoretic Grammar*. Vol. 2, 453–535. Boston: MIT Press.

Wang, Jialing & Norval S.H. Smith (eds.) (1997): *Studies in Chinese Phonology*. – Berlin/New York: Mouton de Gruyter.

Wang, Li (1985): 汉语语音史 *[History of Chinese Phonology]*. Beijing: Zhongguo Shehuikexue Chubanshe.

Weijer, Jeroen M. van de & Jason Zhang (2008): "An X-bar approach to the syllable structure of Mandarin." – In: *Lingua* 118, 1416–1428.

Xu, Ching X. & Yi Xu (2004): "Effects of consonant aspiration on Mandarin tones." – In: *Journal of the International Phonetic Association* 33, 165–181.

Yip, Moira (2002): *Tone*. – Cambridge: Cambridge University Press.

– (2003): "Casting doubt on the onset-rime distinction." – In: *Lingua* 113, 779–816.

Zee, Eric & Ian Maddieson (1979): "Tones and tone sandhi in Shanghai: phonetic evidence and phonological analysis." – In: *UCLA Working Papers in Phonetics* 45, 93–129.

John J. McCarthy, Kevin Mullin & Brian W. Smith

Implications of Harmonic Serialism for lexical tone association*

1. Introduction

One of the properties of the classic version of Optimality Theory (OT) in Prince & Smolensky (1993[2004]) is *parallelism*: output candidates may show the effects of several different phonological changes at once. Harmonic Serialism (HS), a version of OT that Prince & Smolensky also briefly consider, is *serial* or *derivational* rather than parallel: output candidates show the effect of only one phonological change at a time, but the winning candidate is run through the grammar again so it can accumulate additional changes.

Although Prince & Smolensky put HS aside and it received little subsequent attention, the case for it was reopened in McCarthy (2000, 2002: 159–163; 2007). In these and other works (see McCarthy (2010) for a summary), two main kinds of evidence for HS have been identified. One is that it permits generalizations to be stated on its intermediate representations, neither underlying nor surface. For example, the cross-linguistically common process of unstressed vowel syncope cannot be analyzed satisfactorily without access to a level of representation in which stress has been assigned but syncope has not yet occurred (McCarthy 2008). The other kind of evidence is typological: the same constraints can predict different language typologies under parallel OT (P-OT) and HS, and in many cases examined so far these differences favour HS. Section 2 presents one such example and McCarthy (2010) cites a number of others in the HS literature.

Of course, an honest exploration of HS's consequences must include a search for potential problems. Most of the existing arguments for parallelism in the OT literature have been addressed (in, e.g., McCarthy 2008; McCarthy

* We are grateful for comments received from the McCarthy-Pater grant group at UMass Amherst. Thanks to John Goldsmith and David Odden for assistance in understanding the ideas about lexical tone association in early autosegmental phonology discussed in section 6. Thanks to Bert Botma, Jeroen van de Weijer, and an anonymous reviewer for comments on the manuscript.

This research was supported by grant BCS-0813829 from the National Science Foundation to the University of Massachusetts Amherst.

et al. to appear; Pater to appear). But new arguments have also emerged. This paper lays out one such argument, based on the phonology of tone in Kikuyu.

Section 3 describes the basic tonal phonology of Kikuyu, summarizing the analysis in Clements & Ford (1979). Section 4 then goes on to explain how this system can be analyzed in HS using standard tone constraints. A key feature of this analysis is the assumption that candidates can be generated by adding or removing at most one association line at a time. The argument for parallelism is presented in section 5. It consists of a demonstration that lexically linked tones disrupt the analysis in HS but not P-OT. The problem for HS is that removing an unwanted lexical tone association is sometimes impossible in Kikuyu-type systems. This problem does not arise in P-OT, where removing unwanted tone associations and inserting better ones take place simultaneously.

What conclusion can we draw from this result? One possibility is that HS is simply wrong and the parallel theory is right. This is not a very attractive option, however, because it disregards the large and growing body of evidence for HS over parallelism. The alternative, which we explore in section 6, is to return to a view that was prevalent in the early days of autosegmental phonology: tones are never associated in underlying representation. By ensuring that tone association can proceed monotonically, adding links but never deleting them, this move solves the problem identified in section 5.

Finally, section 7 concludes with some discussion of the convergence between our results and those in McCarthy & Pruitt (to appear), where it is shown that lexical foot structure is also incompatible with HS.

2 Harmonic Serialism

In P-OT, GEN can make many changes at once, and as a result the candidate set is large and diverse. In HS, GEN can make only one change at a time, and as a result the candidate set is small and homogeneous. HS makes up for its impoverished GEN by being derivational: the optimal candidate selected by EVAL becomes the input for a new application of GEN. This GEN→EVAL→... loop continues until convergence, when the output of EVAL is identical with the latest input to GEN. The resulting form is the final output of the grammar.

In HS, much depends on precisely how GEN is defined, and so the study of GEN is one of the most important elements of the HS research program. One of our goals in this chapter is to understand what it means for GEN to make 'one change' in autosegmental association lines. Some guidance is provided by restrictive theories of phonological rules, which sought to limit exactly how much a single rule could do. Archangeli & Pulleyblank (1994) define primitive operations INSERT/PATH and DELETE/PATH (a path is an autosegmental association line), and similar ideas are fairly standard in other work on autosegmental phonology. If this proposal is incorporated into HS, it means that GEN includes the operations in (1), but it can only apply them once and one at a time:

(1) Operations on autosegmental association lines in GEN

    a.   Insertion

    b.   Deletion

A consequence of this hypothesis is that the process variously referred to as autosegmental shift, displacement, transfer, or flop can never be done in a single step of a HS derivation. In this process, an association line appears to move from one segment or syllable to another. If (1) is right, then moving an association line can only be accomplished by spreading followed by delinking, as in (2):[1]

(2) Autosegmental shift, given (1)

Esimbi (Niger-Congo, Cameroon) supplies a nice example (Clements 1991; Hyman 1988; Stallcup 1980; Walker 1997, 2001). In this language, the height of a prefix vowel is determined by the underlying height of the root vowel, and the root vowel neutralizes to [+high]. For example, as shown in (3), the

---

[1] Another logical possibility is that a first delinks from X and then reassociates to Y. This is not precisely what is meant by autosegmental shift, however. In HS, any grammar that will cause *a* to delink from *X* will do so regardless of whether *Y* follows. The real process, then, is neutralization: *a* delinks from *X*. Aspiration throwback in Sanskrit is an example (Borowsky & Mester 1983): voiced aspirates in coda position lose aspiration, and aspiration reappears on the preceding onset only if it is also a voiced obstruent.

infinitival prefix is a back rounded vowel that alternates among *u*, *o*, and *ɔ*, depending on the underlying vowel of the following root. Hyman and Walker analyze this as a shift process: the height features of the root vowel are transferred to the prefix syllable, and the root vowel becomes high by default.

(3)   Esimbi vowel alternations

	Underlying root	Infinitive	
	/ri/	u-ri	'to eat'
	/zu/	u-zu	'to kill'
	/se/	o-si	'to laugh'
	/to/	o-tu	'to insult'
	/ʤə/	o-ʤɨ	'to steal'
	/rɛ/	o-ri	'to daub'
	/hɔ/	ɔ-hu	'to knead'
	/ba/	ɔ-bɨ	'to come'

Walker develops a P-OT analysis of Esimbi in which height shifts to the word-initial syllable to satisfy the constraint LICENSE([–high], $_{wd}[σ)$), which requires any token of a [–high] feature value to be linked to a word-initial syllable (cf. Zoll 2004). Shift is required, rather than spreading, because CRISP(σ, [high]) prohibits any token of the feature [high] from being linked to more than one syllable at a time (cf. Ito & Mester 1999). Ranking these two constraints above IDENT(high), as shown in (4), produces the desired result: [2]

---

(4) Esimbi in Walker (2001)

/u-ba/ | [–hi,+lo]	LIC([–high], wd[σ)	CRISP(σ, [high])	ID(high)
a. ☞ ɔ-bɨ 〳 [–hi,+lo]			2
b. u-ba | [–hi,+lo]	1 **W**		**L**
c. ɔ-ba 〵 [–hi,+lo]		1 **W**	1 **L**

The full analysis also accounts for why the root vowel defaults to [+high]; see Walker (2001) for details.

An HS analysis in the manner of (2) is nearly identical, the only difference being the ranking of LICENSE above CRISP:

(5) Esimbi in HS, Step 1

/u-ba/ | [–hi,+lo]	LIC([–high], wd[σ)	CRISP(σ, [high])	ID(high)
a. ☞ ɔ-ba 〵 [–hi,+lo]		1	1
b. u-ba | [–hi,+lo]	1 **W**	**L**	**L**

(6) Esimbi in HS, Step 2

ɔ-ba 〵 [–hi,+lo]	LIC([–high], wd[σ)	CRISP(σ, [high])	ID(high)
a. ☞ ɔ-bɨ 〵 [–hi,+lo]			1
b. ɔ-ba 〵 [–hi,+lo]		1 **W**	**L**

At step 3, this derivation converges on the output of step 2 as the final output, because no further improvement in the harmony of *ɔ-bí* is possible with this grammar. Observe that faithfulness violations are computed anew at each step, relative to the input to the most recent iteration of GEN.

The P-OT analysis in (4) and the HS analysis in (5)-(6) look quite similar, but there is an important difference between them. In the P-OT analysis, *shifting* [–high] from root to prefix in (4a) competes with *spreading* [–high] from root to prefix in (4c). In the HS analysis, however, spreading and shift do not compete at step 1. In HS, given our assumptions about GEN, for a feature to shift it must first spread.

As a consequence, HS offers a more restrictive theory of shift processes than P-OT does, all else being equal. It is more restrictive because shift in HS is limited by the same constraints, hard or violable, that limit spreading. These constraints have been studied throughout the history of autosegmental phonology, starting with the Well-Formedness Condition of Goldsmith (1976a, b) and continuing through much more recent proposals about strict locality (Gafos 1999; Ní Chiosáin & Padgett 2001; Walker 1998, and others). In P-OT, there is no reason to expect constraints on spreading to also govern shift. Indeed, it is incumbent on the proponent of P-OT to demonstrate that this less restrictive theory of shift is necessary or to show how constraints on spreading can be non-stipulatively extended to shift.

It is important to realize that the connection between shift and spreading in HS depends on making the assumption about GEN in (1). If GEN also included a more powerful operation that is able to shift an association line in a single step, then step 1 of the HS derivation would look exactly like the P-OT tableau in (4). This reflects a general property of HS: analysis and typology depend on assumptions about *both* GEN and CON (McCarthy 2009). This point will be revisited in section 5.

3 Tone association in Kikuyu

In Kikuyu, tone association is fully predictable (Clements 1984; Clements & Ford 1979): the first tone is associated with the first two syllables, and each subsequent tone is associated with the syllable immediately following the morpheme that supplied it.

(7)   Example

    a.   Lexical representations

        Segments   Tone

to	L	'we'
ma	H	'them'
rɔr	L	'look at'
ir-ɛ	H	current past tense

    b.   Surface form

```
        L        H  L H
        ⌐⌐⌐⌐⌐⌐⌐  |  | |
        t o m  a r ɔ r i rɛ      'we looked at them'
```

Kikuyu follows this pattern with remarkable regularity (though see Clements 1984: 290, 298 on two non-conforming situations).

In Clements & Ford's analysis, surface structures like (8) are obtained from underlying representations in which tones are lexically listed with morphemes but not autosegmentally associated with them. The underlying forms of the morphemes in (7) are therefore: /to, L/; /ma, H/; /rɔr, L/; and /irɛ, H/. In the first step of the derivation, a language-particular rule associates the initial L with the *second* syllable:

(8)   After initial tone association rule

```
        L        H  L H
         ⟍
        t o m  a r ɔ r i  rɛ
```

From this point forward, universal tone association conventions take over. They cause the remaining unlinked tones to be linked one-to-one, from left to right, to the toneless syllables:

(9)   After one-to-one left-to-right association

```
        L        H  L H
         ⟍       |  | |
        t o m  a r ɔ r i  rɛ      'we looked at them'
```

The universal tone association conventions also cause the initial L to spread to the toneless initial syllable, yielding the surface form in (7b).

It sometimes happens that there are as many tones as syllables. Since the first tone takes up two syllables, a tone is left over after one-to-one left-to-right association. One possible disposition of the left-over tone is that it becomes part of a contour tone. Kikuyu allows rising tones on the final syllable, as in (10):

(10)   Final rising tone (Clements & Ford 1979: 191)

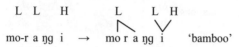

But if the tonal contour is forbidden, then the left-over tone remains floating. For example, Kikuyu does not allow contour tones falling from H to L. As a result, the L tone remains floating in (11), where its presence can be inferred from its role in the downstep system (Clements & Ford 1979: 203ff.):

(11)   Final floating tone

The assumption that tones are lexically unassociated with their sponsoring morphemes is essential to Clements & Ford's analysis. It is precisely because the non-initial tones are unassociated in (8) that the universal tone association conventions produce (9). If, on the contrary, tones were associated in underlying representation, then the immediate output of the initial tone association rule would look like this:

(12)   After initial tone association rule, underlying linked tones

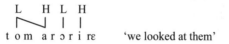

The universal tone association conventions are no guide through the complex chain of operations that would be needed to get from (12) to the surface form in (7b). Thus, the assumption that tones are unassociated in underlying representation is doing real work in Clements and Ford's analysis.[3]

4 Kikuyu tone association in Harmonic Serialism

In the view of Clements and Ford, one-to-one left-to-right association of tones with syllables is the default pattern cross-linguistically. To analyze this pattern in HS (or OT generally), constraints of four types are required:

---

[3] We emphasize this point because non-association of tones in underlying representation is often posited for less weighty reasons, such as considerations of minimal redundancy.

(i) Constraints against floating tones and toneless syllables, which approximate the effects of Goldsmith's (1976b) Well-formedness Condition for autosegmental phonology. These constraints motivate tone-syllable association.

(13) NO-FLOAT (NO-FL)

Assign one violation mark for every tone that is not associated with a syllable.

(14) HAVE-TONE (HAVE-T)

Assign one violation mark for every syllable that is not associated with a tone.

(ii) Constraints against skipping tones or syllables in the process of association. They ensure that association iterates directionally.

(15) NO-SKIP(tone) (NO-SK(t))

Assign one violation mark for every unlinked tone that is preceded and followed (at any distance) by linked tones.

(16) NO-SKIP(syllable) (NO-SK(s))

Assign one violation mark for every unlinked syllable that is preceded and followed (at any distance) by linked syllables.

(iii) A constraint requiring the initial tone to link to the initial syllable. This accounts for the default left-to-right direction.

(17) LINK-INITIAL (LNK-INIT)

Assign a violation mark if the initial tone is not linked to the initial syllable.

(iv) The faithfulness constraint IDENT(tone), which is violated once for each change in an association line. (Because deletion and insertion of tones are not in general at issue here, we assume that MAX(tone) and DEP(tone) are undominated.)

None of these constraints is really new; see Myers (1997) or Yip (2002), among others, for similar proposals.

In HS far more than in P-OT, the details of the candidate generator GEN are important, because GEN determines exactly how much a candidate can differ from its input. The natural assumption for autosegmental phonology is that GEN can insert or delete exactly one association line at a time, as in (1). We also make the standard assumption that GEN cannot produce structures with crossing association lines.

John J. McCarthy, Kevin Mullin & Brian W. Smith

We will illustrate this system with an HS analysis of a hypothetical language with left-to-right tone association. (This language is essentially Kikuyu without tone shift.) The underlying representation consists of segmental material for four syllables and an equal number of unassociated tones. The derivation in (18) is typical of what the analysis has to do:

(18) Derivation for left-to-right language

Underlying	Step 1	Step 2	Step 3	Step 4	Step 5 convergence
L H L H patakasa	L H L H patakasa	L H L H patakasa	L H L H patakasa	L H L H patakasa	L H L H patakasa

The candidates available at the first step of the derivation, some of which are shown in tableau (19), consist of all the ways of applying either of the operations in (1) exactly once, plus the faithful candidate. (Because the input has no associations, only the linking operation in (1) is in fact applicable.) The faithful candidate (19b) loses because the faithfulness constraint IDENT(tone) is ranked below NO-FLOAT and HAVE-TONE. The others (19c,d) lose because LINK-INITIAL favours candidate (19a), where the first tone and first syllable are associated with one another.

(19) Step 1 of one-to-one left-to-right association

L H L H patakasa	NO-FL	HAVE-T	NO-SK(T)	NO-SK(S)	LNK-INIT	ID(T)
a. ☞ L H L H patakasa	3	3				1
b. L H L H patakasa	4 W	4 W			1 W	L
c. L H L H patakasa	3	3			1 W	1
d. L H L H patakasa	3	3			1 W	1

At step 2 (tableau (20)), the no-skipping constraints are important. NO-FLOAT and HAVE-TONE continue to compel tone association, and the no-skipping constraints determine that the next tone and syllable associated must be adjacent to the last tone and syllable associated. The candidates include the unchanged output of step 1, all of the ways of adding a single association line to it, and a candidate that has removed its lone association line (20e):

(20) Step 2 of one-to-one left-to-right association

LHLH | patakasa	No- FL	HAVE- T	No- SK(T)	No- SK(S)	LNK- INIT	ID(T)
a. ☞ LHLH | | patakasa	2	2				1
b. LHLH | patakasa	3 W	3 W				L
c. LHLH | \\ patakasa	2	2		1 W		1
d. LHLH | ╱ patakasa	2	2	1 W			1
e. LHLH patakasa	4 W	4 W			1 W	1

The derivation continues like this until it converges at step 5.

The derivation in (19)-(20) involves an example with equal numbers of tones and syllables. When the number of syllables is larger than the number of tones, as in (21), then the last tone will spread to any toneless syllables because of HAVE-TONE. When the number of tones is larger, as in (22), No-FLOAT will force creation of a contour tone, unless some higher ranking constraint prevents it.

(21) Step 4 from /patakasa, LHL/

LHL | | | patakasa	No- FL	HAVE- T	No- SK(T)	No- SK(S)	LNK- INIT	ID(T)
a. ☞ LHL | | ⋀ patakasa						1
b. LHL | | | patakasa		1 W				L

(22) Step 4 from /pataka, LHLH/

L H L H │ │ │ pataka	NO- FL	HAVE- T	NO- SK(T)	NO- SK(S)	LNK- INIT	ID(T)
a. ☞ L H L H │ │ │/ pataka						1
b. L H L H │ │ │ pataka	1 W					L

Kikuyu follows this pattern in all respects except one: it requires the first tone to be linked to two syllables. Although Clements (1984: 330–331) has an interesting proposal about why this should be so, in the interest of simplicity we will opt here for an *ad hoc* constraint:

(23) INITIAL-PLATEAU (INIT-PLAT) (*ad hoc* constraint)[4]

> Assign a violation mark if the initial tone is linked to fewer than two syllables.

We now have the resources we need to analyze Kikuyu. Since /tomarɔrirɛ, LHLH/ contains five syllables and four tones, there are 20 ways of adding a single association line to it at step 1. Those 20, plus the faithful candidate, form the candidate set. Only one of these candidates satisfies LINK-INITIAL, which is the only constraint (other than faithfulness) that distinguishes among them, as tableau (24) shows.

---

[4] The factorial typology of this constraint set on inputs like the one in (24) was computed with OT-Help (Staubs et al. 2010). The results were consistent with expectations except for a pattern where the contour tone appears on the second syllable. This pattern is produced under rankings where INITIAL-PLATEAU dominates IDENT(t), but the constraints giving one-to-one left-to-right association dominate INITIAL-PLATEAU. This results in a contour tone on the second syllable because satisfaction of INITIAL-PLATEAU is the last step before convergence. This prediction is implausible, and it suggests unsurprisingly that the *ad hoc* constraint INITIAL-PLATEAU is somewhat off the mark.

(24) Step 1 from /tomarɔrirɛ, LHLH/

L H L H tomarɔrirɛ	Have-T	No-Sk(t)	No-Sk(s)	Lnk-Init	Init-Plat	No-Fl	Id(t)
a. ☞ L H L H | tomarɔrirɛ	4				1	3	1
b. L H L H tomarɔrirɛ	5 W			1 W	1	4 W	L
c. L H L H \ tomarɔrirɛ	4			1 W	1	3	1
d. L H L H | tomarɔrirɛ	4			1 W	1	3	1

At the second step, the available options include spreading the first tone (25a), doing nothing (25b), one-to-one linking (25c), creation of a contour tone (25d), and delinking (25e). Spreading of the first tone is required by INITIAL-PLATEAU. For it to take precedence over one-to-one linking, INITIAL-PLATEAU has to dominate NO-FLOAT:

(25) Step 2 from /tomarɔrirɛ, LHLH/

L H L H | tomarɔrirɛ	Have-T	No-Sk(t)	No-Sk(s)	Lnk-Init	Init-Plat	No-Fl	Id(t)
a. ☞ L H L H ∧ tomarɔrirɛ	3					3	1
b. L H L H | tomarɔrirɛ	4 W				1 W	3	L
c. L H L H | | tomarɔrirɛ	3				1 W	2 L	1
d. L H L H V tomarɔrirɛ	4 W				1 W	2 L	1
e. L H L H tomarɔrirɛ	4 W			1 W	1 W	4 W	1

Observe that delinking of the previously associated tone, as in (25e), is harmonically bounded by the winner (25a). This will become important when we consider the effects of lexical associations.

One-to-one left-to-right association prevails at the next step of the derivation, where it is favoured by the no-skipping constraints. In this respect, the Kikuyu step-3 tableau (26) is identical with the step-2 tableau of the hypothetical example in (20).

(26) Step 3 from /tomarɔrirɛ, LHLH/

L H L H ∧ tomarɔrirɛ	HAVE-T	No-SK(T)	No-SK(S)	LNK-INIT	INIT-PLAT	No-FL	ID(T)
a. ☞ L H L H ∧ | tomarɔrirɛ	2					2	1
b. L H L H ∧ tomarɔrirɛ	3 W					3 W	L
c. L H L H ∧ | tomarɔrirɛ	2	1 W	1 W			2	1
d. L H L H ∧ | tomarɔrirɛ	2		1 W			2	1
e. L H L H ∧ | tomarɔrirɛ	2	1 W				2	1

The pattern of one-to-one left-to-right association continues at step 4:

(27) Step 4 from /tomarɔrirɛ, LHLH/

L H L H (tomarɔrirɛ)	HAVE-T	NO-SK(T)	NO-SK(S)	LNK-INIT	INIT-PLAT	NO-FL	ID(T)
a. ☞ L H LH (tomarɔrirɛ)	1					1	1
b. L H L H (tomarɔrirɛ)	2 W					2 W	L
c. L H L H (tomarɔrirɛ)	1		1 W			1	1
d. L H L H (tomarɔrirɛ)	1	1 W				1	1

At step 5, the last unlinked tone associates with the last unlinked syllable:

(28) Step 5 from /tomarɔrirɛ, LHLH/

L H L H (tomarɔrirɛ)	HAVE-T	NO-SK(T)	NO-SK(S)	LNK-INIT	INIT-PLAT	NO-FL	ID(T)
a. ☞ L H LH (tomarɔrirɛ)							1
b. L H LH (tomarɔrirɛ)	1 W					1 W	L

Finally, at step 6, the derivation converges on the correct surface form:

(29) Step 6 from /tomarɔrirɛ, LHLH/ — Convergence

L H LH (tomarɔrirɛ)	HAVE-T	NO-SK(T)	NO-SK(S)	LNK-INIT	INIT-PLAT	NO-FL	ID(T)
a. ☞ L H LH (tomarɔrirɛ)							
b. L H LH (tomarɔrirɛ)							1 W

The analysis just presented is strictly structure-building. The original inputs to the system have no tone-syllable associations, and the ultimate outputs have no toneless syllables and floating tones only when contours are impossible. Structure is built in a strictly monotonic fashion: although GEN as defined in (1) includes a delinking operation, at no point in this dervation was it optimal to remove an association line. Kikuyu's monotonic structure-building derivations are, moreover, monotonically harmonically improving with respect to HAVE-TONE and NO-FLOAT. Each added association line improves performance on one or more of these constraints. Removing association lines only degrades performance, making the representation less harmonic rather than more.

5 Effect of lexical tone linking

This analysis, which was worked out under the assumption that tones are unassociated in the lexicon, fails when confronted with lexical associations. To show this, we will examine the threshold case, where every tone is lexically linked, and show that the HS analysis is unable to bring it into conformity with the observed regularities of tone association in Kikuyu.

The phonology of Kikuyu should be able to map the underlying representation in (30a) to the surface representation in (30b):

(30) Effect of lexical linking

    a. Underlying form   b. Desired surface form

       L H L H   L H LH

       | | | | $\diagdown\ |\ \diagup$

       patakasa   patakasa

This requirement follows because the grammar has to capture some basic generalizations about tone in this language: the underying tones of non-initial, non-final morphemes appear one syllable to their right in the surface form; the first two syllables have a level tone; and contour tones are confined to the final syllable. Section 4 presented a grammar that captures these generalizations when the underlying form has only unlinked tones. As we will now show, the same grammar is unable to accomplish the mapping in (30), which means that it is sometimes unable to capture these generalizations when the underlying representation has linked tones.

At step 1, INITIAL-PLATEAU prevails, and the first tone spreads to the second syllable, creating a LH contour tone on it, as in (31):

(31) Step 1 from /paL taH kaL saH/

L H L H | | | | patakasa	HAVE-T	NO-SK(T)	NO-SK(S)	LNK-INIT	INIT-PLAT	NO-FL	ID(T)
a. ☞ L H L H N | | patakasa							1
b. L H L H | | | | patakasa					1 W		L
c. L H L H | | | patakasa	1 W	1 W	1 W		1 W	1 W	1

At step 2, the grammar converges on the output of Step 1:

(32) Convergence at step 2 from /paL taH kaL saH/

L H L H N | | patakasa	HAVE-T	NO-SK(T)	NO-SK(S)	LNK-INIT	INIT-PLAT	NO-FL	ID(T)
a. ☞ L H L H N | | patakasa							
b. L H L H \\ | | patakasa		1 W				1 W	1 W
c. L H L H NN | patakasa							1 W

This is not a welcome result. Starting from an underlying representation where tones and tone-bearers are linked one-to-one, the grammar produces a result with a contour tone on the second syllable. This is at odds with the facts of Kikuyu, which allows contour tones only on the final syllable.

The source of this problem is evident from (32). To get from (32a) to a final result that has a contour tone on the final syllable, the H linked to the second syllable needs to shift to the third syllable, forcing the L on the third syllable to shift to the fourth and final syllable. (In longer words, obviously, more intermediate steps will be required.) The only way to accomplish this within our assumptions about GEN is for one of the losers in (32) to win. But both are harmonically bounded by the winner, which means that no ranking of these constraints can make winners of them.

The harmonic bounding in (32) can be broken by introducing another constraint that favours one of the losers over the unwanted winner. One plausible option is NO-MEDIAL-CONTOUR (NO-MC) (cf. Zoll 2003), which favours (32b) over (32a). It has to be ranked below INITIAL-PLATEAU, since creating the plateau produces a medial contour tone. But if it dominates NO-SKIP(tone) and NO-FLOAT, it can force simplification of the contour tone created at step 1 by delinking the H part of the contour:

(33) Step 2 from /paL taH kaL saH/ with NO-MEDIAL-CONTOUR

L H L H $\diagdown$ | | patakasa	No-Sk(s)	Init-Plat	Lnk-Init	Have-T	No-MC	No-Sk(t)	No-Fl	Id(t)
a. ☞ L H L H $\diagdown$ | | patakasa						1	1	1
b. L H L H $\diagdown$ | | patakasa					1 W	L	L	L

At the next step, the floating H needs to reassociate with the third syllable, but that is impossible under this ranking. The problem (see tableau (34)) is that reassociating the floating H violates NO-MEDIAL-CONTOUR, while the floating H itself violates only NO-SKIP(tone) and NO-FLOAT. As we just saw in (33), these constraints have to be ranked below NO-MEDIAL-CONTOUR to get step 2 to work right.

(34) Convergence at step 3 on output of (33)

L H L H $\diagdown$ | | patakasa	No-Sk(s)	Init-Plat	Lnk-Init	Have-T	No-MC	No-Sk(t)	No-Fl	Id(t)
a. ☞ L H L H $\diagdown$ | | patakasa						1	1	
b. L H L H $\diagdown\!\!\diagup$ | patakasa					1 W	L	L	1 W

Clearly, introducing NO-MEDIAL-CONTOUR does not in general help to map underlying representations with linked tones onto the actual surface tone pattern of Kikuyu. With or without this constraint, the HS analysis only works reliably when underlying representations are limited to unassociated tones.

Analysis in HS depends on assumptions about GEN as well as CON. In section 2, we argued for a maximally simple GEN with just two operations on autosegmental association lines, insertion or deletion of a single line. We specifically argued against including an operation that is able to reassociate, shifting a tone from one syllable to the next in a single step. As it turns out, even if GEN included such an operation, it would not help with the problem of lexically associated tones. This operation adds another relevant candidate to those listed in (33). This candidate, which is shown in (35c), is no improvement — in fact, it is harmonically bounded by (35b), which has no changes at all.[5]

(35) Step 2 from /paL taH kaL saH/ with flop

L H L H N | | patakasa	No-SK(S)	INIT-PLAT	LNK-INIT	HAVE-T	No-MC	No-SK(T)	No-FL	ID(T)
a. ☞ L H L H N | | patakasa						1	1	1
b. L H L H N | | patakasa					1 W	L	L	L
c. L H L H N\\ | patakasa					1 W	L	L	2 W

In contrast, underlying tone associations present no difficulties for a P-OT analysis. As long as IDENT(tone) is ranked low enough, underlying representations with linked and unlinked tones map to the same outputs. Precisely because IDENT(tone) is bottom-ranked, the markedness constraints overwhelm any faithfulness effects and thereby fully determine the tonal pattern of the output, regardless of whether or how tones are linked in the input. Tableaux (36) and (37) illustrate:[6]

---

[5] Another imaginable approach would be to replace NO-MEDIAL CONTOUR with a gradient constraint ALIGN-R(contour tone, word). This constraint would break the harmonic bounding in (35) by favouring (35c) over (35b), because (35c)'s contour tone is one syllable further to the right than (35b)'s. The problem with this constraint is that it makes implausible typological predictions in other grammars. For example, it predicts the existence of a language where the penult can have a contour tone only if the ultima does, where the antepenult can have a contour tone only if the penult and ultima do, and so on. In general, licensing constraints like NO-MEDIAL CONTOUR never seem to be evaluated gradiently (Zoll 1996: 141).

[6] The ranking in (36) and (37) is based on examples like (11), which show that INITIAL-PLATEAU has to dominate NO-FLOAT.

(36) Kikuyu in parallel OT: Underlying linked tones

L H L H / patakasa	NO-SK(S)	INIT-PLAT	LNK-INIT	HAVE-T	NO-MC	NO-SK(T)	NO-FL	ID(T)
a. ☞ L H L H (linked) patakasa								5
b. L H L H |||| patakasa	1 W							L
c. L H L H (linked) patakasa					1 W			1 L
d. L H L H (linked) patakasa						1 W	1 W	2 L

(37) Kikuyu in parallel OT: Underlying unlinked tones

L H L H / patakasa	NO-SK(S)	INIT-PLAT	LNK-INIT	HAVE-T	NO-MC	NO-SK(T)	NO-FL	ID(T)
a. ☞ L H L H (linked) patakasa								5
b. L H L H (linked) patakasa		1 W		4 W			4 W	L
c. L H L H |||| patakasa		1 W						4 L
d. L H L H (linked) patakasa						1 W		5
e. L H L H (linked) patakasa						1 W	1 W	4 L

Why do P-OT and HS analyses differ so sharply in their ability to accommodate underlying representations with linked tones? Why is it that P-OT is able to accomplish the mapping in (38) (repeated from (30)), while HS is not? Because the relationship between an underlying form and its surface form is different in P-OT and HS. In P-OT, a surface form is the most harmonic candidate derived from its underlying form. In HS, a surface form is the most harmonic candidate derived from the form that preceded it in the derivation, which is the most harmonic candidate derived from its predecessor, and so on, all the way back to the underlying form. Whether a particular surface form is accessible from some underlying form in HS depends on whether there is a series of intermediate optima linking them by a succession of small changes — in tone association, those small changes have to be drawn from (1). The mapping in (38) is impossible for the HS analysis because there is no such series of optima, as we saw when we attempted to construct one in (31)-(35).

(38)   Effect of lexical linking

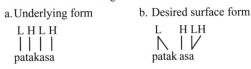

There is clearly a problem for HS here. One obvious solution to this problem is to prohibit linked tones in the Kikuyu lexicon. This is in fact the solution we adopt, but it cannot be true of the lexicon of Kikuyu alone — it must be true of every language or none at all. A fundamental premise of OT is that languages differ in constraint ranking. The null hypothesis is that languages differ *only* in constraint ranking. Lexica are language-particular, of course, but all systematic differences between languages are expressed by the grammar. This thesis is called richness of the base (ROTB), because it holds that the base (= original input to the grammar) is rich in the sense that it is not subject to any language-particular restrictions. ROTB does not rule out language-universal restrictions on inputs, however. For instance, the PARSE/FILL theory of faithfulness in Prince & Smolensky (1993[2004]) relied on the assumption that inputs contain no syllable structure.

ROTB rules out a fairly standard pre-OT analytic move of saying that tones are underlyingly unlinked in languages where tone association is fully predictable, such as Kikuyu, but they are underlyingly linked in languages where tone association is unpredictable, such as Japanese. If we are to say that tones are underlyingly unlinked in the lexicon of Kikuyu, as the argument just presented shows, then we are obliged under ROTB to say that they are underlyingly unlinked in *all* languages.

Although our reasons for taking this position are novel, the position itself is not. According to Odden (1995: 468), "The view that tones and segments are underlyingly separated was pursued in early autosegmental phonology to the point that in Goldsmith (1976a) there are no lexical linkings between tones and vowels." Lexical tone association was seen as unnecessary, and hence excluded by Occam's Razor. The assumptions that made it unnecessary in Goldsmith (1976a) are also relevant to our proposal, as the next section will show.

6 Lexical tone association: evidence and response

Tone association is not always entirely predictable from simple phonological principles like those operative in Kikuyu. In such cases, a surface contrast in tone association has to be encoded in the lexicon. We have argued that direct encoding is not an option. What alternatives are available?[7]

There is a tradition of work on tone in Bantu and Japanese that posits diacritic accent (Goldsmith 1976a, 1982, 1984b; Haraguchi 1977; Hyman 1981, 1982; Hyman & Byarushengo 1980; Odden 1982, 1985). A diacritic accent is a phonetically uninterpretable lexical feature of a vowel that attracts a particular tone, H or L. In the literature on Bantu, the primary purpose of the diacritic accent is to allow for a modular system in which the locations of tones can be manipulated by rules prior to insertion of tone melodies (Goldsmith 1982: 48). In the literature on Japanese, however, diacritic accent is primarily used to mark contrasts in tone association. This idea is revisited and situated in HS in McCarthy & Pruitt (to appear), so we will not develop it further here.

Instead, we will focus here on a purely tonal source for tone-association contrasts. In the early autosegmental literature, apparent contrasts in tone association were sometimes attributed to contrasts in the tone melody itself. In Etung (Niger-Congo, Nigeria), for example, there are contrasting tone patterns like *ákpùgà* 'money' versus *ésébè* 'sand'.[8] If these words are assumed to have the same HL tone melody, then underlying tone association would seem unavoidable. In Goldsmith's (1976a: 221ff.) analysis of Etung, however, these words are analyzed with different melodies: HL in *ákpùgà* and HHL in *ésébè*. If these are the underlying representations, then tone association can be fully determined by the grammar. Venda exemplifies this kind of analysis.

---

[7] Besides the two mentioned in the text, there is a third possible source of surface tone-association contrasts. When contrasts emerge because different parts of the lexicon are subject to different regularities, lexical indexation of ranking and/or constraints may be the best analysis (Inkelas 1999: 143; Pater 2000, 2006; and others).

[8] High tone is indicated by an acute accent and low by a grave accent.

Venda has been cited as a Bantu language with an unusually wide range of contrasting tone patterns (Kisseberth & Odden 2003: 59). It has also provided the basis for an explicit argument in support of underlying tone association (Cassimjee 1992: 77–80). It therefore merits our close attention as representative of the kinds of challenges a theory without underlying tone association must face.

Here, we reanalyze the Venda evidence in HS under ROTB. As we showed in the analysis of Kikuyu, ROTB forces HS to ban underlying tone associations. But ROTB also rules out a key assumption that made underlying tone association necessary in the first place: the assumption that underlying representations are subject to the Obligatory Contour Principle (OCP), which prohibits adjacent identical tones (Goldsmith 1976a; Leben 1973). We argue instead that, although the OCP controls aspects of surface form, like any other markedness constraint it does not and cannot control underlying forms. Once this argument is in place, the need for underlying tone association in Venda disappears.

Venda has two tones, H and L. In noun stems, every combination of H and L is possible (Cassimjee 1992). Thus, monosyllabic nouns are H or L, disyllabic nouns are HH, LL, HL, or LH, and so on. There is complete attestation of the eight possible patterns in trisyllables, and nearly complete attestation of the 16 possible patterns in quadrisyllabic stems.

Cassimjee (1992: 77–80) uses this system of contrasts to argue for underlying tonal association. Her argument starts with a claim about the representation of high tone in Venda: tautomorphemic sequences of H autosegments are prohibited. The evidence for this claim comes from the process known as "Meeussen's Rule" (Goldsmith 1984a and much subsequent work). Meeussen's Rule is a dissimilatory process that changes the second of two adjacent H tones into L. When a stem containing several high-toned syllables in a row undergoes Meeussen's Rule, all of the high-toned syllables become low:

(39)   Effect of Meeussen's Rule (gloss: 'spy')

$$
\begin{array}{llll}
\text{H} & \text{H} & \text{H} & \text{L} \\
| & \wedge & | & \wedge \\
\text{V} \ \# \ \text{tholi} & \rightarrow & \text{V} \ \# \ \text{tholi}
\end{array}
$$

From this observation, Cassimjee infers that sequences of H autosegments are prohibited in underlying representation. If such sequences were allowed in the input to Meeussen's Rule, then only the first H in the sequence would lower:

(40)   Not the effect of Meeussen's Rule

$$
\begin{array}{cccc}
\text{H} & \text{H H} & \text{*H} & \text{LH} \\
| & | \, | & | & | \, | \\
\text{V \# tholi} & \rightarrow & \text{V \# tholi}
\end{array}
$$

Cassimjee goes on to consider whether this result entails lexical tonal association under two different assumptions about L tone, underspecification and full specification. Since Venda presents no good evidence for underspecification of L, we focus on the stronger argument for lexical associations that is based on full specification.

The possible contrasts in quadrisyllables are relevant to this issue. Specifically, in Cassimjee's analysis HLH melodies can contrast in the choice of which H is multiply linked in quadrisyllables:[9]

(41) Contrast in H linking (with L specification)

Near-surface form	Underlying form	
	No lexical association	Lexical association
H L H ∧ | | gokoshomba 'Cape grape'	H L H gokoshomba	H L H ∧ | | gokoshomba
H L H | | ∧ sudzungwane 'shrub species'	H L H sudzungwane	H L H | | ∧ sudzungwane

Since HLH can be associated with a stem in at least two distinct, contrasting ways, lexically specified tone association would appear to be indispensible.

This argument rests on the assumption that the lexical representations of morphemes do not contain sequences of H autosegments. In other words, OCP(H) is a morpheme-structure constraint of Venda (Cassimjee 1992: 122). But OCP(H) is also active dynamically, in the course of phonological derivations. In Cassimjee's analysis, it is responsible for fusion of adjacent Hs between some prefixes and the stem in verbs (Cassimjee 1992: 124, 324). Furthermore, Meeussen's Rule has also been attributed to OCP(H), because it eliminates sequences of adjacent H tones dissimilatorily (Myers 1987, 1997 and others). When a phonological constraint has these dual roles — as a passive restriction on underlying morphemes and as an active participant in derivations — we have what is known as the Duplication Problem (Clayton 1976; Kenstowicz & Kisseberth 1977). The Duplication Problem is a

---

[9] The ultimate surface forms are *gókóshômbá* and *súdzúngw!áné*, as a result of a process that spreads the first H rightward, creating a contour tone on the (long) penult or a floating L otherwise.

problem because the analysis misses a generalization: two different grammatical components have the same constraint, with only its functions differing.

ROTB is OT's solution to the Duplication Problem (see McCarthy 2002: 71–76 for an explanation). By denying the existence of language-particular constraints on the lexicon, ROTB eliminates the possibility of this duplication. In the present instance, ROTB entails the possibility of lexical items with underlying tone sequences like HHLH and HLHH. Indeed, those can be exactly the tones of the lexical items in (41). In other words, a putative contrast in tonal association is reanalyzed as a contrast in tones themselves. Lexical association of tones is not necessary.

The principal challenge to this analysis is the Meeussen's Rule evidence in (39). If [gókóshòmbá] has separate H tones on its first two syllables, why does Meeussen's Rule lower both of them? The answer is that there are two H tones in the lexicon, but there is only one H by the time Meeussen's Rule comes into effect because sequences of H tones on adjacent syllables have already fused to satisfy OCP(H), defined as follows:

(42)   OCP(H) (after Myers 1987: 154)

   Assign one violation mark for every pair of H autosegments that are adjacent on their tier and linked to adjacent syllables.

Although it compels fusion later on, OCP(H) does not affect one-to-one left-to-right association at the initial stages of the derivation. That is because it is ranked below all of the constraints that are responsible for that pattern of association, as shown in tableau (43):[10]

---

[10] Also see Reynolds (1997) for a parallel OT analysis of Venda nouns in a headed domains theory of tone representation.

(43) Step 2 from /gokoshomba, HHLH/

H H L H | gokoshomba	LNK- INIT	NO- FL	HAVE- T	NO- SK(T)	NO- SK(S)	ID(T)	OCP(H)
a. ☞ H H L H | | gokoshomba		2	2			1	1
b. H H L H | gokoshomba	3 W	3 W				L	L
c. H H L H ∧ gokoshomba	3 W	2				1	L
d. H H L H | | gokoshomba		2	2		1 W	1	L
e. H H L H | ╱ gokoshomba		2	2	1 W		1	L

This derivation continues in the same vein, eventually producing
[gókóshòmbá], with one-to-one association between tones and syllables:

(44) /gokoshomba, HHLH/ after step 4

Now that all of the constraints ranked higher than OCP(H) have been
satisfied, attention turns to it. The OCP evokes various responses in the
world's languages, and among them is fusion of the offending elements
(Boersma 1998; Keer 1999; Myers 1987, 1997; Yip 1988). Fusion or
coalescence of identical elements violates no faithfulness constraints except
UNIFORMITY (McCarthy & Prince 1995: 371). We propose that OCP(H)
dominates UNIFORMITY in Venda, so (44) is transformed into a representation
where a single H autosegment is associated with the first two syllables:

(45) Step 5 from /gokoshomba, HHLH/

H H L H | | | | gokoshomba	LNK- INIT	NO- FL	HAVE- T	NO- SK(T)	NO- SK(S)	ID(T)	OCP(H)	UNIF
a. ☞ H L H ∧ | | gokoshomba								1
b. H H L H | | | | gokoshomba							1 W	L

Fusion of identical elements does not violate IDENT (Keer 1999).

All stem-internal sequences of H autosegments will fuse in this fashion. For example, the underlying representation of *bólóngóndó* is /bolongondo, HHHH/ with three OCP(H) violations at step 4 of its derivation. These violations are removed in three steps, each of which effects fusion of one pair of adjacent Hs. The order in which these tones fuse is indeterminate, but the final result is a single H linked to four syllables.

Meeussen's Rule — that is, dissimilation of H to L — competes with fusion as a way of satisfying OCP(H). In nouns, there is a clear division of responsibility, with fusion intramorphemically and dissimilation intermorphemically.[11] The key to the analysis is that fusion is preferred to dissimilation because IDENT(H) dominates UNFORMITY(H). But heteromorphemic fusion is blocked by the constraint MORPHDIS (abbreviated MDIS), which prohibits morphemes from sharing segments, tones, or other phonological elements (Keer 1999: 53, McCarthy & Prince 1995: 310). Tableau (46) illustrates with a schematic example of a heteromorphemic sequence of high tones. (Some constraints have been omitted to save space.) Dissimilation in (46a) competes against fusion in (46c). Since this H sequence arises across word boundary, merger is blocked by MORPHDIS and dissimilation prevails.[12]

---

[11] The situation in verbs is less clear; the choice between fusion and Meeussen's Rule in verbs is perhaps the most important incompletely resolved question in Cassimjee (1992).

[12] Since it is not really relevant to our concerns, we set aside the question of why Meeussen's Rule affects the second H rather than the first. See Myers (1997: 887) for one proposal.

(46)   Meeussen's Rule

At step 3 from /SS,HL/ after H-final word

H # H L | | | S # S S	MDIS	OCP(H)	NO-LNK(T)	ID(H)	UNIF(H)
a. ☞ H # L L | | | S # S S				1	
b. H # H L | | | S # S S		1 W		L	
c. H L ∧ | S # S S	1 W			L	1 W

A final detail. Some sort of cyclic analysis is required to account for cases like (39) where a H-final word is followed by a noun whose underlying representation begins in an H sequence. The stem-internal H sequence is merged on the first or lexical cycle, and then it dissimilates when the preceding H becomes visible on the second or postlexical cycle:

(47)   Cyclicity in H#HH...

$$
\begin{array}{ccccc}
\text{H H} & & \text{H} & & \text{H} \quad \text{L} \\
\text{\textbar\textbar} & \rightarrow & \wedge & \rightarrow & \text{\textbar} \ \wedge \\
\text{tholi} & & \text{tholi} & & \text{V \# tholi}
\end{array}
$$

See Wolf (2008) for a demonstration of how the cycle can be incorporated into a serial version of OT similar to HS.

As we saw in the last section, ROTB forces the conclusion that tone associations are universally absent from the lexicon. This conclusion is challenged by the complex tonal patterns of nouns in Venda, which seem to require lexical associations. But ROTB forces the analysis to include tone melodies that eliminate the need for lexical associations. In short, ROTB not only creates the problem but also solves it.

7 Conclusion

Any interesting linguistic theory has unanticipated consequences. Harmonic Serialism is interesting because it has led to a body of interesting results, such as the one described in section 2 and others cited in McCarthy (2010). Among its unanticipated consequences is its incompatibility with lexical tone linking in languages like Kikuyu where tone association is completely predictable.

As we noted in the introduction, the results in this paper converge with the conclusions about lexical marking of metrical feet in Harmonic Serialism in McCarthy & Pruitt (to appear). This convergence is no accident. In both cases, we are dealing with phonological distinctions that are represented structurally. Furthermore, in both cases there are languages where the properties of that structure are fully predictable, though there are also others where they are not. Most importantly, in both cases there are constraints favouring full parsing of the structure: with metrical feet, the primary full-parsing constraint is PARSE-SYLLABLE, and with tone the constraints are HAVE-TONE and NO-FLOAT. Lexical structure is a kind of pre-existing parse, and removing it degrades performance on these constraints. In Harmonic Serialism, under the assumption that the removal of unwanted structure and the introduction of new structure cannot occur simultaneously, lexical structure is invulnerable precisely because of these pro-parsing constraints.

Dealing with this consequence of Harmonic Serialism led us to explore alternative ways of lexically encoding unpredictable tone association, and this brought us back to ideas that were prevalent in earlier work on tone, particularly lexical violation of the OCP. Under richness of the base, the OCP cannot be a restriction on underlying representations, but once underlying "violations" of the OCP are admitted, an important argument for underlying tone association goes away. Our results, then, emerge from a nexus of Harmonic Serialism, the maximally simple theory of GEN in (1), and the familiar OT principle of richness of the base.

Optimality Theory has, since its outset, focused its attention on constraints on phonological substance. In his research, Norval Smith has long emphasized the importance of phonological representations. Work in Harmonic Serialism, including this chapter, shows that representational matters continue to be important. HS's theory of GEN is, to a great extent, a theory of representations and the operations on them. We therefore are seeing a convergence of two well-established and productive research programs.

Personal remark by John McCarthy

Norval's bad luck is the reason why I am a contributor to this volume. I was invited because I am listed as his co-author on an article in the *Oxford Encyclopedia of Linguistics* (2nd edition). That co-authorship came about through a complicated set of circumstances. In 2001, I was in charge of the phonology articles in the encyclopedia, and Norval was supposed to be revising his article from the first edition. He could not because he was undergoing treatment for cancer, and so I took care of the revisions. As we all know, Norval got well, the encyclopedia was published, and a decade later my collaborators and I have the privilege of honoring someone I have always admired for his broad interests and openness to new ideas.

References

Archangeli, Diana & Douglas Pulleyblank (1994): *Grounded Phonology*. – Cambridge, MA: MIT Press.

Boersma, Paul (1998): "The OCP in functional phonology." – In: *Proceedings of the Institute of Phonetic Sciences*, University of Amsterdam 22, 21–45.

Borowsky, Toni & Armin Mester (1983): "Aspiration to roots: remarks on the Sanskrit diaspirates." – In: *Proceedings of CLS* 19, 52–63. Chicago: Chicago Linguistics Society.

Cassimjee, Farida (1992): *An Autosegmental Analysis of Venda Tonology*. – New York: Garland.

Clayton, Mary L. (1976): "The redundancy of underlying morpheme-structure conditions." – In: *Language* 52, 295–313.

Clements, George N. (1984): "Principles of tone association in Kikuyu." – In: Clements, George N. & John Goldsmith (eds.): *Autosegmental Studies in Bantu Tone*, 281–339. Dordrecht: Foris.

– (1991): "Vowel height assimilation in Bantu languages." – In: Hubbard, Kathleen (ed.): *BLS 17S: Proceedings of the Special Session on African Language Structures*, 25–64. Berkeley: Berkeley Linguistic Society.

Clements, George N. & Kevin C. Ford (1979): "Kikuyu tone shift and its synchronic consequences." – In: *Linguistic Inquiry* 10, 179–210.

Gafos, Adamantios (1999): *The Articulatory Basis of Locality in Phonology*. – New York: Garland.

Goldsmith, John (1976a): *Autosegmental Phonology*. – PhD dissertation, MIT.

– (1976b): "An overview of autosegmental phonology." – In: *Linguistic Analysis* 2, 23–68.

– (1982): "Accent systems." – In: Hulst, Harry van der & Norval S.H. Smith (eds.): *The Structure of Phonological Representations*, 47–63. Dordrecht: Foris.

- (1984a): "Meeussen's rule." – In: Aronoff, Mark & Richard T. Oehrle (eds.): *Language Sound Structure*, 245–259. Cambridge, MA: MIT Press.
- (1984b): "Tone and accent in Tonga." – In: Clements, George N. & John Goldsmith (eds.): *Autosegmental Studies in Bantu Tone*, 19–51. Dordrecht: Foris.

Haraguchi, Shosuke (1977): *The Tone Pattern of Japanese: An Autosegmental Theory of Tonology*. – Tokyo: Kaitakusha.

Hyman, Larry (1981): "Tonal accent in Somali." – In: *Studies in African Linguistics* 12, 169–203.

- (1982): "Globality and the accentual analysis of Luganda tone." – In: *Journal of Linguistic Research* 2, 1–40.
- (1988): "Underspecification and vowel height transfer in Esimbi." – In: *Phonology* 5, 255–73.

Hyman, Larry & Ernest Byarushengo (1980): "Tonal accent in Haya: an autosegmental approach." – Ms., University of Southern California.

Inkelas, Sharon (1999): "Exceptional stress-attracting suffixes in Turkish: representation vs. the grammar." – In: Kager, René, Harry van der Hulst & Wim Zonneveld (eds.): *The Prosody-Morphology Interface*, 134–187. Cambridge: Cambridge University Press.

Ito, Junko & Armin Mester (1999). "Realignment." – In: Kager, René, Harry van der Hulst & Wim Zonneveld (eds.): *The Prosody-Morphology Interface*, 188–217. Cambridge: Cambridge University Press.

Keer, Edward (1999): *Geminates, the OCP, and the Nature of* CON. – PhD dissertation, Rutgers University.

Kenstowicz, Michael & Charles Kisseberth (1977): *Topics in Phonological Theory*. – New York: Academic Press.

Kisseberth, Charles & David Odden (2003): "Tone." – In: Nurse, Derek & Gérard Philippson (eds.): *The Bantu Languages*, 59–70. London/New York: Routledge.

Leben, Will (1973): *Suprasegmental Phonology*. – PhD dissertation, MIT.

McCarthy, John J. (2000): "Harmonic Serialism and parallelism." – In: Hirotani, Masako (ed.): *Proceedings of the North East Linguistics Society* 30, 501–524. Amherst, MA: GLSA Publications.

- (2002): *A Thematic Guide to Optimality Theory*. – Cambridge: Cambridge University Press.
- (2007): "Restraint of analysis." – In: Blaho, Sylvia, Patrik Bye & Martin Krämer (eds.): *Freedom of Analysis*, 203–231. Berlin/New York: Mouton de Gruyter.
- (2008): "The serial interaction of stress and syncope." – In: *Natural Language & Linguistic Theory* 26, 499–546.
- (2009): "Studying GEN." – In: *Journal of the Phonetic Society of Japan* 13, 3–12.
- (2010): "An introduction to Harmonic Serialism." – In: *Language and Linguistics Compass* 4, 1001–1018.

McCarthy, John J., Wendell Kimper & Kevin Mullin (to appear): "Reduplication in Harmonic Serialism." – *Morphology*.

McCarthy, John J. & Alan Prince (1995): "Faithfulness and reduplicative identity." – In: Beckman, Jill, Laura Walsh Dickey & Suzanne Urbanczyk (eds.): *University of Massachusetts Occasional Papers in Linguistics* 18, 249–384. Amherst, MA: GLSA Publications.

McCarthy, John J. & Kathryn Pruitt (to appear): "Sources of phonological structure."
      – In: Vogel, Ralf & Hans Broekhuis (eds.): *Linguistic Derivations and Filtering:
      Minimalism and Optimality Theory*. London: Equinox Publishing.

Myers, Scott (1987): *Tone and the Structure of Words in Shona*. – PhD dissertation,
      University of Massachusetts Amherst.

–   (1997): "OCP effects in Optimality Theory." – In: *Natural Language & Linguistic
      Theory* 15, 847–892.

Ní Chiosáin, Máire & Jaye Padgett (2001): "Markedness, segment realization, and
      locality in spreading." – In: Lombardi, Linda (ed.): *Segmental Phonology in
      Optimality Theory: Constraints and Representations*, 118–156. New York:
      Cambridge University Press.

Odden, David (1982): "Separating tone and accent: the case of Kimatuumbi." – In:
      Flickinger, Daniel P., Marlys Macken & Nancy Wiegand (eds.): *WCCFL* 1, 219–
      230. Stanford: Stanford Linguistic Association.

–   (1985): "An accentual approach to tone in Kimatuumbi." – In: Goyvaerts, Didier
      L. (ed.): *African Linguistics: Studies in Memory of M. W. K. Seminenke*, 345–419.
      Amsterdam: John Benjamins.

–   (1995): "Tone: African languages." – In: Goldsmith, John (ed.): *The Handbook of
      Phonological Theory*, 444–475. Cambridge, MA/Oxford, UK: Blackwell.

Pater, Joe (2000): "Nonuniformity in English secondary stress: the role of ranked and
      lexically specific constraints." – In: *Phonology* 17, 237–274.

–   (2006): "The locus of exceptionality: morpheme-specific phonology as constraint
      indexation." – In: Bateman, Leah, Adam Werle, Michael O'Keefe & Ehren Reilly
      (eds.): *University of Massachusetts Occasional Papers in Linguistics* 32: Papers in
      Optimality Theory III, 259–296. Amherst, MA: GLSA.

–   (to appear): "Serial Harmonic Grammar and Berber syllabification." – In:
      Borowsky, Toni, Shigeto Kawahara, Takahito Shinya & Mariko Sugahara (eds.):
      Prosody Matters: Essays in Honor of Lisa Selkirk. London: Equinox Publishing.

Prince, Alan (2002): "Arguing optimality." – In Carpenter, Angela, Andries Coetzee
      & Paul de Lacy (eds.): *University of Massachusetts Occasional Papers in
      Linguistics 26: Papers in Optimality Theory* II, 269–304. Amherst, MA: GLSA.

Prince, Alan & Paul Smolensky (1993/2004): *Optimality Theory: Constraint
      Interaction in Generative Grammar*. – Malden, MA/Oxford: Blackwell.

Reynolds, William T. (1997): "Post-high tone shift in Venda nominals." – Ms.,
      University of the Witwatersrand.

Stallcup, Kenneth L. (1980): "Noun classes in Esimbi." – In: Hyman, Larry (ed.):
      Noun Classes in the Grassfields Bantu Borderland, 139–153. Los Angeles: Dept.
      of Linguistics, University of Southern California.

Staubs, Robert, Michael Becker, Christopher Potts, Patrick Pratt, John J. McCarthy &
      Joe Pater (2010): "OT-Help 2.0" [computer program]. Amherst, MA: University of
      Massachusetts Amherst.

Walker, Rachel (1997). "Faith and markedness in Esimbi feature transfer." – In:
      Walker, Rachel, Motoko Katayama & Dan Karvonen (eds.): *Phonology at Santa
      Cruz*, 103–115. Santa Cruz, CA: Linguistics Research Center, UC Santa Cruz.

–   (1998): *Nasalization, Neutral Segments, and Opacity Effects*. – PhD dissertation,
      University of California, Santa Cruz.

– (2001): "Positional markedness in vowel harmony." – In: Féry, Caroline, Antony Dubach Green & Ruben van de Vijver (eds.): *Proceedings of HILP 5*, 212–232. Potsdam: University of Potsdam.

Wolf, Matthew (2008): *Optimal Interleaving: Serial Phonology–Morphology Interaction in a Constraint-Based Model.* – PhD dissertation, University of Massachusetts Amherst.

Yip, Moira (1988): "The Obligatory Contour Principle and phonological rules: a loss of identity." – In: *Linguistic Inquiry* 19, 65–100.

– (2002): *Tone.* – Cambridge: Cambridge University Press.

Zoll, Cheryl (1996): *Parsing below the Segment in a Constraint-based Framework.* – PhD dissertation, University of California, Berkeley.

– (2003): "Optimal tone mapping." – In: *Linguistic Inquiry* 34. 225–268.

– (2004): "Positional asymmetries and licensing." – In: McCarthy, John J. (ed.): *Optimality Theory in Phonology: A Reader*, 365–378 Malden, MA/Oxford: Blackwell.

Paul Boersma

A constraint-based explanation of the McGurk effect*

1 Introduction

The *McGurk effect* is a spectacular phenomenon that can arise with manipulated spoken language in the laboratory. It occurs when visual cues to phonological categories override auditory cues. McGurk & MacDonald (1976) devised a videotape on which the visual part of the recording was from a person saying [gɑ], whereas the auditory part of the recording was from a person saying [bɑ]. Listeners were then asked what consonant they heard when watching the video. Although all the auditory information pointed at /bɑ/, they in fact reported hearing /dɑ/.

The McGurk effect is *robust*, i.e. it tends to occur even in cases where the listener knows what is going on, i.e. that the sound is that of somebody saying [bɑ]: "[these effects] do not habituate over time, despite objective knowledge of the illusion involved. By merely closing the eyes, a previously heard /dɑ/ becomes /bɑ/ only to revert to /dɑ/ when the eyes are open again." (McGurk & MacDonald 1976: 747).[1]

McGurk & MacDonald's interpretation was that the main piece of visual information (namely, the open lips when mouthing [gɑ]) was compatible with perceiving either /dɑ/ or /gɑ/, whereas some of the auditory information of a sounding [bɑ] was compatible only with /bɑ/ and /dɑ/ (and not with /gɑ/), so that "the unified percept" /dɑ/ is most compatible with the visual and auditory cues combined. McGurk & MacDonald did not specify what the common auditory cues for /bɑ/ and /dɑ/ could be.

McGurk & MacDonald's observations were the starting point of a surge of interest among speech perception researchers, generally confirming the ro-

---

* Thanks go to Kateřina Chládková for creating the video and testing a group of Czech listeners, and to Jan-Willem van Leussen for testing most of the Dutch listeners.
[1] I adapted the notation in this quote to the one used elsewhere in the present paper, namely with slashes for phonological surface structures such as /bɑ/ and /dɑ/, and with square brackets for auditory or visual peripheral representations such as [bɑ]$_{Aud}$ and [gɑ]$_{Vis}$. McGurk & MacDonald used square brackets throughout, but do make a distinction in the text between auditory and visual on the one hand, and (response or phonological) categories on the other.

bustness that McGurk & MacDonald had anecdotally described, as well as corroborating McGurk & MacDonald's speculative interpretation. As a result, the McGurk effect is nowadays generally seen as a case of low-level multimodal cue integration. The effect has turned out to be stronger in adults than in children (McGurk & MacDonald, 1976), and stronger in English than in several other languages, which also differ with respect to each other (Sekiyama & Tohkura 1991; Grassegger 1995; Burnham 1998).

The present paper provides a description and explanation of the McGurk effect within an integrative formal model of bidirectional phonology and phonetics, in which decisions for speaking and listening are made with the help of ranked constraints that evaluate phonological and phonetic representations and their relations.

2 Representations and constraints

Figure 1 shows a bidirectional model of phonology and phonetics (Boersma 1998, 2007), which contains four connected mental *representations*. The number of *phonological* representations is the minimum that phonologists regard as sensible, namely two: the Underlying Form, which is a sequence of discrete phonological structures stored in the lexicon, and the Surface Form, which is an equally discrete phonological structure consisting of features, segments, syllables, and feet. The number of *phonetic* representations is also minimal, namely two: the continuous Auditory Form (pitch, formants, duration, silence, noise) and the equally continuous Articulatory Form (muscle gestures).

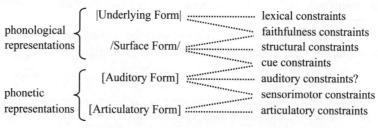

Fig. 1 Representations and constraints (sound only)

Several *processes* can be defined on the representations in the figure. In the process of *comprehension*, the listener is given an auditory form and ultimately has to find underlying forms in the lexicon (which again connect to meaning and world knowledge, not represented in Figure 1). In the process of *production*, the speaker starts with an underlying form (which is itself fed by an intended meaning) and ultimately has to decide on an articulatory form that will generate the sound of speech.

The decisions made in the processes of comprehension and production are guided by *constraints*, which are the elements of the grammar.

The four representations are connected by three types of constraints, which express the speaker-listener's knowledge of the relations between the representations. The faithfulness constraints favour similarity of underlying and surface form in production (McCarthy & Prince 1995) as well as in comprehension (Smolensky 1996). The cue constraints (Escudero & Boersma 2003) express the speaker-listener's knowledge of the relation between phonological features and auditory cues. The sensorimotor constraints express the speaker's knowledge of the relation between muscle commands and sound, and are only needed in production.

The four representations themselves are evaluated by two more kinds of constraints. The articulatory constraints militate against articulatory effort and are used in production alone. The structural constraints disfavour selected surface structures and are used in production (Prince & Smolensky 1993) as well as in comprehension (Tesar 1997). The auditory constraints, if they exist, will militate against loud and otherwise unpleasant sounds.

If visual cues have to be included in the model of Figure 1, it is the Auditory Form that will have to be generalized. The result is in Figure 2, which now contains a general Sensory Form. The cue constraints now express the speaker-listener's knowledge of the relation between phonological features and both auditory and visual cues. The sensorimotor constraints now express the speaker's knowledge of the relation between muscle commands on the one hand and sound and vision (e.g. visible lip closure) on the other. The sensory constraints, if they exist, will now militate as well against flashing and otherwise unpleasant sights.

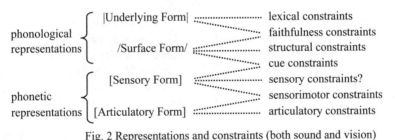

Fig. 2 Representations and constraints (both sound and vision)

3 The McGurk effect as low-level perception

In the case of the McGurk effect, the input to the process is the sensory form that consists of [ba]-like auditory cues and [ga]-like visual cues. The output of the process is a nonsense syllable chosen from the candidates /ba/, /da/, and /ga/. Since these are not lexical items, they are just instances of a Surface Form. Therefore, to describe the McGurk effect as it happens in the laboratory, we only need to consider the Sensory Form and the Surface Form in the figure; the Underlying Form and Articulatory Form are irrelevant (in §4, where an *explanation* for the McGurk effect is given, the Underlying Form will turn out to be relevant as well; and in §6, where *production* is considered, the Articulatory Form may play a role).

In the mapping from Sensory Form to Surface Form, two kinds of constraints could be relevant according to Figure 2, at least if an Underlying Form does not have to be constructed in parallel. These two constraints are the cue constraints and the structural constraints (any sensory constraints would evaluate the input only, but this could never decide between the output candidates). Of these, I propose that the structural constraints are irrelevant, because /ba/, /da/, and /ga/ are all fully legitimate syllables in English. This leaves the cue constraints as the only kind of constraints relevant to the description of the McGurk effect.

Cue constraints tend to be formulated negatively (Boersma 2007). To see this in the McGurk case, consider what the visually present open lips tell the viewer about the possible sounds. A positively formulated constraint would say "[open lips] can be /d/ *or* /t/ *or* /n/ *or* /g/ *or* /k/ *or* /ŋ/", whereas a negatively formulated constraint would say "[open lips] is *not* /b/ *and not* /p/ *and not* /m/". As shown by Boersma & Escudero (2008), the negative formulation can be split into its parts, the positive formulation cannot. The relevant high-ranked visual cue constraints, therefore, are "[open lips] is not /b/", "[open lips] is not /p/", and so on, or in a more symmetric notation (which can be used for production as well, see §7): "*/b/[open lips]" and "*/p/[open lips]". The arbitrariness of the cue constraints (Escudero & Boersma 2003) demands the additional existence of constraints like "*/d/[open lips]", and "*/g/[open lips]", but these must be low ranked in order to describe the McGurk effect (§4 explains how the constraints have become ranked as they are).

A high ranking of "*/b/[open lips]", then, describes the fact that listener-viewers of the McGurk movie are reluctant to perceive /ba/. But what makes them perceive /da/ rather than /ga/? The answer cannot be a visual cue constraint, because the motion was that of somebody mouthing, in fact, [ga]. So the answer must be an auditory cue constraint. An auditory cue that would have favoured the perception of /gɑ/ would have been a close approach of the second and third formants during the transition from the plosive to the vowel (Ladefoged & Maddieson 1996, Stevens 1998). In an auditory [bɑ], F2 and F3 are fairly separated, as they are in [dɑ]. Hence, a high-ranked "*/g/[separated F2 & F3]" could eliminate the candidate /gɑ/. Apparently, the information about F2–F3 separation is more important than the information about F2 alone, which must have been low for the auditory [bɑ] and disfavours the /dɑ/ perception more than the /gɑ/ perception. All these considerations are summarized in perception tableau (1), which shows the formalization of this phenomenon within the decision-making framework of Optimality Theory.

(1) *The McGurk effect (eyes open)*

[open lips, separated F2 & F3, low F2]	*/b/ [open lips]	*/g/ [separated F2 & F3]	*/d/ [low F2]	*/g/ [low F2]	*/b/ [low F2]	*/d/ [open lips]	*/g/ [open lips]
/bɑ/	*!				*		
☞　　/dɑ/			*			*	
/gɑ/		*!		*			*

Tableau (2) shows with the same grammar (constraint ranking) that if the listener has her eyes closed, she will perceive /b/. This is because the visual cue is no longer present.

(2) *The McGurk effect (eyes closed)*

[separated F2 & F3, low F2]	*/b/ [open lips]	*/g/ [separated F2 & F3]	*/d/ [low F2]	*/g/ [low F2]	*/b/ [low F2]	*/d/ [open lips]	*/g/ [open lips]
☞　　/bɑ/					*		
/dɑ/			*!				
/gɑ/		*!		*			

Tableaus (1) and (2) together describe the phenomenon that listener-viewers who alternatingly close and open their eyes while repeatedly watching a McGurk movie alternate between perceiving /bɑ/ and /dɑ/.

4 The explanation of the McGurk effect

The previous section presented a description of the McGurk effect in terms of constraint ranking, but did not provide an explanation of how the constraints have come to be ranked as they are. This section explains the ranking as a result of lexicon-driven acquisition of Optimality-Theoretic perception (Boersma 1998).

The lexicon-driven acquisition algorithm by Boersma (1998) is capable of explaining how constraints for more reliable cues become higher ranked than constraints for less reliable cues. The only assumption needed for explaining the McGurk effect is then that the [open lips] cue, *if present*, is more reliable than the [F2 & F3 separated] cue. This assumption is quite plausible, because acoustic noise is omnipresent.

Now suppose that the visual cue constraints are ranked at a height where they do not contribute much to the perception decision, as in tableau (3). This ranking means that the choice among candidates like /baːn/, /daːn/, and /gaːn/ will usually be made on the basis of the formant cues alone. Assume, moreover, that the [open lips] cue is more reliable than any of the formant cues. This greater reliability means that cases with incorrectly available formant cues are more common than cases with incorrectly available lip cues. One of these more common cases is shown in tableau (3). In this example, an intended underlying |daːn| is incorrectly transmitted as having a [low F2] cue, while the lip cue (open lips) and the [separated F2 & F3] cue are transmitted correctly. The perceived structure is /baːn/.

(3) *Acquiring the McGurk effect*

[open lips, separated F2 & F3, low F2] (intended |daːn|)	*/g/ [separated F2 & F3]	*/d/ [low F2]	*/b/ [open lips]	*/d/ [open lips]	*/g/ [open lips]	*/g/ [low F2]	*/b/ [low F2]
☞ /baːn/			←*				←*
√ /daːn/		*!→		*→			
/gaːn/	*!				*	*	

Now suppose that the listener subsequently accesses meaning in the lexicon, and the lexicon tells her, informed by semantic considerations, that the speaker's intended word was |daːn| 'darn'. The proposal of lexicon-driven acquisition of perception (Boersma 1998: 338) now implies that the listener will consider the candidate /daːn/ to be the *correct candidate* in tableau (3), i.e. the candidate that she should have perceived but didn't. This lexicon-informed knowledge is depicted in tableau (3) by supplying the candidate /dɑːn/ with a check mark.

The fact that the listener's perceived candidate in tableau (3), namely /bɑːn/, differs from the correct candidate means that she has made a *perceptual error*. The fact that the lexicon has told the listener what the correct candidate was, namely /dɑːn/, implies that the listener 'knows' that she has made this error, so that she is 'aware' that her grammar (constraint ranking) may be in need of modification. The fact that the correct candidate occurs in the tableau implies that the listener's Gradual Learning Algorithm 'knows' how the constraint ranking has to be modified. The required modification is that the constraints that prefer the correct candidate, namely "*/b/[open lips]" and "*/b/[low F2]" will have to be raised a bit, and that the constraints that prefer the learner's incorrect winner, namely "*/d/[low F2]" and "*/d/[open lips]", will have to be lowered a bit. These raisings and lowerings are indicated in the table by arrows.

In tableau (3) we can see that the raisings and lowerings indicated by the arrows will ultimately cause the visual cue constraint "*/b/[open lips]" to rise above the auditory cue constraint "*/d/[low F2]", which is enough to produce the McGurk effect, which has therefore now been explained, although two minor issues have to be resolved.

One minor issue is a possibly unwanted side effect predicted by tableau (3), namely the rise of "*/b/[low F2]". This side effect will be counteracted by the lexicon as soon as a too high ranking of this constraint will cause spurious perceptions of intended |b| (with correct [low F2]) as the incorrect categories /d/ or /g/. In the end, the most reliable constraints will emerge on top. The other minor issue is the question how far "*/b/[open lips]" will end up being ranked above "*/d/[low F2]". The answer according to Boersma (1998: 339) is probability matching. If incorrect instances of the auditory cue [low F2] appear 20 times more often than incorrect instances of the visual cue [open lips], the listener's grammar will in the end favour the cue [open lips] over the cue [low F2] 20 times more often than the reverse. The strong reproducibility of the McGurk effect suggests that such high factors are indeed involved. The probability matching property of the learning algorithm does predict that the McGurk effect is less strong for people who are used to watching dubbed movies and have therefore learned to ignore visual cues to some extent.

5 The interaction of structural and cue constraints

Audio-visual perception seems not to be handled by cue constraints alone. Language-specific structural constraints also seem to play a role. This is predicted by Figure 2, where the output of the mapping from Sensory Form to Surface Form can be evaluated by the same structural constraints that phonologists use to model production. Evidence is found in what English viewers-listeners do when the video mouths [ba], but sounds [ga], i.e. the opposite combination of the main McGurk effect described above. McGurk & MacDonald (1976) report that people will often hear /bagba/, where the initial consonant cluster is only labial and the second consonant cluster is both velar and labial. My interpretation is that the visual labiality and the auditory velarity do not conflict intervocalically, because in that position a cluster of two plosives is allowed phonotactically in English (as in the word *rugby*). By contrast, such a cluster is not allowed in initial position, so that viewers-listeners can only decide for a single consonant. Tableau (4) summarizes, and includes syllable boundaries for explicitness. The constraint "[closed lips]⇒/lab/" reads as "*if* the sensory form has closed lips, *then* there must be a labial" (and can be used bidirectionally, as we will see in §7).

(4) *The reverse McGurk effect*

[closed lips]$_{Vis}$ [close F2 & F3]$_{Aud}$	*/.labvel/	*/.C./	[closed lips]$_{Vis}$ ⇒/lab/	[close F2 & F3]$_{Aud}$ ⇒/vel/
/.ga.ga./			*!*	
☞ /.bag.ba./				*
/.gbag.ba./	*!			
/.gba.gba./	*!*			
/.g.bag.ba./		*!		
/.ba.ba./				**!

The constraint "*/.labvel/" is an abbreviation for "no labial-velar sequences in onset". It can be seen that the tableau requires the additional structural constraint "/.C./", which militates against syllables without vowels, which are not allowed in English.

The conclusion is that the asymmetry between initial /ba/ and medial /gba/ is caused by language-specific structural constraints.

6 Why OT and not neural nets? The case of phonological production

The McGurk effect and its acquisition were modelled successfully by using the decision mechanism of Optimality Theory. The question naturally arises why the tried and tested decision mechanism of neural net classification was not used instead. The answer is: because the perceptual decision is influenced by language-specifically ranked structural constraints. These constraints are linguistic because (1) they are language-specific or language-specifically ranked, and (2) they are also used in production, where they interact with faithfulness constraints.

The language-specificity of the constraints and/or their ranking follows both from the language-specificity of the strength of the McGurk effect itself and from the language-specificity of the ranking of *$/$.labvel$/$ in (4). After all, listeners of a Slavic language like Czech should have no trouble perceiving a /bg/ or /gb/ cluster, given the existence of phrases like /.gbr̩.nu./ 'to Brno', and could therefore favour a winner like /.gbɑg.bɑ./, very similar to the third candidate in (4). Likewise, listeners of a Gbe language like Ewe would have no trouble perceiving labial-velar plosives like /g͡b/, and might therefore favour a winner like /.g͡bɑ.g͡bɑ./ somewhat similar to the fourth candidate in (4) (the third candidate would be ruled out by a constraint against coda consonants). To see whether this prediction is true, my colleague Kateřina Chládková manufactured a video of herself saying [bɑbɑ] visually and [gɑgɑ] auditorily.[2] Nine Czech listeners and one Yoruba listener, when asked to write down what they heard, all reported hearing both a velar and a labial consonant, sometimes with the labial first (6 times 'bgabga', 2 times 'mgamga'), sometimes with the velar first (2 times 'gbagba'); a Gbe (Fongbe) listener heard 'bgaga'. By contrast, 25 Dutch listeners displayed a variety of strategies: next to 6 'integrating' perceptions (4 times 'bgabga', 1 time 'mgamga', 1 time 'gbagba'), they failed to report one of the labials or velars in 9 cases (2 times 'gaabgaa', 1 time 'gaapga', 1 time 'gabga', 2 times 'mgaga', 1 time 'mgaagaa', 1 time 'bgaga', 1 time 'bkaka') and failed to report two labials or velars in 10 cases (8 times 'gaga', 1 time 'ganggang', 1 time 'mama').[3] A chi-square test on whether listeners fully integrate or not

---

[2] The recording has her saying the word three times. A listener's response reported in this paper was constructed by noting the listener's most frequently occurring response for the first and second syllable separately. For instance, if a listener wrote 'bgaga gaga gamga', this is counted as 'gaga'. This worked because a listener never reported three different perceptions for the first (or second) syllable.

[3] In addition we tested two teachers of phonetic transcription, including Norval Smith. Reassuringly, both of them reported hearing 'gbagba' or 'bgabga'.

([[10, 1], [6, 19]], $df = 1$), yields a two-tailed p value of 0.0008, indicating that the Dutch group performed differently from the Czech-African group.[4]

The Dutch results may be explained by the idea that people either report an analytical perception ('gbagba'), a true phonological perception ('gabga'), a phonological perception with incorrect localisation of the labial ('bgaga'), or a phonological perception influenced by an idea of repetition ('gaga'); the analytical perception may arise from a listener's individual ranking of "[close F2 & F3]$_{Aud} \Rightarrow$/vel/" above */.labvel/, the other report from a listener's individual high ranking of */.labvel/, as in tableau (4). By contrast, the Czech results are never influenced by phonotactic restrictions such */.labvel/, so that the Czech always report 'bgabga', which is both analytically and phonologically correct. This finding has to qualify the speculation by Mills & Thiem (1980) that "[i]t might be expected that the perception of combinations [i.e. things like /bg/, PB] would be governed by phonotactic rules, but this is not at all the case." Mills & Thiem based their speculation on the analysis of their results with a single language (German, which is very similar to Dutch in this respect), and although my experiment finds that some Dutch listeners do hear 'combinations' like 'bgabga', their number is much smaller than for Czech listeners; thus, language-specific phonotactic restrictions do influence the perceived structures at least probabilistically.

The strongest argument in favour of a linguistic analysis of McGurk perception is the fact that the same structural constraint */.labvel/ is used in production. Suppose that a speaker of English knows the name of the language group Gbe. Her underlying form, partly based on the orthography, will be |gbei| (at least if she has the vowel right). When asked to produce this word, however, she will say [gəbei], suggesting a phonological surface form /.gə.bei./. The tableau that describes this schwa insertion is given in (5). In this tableau, MAX is the usual faithfulness constraint against having underlying segments that do not correspond to anything in the surface form, and DEP is the usual faithfulness constraint against having segments in the surface form that do not correspond to anything in the underlying form (McCarthy & Prince 1995).

---

[4]   The failure of the Gbe listener to perceive a labial-velar plosive can be explained by the fact that the labial-velar [ɡ͡b] does *not* lie auditorily close to [ɡ]; in fact, viewed from [ɡ] it lies even beyond [b]: it has by far the lowest F2 locus of all stops, just like the labial-velar vowel [u] has a lower F2 than the exclusively labial [y] and the exclusively velar [ɯ]. Ladefoged & Maddieson (1996) show spectrograms.

(5) *Schwa insertion in English: the same structural constraints as in perception*

	|ɡbei|	*/.labvel/	*/.C./	Max	Dep
	/.ɡbei./	*!			
	/.ɡ.bei./		*!		
	/.bei./			*!	
☞	/.ɡə.bei./				*

Production tableau (5), therefore, makes it plausible that the candidates that are most faithful to the underlying form (namely, the first and second candidates), are ruled out by the very same constraints that rule out candidates 3, 4, and 5 in perception tableau (4). In Figure 1, we can indeed see that the surface form is the output of both prelexical perception and phonological production, so that the constraints that evaluate this surface form (namely, the structural constraints) must be able to restrict the outputs of both prelexical perception and phonological production. Whereas Prince & Smolensky (1993) and most of the OT literature since stressed the use of structural constraints in production, and Boersma (1998 et seq.) stressed their use in perception, the bidirectional use of these constraints in comprehension as well as production was stressed by Tesar (1997) and Pater (2004), and in (4) and (5) we see another example of this bidirectional use (for a detailed example of this bidirectionality in the phonology of a single language, see Boersma & Hamann 2009).

If, now, the interaction between structural and faithfulness constraints is uncontroversially linguistic and therefore has to be modelled with OT (and not with neural nets), then the interaction between structural and cue constraints must also be linguistic and has to be modelled with OT as well. Otherwise, the strength of the same entities (namely, the structural constraints) would at the same time be measured in terms of ranking (in production) and in terms of weighting (in comprehension), an unwanted duplication of theoretical elements. Of course, language is ultimately performed by the brain, so the ultimately correct theory of language processing will involve neural networks, but these will then have to implement structural constraints as well as an OT-like decision mechanism (if that is how language works).

7 OT in phonetic production

If structural constraints can be used bidirectionally, then perhaps the cue constraints can be used bidirectionally as well, namely to specify what auditory cues the speaker should produce for a given underlying form.

This turns out to be correct. Suppose that the speaker wants to produce the underlying form |baɡa|. The cue constraints will explain why she pronounces this as [baɡa] (i.e. [closed lips, separated F2 & F3, low F2] followed by [a] followed by [open lips, close F2 & F3] followed by [a]) rather than as [baba] or [ɡaba]. Tableau (6) gives all 16 relevant candidates, assuming that the surface form, the auditory form, and the articulatory form are evaluated in parallel, i.e., that every output candidate is a triplet of surface, auditory, and articulatory forms. The constraint IDENT is the usual faithfulness constraint that evaluates the identity of a pair of corresponding Underlying and Surface segments (McCarthy & Prince 1995); the subscript Sens is short for both Vis and Aud; and the articulatory representations look very similar to the sensory representations because I assume that sensorimotor knowledge is perfect. An example of the workings of cue constraints in production is that the fifth candidate, /.ba.ɡa./ [baba]_Sens, violates "[closed lips]_Vis⇒/lab/" because the second sensory [b]_Sens must have been pronounced with visibly closed lips, although the corresponding surface segment /ɡ/ (the onset of the second syllable) is not labial.

(6) *Phonetic production of plosives: the same cue constraints as in perception*

|baɡa|	IDENT	[closed lips]_Vis ⇒/lab/	[close F2 & F3]_Aud ⇒/vel/
/.ba.ba./ [baba]_Sens [baba]_Art	*!		
/.ba.ba./ [baɡa]_Sens [baɡa]_Art	*!		*
/.ba.ba./ [ɡaba]_Sens [ɡaba]_Art	*!		*
/.ba.ba./ [ɡaɡa]_Sens [ɡaɡa]_Art	*!		**
/.ba.ɡa./ [baba]_Sens [baba]_Art		*!	
☞ /.ba.ɡa./ [baɡa]_Sens [baɡa]_Art			
/.ba.ɡa./ [ɡaba]_Sens [ɡaba]_Ar		*!	*
/.ba.ɡa./ [ɡaɡa]_Sens [ɡaɡa]_Ar			*!
/.ɡa.ba./ [baba]_Sens [baba]_Art	*!	*	
/.ɡa.ba./ [baɡa]_Sens [baɡa]_Art	*!	*	*
/.ɡa.ba./ [ɡaba]_Sens [ɡaba]_Art	*!		
/.ɡa.ba./ [ɡaɡa]_Sens [ɡaɡa]_Art	*!		*
/.ɡa.ɡa./ [baba]_Sens [baba]_Art	*!*	**	
/.ɡa.ɡa./ [baɡa]_Sens [baɡa]_Art	*!*	*	
/.ɡa.ɡa./ [ɡaba]_Sens [ɡaba]_Art	*!*	*	
/.ɡa.ɡa./ [ɡaɡa]_Sens [ɡaɡa]_Art	*!*		

This ranking, then, makes sure that an Underlying |b| is realized as a Surface /b/ because of the faithfulness constraints, and as a Sensory [b] because of the cue constraints (at least if there is no high ranked articulatory constraint, i.e. *[b]$_{Art}$, against producing labials). Note that in case some phonological rule had turned an underlying |g| into a Surface /b/, the cue constraints would have made sure that the Sensory form would have been pronounced as [b], as most phonologists would expect.

What tableau (6) shows, then, is that OT can handle both phonological and phonetic production, by using the same cue constraints as in perception.

8 Conclusion

The McGurk effect in prelexical ('phonetic') perception can be described as an interaction of the same structural and cue constraints that also regulate phonological and phonetic production, respectively.

References

Boersma, Paul (1998): *Functional Phonology: Formalizing the Interactions between Articulatory and Perceptual Drives*. PhD dissertation, University of Amsterdam. – The Hague: Holland Academic Graphics.

Boersma, Paul (2007): "Some listener-oriented accounts of *h*-aspiré in French." – In: *Lingua* 117, 1989–2054.

Boersma, Paul & Paola Escudero (2008): "Learning to perceive a smaller L2 vowel inventory: an Optimality Theory account." – In: Peter Avery, Elan Dresher & Keren Rice (eds.): *Contrast in Phonology: Theory, perception, acquisition*, 271–301. Berlin & New York: Mouton de Gruyter.

Boersma, Paul & Silke Hamann (2009): "Loanword adaptation as first-language phonological perception." – In: Andrea Calabrese & W. Leo Wetzels (eds.): *Loanword Phonology*, 11–58. Amsterdam: John Benjamins.

Burnham, Denis (1998): "Language specificity in the development of auditory-visual speech perception." – In: Ruth Campbell, Barbara Dodd & Dennis K. Burnham (eds.) *Hearing by Eye II: Advances in the Psychology of Speechreading and Auditory-visual Speech*, 27–60. Hove, UK: Psychology Press.

Escudero, Paola & Paul Boersma (2003): "Modelling the perceptual development of phonological contrasts with Optimality Theory and the Gradual Learning Algorithm." – In Sudha Arunachalam, Elsi Kaiser & Alexander Williams (eds.):

Proceedings of the 25th Annual Penn Linguistics Colloquium. Penn Working Papers in Linguistics 8.1, 71–85.

Grassegger, Hans (1995): "McGurk effect in German and Hungarian listeners" – In: *13th International Congress of Phonetic Sciences*, Vol. 3, 210–213.

Ladefoged, Peter & Ian Maddieson (1996): *The Sounds of the World's Languages*. – Oxford: Blackwell.

McCarthy, John & Alan Prince (1995): "Faithfulness and reduplicative identity." – In: Jill Beckman, Laura Walsh Dickey & Suzanne Urbanczyk (eds.): *Papers in Optimality Theory*. University of Massachusetts Occasional Papers 18, 249–384. Amherst, Mass.: Graduate Linguistic Student Association. [ROA-60].

McGurk, Harry & John MacDonald (1976): "Hearing lips and seeing voices." *Nature* 264: 746–748.

Mills, Anne E. & Rudolf Thiem (1980): "Auditory-visual fusions and illusions in speech perception." – In: *Linguistische Berichte* 68, 85–108.

Pater, Joe (2004): "Bridging the gap between receptive and productive development with minimally violable constraints." – In: René Kager, Joe Pater & Wim Zonneveld (eds.) *Constraints in Phonological Acquisition*, 219–244. Cambridge: Cambridge University Press.

Prince, Alan & Paul Smolensky (1993): *Optimality Theory: Constraint interaction in Generative Grammar*. Technical Report TR-2, Rutgers University Center for Cognitive Science.

Sekiyama, Kaoru, & Yoh'ichi Tohkura (1991): "McGurk effect in non-English listeners." – In: *Journal of the Acoustical Society of America* 90, 1797–1805.

Smolensky, Paul (1996): "On the comprehension/production dilemma in child language." – In: *Linguistic Inquiry* 27, 720–731.

Stevens, Kenneth N. (1998): *Acoustic Phonetics*. – Cambridge, Mass. & London: MIT Press.

Tesar, Bruce (1997): "An iterative strategy for learning metrical stress in Optimality Theory." – In: Elisabeth Hughes, Mary Hughes & Annabel Greenhill (eds.): *Proceedings of the 21st Annual Boston University Conference on Language Development*, 615–626. Somerville, Mass.: Cascadilla.

Frans Hinskens

Liquids in a case of unfolding early L1 Dutch: from null realizations through free variation through probabilistically bound variation to lexical contrast*

1 Introduction

The study of first-language (L1) acquisition is largely the domain of psychologists and psycholinguists, especially where perceptual factors are concerned. Within linguistics, most research on L1 acquisition deals with syntactic aspects. Phonological research has by and large been restricted to the development of segment inventories and phonotactics, and has focused mainly on the relative order of acquisition. Attempts to account for this are usually based on general insights about the organisation of features and natural classes (see e.g. Beers 1995; Van der Linde 2001; Levelt & Van Oostendorp 2007). For example, Levelt & Van Oostendorp provide an interesting OT account where implicational relationships in growing segment inventories are modeled in terms of the stepwise introduction, addition, and (in some cases) demotion of feature co-occurrence constraints.

The general assumption in most phonological work on L1 acquisition appears to be that a given segment, once it has been produced for the first time, shows hardly any variability in its production – in other words, that the segment has immediately gained categorical status.[1] While many of these studies note that the acquisition of segments involves variation,[2] this issue is hardly ever studied as such. This is remarkable, since variation is a property of each of the phases in the acquisition process. Despite this observation,

---

* Many thanks to Wilbert Heeringa, Aniek IJbema, Claartje Levelt, Marc van Oostendorp, Marijn van der Veer as well as to the editors for their help, advice, suggestions and corrections. Special thanks to reviewer Yvan Rose and to an anonymous reviewer for their highly valuable input as well as to Bert Botma for carefully polishing my grammar and style. Of course, none of these people is to be blamed for any shortcomings this paper may have. This paper is dedicated to Norval Smith, by way of a Thank You for everything he taught me.

[1] Though see Beers (1995) for a contrasting view.

[2] For example, Fikkert & Levelt (2008), in their study of the stepwise development in the acquisition of place, pay some attention to variation within the separate developmental stages.

acquisition data are typically analyzed in the literature as if they involve static and homogeneous phenomena, even in those studies that address the order of acquisition of specific elements, structures, and processes. This point is also made in recent overviews of the field. For example, Rose & Inkelas (2011: 2428) note that the majority of approaches to the acquisition of L1 phonology "often neglect to situate the patterns observed in their larger context, that of an emerging system influenced by a variety of independent factors." The same criticism can be raised against many studies that deal with the unfolding of (natural classes of) segments in early L1 acquisition.

The framework of OT should in principle be able to model the continuous development of L1 acquisition by means of a gradual re-ranking of faithfulness and markedness constraints. Van der Linde (2001: 106–134) offers such an approach for Dutch. She starts from the assumption that at the beginning of the acquisition process, markedness constraints dominate faithfulness constraints; this is the 'default ranking'. The constraints in Van der Linde's approach all refer to specific phonological features. However, the empirical tests of the developmental model that she proposes mainly involve finding data on segment substitutions which fit the picture for each predictable phase in the development.[3] In addition, Van der Linde often presents these data without making explicit how many non-fitting data there are for each phase, and of which type. However, she does note on several occasions that there is more variation within the phases, and more overlap between the phases, than is predicted. At one point in her analysis, Van der Linde (2001: 135) observes that "a particular stage of acquisition was shown that forced a complete avoidance of any dominance order of constraints. This stage was best accounted for by means of an analysis in accordance with the random conception [of free ranking]. These considerations led to the assumption that the initial ranking is random but with an inclination towards a certain default ranking". Van der Linde formalizes this by weighing the relevant correspondence constraints.

The present paper is another attempt to get to grips with what Rose & Inkelas call "an emerging system influenced by a variety of independent factors" (see above). The paper reports the results of a (partly quantitative) case study on the growth of the liquid system (i.e., /l r/) of a girl (my daughter Nynke) growing up with Dutch as her mother tongue. The study covers the period between roughly 1;7 and 3;3 in the girl's life; by the end of this period, the liquid system was fully acquired and fixed. The study shows that acquisition (of liquids at least) proceeds considerably less linearly than is often assumed, and that the variation observed in production displays

---

[3] From several different sources for four different young children.

interesting patterns. As we will see, these patterns are by and large plausible from a phonological point of view.[4]

In their studies on the acquisition of variable phenomena, Guy & Boyd (1990), Roberts (1993) and Labov (1994: 578-83) show that 3–5-year-olds master the adult system of their surroundings, including the probabilistic fine-tuning of the occurrence of the variants and the internal constraints.

However, not all aspects of L1 acquisition concern phenomena which are variable in the adult system. Labov & Labov (1976) demonstrated this for one of the phases in the acquisition of English wh-questions, by their 3-year-old daughter Jessie. Of the syntactic processes involved (wh-fronting and inversion), the latter showed variability in this phase. On the basis of ample data, a variable rule is formulated and the probability of the application of the rule[5] is computed. The case study reported in the present paper does not deal with the acquisition of a variable phenomenon either, but rather with the acquisition of a natural class of contrasting segments, viz. /l/ and /r/. The way in which these segments are acquired is similar to the former Echternach procession (i.e., two steps ahead, one step back), in that the production of the sounds is not yet categorical after their first 'successful' realization. Instead, several stages in the acquisition of /l/ and /r/ show quantitative variation between variants, some of which exist as segments of Dutch and some of which do not.

The study of the early L1 acquisition of liquids is interesting for a number of reasons. One is its relation to the cross-linguistic typology of liquids. Not all languages have liquids, let alone a phonemic contrast between laterals and rhotics. According to Maddieson (1984), 81% of the languages in UPSID have laterals while 76% have rhotics. The relationship between typology and acquisition resides among other things in markedness theory. On the external level, markedness is defined by cross-linguistic frequency of occurrence (unmarked > marked) and order of acquisition (unmarked > marked). One would therefore expect acquisition to mirror cross-linguistic frequency, with laterals being acquired before rhotics.[6]

Another issue concerns the degree of cross-linguistic overlap. The online version of UPSID (an expanded version of Maddieson 1984) contains 352 languages with lateral approximants and 209 with rhotics/trills; of these, 183

---

[4] The observed variation was analyzed in connection with internal factors only; extra-linguistic factors were not taken into consideration.

[5] Both generally and under specific conditions.

[6] Cf. Beers (1995: 71). Van der Linde (2001) attaches different weights to the relevant correspondence constraints. The liquids, which are argued to be maximally marked (cf. also Gilbers 2002: 25), have the lowest weight; within the class of the liquids, the rhotic has the lowest weight (cf. Van der Linde 2001: 133–134).

have both lateral approximants and rhotics/trills.[7] It will be clear that aspects of the acquisition of these segments have been investigated for very few of these languages. The present study is a small step in this direction.

On the basis of UPSID it cannot be established how many 'one-liquid languages' display free or allophonic variation of the liquid. It is clear that such languages exist. Examples of languages with free variation include the various dialects of Chinese (Jakobson 1941/1968: 40) and the Papuan languages Hatam (Reesink 1999) and Sentani (Cowan 1965). The latter two are described as having free variation across the board, which includes trilled realizations in Sentani. The Niger-Congo language Jita has a single liquid whose realization varies freely morpheme-initially (Downing 2001). Other languages display neutralization of contrastive liquids. For example, Kikongo Kituba (Mufwene 2001), a Bantu language spoken in Congo, and Hausa (Newman 2000) have several liquid phonemes, which neutralise across the board in Kikongo Kituba, and in final position in Hausa. For a useful cross-linguistic overview of such patterns, see Proctor (2009: 38–39).

The study reported in this paper is also interesting for another reason. Dutch is a language in which the standard norm allows several co-existing variants of /r/. The main variants are uvular and apical, which do not differ in terms of their prestige. In the case study to be described, the girl's father is a native speaker of a variety of standard Dutch with a uvular /r/, while her mother has an apical /r/. Given that the girl has been exposed to a reasonably balanced input from both parents[8], the question was which variant the girl would 'choose' in her emergent Dutch.

2 The hypothetical development

In his famous *Kindersprache, Aphasie und allgemeine Lautgesetze* from 1941, Roman Jakobson posits a relationship between L1 acquisition and certain types of aphasic speech which can be described as the "first in, last out" law of cybernetics. The ordering which guides both processes is taken to be a matter of universal principles. In the fourth of his Six Lectures on Sound

---

[7] See e.g. http://web.phonetik.uni-frankfurt.de/upsid_info.html. The database contains 48 languages with 'r-sounds'; of these, 34 also have a lateral approximant. 161 of the languages in the database have 'trill sounds'; of these, 149 also have a lateral approximant. There is no overlap between the languages with 'r-sounds' and those with 'trill sounds'.

[8] Thanks to fairly equally shared caretaking, made possible by an advanced parental leave system.

and Meaning from 1942, Jakobson (1978: 116) paraphrases his insights as follows:

> It is the structural analysis of language in the process of development -the analysis of children's language and its general laws- and of language in the process of disintegration -aphasic language- which enables us to throw light on the selection of phonemes, the distinctive features, and their mutual relations, and to get closer to the main principles of this selection and of this interdependence so as to be in a position to establish and explain the universal laws which underlie the phonological structure of the world's languages.

With regard to liquids, Jakobson (1941/1968: 90) notes that these

> ...are similar to the nasal consonants in that they add a vocalic opening to the consonantal closure, except that in the nasal consonants two cavities each perform a single function, while in the liquids the two opposing functions belong at the same time to one and the same cavity. The oral quality of the liquids ... consists of a coupling of the consonantal and vocalic features, as a result of which the opposition of a liquid and another consonant is much more complex. This explains the fact that the liquids remain unknown to many languages ... and appear in child language considerably later than the universal nasal consonants.

This claim is corroborated by the statistical patterns in UPSID. However, Jakobson (1941/1968: 57) makes a further claim about the acquisition of liquids:

> The number of languages with a single liquid (whether *l* or *r*) is extraordinarily large, and in this connection Benveniste (1939) justly points out that the child has only a single liquid for a long time and acquires the other liquid as one of his last speech sounds.

This claim will serve as the first hypothesis to be tested in the present study.

While monitoring and transcribing the girl's utterances, it occurred to me that the unfolding of her liquid subsystem, although seemingly chaotic, in fact proceeded very smoothly. More specifically, the development seemed to proceed from a phase that was characterized by a predominance of null realizations, via a phase of free variation and a phase in which the variation was quantitatively conditioned by the phonological and prosodic context, to the categorical lexical contrast typical of the adult system. This impression, which took shape during longitudinal observation, forms the second hypothesis guiding the study.

3 Case study

This section offers a brief outline of the essentials of the process of data collection, the internal organization of the database, and the main steps in the analysis of the data. This sets the stage for section 4, which presents the main findings of the study.

3.1 Data collection

Almost all observations were made during family dinners in the early evening. The observations were noted down, usually in the form of phonetic transcriptions of (parts of) the girl's utterances. The notes were not confined to items containing one or more liquids. Notes were made fairly regularly, in general at least as often as once a week.

In addition to these notes, sound recordings of indoor family activities were made at 3-month intervals, usually for the duration of almost an entire day, during those hours that the girl was awake. For the present study, no use has been made of these recordings (though see section 5).

3.2 The database

The database contains notes taken of 420 relevant observations, i.e. items containing one or more liquids in the adult system (cf. Inkelas & Rose 2011: 2424). Excluded from the analysis are therefore those liquids which were 'out of place', as in [bʀenə], *beneden*, 'downstairs' (2;4.11); [klɑpəmɛit], *knappe meid*, 'smart girl' (2;6.25); [pʀɑmiʲa], *pyjama*, 'pyjamas' (2;7.15); [sleːu] *sneeuw* 'snow' (3;0.10); [watəʀplɔkə], *waterpokken*, 'chicken pox, varicella' (3;2.15). Unclear cases of liquids were also excluded. This concerned, for example, the liquids in [fɛlɛkədə] and [vølɜkədə], *veel lekkerder*, '(tasting) much better' (2;6.6), since the adjacent /l/s may have well been degeminated (categorical in the adult system), even though in the same period (2;6.6) the compound *tafellaken*, 'table cloth' (morphologically ##tafel#lake(n)##) was realised as [tafəlʀakə], showing that adjacent /l/s separated by a grammatical boundary are not always degeminated.

The number of relevant observations over the entire period comes down to an average of 21 observations per month, and 5 observations per week. The observations were entered into the database, together with some linguistic context, viz. the following phonological parameters: left-hand environment, right-hand environment, part of consonant cluster (yes/no), position in the syllable.

The nature of the immediate left-hand and right-hand environment has been coded phonemically. (These parameters have not been operationalised phonetically, as the focus was always on (what seemed to be) the planned output from the perspective of the adult system.) For both parameters, distinctions were made between pause (if the item is in the initial or final position of an utterance), obstruent, sonorant, and vowel.

For each observed occurrence of an item with a liquid, it was determined whether or not the liquid formed part of a consonant cluster. Here the relevant unit of analysis was taken to be the grammatical (rather than the prosodic) word. Thus, [trakə], /(ə)t ## lakə(n)/, *het laken*, 'the sheet' (2;7.3), with a procliticized definite article, was not considered to contain a consonant cluster, for example.

Finally, with regard to prosodic position, liquids were considered to be in nuclear position if they followed a tautosyllabic lax/short vowel, and in coda position if they followed a tense/long vowel or a diphthong. In items such as *hallo* 'hello' and *sterretje,* 'star-DIM', the liquid was analyzed as ambisyllabic.

3.3 Analysis

The analysis consisted mainly of categorizing and sorting the data, and of counting and comparing the numbers (totals or means). For the latter, tests of significance were applied to determine to which extent chance could be excluded.

The principal aim of the study was to uncover and explain the distribution of variants of /l r/ across the different developmental phases on the one hand, and the different phonological contexts (as defined by the parameters described in section 3.2) on the other.

4 Main findings

The quantitative distribution of both liquids over the full range of phonetic realizations is summarized in Table 1 (next page), aggregated over the entire 20-month period in the girl's early acquisition of Dutch, along with some examples of realizations which do not match the adult system.

Conveniently, the total numbers of observations for /l/ and /r/ do not differ too much.

		[ ]	/l/	e.g.	/r/	e.g.	total
null			49	tu, *stoel*, 'chair'	91	daiʲə, *draaien*, 'turn'	140
obstr	plos +vce	d	3	fodipɑp, *olifant*, 'elephant'	3	odiʲa, *gloria*, 'glory'	6
		dʲ	1	Rɔmədʲə, *rommelen*, 'muddle'	0		1
	fric +vce	z	0		2	zozɛin, *rozijn*, 'raisin'	2
		γ	0		1	wɑkəɣ, *wakker*, 'awake'	1
	-vce	x	0		1		1
nasal		n	3	kʏfənə, *knuffelen*, 'cuddle'	0	lu, *roe*, 'rod'	3
liquid		l	77		2		80
		/l	4		0		4
		lʷ	1		0		1
		R	46	Ropt, *loopt*, 'walks'	112		157
		/R	0		8		8
glide		j	4	hɑjo, *hallo*, 'hello'	3	hoi, *hoor*, 'hear'	7
		w	9	hœywə, *huilen*, 'cry'	0		9
total			197		223		420

Table 1. The quantitative distribution of the realizations of both liquids aggregated over the entire 20-month period. /l and /R indicate 'half-articulated' realizations.

Table 1 shows that /l/ has 10 different realizations and /r/ 9; the overlap adds up to 5, viz. null, [d], [l], [R] and [j]. During this 20-month period /r/ has many more null-realizations than /l/ (77/197 = 39% for /l/ *vs.* 112/223 = 50% for /r/), a statistically significant difference.[9] It is also remarkable that /l/ is realized as [R] no fewer than 46 times (almost 25% of the total number of relevant observations), whereas the opposite occurs only 2 times. This part of the variation is therefore definitely not symmetrical.[10] In addition, /l/ was

[9] Tested with chi square for the significance of differences between correlated proportions: χ^2=6.15 df=1 p<.02.

[10] The data therefore differ from Jonathan Swift's perception and imitation of 'baby language', used by the author in a series of letters to two women (e.g. *I expect a Rettle vely soon; & that MD is vely werr*) which were recently unearthed by Dr

realized as [w] 9 times, while /r/ was realized as [j] only 3 times. All other realizations (for /l/, [dʲ] and [lʷ]; for /r/, [x] and [ɣ]) are marginal.

Only 10 (or so) cases can be argued to involve consonant harmony (for this term, see Goad 1997). These occurred mainly in the earlier phases. Examples include [dɔus], *proost*, 'cheers', [zozεin], *rozijn*, 'raisin'; [bɑw], *bal*, 'ball'; [ɑmaw], *allemaal*, 'everybody'. The realizations [lεkəx], *lekker*, '(tasting) good' and [wɑkəɣ], *wakker*, 'awake', may be further instances of consonant harmony, although here the articulatory and acoustic similarity of [ʀ] to the velar fricatives may also have played a role.

If we disregard both null realizations and 'half-articulated' liquids, then there seems to be something of an inverse relation between the deviation from the liquid target (as measured in terms of the number of different feature specifications) and the number of times this deviation occurs in the data. This correlation is not significant on any level (neither overall nor for the realization of /l/ and /r/ separately) if we use the feature matrices for Dutch segments of Booij (1995: 20–21). However, the picture changes if the deviation is measured on the universal sonority scale, in (1):

(1)   Obstruent < Nasal < Liquid < Glide < Vowel
              1   2   3   4   5

Given (1), a value of –2 is assigned to the realization of /l/ as [z], a value of –1 to the realization of /l/ as [n], and a value of +1 to the realization of /l/ as [w], say. This results in a highly significant correlation between the number of occurrences of a particular realization on the one hand, and its sonority distance to the relevant liquid on the other (an overall correlation of –.710 (two-tailed p=.000), –.749 (p=.006) for /l/, and –.738 (p=.007) for /r/; all correlations are strong). The correlations are still highly significant (a relatively strong r of –.678 (p=.001) overall and of –.738 (p=.007) for /r/) if we factor in the small distance in sonority between /r/ and /l/ (for this, see van der Hulst 1984).[11] In general, the larger the sonority distance between the liquid and its actual realization, the less frequent it is. Therefore, since the number of each deviant realization is determined by its sonority distance, we can conclude that the production of liquids in this stage is clearly not random.

Abigail Williams of Oxford University (see http://www.bbc.co.uk/news/entertainment-arts-12306109). Interestingly, Jakobson (1941/1968: 17) notes that a similar phenomenon is found elsewhere: "When we observe, e.g., in the coquettish, precious, love language of Russian peasant women in Northeast Siberia (near Lower Kolyma), a *j* in place of a liquid, this so-called 'sweet-talk' (*sladkojazyčije*) is a deliberate infantilism."

[11] /r/ is slightly more sonorous than /l/. This is also corroborated by some of Taeldeman's (1985) observations about morpheme structure constraints.

As Table 1 shows, all realizations of both /r/ and /l/ as [ʀ] have uvular place (i.e., IPA [ʀ] or [ʁ]). This is all the more remarkable since, as was already noted, the girl's mother has an apical /r/ and her father a uvular /r/. In order to find out what the girl would do if her father pronounced a word which the girl had not yet acquired with an apical /r/, a little experiment was designed. A few nonsense words (whose meaning seemed to fit the girl's world and priorities) were coined, viz. *riki-ijsje* 'riki ice-cream', *ruku-ijsje* 'ruku ice-cream', and *raka-ijsje* 'raka ice-cream' (where *riki, ruku,* and *raka* are nonce items). These words were introduced and pronounced by the father using an apical /r/, in sentences like "Would you like to have a *riki-ijsje* or a *ruku-ijsje?*" and "Or how about a *raka-ijsje?*". The girl repeated the relevant words several times, consistently using unmistakably uvular /r/s.

The database contains a total of two /r/ → [l] substitutions. Interestingly, one occurred at the beginning of the 20-month period ([lɔus] for *proost* 'cheers'), and the other ([lu] for *roe,* 'rod') almost at the end, a word which most speakers of modern Dutch probably only know from a popular song sung during Sinterklaas season, early December.[12] /l/ → [ʀ] substitutions occurred much more often, and will be discussed in section 4.1. There and in section 4.2 I focus on the different stages that can be identified in the development of each of the two liquids.

4.1 The lateral

The girl's first realization of /l/ as [l] was observed at the age of 1;9.17. From that point on [l] was rather rare, however: in the first half of the 20-month period under investigation, no more than 6 of the total of 77 [l]s occurred, and in the third quarter no more than 11.

Slightly less than 25% of the total number of realizations of /l/ in the entire 20-month period are [ʀ]s. It is worth noting that in those cases we also observe centralisation of preceding tautomorphemic non-low vowels, as is typical of Dutch. An example from the database is [tuᵊʀ], *stoel* 'chair' (2;3.5).

In this section the analysis of /l/ → [ʀ] substitutions will initially be confined to the 46 cases observed. After this, these cases will be statistically analysed in combination with all other /l/ realizations occurring in the phase during which /l/ was occasionally pronounced as [ʀ]. For the sake of the analysis, I will divide this phase into two sub-phases.

---

[12] Sinterklaas is a traditional Dutch family feast and Sinterklaas folklore consists among other things of special songs. Sinterklaas songs are infamous for their specialised and largely archaic vocabulary.

It turns out that /l/ → [ʀ] occurs no more than 4 times in the context of a preceding obstruent in the same onset, as in [vles] ~ [vʀes], *vlees* 'meat', which occurred in the same utterance (2; 7. 7). When we divide the 46 occurrences of /l/ as [ʀ] in 4 portions of 11 or 12, then an interesting pattern emerges in post-pausal context.[13] During the entire period in which /l/ is occasionally realised as [ʀ], a total of 95 realizations of /l/ were observed, 12 of which after pause. In this context we find only 3 other realizations occur, each [l]. The remaining cases all involve /l/ → [ʀ] substitutions, and these pattern numerically as 5-2-1-1, respectively. In part, this is due to chance, as the total number of /l/-initial items in utterance-initial position drops. Yet, we observe that in the last of the four analyzed portions /l/ → [ʀ] is losing to ground to [l], which utterance-initially (a prosodically strong position) is a better onset, as it is slightly less sonorous (cf. van der Hulst 1984: 84–93).

As to the right-hand environment, we observe that /l/ → [ʀ] never occurs before a sonorant (suggesting that high-sonority clusters are avoided), and only twice before an obstruent.

/l/ → [ʀ] occurs only once in nuclear position. However, if /l/ is in the nucleus and at the same time part of a consonant cluster, as in *melk*, 'milk', then [ʀ] does not occur.

To check whether the realization of /l/ as [ʀ] starts out as free or as conditioned variation, the first 30 realizations of /l/ were analyzed (for this method, see Sankoff 1987).[14] Out of the 30 tokens, 13 were produced as [ʀ], 7 had a null realization, 4 were realized as [w] (all of them in postvocalic position), and 1 as [j]. [n] and [dʲ] also occurred once, and [l] three times.

It turned out that during the earliest part of this sub-phase, i.e. in the period when the first 30 /l/s were realised (2;2.7 until 2;3.21), there was free variation. Breaking down the realization of /l/ as either [ʀ] or 'other', the patterning was studied for each of the four parameters (left-hand environment, right-hand environment, part of consonant cluster (yes/no), syllable position). None of these showed a statistically significant effect on the occurrence of either [ʀ] or other realization types. The parameter consonant cluster (yes/no) has an effect of .05<p<.10, however. The nature of this 'trend towards significance' (as some would call it) is that in clusters [ʀ] occurs only once on a total of 7 realizations; in all cases where /l/ does not form part of a cluster the numbers are almost identical (viz. 12 and 11, respectively). It should be kept in mind that this effect is just outside the regular .05 significance level, however.[15] In a more advanced statistical

---

[13] The shortest portion is almost one month long; the longest slightly more than two months.

[14] Rose & Inkelas (2011: 2416) refer to "conditioned" as "context-sensitive".

[15] χ^2=3.13 df=1.

analysis, the significance of the effect of this parameter turns out to be .105, i.e. not even a trend towards significance.[16]

In short, there does not appear to be an allophonic division of labour among [R] and the other realizations of /l/, for any of the four parameters studied. Not only are there no categorical effects, but we even observe free variation in the early stages of the period during which /l/ is occasionally realized as [R]. This is confirmed by a comprehensive (multivariate) analysis of the simultaneous effects of all four parameters: no single parameter value is included in the final equation.[17] In other words, in the first sub-phase there does not appear to be any (dis-)preference for the realization of /l/ as [R] in any phonological environment.

In the following sub-phase in the girl's development (before the variable realization of /l/ as [R] came to an end, at 2;8.17), another 65 observations were made. During this period the choice between [R] and other realization types appears to become probabilistically conditioned by the left-hand environment. Whereas only [R] occurs following sonorants, and is clearly preferred after pauses and obstruents, other realization types dominate after vowels (26 out of 37 cases).[18] Of these, zero and [l] are the most frequently encountered realizations (with 7 and 8 occurrences, respectively). In other words, both utterance-initially and following a consonant, /l/ is mainly or exclusively realized as [R], while after vowels mainly null and [l] occur. Since these realizations are both less sonorous than [R], this distribution could be motivated by the sonority distance from the left-hand environment. But whatever the explanation, in this sub-phase the variation in /l/ → [R] is no longer free.

The trend towards significance of the parameter consonant cluster (yes/no), for which some indication was found in the first 30 observations in the first sub-phase (i.e., the one with occasional /l/ → [R] substitutions), did not persevere in the second sub-phase. On the contrary, it disappeared completely.

After the phase in which /l/ is occasionally realised as [R], another 62 realizations of /l/ were observed. All except one of these were [l]. The only exception is [d], which differs from /l/ in terms of two major class features; it

---

[16] Logistic regression with consonant cluster (yes/no) as a categorical predictor.

[17] Logistic regression in which the four parameters are categorical predictors (consonant cluster yes/no treated as an 'indicator' and the three four-value parameters as 'deviations' with the overall parameter effect as point of reference) and for which the backward Wald method was used.

[18] This patterning is statistically significant: $\chi^2=15.87$ df=3 p=.001; contingency .443. Logistic regression with left-hand environment as a categorical predictor shows that the variable as such has a significant effect (.009), but the single values of this variable do not.

occurred in the item *vervelend* ('annoying'), where its presence may be the result of consonant harmony.

4.2 The rhotic

Subdividing the total period into four equal phases of five months and limiting the perspective per phase to those realization of /r/ which occur at least 5 times, /r/ shows an overall entirely different development than /l/.

The girl's first realization of /r/ as [ʀ] was observed when at 1;9.21, less than a week after the first [l] for /l/;[19] almost all other realizations in the first phase are null-realizations (26 out of a total of 31 observations). Preceding non-low vowels are centralized relatively often, as in [meːə] or even [meːɑ], *meer* 'more' (1;9;28 and later). In the second phase (N observations = 67), null (occurring 46 times) is no longer the only numerically striking variant, since [ʀ] already occurs 14 times. During the third phase (N=61), the proportions between both realizations have been more or less reversed (18 occurrences of null, 38 of [ʀ]). In the fourth phase (N=63), null has disappeared entirely (also as a realization of /l/, for that matter) and [ʀ] occurs 59 times.

By the end of phase 2, /r/ is realized several times as [ʀ] in initial clusters, in particular following a plosive (in the items *trui* 'sweater', *trap* 'stairs' and *broek* 'pants'), with the cluster broken up by svarabakthi.

As was mentioned above, variation between null and [ʀ] was observed in phases 2 and 3 only (with a total number of occurrences of null plus [ʀ] of 60 and 57, respectively). In both phases there are statistically significant relationships between the variation between null and [ʀ] on the one hand, and the left-hand environment, the right-hand environment, and the position in the syllable on the other.[20] In none of the phases does there seem to be any free variation. There does not appear to be any continuity in the transition from phase 2 to phase 3 with regard to the nature of left-hand environment effects. There is some continuity with regard to the nature of the right-hand environment: in phase 2, an obstruent almost always co-occurs with a preceding null realization, while in phase 3 obstruents mainly co-occur with null realizations. The effect of syllable position in the transition from phase 2

---

[19] This matches the order of acquisition as predicted and observed for Dutch by Beers (1995: 79, 176-7, 184, 190-1, 198-9) and Van der Linde (2001: 134).

[20] Phase 2: χ^2=17.28 df=2 (no preceding sonorants) p=.000, contingency .472; χ^2=23.14 df=3 p=.000, contingency .528; χ^2=22.56 df=3 p=.000, contingency .523, respectively. Phase 3: χ^2=13.39 df=3 p=.004; contingency .436; χ^2=20.99 df=3 p=.000; contingency .519; χ^2=18.96 df=3 p=.000; contingency .500.

to 3 shows even more continuity. In phase 2, onsets prefer [ʀ] while nuclei and codas almost only contain null realizations; in phase 3, onsets strongly prefer [ʀ] while codas mainly show null realizations.

To determine whether the effects of the three parameters survive in a comprehensive analysis and to ascertain the mutual weights of the parameters and the separate parameter values (in case several parameter values turn out to have significant effects), a multivariate analysis was carried out for each phase.[21] In phase 2, none of the parameters show a significant effect for any single value, meaning that none of the environments appear to display any (dis-)preference for the realization of /r/ as null. For phase 3, only the right-hand environment after obstruents appears to have a (negative) significant effect on the occurrence of [ʀ].[22]

Thus, it would seem to be the case that in phase 2 of the development of /r/ the variation between [ʀ] and null is free, but becomes linguistically conditioned in phase 3. The relevant condition (a dispreference for [ʀ] in case an obstruent follows) leads to cluster reduction, and so would seem to be phonotactically motivated.

5 Discussion and questions for further research

Consonant harmony occurs mainly in the first half of the 20-month period covered by this longitudinal case study. However, numerically its role in the realization of /l r/ seems to be marginal. The number of occurrences of the various realization types was shown to be inversely proportional to the sonority distance of each type vis-à-vis the two liquids.

Dividing the 20-month period into four 5-month phases and zooming in on the growth of the adult part of the consonant inventory results in the patterns in Table 2.

---

[21] Logistic regression in which the four parameters are categorical predictors (as 'deviation' with the overall parameter effect as point of reference) and the backward Wald method was used.
[22] B= –1.633 df=1 sign=.002.

phase	/l/	[l]		/r/	[ʀ]	
	n	%	cumulative %	n	%	cumulative %
1	3	4	4	1	1	1
2	3	4	8	14	12,5	13,5
3	11	13	21	38	34	47,5
4	61	79	100	59	52,7	100

Table 2. Numbers and proportions of realization of the adult variant per 5-month phase

As we have seen above, [l] had a slightly better start, but from phase 2 onwards [ʀ] showed a much stronger growth. Levelt et al. (2000) established that monolingual Dutch-learning children acquire syllable structure in the order CV > CVC > CCV. From the perspective of syllable structure (with CV being the main and earliest syllable type) and sonority, then, the opposite finding might rather have been expected. If, as was assumed, /l/ is less sonorous than /r/, and so a 'better' onset, we would probably expect /l/ to be more easily acquired. On the other hand, measured over the entire period /r/ showed considerably more null realizations. This would seem to tally with the sonority-based expectations, as well as with the more general claim of Benveniste and Jakobson that served as one of the hypotheses guiding this study, viz. that "the child has only a single liquid for a long time and acquires the other liquid as one of his last speech sounds" (see Section 2).

The development of the acquisition of /l/ and /r/ show partly overlapping phases. Superficially, the developmental phases in the acquisition of /l/ resemble those of /r/, but closer inspection reveals a number of non-trivial differences. Time-wise, the (sub-)phases in the development of the liquids do not always coincide; for /l/, it may be necessary to identify specific sub-phase, for example to account for the pattern in utterance-initial position.

A more detailed examination shows that the acquisition of /l/ proceeds in four phases. During phase 1, the main realization type was null. Phase 2 was characterized by free variation in the realization of /l/ as [ʀ]. In phase 3, this variation became linguistically conditioned, although probabilistically rather than categorically. At the same time, the constraining effect of a preceding pause was gradually relaxed, as a result of which the domain of /l/ → [ʀ] became more restricted. During phase 4, finally, /l/ was realized as [l] almost without exception.

As far as /r/ is concerned, phase 1 showed almost only null realizations. Null was also the main realization type during phase 2, although [ʀ] showed a strong start; both variants were in free variation during this phase. In phase 3, [ʀ] became more frequent than null and the variation between both variants became linguistically conditioned. Finally, in phase 4 null had disappeared completely, and /r/ was realised as [ʀ] in almost all cases. In the last phase, both liquids were therefore close to reaching the adult stage of lexical contrast.

Given these findings, the second hypothesis, as formulated in Section 2, can be said to be supported by the data.

The asymmetry observed in the substitution patterns during phases 2 and 3 deserves special attention. As was pointed out in Section 1, the girl's mother is a native speaker of a variety of standard Dutch with an apical /r/, while her father has a uvular /r/. Given that apical [r] is articulatorily closer to /l/ than [ʀ], the child probably learned [ʀ] as different from /l/ but possibly confused apical [r] and /l/, and may thus have constructed representations in which /r/ has been replaced by /l/. But this would then have led her to realize adult /r/ as [l] rather realize /l/ as [ʀ]. So, the asymmetry in the substitution patterns probably has another explanation.

During both the period in which phase 2 in the development of both liquids overlapped and the period in which phase 3 in the development of both liquids overlapped, the main variant of /l/ was [ʀ], while the main variant of /r/ was null. This could be taken to suggest that the two segments-in-the-making were subject to a chain shift. However, there are a number of arguments against this:

i.   during this period, both /l/ and /r/ varied strongly in their realization;

ii. during this period, /l/ also had a (numerically non-negligible) null realization. This would also make it impossible to decide whether the chain shift involves a push chain or a pull chain;

iii. the development of both /l/ and /r/ involved free variation in phase 2 but conditioned variation in phase 3; the relevant conditioning concerns the left-hand environment for /l/ and the right-hand environment for /r/. So, the conditioning did not contribute to mutual feeding relationships.

Categorical allophonic distributions did not occur at any point during the development, unlike in the phonological study of Steven described in Gilbers (2002). Gilbers (2002: 25) observes that

> "until the age of four, Steven still had trouble with the pronunciation of /l/ in syllable-final position ... At this stage, he did not have any difficulties with the realization of /l/ in onset position anymore, which indicates that positional markedness plays an important role in the acquistion."

Insofar as positional markedness played a role in Nynke's acquisition of both liquids, it did so only gradiently (and to statistically significant extents) in the third phase of the development of both /l/ and /r/. Whereas /l/ was mainly realised as [ʀ] utterance-initially, after both obstruents and sonorants, /r/ was mainly realized as null before obstruents.

In conclusion, it is clear that the present case study raises a number of issues that require further investigation. These include at least the following:

i. Does the quality of adjacent vowels affect the acquisition process of /l/ and /r/? It should be possible to address this question on the basis of the relevant data collected for the present study.

ii. In the present study, both the liquids and the left/right-hand environments were defined in phonemic rather than phonetic terms. However, it is possible that a phonetic implementation of the left/right-hand contexts would show sharper effects, especially with respect to the svarabhakti cases (cf. Section 4.2) and in cases such as [ɔmbʀax], *omlaag* 'down' (2;4;11 and 2;4;28), with an intrusive [b].

iii. More generally, the present study implicitly assumes 'adult-like phonological representations' as are used in generative approaches to phonology, which draw on formal relationships between inputs and outputs (cf. Rose & Inkelas 2011: 2424). The question is a) how the data in this paper would have been analyzed without that assumption, and b) to what extent this would have yielded comparable findings.

iv. Levelt et al. (2000) have shown that the order of acquisition of syllable types in Dutch reflects their distributional frequency in the adult system. Similarly, Fikkert & Levelt (2008: 246) have shown that in segmented words, "the most frequent pattern in the input ... appears first [while] patterns of low frequency ... appear late." Levelt & van Oostendorp (2007) were able to exclude effects of token frequency in child-directed speech, but their study concerned the chronology of the acquisition of the Dutch consonant inventory. To what extent do type and/or token frequencies in the input play a role in the gradual unfolding of the liquid subsystem? And to the extent that there are frequency effects, how do they relate to structural constraints of the type studied above?

v. Do the sound recordings which were made at 3-month intervals (cf. Section 3.1) confirm the patterns in the developmental phases in this period of the acquisition process? This question concerns the internal validity of this study. Another question concerns the external validity. A general question which confronts case studies (as well as corpus studies) is how representative the data are, and thus how generalizable the findings can be. I do not have an answer to this question, but its impact is considerably lessened if such studies are based on random selections of speakers. This is one reason why it would be good to have comparable research on the basis of similar data, collected in random samples of comparable speakers, i.e. children growing up with Dutch as their mother tongue.

vi. The realization of liquids is highly variable across languages, and as Yvan Rose (p.c.) points out, liquids are also notoriously difficult for children. Would the acquisition of other segment types, such as stops and (certain) fricatives, have followed more categorical-looking developmental paths?

The electronic database that has been constructed for the purposes of this paper will soon be made available, so that anybody who is interested can address questions 1 through 4 using the data underlying the present study.

References

Beers, Mieke (1995): *The Phonology of Normally Developing and Language-impaired Children.* – PhD dissertation, University of Amsterdam.

Booij, Geert (1995): *The Phonology of Dutch.* – Oxford: Clarendon Press.

Cowan, Hendrik (1965): *Grammar of the Sentani language, with specimen texts and vocabulary.* – The Hague: Nijhoff. (Verhandelingen van het Koninklijk Instituut voor Taal-, Land- en Volkenkunde, deel 47.)

Downing, Laura. (2001): "Liquid spirantization in Jita." – In: *Maililime: Malawian Journal of Linguistics* 2, 1–27.

Fikkert, Paula & Claartje Levelt (2008): "How does place fall into place? The lexicon and emergent constraints in children's developing Grammars." – In: Peter Avery, B. Elan Dresher & Keren Rice (eds.): *Contrast in Phonology: Theory, Perception, Acquisition*, 231– 268. Berlin: Mouton de Gruyter.

Gilbers, Dicky (2002): "Conflicting phonologically based and phonetically based constraints in the anlysis of /l/-substitution". In: Beers, Mieke, Petra Jongmans & A. Wijnands (eds.): *Netwerk Eerste Taalverwerving, Net-bulletin 2001*, 22-40.

Goad, Heather (1997): "Consonant harmony in child languae: an optimality-theoretic account." – In: Hannahs, S.J. & Martha Young-Scholten (eds): *Focus on Phonological Acquisition*, 113-142. Amsterdam & Philadelphia: Benjamins.

Guy, Gregory & Sally Boyd (1990): "The development of a morphological class." – In: *Language Variation and Change* 2(1), 1–18.

Jakobson, Roman (1941): *Kindersprache, Aphasie und allgemeine Lautgesetze.* English translation by Alan R. Keiler (1968): *Child language, aphasia and phonological universals.* – The Hague: Mouton.

Jakobson, Roman (1942): *Six Lectures on Sound and Meaning.* Translated by John Mepham; preface by Claude Lévi-Strauss. – Brighton, UK: Harvester Press.

Labov, William (1994): *Principles of Linguistic Change. Volume 1: Internal Factors.* – Oxford: Basil Blackwell.

Labov, William & Teresa Labov (1976): "Learning the syntax of questions." – In: R. Campbell, Robin N. & Philip T. Smith (eds.): *Recent Advances in the Psychology of Language.* New York: Plenum Press.

Levelt, Claartje, Niels Schiller & Willem Levelt (2000): "The acquisition of syllable types." – *Language Acquisition* 8, 237–264.

Levelt, Claartje & Marc van Oostendorp (2007): "Feature co-occurrence constraints in L1 acquisition." – In: Bettelou Los & Majo van Koppen (eds.): *Linguistics in the Netherlands 2007*, 162–172. Amsterdam & Philadelphia: Benjamins.

Maddieson, Ian (1984): *Patterns of Sounds.* – Cambridge: Cambridge University Press.

Mufwene, Salikoko (2001): "Kikongo Kituba." – In: J. Garry & C. Rubino (eds.): *Facts About the World's Languages: an Encyclopedia of the World's Major Languages, Past and Present.* New York: H.W. Wilson.

Newman, Paul (2000): *The Hausa Language. An Encyclopedic Reference Grammar.* – New Haven CT: Yale University Press.

Proctor, Michael (2009): *Gestural Characterization of a Phonological Class: the Liquids.* – PhD dissertation, Yale University.

Reesink, Ger (1999): *A Grammar of Hatam, Bird's Head Peninsula, Irian Jaya.* – Canberra: Australian National University, Pacific Linguistics.

Roberts, Julia (1993): *The Acquisition of Variable Rules: t, d Deletion and -ing Production in Preschool Children.* – PhD dissertation, University of Pennsylvania.

Rose, Ivan & Sharon Inkelas (2011): "The interpretation of phonological patterns in first language acquisition." – In: Van Oostendorp, Marc, Colin Ewen, Elisabeth Hume & Keren Rice (eds.): *The Blackwell Companion to Phonology.* Vol. IV, *Phonological interfaces*, 2414–2438.

Sankoff, David (1987): "Problems of representativeness." – In: Ammon, Ulrich, Norbert Dittmar & Klaus J. Mattheier (eds.): *Sociolinguistics. An International handbook of the Science of Language and Society*, 899–903. Berlin: De Gruyter.

Taeldeman, Johan (1985): "Likwiditeiten. Over likwieden en syllabeteorieën." In: Ryckeboer, Herman et al. (eds.): *Hulde-album Prof. Dr. Marcel Hoebeke*, 341–351. Gent : RUG, Seminarie voor Nederlandse Taalkunde.

Van der Hulst, Harry (1984): *Syllable structure and stress in Dutch.* – Dordrecht: Foris.

Van der Linde, Klarien (2001): *Sonority substitutions.* PhD dissertation, University of Groningen.

Diana Apoussidou

The Tibetan numerals segmentation problem and how virtual learners solve it*

1 Introduction

Spoken language is continuous: there are no breaks to indicate word boundaries corresponding to something as unambiguous as white space in written language. Yet finding the correct word boundaries to extract meaningful units such as words or morphemes is crucial for understanding an utterance. There exist different cues in a language that signal word boundaries to the listener. Known cues are, among others, word stress, phonotactics, statistical cues such as transitional probabilities, or lexical information (if you are able to recognize a word out of the speech stream, you are able to set a boundary, which in turn will signal the beginning of a new word): Different languages use different cues, though, and the right segmentation of a word into its subunits is language specific. Therefore, a learner of a language (be it L1 or L2) needs to find out the proper cues in order to be able to segment spoken language. Learning the morphemes of a word is just as language specific, and for the most part depends on a lexical learning device.

In this paper, I present such a lexical approach of how L1 learners (and possibly L2 learners as well) acquire the segmentation of a word into its morphemes. A well-known segmentation problem is, for instance, the segmentation of numerals in Lhasa Tibetan (as described in Halle & Clements 1983): In Lhasa Tibetan, numerals vary depending on their position within a word. For instance, 'fourteen' surfaces as *ʤubʃi* (composed of the words 'ten' and 'four'), whereas 'forty' surfaces as *ʃibʤu* (composed of 'four' and 'ten'): The words for 'four' and 'ten' in isolation surface as *ʃi* and *ʤu*. The segmentation question is therefore whether *ʤubʃi* and *ʃibʤu* are

---

* The author especially thanks Joe Pater and Karen Jesney for their insights and valuable comments during the emergence of this work, as well as Tamás Biró and Andries Coetzee for their thorough and thoughtful reviews. The author furthermore thanks the audiences of the Sound Circle at the University of Amsterdam and at Brown University for their attention and input. This research was made possible with the support of the NWO Rubicon grant 446-07-030. Errors and misconceptions remain the author's very own responsibility, of course.

analyzed as *ʤu-bʃi* and *ʃi-bʤu*, or as *ʤub-ʃi* and *ʃib-ʤu* (or maybe even as *ʤu-b-ʃi* and *ʃi-b-ʤu*, with an epenthetic *b*), respectively, and furthermore whether the medially occurring [b] is the result of an epenthetic process, or subject to deletion word-initially. Because the morphemes alternate on the surface, a language learner is faced with the problem to determine a) the underlying representation of morphemes such as 'four' and 'ten' and b) whether and what phonological processes are involved that lead to the alternation, in order to successfully comprehend and produce the words. In more general terms, the learner needs to acquire parts of the lexicon and parts of the grammar. The problem is that in order to acquire the lexicon, the learner depends on grammar, and in order to acquire the grammar, the learner depends on information from the lexicon. An appropriate learning model hence needs to be able to bootstrap into grammar and lexicon. In the lexical learning model proposed here, the morphemes and their allomorphs are encoded as lexical constraints that compete with each other in an optimality-theoretic fashion. Their formulation as constraints furthermore enables a straightforward interaction with the phonological grammar (which consists itself of constraints): The learner thus develops lexicon and grammar in parallel, and, as I will show, this leads to a correct segmentation of the Tibetan numeral system.

The learnability model will be computationally implemented and tested. The results contribute to understanding the nature of grammar and the mental lexicon and to the debate of how much and what parts of language need to be hard-wired into our brains. It furthermore shows how learners might be able to deal with linguistic variation. Computational modelling complements psycholinguistic experiments and language acquisitional data by spelling out predictions of the involved theoretical frameworks, and enables the handling of large amounts of data. The phenomena can be tested in isolation and influence from other factors can easily be excluded.

Here, two types of virtual learners will be compared: Optimality Theory (OT) learners with Harmonic Grammar learners (as described in Boersma & Pater 2008): Faced with the surface alternations, the OT-learners are able to acquire a restrictive lexicon along with a grammar that correctly produces the observed data, and are moreover able to segment new words correctly. The HG-learners produce the correct surface forms just as well, but show cases of allomorphy.

2 Tibetan numerals: an analysis

In the following, I describe the numeral system of Lhasa Tibetan and present a general analysis of the data. I proceed by outlining the model, followed by a description of the computer settings of the simulations and the results, before I conclude in the last section. 2 Tibetan numerals: an analysis

The correct segmentation of an utterance is crucial for its understanding, because different segmentations can lead to access of different lexical entries and therefore render different meanings (cf. e.g. *...bartending...* with *...Bart ending...*): Some of the problems with segmentation can be very nicely demonstrated with Tibetan numerals (Halle & Clements 1983): In this case, the numeral morphemes alternate on the surface, depending on whether they appear in word-final position or not:

(1) The segmentation problem of Tibetan numerals[1]

[dʒig]	'one'	[dʒu]	'ten'	[dʒugdʒig]	'eleven'
[ʃi]	'four'	[ʃibdʒu]	'forty'	[dʒubʃi]	'fourteen'
[ŋa]	'five'	[ŋabdʒu]	'fifty'	[dʒuŋa]	'fifteen'
[gu]	'nine'	[gubdʒu]	'ninety'	[dʒurⁿu]	'nineteen'

The morphemes seem to be freely combinable with each other and surface with at least two different forms. A full list of alternations is given in (2):

(2) Alternations:

Morpheme	In isolation	Word-finally	Word-initially
'one'	[dʒig]	[-gdʒig]	
'four'	[ʃi]	[-bʃi]	[ʃib-]
'five'	[ŋa]	[-ŋa]	[ŋab-]
'nine'	[gu]	[-rgu]	[gub-]
'ten'	[dʒu]	[-bdʒu]	[dʒub-], [dʒug-], [dʒur-]

---

[1] In this paper, I diverge in my notation for underlying representations and surface forms from standard phonological theory because I work in a framework close to Boersma (1998 and after) which connects not only underlying representations with surface structure, but also incorporates phonetic forms and meaning. I therefore write underlying representations in pipes. However, because I limit myself just to two levels of representation and conflate, for simplicity's sake, 'surface' and 'phonetic' forms, I also divert from Boersma's notation, and therefore write the 'surface forms' in brackets (also, if I wrote them in slashes, people might confuse them for underlying representations, which they are not):

In isolation, the morphemes 'four' and 'ten' surface as [ʃi] and [dʒu], whereas, when combined to form 'fourteen' (as in example (3)), and 'forty' (as in example (4)), a [b] appears word-medially:

(3) [dʒu] + [ʃi] = [dʒubʃi]
    'ten' 'four' 'fourteen'

The questions are, a) where in the compounds the morpheme boundary is and b) what status the [b] has. Two segmentation possibilities are that 1) the [b] belongs to the initial morpheme, or 2) it belongs to the final morpheme.[2] Hence, confronted with the data in (3) and (4), a learner could come up with two hypotheses about the segmentation:

(4) Hypothesis 1: the morpheme boundary splits the consonants of a word-internal cluster, i.e.
    a)   [dʒubʃi] → |dʒub+ʃi|
    b)   [ʃibdʒu] → |ʃib+dʒu|

(5) Hypothesis 2: the morpheme boundary is before the word-internal cluster, i.e.
    a)   [dʒubʃi] → |dʒu+bʃi|
    b)   [ʃibdʒu] → |ʃi+bdʒu|

If Hypothesis 1 is correct, the grammatical consequence would be that word-*final* consonants delete on the surface: |dʒub| → [dʒu_#]. However, this is inconsistent with other forms of the language: i) [dʒig] 'one' ends in a consonant and ii) other variants such as [dʒur-] and [dʒug-] are also observed (in e.g. [dʒurgu] 'nineteen' and [dʒugdʒig] 'eleven'): A learner going for this analysis would end up with an extensive list of allomorphs in the lexicon and little grammar, shifting the workload more or less completely to the lexicon. This is not the most elegant solution.

If Hypothesis 2 is correct, the grammatical consequence would be that the language prohibits word-*initial* consonant clusters and resolves them by deleting the first segment in the cluster: |bdʒu| → [#_dʒu]. There are no data contradicting this analysis, and it does without allomorphy. It can be

---

[2] A third possibility is to assume that the medial [b] belongs to neither morpheme, but is inserted for some phonological reason. An argument against this possibility is given by the forms for 'eleven' [dʒugdʒig], 'fifteen' [dʒuɲa], and 'nineteen' [dʒurgu], where either no consonant (*dʒuɲa*) or other consonants than [b] (*dʒugdʒig, dʒurgu*) are inserted. It is unlikely that there is a phonological reason for assuming that [g] and [r] are additional epenthetic consonants, especially in the light of the fact that in [dʒugdʒig], a [g] appears before [dʒ], but in [ʃibdʒu], a [b] appears before the very same consonant. We therefore want to a priori exclude this analysis, although, in a comprehensive learnability account, one would have to include the possibility for this analysis.

modelled with a simple, traditional OT-analysis involving a well-established structural constraint[3] *#CC (going back to Prince & Smolensky 1993/2004, Kager 1999) and a simple faithfulness constraint MAX-C (e.g. McCarthy & Prince 1995), listed in (6) and (7):

(6) *#CC: No word-initial consonant clusters on the surface.

(7) MAX-C: Consonants in the underlying representation are not deleted on the surface.

A simple, traditional OT-tableau in (8) for Tibetan 'eleven' illustrates how the surface form comes about. The input consists of two morphemes that both start with a consonant cluster (the morpheme boundary is indicated by a '+'): Candidates are surface structures (dots represent syllable boundaries): a faithful one, one with word-initial cluster reduction and one where both clusters are resolved. With a ranking of *#CC >> MAX-C, candidate (8b) is chosen, i.e. the one in which the first element of the word-initial cluster is deleted but the medial one is preserved.

(8) Production of 'eleven' with known underlying representation

	|bdʒu+gdʒig|	*#CC	MAX-C
a.	[bdʒug.dʒig]	*!	
☞ b.	[dʒug.dʒig]		*
c.	[dʒu.dʒig]		**!
d.	[bdʒu.gdʒig]	*!	

This analysis reduces the number of assumed underlying representations to one for each morpheme and gets away with a simple deletion mechanism word-initially. Adult speakers of Tibetan would, according to this analysis, segment the numerals as follows:

(9) Assumed segmentation for Tibetan numerals

	Underlying	Surface
'eleven'	|bdʒu+gdʒig|	[dʒugdʒig]
'fourteen'	|bdʒu+bʃi|	[dʒubʃi]
'forty'	|bʃi+bdʒu|	[ʃibdʒu]
'fifteen'	|bdʒu+ŋa|	[dʒuŋa]
'fifty'	|ŋa+bdʒu|	[ŋabdʒu]
'nineteen'	|bdʒu+rgu|	[dʒurgu]
'ninety'	|rgu+bdʒu|	[gubdʒu]

---

[3] In this paper, I use the terms structural and markedness constraint interchangeably.

How does a learner of Tibetan figure out that the segmentation is *dʒu+bʃi* and not *dʒub+ʃi*? How does a learner find out that [dʒu] is underlyingly |bdʒu| and does not additionally have the allomorphs |dʒur|, |dʒug| and |dʒu|?

3 Learning alternations

As indicated in the hypotheses in (4) and (5), there are basically two opposing solutions to learn the alternations in the numerals (and comparable cases): a) total allomorphy (i.e. for each instance of a surface structure there exists a faithful underlying representation) and b) a restrictive grammar and lexicon, with one grammar and one underlying representation for each morpheme. The latter is a traditional generative stance, arguing for a restrictive mechanism with the highest possible generalizability (e.g. Kenstowicz & Kisseberth 1979): There are several (computationally imple- mented) approaches to similar problems. Most of them involve batch learning from paradigmatic information, where the learner has access to all surface structures and all possible underlying representations at once (e.g., Tesar et al. 2003; Tesar 2004; Alderete et al. 2005; Jarosz 2006): Others focus on different learning problems (e.g. Albright 2000, Merchant 2008), and their application to the segmentation problem presented here is not straight- forward. To test the case of Tibetan numerals and their segmentation, we need a model that is both capable of learning a restrictive lexicon and grammar and at the same time is able to handle allomorphy, and preferably in an incremental fashion (because it seems to be more realistic to process input the moment it occurs): I therefore use Apoussidou's (2007) bootstrapping model (which is based on Boersma's 1998 bidirectional model of phonology and phonetics) that has been developed for learning underlying forms in general and that is capable of handling allomorphy as well as learning a restrictive lexicon and grammar (Apoussidou 2008a,b, 2009):

First, we can assume that the learner is able to make similar observations as linguists can. Initially, then, the learner might simply observe and stipulate completely faithful underlying representations for each surface form it encounters. After a while, the learner might have one allomorph for each occurrence of a form, i.e. use the 'total-allomorphy' approach. For one meaning, e.g. for the numeral 'one', the learner will create different representations (depending on the context: in isolation, word-initially, word- finally) and store them in form of *lexical constraints* (Boersma 2001,

Apoussidou 2007):[4] Lexical constraints are here formulated as 'map a <meaning> onto a phonological |under+ly+ing#re+present+ation|'. Initially, all constraints are equally important. In order to get to a restrictive lexicon and grammar, the learner needs to be able to change the representations and the initial grammar. Because grammar and lexicon are encoded as constraints, this means that the initial ranking of constraints has to be changed. In the model here, the learner will be able to make an informed, error-driven change: the learner will create an underlying representation in the comprehension step, and will use this representation to virtually produce the form. The resulting surface form is compared to the comprehended form. If the virtual production is equal to this observed form, grammar and lexicon remain unchanged. If there is a mismatch, i.e. error, grammar and lexicon are adjusted:

(10) A simplified model of comprehension and production

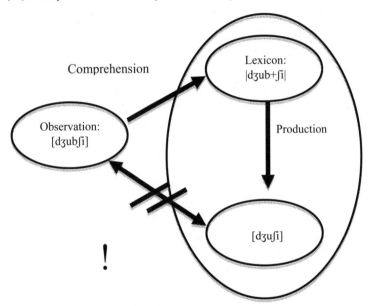

In both production and comprehension, the same ranking of constraints is applied. A mismatch is possible because the two processes have different inputs. In production, morphemes are the input, and in comprehension,

---

[4] One could argue that language learners such as infants are not starting out to acquire underlying representations by learning numerals, but I hope the friendly reader will be able to abstract away from that and focus on the type of morphemic learning involved.

surface forms are the input. Constraints that are crucial in one process can be vacuously satisfied in the other.

In the following, I will go through the steps of the model one by one. In the comprehension process, the learner chooses between candidates that consist of pairs of underlying representations and surface structures. For an incoming form such as 'eleven' [dʒug.dʒig] (11), there is only one surface structure (because we assume here that the learner cannot misperceive anything), but there are several possible underlying structures. Given lexical constraints <one>|dʒig| and <ten>|dʒu| with the ranking in (11) (due to some previous learning, e.g., if both numerals occurred in isolation before), the decision is made for candidate (12a), where the underlying representation for <ten> is |dʒug|. The structural and faithfulness constraints are vacuously satisfied:

(11) Comprehension

[dʒug.dʒig]	*#CC	<one>|dʒig|	Max-C	<ten>|dʒu|
☞ a. |dʒug+dʒig| [dʒug.dʒig]				*
b. |dʒu+gdʒig| [dʒug.dʒig]		*!		

The underlying representation |dʒug| that this produces has not occurred before, but since it won in the evaluation of 'eleven', a lexical constraint <ten>|dʒug| is invoked and inserted at a neutral position in the constraint hierarchy. In general, lexical constraints are language specific and therefore have to be created by the learner. They are assumptions about possible underlying representations of a surface structure. The idea is that for each instance of a morpheme, a lexical constraint is created. In the simulations here, the lexical constraints are already implemented. In our case, this means that our learners here will have 15 lexical constraints, one for each surface form of a morpheme (based on the observations in (2)): The list in (12) is an initial guess of what the lexicon might look like, where for each meaning there are as many underlying representations as observed (limiting it to the relevant ones):

(12) An initial lexicon

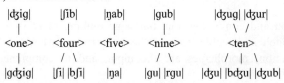

Being constraints, the lexical entries can be ranked with each other (and with the grammatical constraints): What the learner should end up with is a lexicon where each underlying representation corresponds to only one morpheme, in combination with a grammar as proposed in the tableau in (8): This is demonstrated in the (simplified) tableau in (13), where the *morphemes* are the input to the production evaluation, and the candidates consist again of pairs of underlying representations and surface structures (cf. also Zuraw 2000; Apoussidou 2007; and Wolf 2008 for similar evaluation mechanisms in OT): Contrary to the tableau in (8) (where the underlying representation was the input to the evaluation), now a lexical constraint <one>|dʒig| decides between the competing underlying representations, and in combination with the grammar determines the appropriate surface structure:

(13) Production with morphemes as input

<ten>+<one>	*#CC	<one> |dʒig|	MAX-C	<ten> |dʒu| →	<ten> |dʒug| ←
☞ |dʒu+dʒig| [dʒu.dʒig]					*
|dʒu+gdʒig| [dʒu.dʒig]		*!	*		*
|dʒu+gdʒig| [dʒug.dʒig]		*!			*
|dʒug+dʒig| [dʒu.dʒig]			*!	*	
👂 |dʒug+dʒig| [dʒug.dʒig]				*!	

The winning candidate in (13) is the first one, |dʒu+dʒig| [dʒu.dʒig] (indicated by '☞'), which clashes with the form that the learner has heard in the tableau in (11) (indicated by '👂'): This is an error that causes the learner to change the ranking of constraints: the constraint violated by the comprehended candidate is lowered, and the constraint violated by the produced candidate is raised by a specified amount. By going through several such comprehension/virtual-production loops with different forms, the learner zooms in on a grammar/lexicon that should result in a state where no errors are produced. Once the learner reliably produces no errors, learning terminates.

In the case of Tibetan numerals, the learners should end up with only one underlying representation (and thus only one lexical constraint) for each morpheme. The lexical constraints that were evoked in the learning process, but that proved unnecessary (e.g. the low-ranked constraint <ten>|dʒu| in the tableau in (13)) could then be discarded.[5] In cases of languages with true allomorphy, the different allomorphs of a morpheme could be expressed with conflicting lexical constraints, where the grammar takes care of choosing the right allomorph.

---

[5] The discarding procedure could be implemented by checking, after learning terminated, which constraints are actively involved in generating the different forms. The lexical constraints not being involved could then be deleted.

The OT-framework in general has already been very successfully applied to model acquisitional data (Boersma 1997; Boersma & Levelt 1999; Tesar & Smolensky 2000; Curtin & Zuraw 2001; Boersma & Hayes 2001; Escudero & Boersma 2003; Jäger 2003; Jarosz 2006): Recently, its predecessor Harmonic Grammar (henceforth HG; Legendre et al. 1990), has also been successfully applied to learnability problems (Boersma & Pater 2008): I will therefore compare the behaviour of two different kinds of learners in our simulations, noisy Harmonic-Grammar learners and stochastic Optimality-Theoretic learners (as in Boersma & Pater 2008): They share the gradual learning algorithm GLA introduced by Boersma (1997): The following section presents a small introduction to Harmonic Grammar.

4 Harmonic Grammar in a nutshell

Harmonic Grammar works with constraints, inputs and a list of possible outputs similar to OT. In contrast to standard OT (Prince & Smolensky 1993/2004) and in contrast to Stochastic OT (Boersma 1997), constraints in HG are assigned positive *weights*, and constraint violations are represented by negative integers instead of asterisks (e.g. -1 for one violation of the constraint, -2 by two violations etc.): The candidates are evaluated by multiplying the violations of a constraint with its corresponding weight. The sum of these products is then the harmony score of a candidate, a negative value. The candidate with the largest harmony (i.e. with a score closest to zero) wins. In order to enable a choice between an allomorphic analysis and a restrictive lexicon, noise is added to the constraint weights, which gives a slightly different outcome of the harmony scores every time an input is evaluated.

An example is given in (14): There are two constraints, with rank 0.935 for markedness constraint M and rank 0.138 for faithfulness constraint F (an assumed weighting of constraints which e.g. might have come about with a previous learning step): Evaluation noise is added by sampling it from a Gaussian distribution with a standard deviation of 0.2, resulting in the ranks 1.050 for M and 0.160 for F. To get the weight of a constraint, the exponential is taken (Prince & Smolensky 1993/2004, Smolensky & Legendre 2006, Biró 2006), resulting in weight 2.858 for M and weight 1.173 for F in (15). I adopt the same notation as used in Legendre et al. (2006) and Boersma & Pater (2008): In a HG-tableau, the weights of the constraints are written under the constraint name and the score is at the end of the candidate row. The remaining notation should be familiar from the OT literature, with the input in the upper left corner, a list of candidates, and a pointing hand indicating the winner of the evaluation. In the example tableau (14), the first candidate violates the markedness constraint once, which has a bigger weight than the faithfulness constraint. Its harmony score is $(-1) \times 2.85 = -2.85$. The second candidate violates the lower weighted faithfulness constraint three times: $(-3) \times 1.17 = -3.51$. Because the first candidate has a higher harmony (-2.85), it beats the second candidate (that has a harmony of -3.51): The third candidate violates both constraints once, and has the worst harmony score. So although the first candidate violates the constraint with the heavier weight, it wins over the second one. This is a different outcome than an OT-like evaluation would render, where the second candidate in the tableau in (14) would win.

(14) A HG-tableau

[abd]	M 2.85	F 1.17	
☞ [abd]	−1		−2.85
[efg]		−3	−3.51
[hij]	−1	−1	−4.05

HG can therefore express an effect that OT cannot: this is the gang-up effect of constraints which, though lower-ranked (or rather, lower-weighted), can still outperform higher-ranked ones.

Our HG-learners will apply the weighting strategy with possible gang-up effects, whereas our OT-learners will work with stochastic ranking values. A comparison of the results should reveal learnability differences of the two models.

5 The simulations

Because noise was included in both types of learners to handle variation and different frequencies, and because the learning data were picked randomly from the training set, slight differences in outcomes were possible. I therefore created ten virtual learners (henceforth VL) for each type of learner (ten noisy HG/GLA vs. ten noisy OT/GLA-learners): All VLs were trained on pairs of meaning and surface forms (e.g. <one> [dʒig]), listed in (15): The meaning component ensured the identity of the morphemes.

(15) Input to the learners

monomorphemic	bimorphemic
<one> [ʤig]	<ten+one> [ʤugʤig]
<four> [ʃi]	<ten+four> [ʤubʃi]
<five> [ŋa]	<ten+five> [ʤuŋa]
<nine> [gu]	<ten+nine> [ʤurgu]
<ten> [ʤu]	<four+ten> [ʃibʤu]
	<five+ten> [ŋabʤu]
	<nine+ten> [gubʤu]

The virtual learners had to choose an underlying representation (e.g. <one> |ʤig|) according to their current grammar and lexicon. In our case here, it means that the underlying representations were encoded and pre-implemented as lexical constraints, and that the VLs could choose from among them according to the factual rankings of the lexical constraints in the comprehension-step. For instance, if the lexical constraint <one> |ʤig| had a ranking value (or weight) of 1 and the allomorphic constraint <one> |bʤig| had a ranking value of 2, |bʤig| had a higher chance to be chosen as the underlying representation. This underlying representation would serve as the input for virtual production to the VL. When the produced output of the VL (the surface structure) diverted from the original surface structure, learning (i.e. a re-weighting or -ranking of the lexical and grammatical constraints) took place. Because underlying representations are hidden structures that learners can only speculate about, the successful learner is defined as one who consistently produces the same surface structures that were used in training.

The virtual learners were endowed with a set of lexical constraints (listed in (13)) and the markedness and faithfulness constraints of (6) and (7), resulting in 17 constraints in total. The learners were free to combine the different observed allomorphs for a given meaning in production, i.e. when they analysed an incoming form [gubʤu] 'ninety' as underlying |gub| and |ʤu|, they were allowed to use these allomorphs for producing 'nineteen' as e.g. |ʤu+gub|. In this way, the learners could test their knowledge and compare it to what they heard. If there was an error, the learners would assume that their production is not correct and change something in their grammar and/or lexicon (depending on which constraints were violated):

5.1 The OT/GLA-learners

The noisy OT/GLA-learners used the settings listed in the appendix, which happen to be the standard settings in Praat (Boersma & Weenink 1992-2012) for this kind of learner (also listed in the appendix as (24)): All constraints were initially ranked at the same ranking value 0, with initial learning steps of 1.0 (meaning that after a reranking step a constraint would move up or down the hierarchy by 1.0. This plasticity decreased over time with a factor of 0.1 (i.e. the learning steps became smaller the more input the learners had processed): This has a reflection in real life, if one assumes that infants and children learn faster than adults, but it has also a computational reason: the bigger the learning steps, the faster the learner might acquire a grammar, but the smaller the steps, the less sensitive the learner is to errors in the data and is furthermore better capable of matching the frequency distributions of the input. In total, each learner was confronted with 400,000 learning items. Evaluation noise (a standard deviation of a Gaussian distribution), i.e. the value that enables different ranking values for different evaluations of a form, was 2.0. The evaluation noise was incorporated in the simulations in order to let the learner be able to choose between an allomorphic analysis of the data and a restrictive lexicon.

5.1.1 Results

The resulting output distribution of the ten noisy OT/GLA-learners is listed in table (16): A resulting example ranking is listed in the appendix as (25): All learners can be regarded as successful. The surface forms were produced correctly to a full 100%.[6] With respect to the grammar, all underlying initial clusters were resolved on the surface. The numbers indicate the percentiles that a respective form was chosen in 100,000 production trials. With respect to the underlying representations, slight cases of allomorphy occurred. Table (16) shows that the numbers in the tens ('ten', 'eleven', 'fourteen', 'fifteen' and 'nineteen') plus the numerals involving 'five' practically never alternate, and table (17) shows that in the higher numbers very slight cases of allomorphy occur. For the most part, though, the learners chose the same underlying representations as linguists would, i.e. underlying representations with an initial consonant cluster (such as |rgu|): In sum, the few cases of allomorphy involved underlying representations with resolved clusters (such as |gu|): Interestingly, no allomorphs such as |dʒub| occurred.

---

[6] Learning actually ended long before the virtual learners had encountered the 400,000 items of the training phase.

(16) Resulting output distributions with non-alternating underlying representations

Gloss	SFs	URs
'five'	[ŋa]	|ŋa|
'ten'	[dʒu]	|bdʒu|
'eleven'	[dʒugdʒig]	|bdʒu+gdʒig|
'fourteen'	[dʒubʃi]	|bdʒu+bʃi|
'fifteen'	[dʒuŋa]	|bdʒu+ŋa|
'nineteen'	[dʒurgu]	|bdʒu+rgu|
'fifty'	[ŋabdʒu]	|ŋa+bdʒu|

(17) Resulting output distributions with alternating underlying representations

Gloss	SFs	URs	%
'one'	[dʒig] ⟨	|dʒig| |gdʒig|	> 0.07 < 0.93
'four'	[ʃi] ⟨	|ʃi| |bʃi|	< 0.01 > 0.99
'nine'	[gu] ⟨	|gu| |rgu|	< 0.01 > 0.99
'forty'	[ʃibdʒu] ⟨	|ʃi+bdʒu| |bʃi+bdʒu|	< 0.01 > 0.99
'ninety'	[gubdʒu] ⟨	|gu+bdʒu| |rgu+bdʒu|	< 0.01 > 0.99

An example production of 'forty' from one of the virtual learners is shown in (18): The tableau in (18) shows the competing pairs of underlying representations and surface structures with the actual ranking values of the constraints (i.e. without adding evaluation noise to this evaluation):

(18) Production of 'forty' by virtual OT/GLA-learner no. 1[7]

		<ten> |bdʒu|	<four> |bʃi|	*#CC	<ten> |dʒu|	<four> |ʃi|	Max-C
	<four+ten>	10.181	8.309	1.975	-0.095	-5.482	-18.749
	|ʃib+dʒu| [ʃibdʒu]	*!	*			*	
≈0.01	|ʃi+bdʒu| [ʃibdʒu]		*!		*		
≈0.99	|bʃi+bdʒu| [ʃibdʒu]				*	*	*
	|bʃi+bdʒu| [bʃibdʒu]			*!	*	*	

The numbers on the left of the tableau indicate the proportion of the number of times (out of 100,000) a candidate was chosen. In this particular case, they show that even with a noise of 2.0, the learner pretty much always produced the candidate that underlyingly has both consonant clusters, but deletes the

---

[7] Some suboptimal candidates are left out of the tableau for reasons of readability. The complete tableau with all candidates and all relevant constraints appears in the appendix as (27):

initial one on the surface: |bʃi+bdʒu| [ʃibdʒu]. This is also the solution a linguist would choose, and comes about with the ranking between the lexical constraints (|bdʒu| >> |dʒu| and |bʃi| >> |ʃi|) in combination with the ranking of *#CC >> Max-C, which rules out any candidates with initial consonant clusters. The only other candidate that ever got chosen (a tiny percentage of times) is the one which has a completely faithful underlying representation, |ʃi+bdʒu| [ʃibdʒu].

5.1.2 Testing the richness of the base

In addition, the learners passed the "richness-of-the-base" test: no matter what the input is, the final state grammar filters out any structure that is disallowed in the target language, i.e. *#CC-structures. Consider a previously unheard form with an initial and medial consonant cluster in the tableau in (19): Lexical constraints do not play a role in this case, because there is probably no meaning yet associated with this form, hence the input is a stipulated underlying representation:

(19) Never-before-heard form

	*#CC	Max-C
|gdʒu+bdʒi|	1.975	−18.749
[gdʒubdʒi]	*!	
☞ [dʒubdʒi]		*
[dʒudʒi]		**!

In this case, where the first occurrence of the word (comparable to a situation where a word is borrowed from another language with different structure) could be taken as the input to the grammar, the surface structure with the initial cluster resolution is picked.

In sum, it can be said that the OT/GLA-learners acquired both the segmentation of morphemes and grammar successfully: on the surface, no word-initial clusters occur. The lexicon itself is fairly restrictive: the learners opted for an allomorphic analysis only a minimal amount of times.

5.2 The HG/GLA-learners

For the ten noisy HG/GLA-learners, a M > F-bias as in Jesney & Tessier (2009) was imposed, because a pilot simulation revealed poor learning without this bias. The markedness constraint was initially heavier-weighted than the lexical and faithfulness constraints (with a weight of 1 for the structural constraint and 0 for all other constraints): In addition, the weight for the structural constraint changed with higher plasticity in learning than the weights for the other constraints (with a learning rate of 0.01 and 0.001, respectively): All HG/GLA-learners experienced in a first trial a total of 100,000 learning items (cf. appendix (24) again for the exact settings): The initial amount of learning items was smaller than in the OT-learners, because quicker learning due to the gang-up effect was expected.

5.2.1 Results

All noisy HG/GLA-learners can be regarded as being successful as well, as surface forms were produced correctly most of the times (but see (24) for some exceptions): The resulting output distributions (again, 100,000 production trials) can roughly be divided into two groups, similar to the OT-learners. But where the OT-learners arrived at a restrictive lexicon, the case with the HG-learners is less clear. One group makes very little use of allomorphy (in analogy to the OT-group that practically makes no use of it), the other shows mixed results with a pretty equal distribution of underlying representations with vs. without initial clusters, as table (20) shows.

(20) Resulting output distribution of the ten HG/GLA-learners

SFs URs		%	SFs URs		%
[ʤu] ⟨	|ʤu|	< 0.03	[ʤig] ⟨	|ʤig|	> 0.72
	|bʤu|	< 0.97		|gʤig|	< 0.28
[ʤugʤig] ⟨	|ʤu+gʤig|	> 0.03	[ʃi] ⟨	|ʃi|	< 0.47
	|bʤu+gʤig|	< 0.98		|bʃi|	> 0.53
[ʤubʃi] ⟨	|ʤu+bʃi|	< 0.03	[gu] ⟨	|gu|	< 0.50
	|bʤu+bʃi|	> 0.97		|rgu|	> 0.50
[ʤuŋa] ⟨	|ʤu+ŋa|	< 0.03	[ʃibʤu] ⟨	|ʃi+bʤu|	< 0.47
	|bʤu+ŋa|	> 0.97		|bʃi+bʤu|	> 0.53
[ʤurgu] ⟨	|ʤu+rgu|	< 0.03	[gubʤu] ⟨	|gu+bʤu|	< 0.50
	|bʤu+rgu|	> 0.97		|rgu+bʤu|	> 0.50
[ŋa]	|ŋa|	≈ 1.00			
[ŋabʤu]	|ŋa+bʤu|	≈ 1.00			

The only words without allomorphy were |ŋa| [ŋa] (< 1.00) and |ŋa+bʤu| [ŋabʤu] (< 1.00), which is not surprising because [ŋa] only alternates (here) with [ŋab].

A resulting grammar, with exponential (weight) values, is shown in the tableau in (21): In this tableau, the candidate with the best harmonic score is the one which has underlyingly both consonant clusters and deletes the initial one on the surface. Without evaluation noise, this would be the candidate that would always win. With an evaluation noise of 2.0 and 100,000 production trials, this candidate wins only a little bit more than half of the time (53%), while an alternative candidate with a faithful underlying representation wins 47% of the time.

(21) A HG-learner displaying allomorphy in production

		|bdʒu|	*#CC	|bʃi|	|dʒu|	|ʃi|	Max-C
'forty'		3.17	2.59	1.96	1.06	0.96	0.9
	|ʃib+dʒu| [ʃibdʒu]	−1		−1		−1		−5.13
< 0.47	|ʃi+bdʒu| [ʃibdʒu]				−1	−1		−3.02
> 0.53	|bʃi+bdʒu| [ʃibdʒu]				−1	−1	−1	−2.11
	|bʃi+bdʒu| [bʃibdʒu]		−1		−1	−1		−4.61

Nonetheless, all HG-learners preserved the bias of M > F, and rule out ungrammatical outputs (i.e. they make correct generalizations):

(22) Never-before-heard form for a HG-learner

	*#CC	Max
|gdʒu+bdʒi|	2.59	0.9
[gdʒubdʒi]	−2		−5.18
☞ [dʒubdʒi]		−1	−0.9
[dʒudʒi]		−2	−1.8

The HG/GLA-learners produced a tiny percentage of errors, i.e., diverging surface structures, shown in (24) (all less than a fraction of 0.05): They were all based on a wrong segmentation and occurred mainly in the production of the monomorphemic numerals. Interestingly, this analysis (including a final [b], [g] or [r]) never occurred in the bimorphemic (correctly or incorrectly surfacing) numerals. In contrast, the errors in the bimorphemic numerals included only forms that had no clusters in the underlying representation and therefore lacked clusters on the surface.

(23) Errors on the surface

monomorphemic		bimorphemic	
'four'	|ʃib| [ʃib]	'fourteen'	|dʒu+ʃi| [dʒuʃi]
'five'	|ŋab| [ŋab]	'nineteen'	|dʒu+gu| [dʒugu]
'nine'	|gub| [gub]		
'ten'	|dʒub| [dʒub]		
	|dʒug| [dʒug]		
	|dʒur| [dʒur]		

5.2.2 Results with additional data

The behaviour of the HG/GLA-learners could be due to the fact that they were trained on only 100,000 learning items. To see whether more training improves performance, ten new HG/GLA-learners were run with 400,000 and ten more HG/GLA-learners were run with 1,000,000 data. As the table (27) shows (see appendix), learning could be improved (in the sense that the learners created a more restrictive lexicon), but allomorphy persisted even after 1,000,000 learning data.

6 Discussion

On the surface, the HG/GLA-learners' performance was comparable to that of the OT/GLA-learners in that for the most part, they produced the same surface forms as they were trained on, and both groups of learners were able to apply their learned grammar to new forms in a way that yielded well-formed outputs.

With respect to the underlying representations, though, there was a qualitative difference in analysis. Where the OT-learners preferred an analysis with a rather strict lexicon practically without allomorphy, the HG-learners allowed for substantial use of allomorphy. Even with an initial bias of markedness over faithfulness, the HG-learners regarded faithful parses as a valid analysis. Two factors probably contributed to this. First, the stochastic feature of both learning algorithms allows in general for variation between evaluations of a form (recall that even the OT-learners had a marginal amount of allomorphy, albeit less than the HG-learners): A bigger factor, though, seemed to be the crucial difference between Optimality Theory vs. Harmonic grammar, namely the 'gang-up' effect of HG: taken together, lighter-weighted constraints can outweigh a heavier-weighted constraint. This effect, in combination with the stochastic feature, probably caused the faithfulness constraint to team up with the respective lexical constraints to outweigh the heavier-weighted lexical constraint (cf. the tableau in (21)) a considerable amount of times. This probably also led to the production of the errors that the HG-learners made.

7 Conclusion

The OT-learners produced practically no errors and hardly made use of allomorphy, despite a lack of an initial bias of markedness over faithfulness. If one were to include a mechanism with which lower-ranked lexical constraints decayed over time, no underlying allomorphy would be produced at all. This is contrary to the HG-learners, who produced a tiny percentage of errors on the surface and used allomorphy to the cost of a restrictive lexicon.

While the OT-learners (here) opted for what can be seen as a more elegant analysis, the HG-learners' analyses cannot be discarded as wrong either.

Allomorphy is a valid analysis simply because there are phenomena in languages which are best treated in this way, and which are difficult to analyze in other terms (cf. e.g. Kager 2009). In addition, even experimental evidence is not entirely conclusive about whether speakers employ a relatively restrictive lexicon, like the OT-learners, or a relatively high degree of allomorphy, like the HG-learners.

Whether the OT-learners or the HG-learners come closer to a psycholinguistic truth cannot be decided here. Even the minor errors that the HG-learners made can be an expression of a developmental stage (maybe the amount of learning items was not enough) or simply of slips of the tongue. Quantitative data on Lhasa Tibetan slips of the tongue and language acquisitional data could shed light on this issue, but are not available at this point in time. However, from other languages such as French, it is already known that infants and children produce a certain amount of errors that indicate an allomorphic analysis of articles at least in the developmental stage (e.g. Chevrot et al. 2009): Modelling of the French data (Apoussidou 2009) and also comparable cases in English and Dutch (Apoussidou 2008a,b) indicate that OT-learners comparable to the ones here were able to simulate the allomorphic analysis.

As to the question how much needs to be hard-wired into a human brain to segment Lhasa Tibetan numerals (or plurimorphemic words in general) we can conclude that there exist learners that do not need a markedness-over-faithfulness bias (the OT-learners): The question remains whether the structural constraints have to be hard-wired or not. Research on phonotactic constraints indicates that even structural constraints could in principle be acquired (e.g. Hayes & Wilson 2008; Adriaans & Kager 2010): If this can be combined with the approach of lexical learning tested here, we would have a strong bootstrapping mechanism that does without heavy innate assumptions.

References

Adriaans, Frans & René Kager (2010): Adding generalization to statistical learning: the induction of phonotactics from continuous speech. – In: *Journal of Memory and Language* 62, 311–331.

Albright, Adam (2000): *The Identification of Bases in Morphological Paradigms.* – Ph.D. dissertation, UCLA.

Alderete, John, Adrian Brasoveanu, Nazarré Merchant, Alan Prince & Bruce Tesar (2005): "Contrast analysis aids the learning of phonological underlying forms." – In: John Alderete, Chung-Hye Han & Alexei Kochetov (eds.): *Proceedings of WCCFL 24*, 34–42. Somerville, MA: Cascadilla Press,

Apoussidou, Diana (2007): *The learnability of Metrical Phonology.* – PhD dissertation, University of Amsterdam (LOT Dissertation Series nr. 148).

– (2008a): Final devoicing, allomorphy, and Freedom of the Lexicon: An online learning approach to underlying representations. – Talk presented at CLAY, Yale University, October 30th.

– (2008b): Modelling allomorphy with lexical constraints. – Talk presented at UMMM, University of Massachusetts, November 20th.

– (2009): Modelling the acquisition of French liaison with allomorphy. – Talk presented at the Acquisition Lab Meeting of the Linguistics Department of the University of Massachusetts, April 13th.

Biró, Tamás (2006): *Finding the Right words: Implementing Optimality Theory with Simulated Annealing.* – PhD disseration, University of Groningen (Groningen Dissertations in Linguistics Series nr. 62).

Boersma, Paul (1997): "How we learn variation, optionality, and probability." – In: *Proceedings of the Institute of Phonetic Sciences* 21, 43–58. University of Amsterdam.

– (1998): *Functional Phonology.* – PhD dissertation, University of Amsterdam (LOT Dissertation Series nr. 11).

– (2001): "Phonology-semantics interaction in OT, and its acquisition." – In: Kirchner, Robert, Wolf Wikeley & Joe Pater (eds.): *Papers in Experimental and Theoretical Linguistics* 6, 24 –35. Edmonton: University of Alberta.

– (2008): "A programme for bidirectional phonology and phonetics and their acquisition and evolution." ROA-868.

Boersma, Paul & Joe Pater (2007): Constructing constraints from language data: The case of Canadian English diphthongs. – Paper presented to the North Eastern Linguistic Society. Available at: http://people.umass.edu/pater/boersma-pater-nels.pdf.

– (2008): Convergence properties of a gradual learning algorithm for Harmonic Grammar. ROA-970.

Boersma, Paul & David Weenink (1992-2012): Praat: Doing phonetics by computer. – http://www.praat.org

Chevrot, Jean-Pierre, Celine Dugua & Michel Fayol (2009): Liaison acquisition, word segmentation and construction in French: a usage-based account. – In: *Journal of Child Language* 36, 557–596.

Halle, Morris & George N. Clements (1983): *Problem Book in Phonology: A Workbook for Introductory Courses in Linguistics and in Modern Phonology.* – Cambridge, MA: MIT Press.

Hayes, Bruce & Colin Wilson (2008): "A maximum entropy model of phonotactics and phonotactic learning." – In: *Linguistic Inquiry* 39, 379–440.

Jarosz, Gaja (2006): *Rich Lexicons and Restrictive Grammars – Maximum Likelihood Learning in Optimality Theory.* – PhD dissertation, Johns Hopkins University.

Jesney, Karen & Anne-Michelle Tessier (2009): Gradual learning and faithfulness: consequences of ranked vs. weighted constraints. – In: Schardl, Anisa, Martin Walkow & Muhammad Abdurrahman (eds.): *Proceedings of the 38th Meeting of the North East Linguistics Society (NELS 38).* ROA-967.

Kager, René (1999): *Optimality Theory.* – Cambridge: Cambridge University Press.

– (2009): "Lexical irregularity and the typology of contrast." – In: Hanson, Kristin & Sharon Inkelas (eds.): *The Nature of the Word: Essays in Honor of Paul Kiparsky.* Cambridge, MA: MIT Press. Available at: http://www.let.uu.nl/~Rene.Kager/ personal/ Papers/contrast.pdf.

Kenstowicz, Michael & Charles Kisseberth (1979): *Generative Phonology: Description and Theory.* – New York: Academic Press.

Legendre, Géraldine, Yoshiro Miyata & Paul Smolensky (1990): *Harmonic Grammar: A Formal Multi-level Connectionist Theory of Linguistic Well-Formedness: Theoretical Foundations.* – Report CU-CS-465-90, Computer Science Department, University of Colorado at Boulder.

McCarthy, John & Alan Prince (1995): Faithfulness and reduplicative identity. – In: Beckman, Jill, Suzanne Urbanczyk & Laura Walsh (eds.): *University of Massachusetts Occasional Papers in Linguistics 18: Papers in Optimality Theory,* 249–384.

Merchant, Nazarré (2008): *Discovering Underlying Forms: Contrast Pairs and Ranking.* – PhD dissertation, Rutgers University.

Prince, Alan & Paul Smolensky (1993/2004): *Optimality Theory: Constraint Interaction In Generative Grammar.* Malden MA/Oxford: Blackwell. Version of 1993 as Technical Report CU-CS-696-93, Department of Computer Science, University of Colorado at Boulder, and Technical Report TR-2, – Rutgers Center for Cognitive Science, Rutgers University, New Brunswick, NJ.

Smolensky, Paul & Géraldine Legendre (2006): *The Harmonic Mind: From Neural Computation to Optimality-Theoretic grammar.* – Cambridge, MA: MIT Press.

Tesar, Bruce (2004): Contrast analysis in phonological learning. – Ms., Linguistics Department, Rutgers University. ROA-964.

– (2009): Learning Phonological Grammars for Output-Driven Maps. – Ms., Linguistics Department, Rutgers University. ROA-1013.

Tesar, Bruce, John Alderete, Graham Horwood, Nazarré Merchant, Koichi Nishitani & Alan Prince (2003): "Surgery in language learning." – In: Garding, Gina & Mimu Tsujimura (eds.): *Proceedings of WCCFL 22.* Somerville, MA: Cascadilla Press, pp 477–490.

Wolf, Matthew (2008): *Optimal Interleaving: Serial Phonology-Morphology Interaction in a Constraint-Based Model*. – PhD dissertation, University of Massachusetts, Amherst. ROA-996.

Zuraw, Kie (2000): *Patterned Exceptions in Phonology*. – PhD dissertation, University of California, Los Angeles.

Appendix

(24) Praat settings of the simulations:

	Noisy OT/GLA	Noisy HG/GLA
Reranking strategy	bidirectionally	symmetric all
Evaluation noise	2.0	0.2
Initial ranking values/weights:	All equal at 0	*#CC = 1; all others at 0
Initial plasticity/Learning rate	1.0	0.01
Replications per plasticity	100,000	100,000/400,000/1,000,000
Plasticity decrement	0.1	1
Number of plasticities	4	1
Rel. plasticity spreading	0.1	0

(25) Resulting example grammars

A resulting OT/GLA-grammar	
<ten> |bdʒu|	10.181
<nine> |rgu|	8.868
<four> |bʃi|	8.309
<five> |na|	5.498
<one> |gdʒig|	3.686
*#CC	1.975
<ten> |dʒu|	−0.095
{Remaining lexical constraints}	
<nine> |gu|	−6.179
MAX-C	−18.749

A resulting HG/GLA-grammar	
<ten> |bdʒu|	1.153
*#CC	0.953
<four> |bʃi|	0.673
<nine> |rgu|	0.623
<five> |na|	0.403
<one> |gdʒig|	0.283
<ten> |dʒu|	0.063
<nine> |gu|	0.003
<four> |ʃi|	-0.037
MAX-C	-0.103
{Remaining lexical constraints}	< -0.1

(26) The whole of 'forty', with zero evaluation noise and all relevant constraints:

<four+ten>	<ten> |bdʒu| 10.2	<four> |bʃi| 8.3	*#CC 2.0	<ten> |dʒu| −0.1	<four> |ʃib| −2.8	<ten> |dʒub| −3.0	<ten> |dʒug| −3.1	<ten> |dʒur| −4.0	<four> |ʃi| −5.5	Max −18.7
|ʃi+dʒu| [ʃi.dʒu]	*!	*				*	*	*	*	
|ʃi+bdʒu| [ʃib.dʒu]		*!		*	*	*	*	*		
|bʃi+bdʒu| [bʃib.dʒu]			*!	*	*	*	*	*	*	
☞|bʃi+bdʒu| [ʃib.dʒu]				*	*	*	*	*	*	*
|ʃib+dʒu| [ʃib.dʒu]	*!	*				*	*	*	*	
|ʃi+dʒub| [ʃi.dʒub]	*!	*		*	*		*	*		
|ʃi+dʒug| [ʃi.dʒug]	*!	*		*	*	*		*		
|ʃi+dʒur| [ʃi.dʒur]	*!	*		*	*	*	*			

(27) Resulting output distribution of the HG-learners after 100,000, 400,000 and 1,000,000 learning data:

			100,000	400,000	1,000,000
<one>	|dʒig|	[dʒig]	0.72	0.67	0.63
<one>	|gdʒig|	[dʒig]	0.28	0.33	0.37
<four>	|ʃi|	[ʃi]	0.47	0.40	0.32
<four>	|bʃi|	[ʃi]	0.53	0.60	0.68
<five>	|ŋa|	[ŋa]	1.00	1.00	1.00
<nine>	|gu|	[gu]	0.50	0.40	0.34
<nine>	|rgu|	[gu]	0.50	0.60	0.66
<ten>	|dʒu|	[dʒu]	0.03	0.01	
<ten>	|bdʒu|	[dʒu]	0.97	0.99	1.00
<ten+one>	|dʒu+gdʒig|	[dʒug.dʒig]	0.03	0.01	
<ten+one>	|bdʒu+gdʒig|	[dʒug.dʒig]	0.98	0.99	1.00
<ten+four>	|dʒu+bʃi|	[dʒub.ʃi]	0.03	0.01	
<ten+four>	|bdʒu+bʃi|	[dʒub.ʃi]	0.97	0.99	1.00
<ten+five>	|dʒu+ŋa|	[dʒu.ŋa]	0.03	0.01	
<ten+five>	|bdʒu+ŋa|	[dʒu.ŋa]	0.97	0.99	1.00
<ten+nine>	|dʒu+rgu|	[dʒur.gu]	0.03	0.01	
<ten+nine>	|bdʒu+rgu|	[dʒur.gu]	0.97	0.99	1.00
<four+ten>	|ʃi+bdʒu|	[ʃib.dʒu]	0.47	0.40	0.32
<four+ten>	|bʃi+bdʒu|	[ʃib.dʒu]	0.53	0.60	0.68
<five+ten>	|ŋa+bdʒu|	[ŋab.dʒu]	1.00	1.00	1.00
<nine+ten>	|gu+bdʒu|	[gub.dʒu]	0.50	0.40	0.34
<nine+ten>	|rgu+bdʒu|	[gub.dʒu]	0.50	0.60	0.66